Lecture Notes in Computer Science 6993

Commenced Publication in 1973
Founding and Former Series Editors:
Gerhard Goos, Juris Hartmanis, and Jan van Leeuwen

Editorial Board

David Hutchison
  Lancaster University, UK

Takeo Kanade
  Carnegie Mellon University, Pittsburgh, PA, USA

Josef Kittler
  University of Surrey, Guildford, UK

Jon M. Kleinberg
  Cornell University, Ithaca, NY, USA

Alfred Kobsa
  University of California, Irvine, CA, USA

Friedemann Mattern
  ETH Zurich, Switzerland

John C. Mitchell
  Stanford University, CA, USA

Moni Naor
  Weizmann Institute of Science, Rehovot, Israel

Oscar Nierstrasz
  University of Bern, Switzerland

C. Pandu Rangan
  Indian Institute of Technology, Madras, India

Bernhard Steffen
  TU Dortmund University, Germany

Madhu Sudan
  Microsoft Research, Cambridge, MA, USA

Demetri Terzopoulos
  University of California, Los Angeles, CA, USA

Doug Tygar
  University of California, Berkeley, CA, USA

Gerhard Weikum
  Max Planck Institute for Informatics, Saarbruecken, Germany

Sebastian Mödersheim
Catuscia Palamidessi (Eds.)

Theory of Security and Applications

Joint Workshop, TOSCA 2011
Saarbrücken, Germany, March 31 - April 1, 2011
Revised Selected Papers

 Springer

Volume Editors

Sebastian A. Mödersheim
DTU Informatics
Richard Petersens Plads
2800 Kgs. Lyngby, Denmark
E-mail: samo@imm.dtu.dk

Catuscia Palamidessi
INRIA / Ecole Polytechnique
Rue de Saclay
91128 Palaiseau Cedex, France
E-mail: catuscia@lix.polytechnique.fr

ISSN 0302-9743   e-ISSN 1611-3349
ISBN 978-3-642-27374-2   ISBN 978-3-642-27375-9 (eBook)
DOI 10.1007/978-3-642-27375-9
Springer Heidelberg Dordrecht London New York

Library of Congress Control Number: 2011943626

CR Subject Classification (1998): D.4.6, K.6.5, C.2, E.3, D.2, F.3

LNCS Sublibrary: SL 4 – Security and Cryptology

Typesetting: Camera-ready by author, data conversion by Scientific Publishing Services, Chennai, India

Printed on acid-free paper

Springer is part of Springer Science+Business Media (www.springer.com)

Preface

It is our pleasure to welcome you to the proceedings of TOSCA 2011, a meeting on the Theory of SeCurity and Applications that was held in Saarbrücken from March 31 to April 1, 2011, in conjunction with ETAPS 2011.

TOSCA is the 2011 edition of an annual series of events formerly known as ARSPA-WITS. The aim of TOSCA is to provide a forum for continued activity in different areas of computer security, bringing computer security researchers in closer contact with the ETAPS community and giving ETAPS attendees an opportunity to talk to experts in computer security, on the one hand, and contribute to bridging the gap between logical methods and computer security foundations, on the other.

ARSPA (Automated Reasoning for Security Protocol Analysis) was a series of workshops aiming at bringing together researchers and practitioners from both the security and the formal methods communities, from academia and industry, interested in developing and applying automated reasoning techniques and tools for the formal specification and analysis of security protocols. The first two ARSPA workshops were held as satellite events of IJCAR 2004 and ICALP 2005, respectively. ARSPA then joined forces with the workshop FCS (Foundations of Computer Security): FCS-ARSPA 2006 was affiliated with LICS 2006, in the context of FLoC 2006, and FCS-ARSPA 2007 was affiliated with LICS 2007 and ICALP 2007.

WITS (Workshop on Issues in the Theory of Security) was the official annual event organized by the IFIP WG 1.7 on "Theoretical Foundations of Security Analysis and Design," established to encourage the investigation on the theoretical foundations of security, by discovering and promoting new areas of application of theoretical techniques in computer security and by supporting the systematic use of formal techniques in the development of security-related applications.

In 2008, ARSPA and WITS joined with FCS for a joint workshop – FCS-ARSPA-WITS 2008 – associated with LICS and CSF. In 2009, ARSPA and WITS merged in the joint workshop ARSPA-WITS which has been associated with ETAPS since then.

Starting from next year, TOSCA will also join forces with the workshops FAST (Formal Aspects of Security & Trust) and SecCo (Security Issues in Concurrency) to form the new sixth ETAPS conference *POST: Principles of Security and Trust*, and we wish this new conference great success.

In the 2011 edition of TOSCA there were 24 submissions. All the submissions were thoroughly evaluated on the basis of at least three referee reports, and an electronic Program Committee meeting was held by using the EasyChair on-line conference system. The committee decided to accept the nine papers included in this volume. The program was enriched with invited talks by Michael

Backes (ETAPS plenary speaker), Veronique Cortier, Ueli Maurer, Sjouke Mauw, and David Sands. We are delighted that Michael Backes and Ueli Maurer have presented novel results and have contributed full papers to this volume.

We would like to thank all the people who contributed to the organization of TOSCA. In particular, we are very grateful to the members of the Program Committee and the additional referees. Last but not least, warm thanks to the organizers of ETAPS 2011.

July 2011   Sebastian Mödersheim
                                                                 Catuscia Palamidessi

Organization

Program Committee

Alessandro Armando	Università di Genova & Fondazione Bruno Kessler, Italy
Lujo Bauer	CMU, USA
Achim D. Brucker	SAP Research, Germany
Yannick Chevalier	Université de Toulouse, France
Luca Compagna	SAP Research, France
Cas Cremers	Siemens AG, Germany
Jorge Cuellar	ETH Zrich, Switzerland
Pierpaolo Degano	Università di Pisa, Italy
Riccardo Focardi	Università Ca' Foscari di Venezia
Dieter Gollman	Hamburg University of Technology, Germany
Joshua Guttman	Worcester Polytechnic Institute, USA
Jan Jürjens	TU Dortmund and Fraunhofer ISST, Germany
Gavin Lowe	Oxford University, UK
Catherine Meadows	Naval Research Laboratory, USA
John Mitchell	Stanford University, USA
Sebastian Alexander Mödersheim (Chair)	Technical University of Denmark
Catuscia Palamidessi (Chair)	INRIA and LIX, France
Michael Rusinowitch	INRIA-Lorraine, France
Mark Ryan	University of Birmingham, UK
Geoffrey Smith	Florida International University, USA
Graham Steel	LSV, INRIA & CNRS & ENS-Cachan, France
Luca Viganò	Università di Verona, Italy
Bogdan Warinschi	University of Bristol, UK

Additional Reviewers

Misha Aizatulin	Martin Ochoa
Chiara Bodei	Giancarlo Pellegrino
Mario Bravetti	Serena Ponta
Roberto Carbone	Silvio Ranise
Matteo Centenaro	Ben Smyth
Morten Dahl	Roberto Zunino
Gian-Luigi Ferrari	

Table of Contents

Union and Intersection Types
for Secure Protocol Implementations

Michael Backes[1,2], Cătălin Hrițcu[1], and Matteo Maffei[1]

[1] Saarland University
[2] Max Planck Institute for Software Systems (MPI-SWS)

Abstract. We present a new type system for verifying the security of cryptographic protocol implementations. The type system combines prior work on refinement types, with union, intersection, and polymorphic types, and with the novel ability to reason statically about the disjointness of types. The increased expressivity enables the analysis of important protocol classes that were previously out of scope for the type-based analyses of protocol implementations. In particular, our types can statically characterize: (i) more usages of asymmetric cryptography, such as signatures of private data and encryptions of authenticated data; (ii) authenticity and integrity properties achieved by showing knowledge of secret data; (iii) applications based on zero-knowledge proofs. The type system comes with a mechanized proof of correctness and an efficient type-checker.

1 Introduction

Modern applications are mostly distributed and they rely on complex cryptographic protocols to transmit data over potentially insecure networks (e.g., e-banking, e-commerce, social networks, and mobile applications). Protocol designers struggle to keep pace with the variety of possible security vulnerabilities, which have affected early authentication protocols like Needham-Schroeder [26, 37], carefully designed de facto standards like SSL and PKCS [17, 45], and even widely deployed products like Microsoft Passport [30] and Kerberos [19]. Even if the underlying cryptographic protocols are properly designed, security vulnerabilities may still arise due to flaws in the implementation. Manual security analyses of cryptographic protocols, and even more so protocol implementations, are extremely difficult and error-prone. Therefore, it is important to devise automated analysis techniques that can provide security guarantees for protocol implementations and, more generally, for the source code of distributed applications.

An effective approach for analyzing protocol implementations is to rely on software verification techniques, such as model checking and type theory, and to adapt them to the security problem. Type systems, in particular, proved successful in the automated analysis of both cryptographic protocol models [1, 2, 31] and protocol implementations [12, 14]. Type systems provide security proofs for an unbounded number of runs. Furthermore, the analysis is modular and has a predictable termination behavior. Finally, type systems were designed from the beginning to efficiently deal with programming language features such as data structures, recursion, state, and higher-order functions: consequently, type systems are more efficient and scale better than many

S. Mödersheim and C. Palamidessi (Eds.): TOSCA 2011, LNCS 6993, pp. 1–28, 2012.

state-of-the-art protocol verifiers (e.g., ProVerif [16] used as a back end by fs2pv [15]) in the analysis of source code [14].

Despite these promising features, the type-based analysis of the source code of modern distributed applications is still an open issue. The first problem is that many of these applications (e.g., trusted computing [18], electronic voting [22], and social networks [9]) rely on complex cryptographic schemes, such as zero-knowledge proofs. Although the automated verification of protocols based on some of these schemes is possible in process calculi for abstract protocol specifications, which provide convenient mechanisms to symbolically abstract these schemes (e.g., flexible equational theories), this is not the case for standard programming languages, where one needs to encode these abstractions using the primitives provided by the language. These primitives were, however, not designed for abstractly representing cryptographic primitives, which makes providing encodings that are suitable for automatic analysis and capture all potential usages of cryptographic schemes a challenging task. The second, somewhat similar, problem is that some interesting security properties are obtained by specific cryptographic patterns that are difficult to encode in type systems for programming languages. For instance, authenticity and integrity properties can be achieved by showing the knowledge of secret data, as in the Needham-Schroeder-Lowe public-key protocol [37] that relies on the exchange of secret nonces to authenticate the participants or as in most authentication protocols based on zero-knowledge proofs (e.g., Direct Anonymous Attestation [18] and Civitas [22]).

1.1 Contributions

This paper presents a new type system for the verification of the source code of protocol implementations. The underlying type theory combines refinement types [12] with union, intersection, and polymorphic types. Additionally, we introduce a novel relation for statically reasoning about the disjointness of types. This expressive type system extends the scope of existing type-based analyses of protocol implementations [12, 14] to important protocol classes that were not covered so far. In particular, our types statically characterize: (i) more usages of asymmetric cryptography, such as signatures of private data and encryptions of authenticated data; (ii) authenticity and integrity properties achieved by showing knowledge of secret data; (iii) applications based on zero-knowledge proofs.

Protocols are implemented in $\text{RCF}_{\wedge\vee}^{\forall}$ [12], a concurrent lambda-calculus, and cryptographic primitives are considered fully reliable building blocks and represented symbolically using a sealing mechanism [12, 35, 43]. In addition to hashes, symmetric cryptography, public-key encryption, and digital signatures, our approach supports zero-knowledge proofs. Since the realization of zero-knowledge proofs changes according to the statement to be proven, we provide a tool that, given a statement, automatically generates a symbolic implementation of the corresponding zero-knowledge primitive.

Our type-based analysis is automated, modular, efficient, and provides security proofs for an unbounded number of sessions. We have implemented a type-checker that performed very well in our experiments: it type-checks all our symbolic libraries and samples totaling more than 1500LOC in around 12 seconds, on a normal laptop. The type-checker features a user-friendly graphical interface for examining typing derivations. The tool-chain we have developed additionally contains an automatic code generator for zero-knowledge proofs, an interpreter, and a visual debugger.

We have formalized the type system, and all the important parts of the soundness proof in the Coq proof assistant. The formalization and the implementation are available online [7].

1.2 Related Work

Our type system extends the refinement type system by Bengtson et al. [12] with union, intersection, and polymorphic types. We also encode a novel type Private, which is used to characterize data that are not known to the attacker. A crucial property is that the set of values of type Private is disjoint from the set of values of type Un, which is the type of the messages known to the attacker. This property allows us to prune typing derivations following equality tests between values of type Private and values of type Un. This technique was first proposed by Abadi and Blanchet in their seminal work on secrecy types for asymmetric cryptography [1], but later disappeared in the more advanced type systems for authorization policies. Our extension is necessary to deal with protocols based on zero-knowledge proofs and to verify integrity and authenticity properties obtained by showing knowledge of secret data (e.g., the Needham-Schroeder-Lowe public-key protocol). In addition, our extension removes the restrictions that the type system proposed in [12] poses on the usage of standard cryptographic primitives. For instance, if a key is used to sign a secret message, then the corresponding verification key cannot be made public. These limitations were preventing the analysis of many interesting cryptographic applications, such as the Direct Anonymous Attestation protocol [18], which involves digital signatures on secret TPM identifiers.

In recent parallel work, Bhargavan et al. [14] have developed an additional cryptographic library for a simplified version of the type system proposed in [12]. This library does not rely on sealing but on datatype constructors and inductive logical invariants that allow for reasoning about symmetric and asymmetric cryptography, hybrid encryption, and different forms of nested cryptography. The aforementioned logical invariants are, however, fairly complex and have to be proven manually. Moreover, these logical invariants are global, which means that adding new cryptographic primitives could require reproving the previous established invariants. Therefore, extending a symbolic cryptographic library in the style of [14] to new primitives requires expertise and a considerable human effort. In contrast, extending our sealing-based library does not involve any additional proof: one has just to find a well-typed encoding of the desired cryptographic primitive, which is relatively easy[1].

The main simplification Bhargavan et al. [14] propose over [12] is the removal of the kinding relation, which classifies types as public or tainted, and allows values of public types to also be given any tainted type by subsumption. While this simplification removes the last security-specific part of the type system, therefore making it more

---

[1] A master's student encoded the sophisticated cryptographic schemes used in the Civitas [22] electronic voting protocol (i.e., distributed decryption, plaintext equivalence tests, homomorphic encryptions, mix nets, and a variety of zero-knowledge proofs) in about three weeks [29].

standard, this change also requires attackers to be well-typed with respect to a carefully constructed attacker interface. In contrast, by retaining the kinding relation from [12] we also retain the property that *all* attackers are well-typed with respect to our type system (this property is usually called opponent typability). Despite these disadvantages, Bhargavan et al. [14] manage to solve some of the problems we address in this paper, without relying on union and intersection types, but instead using the logical connectives inside the refinement types. It would be interesting future work to try to combine the advantages of both approaches in a unified framework.

Backes et al. [11] have recently established a semantic correspondence for asymmetric cryptography between a library based on sealing and one based on constructors, showing that both libraries enjoy computational soundness guarantees.

Backes et al. [8] proposed a type system for statically analyzing security protocols based on zero-knowledge proofs in the setting of the Spi calculus. Zero-knowledge proofs are modeled using constructors and destructors. In an extension of this type system [6], union and intersection types are used to infer precise type information about the secret witnesses of zero-knowledge proofs. This is captured in a separate relation called statement verification, which is fairly complex and tailored to zero-knowledge proofs. In contrast, in our paper we encode zero-knowledge proofs symbolically using standard programming language primitives, and we type-check them using general typing rules.

Goubault-Larrecq and Parrennes developed a static analysis technique [32] based on pointer analysis and clause resolution for cryptographic protocols implemented in C. The analysis is limited to secrecy properties, it deals only with standard cryptographic primitives, and it does not offer scalability since the number of generated clauses is very high even on small protocol examples.

Chaki and Datta have proposed a technique [21] based on software model checking for the automated verification of protocols implemented in C. The analysis provides security guarantees for a bounded number of sessions and is effective in discovering attacks. It was used to check secrecy and authentication properties of the SSL handshake protocol for configurations of up to three servers and three clients. The analysis only deals with standard cryptographic primitives, and offers only limited scalability.

Bhargavan et al. proposed a technique [15] for the verification of F# protocol implementations by automatically extracting ProVerif models [16]. The technique was successfully used to verify implementations of real-world cryptographic protocols such as TLS [13]. The analysis, however, is not compositional and is significantly less scalable than type-checking [14]. Furthermore, the considered fragment of F# is restrictive: it does not include higher-order functions, and it allows only for a very limited usage of recursion and state.

The more technical discussion about the related work on union and intersection types is postponed to §8.

1.3   Outline

The remainder of the paper is structured as follows. §2 gives an intuitive overview of our type system and exemplifies the most important concepts on a simple authentication protocol. §3 introduces the syntax of $\mathrm{RCF}_{\wedge\vee}^{\forall}$, the language supported by our type-checker. §4 presents the type system. §5 and §6 show how our type system can be used to obtain an expressive characterization of asymmetric cryptography and zero-knowledge proofs, respectively. §7 describes our implementation and experiments. §8 discusses some related work on union and intersection types. §9 concludes and gives some interesting research directions. We refer to the long version for the results of our Coq formalization, a more technical presentation of our encoding for zero-knowledge proofs, and other details [7].

2 Our Type System at Work

Before giving the details of the calculus and the type system, we illustrate the main concepts of our static analysis technique on the Needham-Schroeder-Lowe public-key protocol [37] (NSL), which could not be analyzed with previous refinement type systems for protocol implementations [12, 14]. For convenience, throughout this section we use some syntactic sugar that is supported by our type-checker and can be obtained from the core calculus presented in §3 by standard encodings [12].

2.1 Protocol Description and Security Annotations

The Needham-Schroeder-Lowe protocol is depicted below:

$$A \qquad\qquad\qquad\qquad\qquad\qquad\qquad\qquad\qquad B$$

$$\longleftarrow\!\!\!-\!\!\!-\!\!\!-\!\!\!-\!\!\!-\!\!\!-\!\!\!-\!\!\!-\!\!\!-\ \{B,n_B\}_{k_A^+}\ -\!\!\!-\!\!\!-\!\!\!-\!\!\!-\!\!\!-\!\!\!-\!\!\!-\!\!\!-\!\!\!-$$

assume $\mathsf{auth}_r(A, B, n_B, n_A)$

$$-\!\!\!-\!\!\!-\!\!\!-\!\!\!-\!\!\!-\!\!\!-\!\!\!-\ \{A,n_B,n_A\}_{k_B^+}\ -\!\!\!-\!\!\!-\!\!\!-\!\!\!-\!\!\!-\!\!\!\longrightarrow$$

$$\qquad\qquad\qquad\qquad\qquad\qquad\qquad\qquad \text{assert } \mathsf{auth}_r(A, B, n_B, n_A)$$

$$\qquad\qquad\qquad\qquad\qquad\qquad\qquad\qquad \text{assume } \mathsf{auth}_i(B, A, n_B, n_A)$$

$$\longleftarrow\!\!\!-\!\!\!-\!\!\!-\!\!\!-\!\!\!-\!\!\!-\!\!\!-\!\!\!-\ \{n_A\}_{k_A^+}\ -\!\!\!-\!\!\!-\!\!\!-\!\!\!-\!\!\!-\!\!\!-\!\!\!-$$

assert $\mathsf{auth}_i(B, A, n_B, n_A)$

The goal of this protocol is to allow A and B to authenticate with each other and to exchange two fresh nonces, which are meant to be private and be later used to construct a session key. B creates a fresh nonce n_B and encrypts it together with his own identifier with A's public key. A decrypts the ciphertext with her private key. At this point of the of the protocol, A does not know whether the ciphertext comes from B or from the opponent as the encryption key used to create the ciphertext is public. A continues the protocol by creating a fresh nonce n_A, and encrypts this nonce together with n_B and her own identifier with B's public key. B decrypts the ciphertext and, although the encryption key used to create the ciphertext is public, if the nonce he received matches the one he has sent to A then B does indeed know that the ciphertext comes from A, since the nonce n_B is *private* and only A has access to it. Finally, B encrypts the nonce n_A received from A with A's public key, and sends it back to A. After decrypting the ciphertext and checking the nonce, A knows that the ciphertext comes from B as the nonce n_A is *private* and only B has access to it.

Following [12], we decorate the code with assumptions and assertions. Intuitively, assumptions introduce new hypotheses, while assertions declare formulas that should logically follow from the previously introduced hypotheses. A program is safe if in all program runs the assertions are entailed by the assumptions. The assumptions and assertions of the NSL protocol capture the standard mutual authentication property.

2.2   Types for Cryptography

Before illustrating how we can type-check this protocol, let us introduce the typed interface of our library for public-key cryptography. Intuitively, since encryption keys are public, they can be used by honest principals to encrypt data as specified by the protocol, or by the attacker to encrypt arbitrary data. This intuitive reasoning is captured by the following typed interface:

$$encrypt : \forall \alpha. \, \mathsf{PubKey}\langle \alpha \rangle \rightarrow \alpha \vee \mathsf{Un} \rightarrow \mathsf{Un}$$
$$decrypt : \forall \alpha. \, \mathsf{Un} \rightarrow \mathsf{PrivKey}\langle \alpha \rangle \rightarrow \alpha \vee \mathsf{Un}$$

Like many of the functions in our cryptographic library, the *encrypt* and *decrypt* functions are polymorphic. Their code is type-checked only once and given an universal type. The type variable α stands in this case for the type of the payload that is encrypted, and can be instantiated with an arbitrary type when the functions are used.

Type Un describes those values that may be known to the opponent, i.e., data that may come from or be sent to the opponent. The type $\mathsf{PubKey}\langle \alpha \rangle$ describes public keys. Since the opponent has access to the public key and to the encryption function, the type system has to take into account that the library may be used by honest principals to encrypt data of type α or by the opponent to encrypt data of type Un. The *encrypt* function takes as input a public key of type $\mathsf{PubKey}\langle \alpha \rangle$ a message of type $\alpha \vee \mathsf{Un}$, and returns a ciphertext of type Un. The *decrypt* function takes as input a ciphertext of type Un, a private key of type $\mathsf{PrivKey}\langle \alpha \rangle$ and returns a payload of type $\alpha \vee \mathsf{Un}$. Without union types, the type of the payload is constrained to be Un or a supertype thereof [12], which severely limits the expressiveness of the type system and prevents the analysis of a number of protocols, including this very simple example.

2.3   Type-Checking the NSL Protocol

We first introduce the type definitions[2] for the content of the three ciphertexts:

$$
\begin{aligned}
\mathsf{msg1} \quad &= (\mathsf{Un} * \mathsf{Private}) \\
\mathsf{msg2}[x_B] &= (x_A : \mathsf{Un} * x_{nB} : \mathsf{Private} \vee \mathsf{Un} \, * \, \{x_{nA} : \mathsf{Private} \mid \mathsf{auth_r}(x_A, x_B, x_{nB}, x_{nA})\}) \\
\mathsf{msg3} \quad &= \{x_{nA} : \mathsf{Private} \mid \exists x_A, x_B, x_{nB}. \\
&\qquad \mathsf{auth_r}(x_A, x_B, x_{nB}, x_{nA}) \, \wedge \, \mathsf{auth_i}(x_B, x_A, x_{nB}, x_{nA})\}
\end{aligned}
$$

The first ciphertext contains a pair composed of a public identifier of type Un and a nonce of type Private. Type Private describes values that are not known to the attacker: the set of values of type Un is disjoint from the set of values of type Private. Type $\mathsf{msg2}[x_A]$ is a combination of two dependent pair types and one refinement type. This type describes a triple composed of an identifier x_A of type Un, a first nonce x_{nB} of type Private $\vee$ Un, and a second nonce x_{nA} of type Private such that the predicate $\mathsf{auth_r}(x_A, x_B, x_{nB}, x_{nA})$ is entailed by the assumptions in the system (A assumes

---

[2] Type definitions are syntactic sugar, and are inlined by the type-checker.

Table 1. NSL Initiator Code and Responder Code

$\text{init} = \lambda x_B : \text{Un}. \ \lambda x_A : \text{Un}.$	$\text{resp} = \lambda x_A : \text{Un}. \ \lambda x_B : \text{Un}.$
$\quad \lambda k_B : \text{PrivKey}\langle\text{payload}[x_B]\rangle.$	$\quad \lambda pk_B : \text{PubKey}\langle\text{payload}[x_B]\rangle.$
$\quad \lambda pk_A : \text{PubKey}\langle\text{payload}[x_A]\rangle.$	$\quad \lambda k_A : \text{PrivKey}\langle\text{payload}[x_A]\rangle.$
$\quad \lambda ch : \text{Ch}(\text{Un}).$	$\quad \lambda ch : \text{Ch}(\text{Un}).$
$\text{let } n_B = \textit{mkPriv}() \text{ in}$	$\text{let } m_1 = \textit{recv}\langle\text{Un}\rangle \ ch \text{ in}$
$\text{let } p_1 = (\text{Msg1 } (x_B, n_B)) \text{ in}$	$\text{let } x_1 \text{ in } \textit{decrypt}\langle\text{payload}[x_A]\rangle \ k_A \ m_1$
$\text{let } m_1 = \textit{encrypt}\langle\text{payload}[x_A]\rangle \ pk_A \ p_1 \text{ in}$	$\text{case } y_1 = x_1 : \text{payload}[x_A] \lor \text{Un in}$
$\textit{send}\langle\text{Un}\rangle \ ch \ m_1;$	$\text{match } y_1 \text{ with Msg1 } z_1 \Rightarrow$
$\text{let } z = \textit{recv}\langle\text{Un}\rangle \ ch \text{ in}$	$\text{let } (y_B, x_{nB}) = z1 \text{ in}$
$\text{let } x = \textit{decrypt}\langle\text{payload}[x_B]\rangle \ k_B \ z \text{ in}$	$\text{if } y_B = x_B \text{ then}$
$\text{case } x_1 = x : \text{payload}[x_B] \lor \text{Un in}$	$\text{let } n_A = \textit{mkPriv}() \text{ in}$
$\text{match } x_1 \text{ with Msg2 } x_2 \Rightarrow$	$\text{assume auth}_r(x_A, x_B, x_{nB}, n_A);$
$\text{let } (y_A, y_{nB}, y_{nA}) = x_2 \text{ in}$	$\text{let } p_2 = \text{Msg2}(x_A, x_{nB}, n_A) \text{ in}$
$\text{if } y_A = x_A \text{ then}$	$\text{let } m_2 = \textit{encrypt}\langle\text{payload}[x_B]\rangle \ pk_B \ p_2 \text{ in}$
$\text{if } y_{nB} = n_B \text{ then}$	$\textit{send}\langle\text{Un}\rangle \ ch \ m_2;$
$\text{assert auth}_r(x_A, x_B, y_{nB}, y_{nA});$	$\text{let } m_3 = \textit{recv}\langle\text{Un}\rangle \ ch \text{ in}$
$\text{assume auth}_i(x_B, x_A, y_{nB}, y_{nA});$	$\text{let } x_3 = \textit{decrypt}\langle\text{payload}[x_A]\rangle \ k_A \ m_3 \text{ in}$
$\text{let } p_3 = (\text{Msg3 } y_{nA}) \text{ in}$	$\text{case } y_3 = x_3 : \text{payload}[x_A] \lor \text{Un in}$
$\text{let } m_3 = \textit{encrypt}\langle\text{payload}[x_A]\rangle \ pk_A \ p_3 \text{ in}$	$\text{match } y_3 \text{ with Msg3 } y_{nA} \Rightarrow$
$\textit{send}\langle\text{Un}\rangle \ ch \ m_3$	$\text{if } y_{nA} = n_A \text{ then}$
	$\text{assert auth}_i(x_B, x_A, x_{nB}, n_A)$

$\text{auth}_r(A, B, n_B, n_A)$ before creating the second ciphertext). The free occurrence of x_B is bound in the type definition. Notice that x_{nB} is given type Private $\lor$ Un since A does not know whether the nonce received in the first ciphertext comes from B or from the opponent. Type msg3 is a refinement type describing a nonce x_{nA} of type Private such that the formula $\exists x_A, x_B, x_{nB}. \ \text{auth}_r(x_A, x_B, x_{nB}, x_{nA}) \land \text{auth}_i(x_B, x_A, x_{nB}, x_{nA})$ is entailed by the assumptions in the system. Indeed, before creating the third ciphertext, B has asserted $\text{auth}_r(A, B, n_B, n_A)$ and assumed $\text{auth}_i(B, A, n_B, n_A)$. Since the payload of the third message only contains x_{nA} we existentially quantify the other variables. The overall type of the payload is obtained by combining the three previous types:

$$\text{payload}[x] = \text{Msg1 of msg1} \mid \text{Msg2 of msg2}[x] \mid \text{Msg3 of msg3}$$

The type of A's public key is defined as $\text{PubKey}\langle\text{payload}[A]\rangle$ and the type of B's public key is defined as $\text{PubKey}\langle\text{payload}[B]\rangle$.

The code of the initiator (B in our diagram) and the code of the responder (A) abstract over the principal's identity and they are type-checked independently of each other.

Since library functions such as *encrypt, decrypt, send* and so on are polymorphic, they are instantiated with a concrete types in the code (e.g., the encryptions in the initiator's code are instantiated with type payload$[x_A]$ since they take as argument x_A's public key). The initiator creates a fresh private nonce by means of the function *mkPriv*. The nonce is encrypted together with B's identifier and sent on the network. The message x obtained by decrypting the second ciphertext is given type payload$[x_B] \lor$ Un, which reflects the fact that B does not know whether the first ciphertext comes from

A or from the attacker. Since we cannot statically predict which of the two types is the right one, we have to type-check the continuation code twice, once under the assumption that x has type payload$[x_B]$ and once assuming that x has type Un. This is realized by the expression case $x_1 = x$: payload$[x_B] \vee$ Un in . . ..

If x has type payload$[x_B]$, then its components are given strong types: y_A is given type Un, y_{nB} is given type Private $\vee$ Un, and y_{nA} is given the refinement type $\{y_{nA} :$ Private $|$ auth$_r(x_A, x_B, y_{nB}, y_{nA})\}$. This refinement type ensures that auth$_r(x_A, x_B, y_{nB}, y_{nA})$ will be entailed at run-time by the assumptions in the system and thus justifies the assertion assert auth$_r(x_A, x_B, y_{nB}, y_{nA})$. Finally, the assumption assume auth$_i(x_B, x_A, y_{nB}, y_{nA})$ allows us to give y_{nA} type msg3 and thus to type-check the final encryption.

If x has type Un then y_A, y_{nB}, and y_{nA} are also given type Un. The following equality check between the value y_{nB} of type Un and the nonce n_B of type Private makes type-checking the remaining code superfluous: since the set of values of type Un is disjoint from the set of values of type Private, it cannot be that the equality test succeeds. So type-checking the initiator's code succeeds.

Type-checking the responder's code is similar. The code contains two case expressions to deal with the union types introduced by the two decryptions. In particular, the code after the second decryption has to be type-checked under the assumption that the variable y_{nA} has type msg3 and under the assumption that y_{nA} has type Un.

In the former case, the assertion assert auth$_i(x_B, x_A, x_{nB}, n_A)$ is justified by the previously assumed formula auth$_r(x_A, x_B, x_{nB}, n_A)$, the formula in the above refinement type, and the following global assumption, stating that there cannot be two different assumptions auth$_r(x_A, x_B, x'_{nB}, x'_{nA})$ and auth$_r(x'_A, x'_B, x'_{nB}, x'_{nA})$ with the same nonce x_{nB}.

$$\text{assume } \forall x_A, x_B, x'_A, x'_B, x_{nA}, x'_{nA}, x_{nB}.$$
$$\text{auth}_r(x_A, x_B, x_{nB}, x_{nA}) \wedge \text{auth}_r(x'_A, x'_B, x_{nB}, x'_{nA})$$
$$\Rightarrow x_A = x'_A \wedge x_B = x'_B \wedge x_{nA} = x'_{nA}$$

This assumption is justified by the fact that the predicate auth$_r$ is assumed only in the responder's code, immediately after the creation of a fresh nonce x_{nB}.

If y_{nA} is given type Un then type-checking the following code succeeds because the equality check between y_{nA} and the value n_A of type Private cannot succeed.

The functions init and resp take private keys as input, so they are not available to the attacker. We provide two public functions that capture the capabilities of the attacker.

Attacker's Interface for NSL

```
createPrincipal = λx : Un.
    let k = mkPrivKey⟨payload[x]⟩ () in addToDB x k; getPubKey⟨payload[x]⟩ k

startNSL = λ(role : Un)(x_A : Un)(x_B : Un)(c : Un).
    let k_A = getFromDB x_A in let pk_A = getPubKey⟨payload[x_A]⟩ k_A in
    let k_B = getFromDB x_B in let pk_B = getPubKey⟨payload[x_B]⟩ k_B in
    match role with inl _ ⇒ (init x_A x_B k_A pk_B c)
    | inr _ ⇒ (resp x_B x_A pk_A k_B c)
```

We allow the attacker to create arbitrarily many new principals using the createPrincipal function. This generates a new encryption key-pair, stores it in a private database, and then returns the corresponding public key to the attacker. The second function, startNSL, allows the attacker to start an arbitrary number of sessions of the protocol, between principals of his choice. When calling startNSL, the attacker chooses whether he wants to start an initiator or a responder, the principals to be involved in the session, and the channel on which the communication occurs. One principal can be involved in many sessions simultaneously, in which it may play different roles.

The two functions above express the capabilities of the attacker for verification purposes, and would not be exposed in a production setting. However, they can also be useful for testing and debugging the code of the protocol: for instance we can execute a protocol run using the following code.

Test Setup for NSL

```
createPrincipal "Alice"; createPrincipal "Bob";
let c = mkChan⟨Un⟩ () in
(startNSL (inl ()) "Alice" "Bob" c) ⌒ (startNSL (inr ()) "Alice" "Bob" c)
```

Since the code of the NSL protocol is well-typed, the soundness result of the type system ensures that in all program runs the assertions are entailed by the assumptions, i.e., the code is safe when executed by an arbitrary attacker. In addition, the two nonces are given type Private and thus they are not revealed to the opponent.

3   The $RCF^\forall_{\wedge\vee}$ Calculus

The Refined Concurrent FPC (RCF) [12] is a simple programming language extending the Fixed Point Calculus with refinement types and concurrency [4]. This core calculus is expressive enough to encode a considerable fragment of an ML-like programming language [12]. In this paper, we further increase the expressivity of the calculus by adding intersection types [40], union types [39], and parametric polymorphism. We call the extended calculus $RCF^\forall_{\wedge\vee}$ and describe it in this and the following section.

We start by presenting the surface syntax of $RCF^\forall_{\wedge\vee}$, which is a subset of the syntax supported by our type-checker. In the surface syntax of $RCF^\forall_{\wedge\vee}$ variables are named, which makes programs human-readable. The surface syntax also contains explicit typing annotations that guide type-checking. It is given semantics by translation (i.e., type erasure) into a core implicitly-typed calculus, which we have formalized in Coq [7]. The syntax comprises the four mutually-inductively-defined sets of values, types, expressions, and formulas. We mark with star (*) the constructs that are completely new with respect to RCF [12].

Surface syntax of $RCF^\forall_{\wedge\vee}$ values

x, y, z	variable
$h ::= $ inl $\mid$ inr	constructor for sum types
$M, N ::=$	value
$\quad x$	variable
$\quad ()$	unit
$\quad \lambda x : T. A$	function (scope of x is A)
$\quad (M, N)$	pair

$h\ M$	value of sum type
$\mathsf{fold}_{\mu\alpha.\,T}\ M$	recursive value
$\Lambda\alpha.\,A$	type abstraction* (scope of α is A)
for $\widetilde{\alpha}$ in $\widetilde{T};\widetilde{U}.\,M$	value of intersection type* (scope of $\widetilde{\alpha} = \alpha_1, .., \alpha_n$ is M)

The set of *values* is composed of variables, the unit value, functions, pairs, and introduction forms for disjoint union, recursive, polymorphic, and intersection types.

Surface syntax of RCF$_{\wedge\vee}^{\forall}$ types

α, β		type variable
$T, U, V ::=$		type
	unit	unit type
	$x : T \to U$	dependent function type (x bound in U)
	$x : T * U$	dependent pair type (x bound in U)
	$T + U$	disjoint sum type
	$\mu\alpha.\,T$	iso-recursive type (α bound in T)
	α	type variable
	$\{x : T \mid C\}$	refinement type (x bound in C)
	$T \wedge U$	intersection type*
	$T \vee U$	union type*
	$\top$	top type*
	$\forall\alpha.\,T$	polymorphic type* (α bound in T)

The unit value () is given type unit. Functions $\lambda x : T.\,A$ taking as input values of type T and returning values of type U are given the dependent type $x : T \to U$, where the result type U can depend on the input value x. Pairs are given dependent types of the form $x : T * U$, where the type U of the second component of the pair can depend on the value x of the first component. If U does not depend on x, then we use the abbreviations $T \to U$ and $T * U$. The sum type $T + U$ describes values $\mathsf{inl}(M)$ where M is of type T and values $\mathsf{inr}(N)$ where N is of type U. The iso-recursive type $\mu\alpha.\,T$ is the type of all values $\mathsf{fold}_{\mu\alpha.\,T}\ M$ where M is of type $T\{\mu\alpha.\,T/\alpha\}$. We use refinement types [12] to associate logical formulas to messages. The refinement type $\{x : T \mid C\}$ describes values M of type T for which the formula $C\{M/x\}$ is entailed by the current typing environment. A value is given the intersection type $T \wedge U$ if it has both type T and type U. A value is given a union type $T \vee U$ if it has type T or if it has type U, but we do not necessarily know what its precise type is. The top type $\top$ is supertype of all the other types, and contains all well-typed values. The universal type $\forall\alpha.\,T$ describes polymorphic values $\Lambda\alpha.\,A$ such that $A\{U/\alpha\}$ is of type $T\{U/\alpha\}$ for all types U.

Surface syntax of RCF$_{\wedge\vee}^{\forall}$ expressions

a, b		name
$A, B ::=$		expression
	M	value
	$M\ N$	function application
	$M\langle T\rangle$	type instantiation*
	let $x = A$ in B	let (scope of x is B)
	let $(x, y) = M$ in A	pair split (scope of x, y is A)
	match M with inl $x \Rightarrow A \mid$ inr $y \Rightarrow B$	pattern matching (scope of x is A, of y is B)

$\text{unfold}_{\mu\alpha.\,T}\ M$	use recursive value
$\text{case } x = M : T \vee U \text{ in } A$	elimination of union types* (scope of x is A)
$\text{if } M = N \text{ as } x \text{ then } A \text{ else } B$	equality check with type cast* (scope of x is A)
$(\nu a \uparrow T)A$	restriction (scope of a is A)
$A \upharpoonright B$	fork off parallel expression
$a!M$	send M on channel a
$a?$	receive on channel a
$\text{assume } C$	add formula C to global log
$\text{assert } C$	formula C must hold

The syntax of expressions is mostly standard [12, 39]. A type instantiation $M\langle T\rangle$ specializes a polymorphic value M with the concrete type T. The elimination form for union types case $x = M : T \vee U$ in A substitutes the value M in A. The conditional if $M = N$ as x then A else B checks if M is syntactically equal to N, if this is the case it substitutes x with the common value. Syntactic equality is defined up to alpha-renaming of binders and the erasure of typing annotations and constructs such as for. During type-checking the variable x is given the intersection of the types of M and N. When the variable x is not necessary we omit the as clause, as we did in §2. The restriction $(\nu a \uparrow T)A$ generates a globally fresh channel a that can only be used in A to convey values of type T. The expression $A \upharpoonright B$ evaluates A and B in parallel, and returns the result of B (the result of A is discarded). The expression $a!M$ outputs M on channel a and returns the unit value (). Expression $a?$ blocks until some message M is available on channel a, removes M from the channel, and then returns M. Expression assume C adds the logical formula C to a global log. The assertion assert C returns () when triggered. If at this point C is entailed by the multiset S of formulas in the global log, written as $S \models C$, we say the assertion *succeeds*; otherwise, we say the assertion *fails*.

Intuitively, an expression A is *safe* if, once it is translated into Formal-RCF$^{\forall}_{\wedge\vee}$, all assertions succeed in all evaluations. When reasoning about implementations of cryptographic protocols, we are interested in the safety of programs executed in parallel with an arbitrary attacker. This property is called *robust safety* and is statically enforced by our type system from §4.

We consider a variant of first-order logic with equality as the authorization logic. We assume that RCF$^{\forall}_{\wedge\vee}$ values are the terms of this logic, and equality $M = N$ is interpreted as syntactic equality between values.

4   Type System

This section presents our type system for enforcing authorization policies on RCF$^{\forall}_{\wedge\vee}$ code. This extends the type system proposed by Bengtson et al. [12] with union, intersection, and polymorphic types. Additionally, we encode a new type Private, which is used to characterize data that are not known to the attacker, and introduce a novel relation for statically reasoning about the disjointness of types. In the following we explain the typing judgements and present the most important typing rules.

4.1 Typing Environment and Entailment

A typing environment E is a list of bindings for variables $(x : T)$, type variables (α or $\alpha :: k$), names ($a \uparrow T$, where the name a stands for a channel conveying values of type T), and formulas (bindings of the form $\{C\}$). An environment is well-formed ($E \vdash \diamond$) if all variables, names, and type variables are defined before use, and no duplicate definitions exist. A type T is well-formed in environment E (written $E \vdash T$) if all its free variables, names, and type variables are defined in E.

A crucial judgment in the type system is $E \vdash C$, which states that the formula C is derivable from the formulas in E. Intuitively, our type system ensures that whenever $E \vdash C$ we have that C is logically entailed by the global formula log at execution time. This judgment is used for instance when type-checking assert C using (Exp Assert): type-checking succeeds only if C is entailed in the current typing environment.

4.2 Subtyping and Kinding

Intuitively, all data sent to and received from an untrusted channel have type Un, since such channels are considered under the complete control of the adversary. However, a system in which only data of type Un can be communicated over the untrusted network would be too restrictive, e.g., a value of type $\{x : \mathsf{Un} \mid Ok(x)\}$ could not be sent over the network. We therefore consider a *subtyping relation* on types, which allows a term of a subtype to be used in all contexts that require a term of a supertype. This preorder is most often used to compare types with type Un. In particular, we allow values having type T that is a subtype of Un, denoted $T <: \mathsf{Un}$, to be sent over the untrusted network, and we say that the type T has *kind public* in this case. Similarly, we allow values of type Un that are received from the untrusted network to be used as values of type U, provided that $\mathsf{Un} <: U$, and in this case we say that type U has *kind tainted*. We outline some important rules for kinding and subtyping (let k range over pub and tnt).

Kinding and subtyping for refinement types

(Kind Refine Pub)
$$\frac{E \vdash \{x : T \mid C\} \quad E \vdash T :: \mathsf{pub}}{E \vdash \{x : T \mid C\} :: \mathsf{pub}}$$

(Kind Refine Tnt)
$$\frac{E \vdash T :: \mathsf{tnt} \quad E, x : T \vdash C}{E \vdash \{x : T \mid C\} :: \mathsf{tnt}}$$

(Sub Refine Left)
$$\frac{E \vdash \{x : T \mid C\} \quad E \vdash T <: T'}{E \vdash \{x : T \mid C\} <: T'}$$

(Sub Refine Right)
$$\frac{E \vdash T <: T' \quad E, x : T \vdash C}{E \vdash T <: \{x : T' \mid C\}}$$

The refinement type $\{x : T \mid C\}$ is a subtype of T. This allows us to discard logical formulas when they are not needed. For instance, a value of type $\{x : \mathsf{Un} \mid Ok(x)\}$ can be sent on a channel of type Un. Conversely, the type T is a subtype of $\{x : T \mid C\}$ only if $\forall x.C$ is entailed in the current typing environment, so by subtyping we can only add universally valid formulas.

Kinding for pair and function types

(Kind Pair)
$$\frac{E \vdash T :: k \quad E, x : T \vdash U :: k}{E \vdash (x : T * U) :: k}$$

(Kind Fun)
$$\frac{E \vdash T :: \overline{k} \quad E, x : T \vdash U :: k}{E \vdash (x : T \to U) :: k}$$

A pair type $T * U$ is public (or tainted) only if both T and U are public (respectively tainted). On the other hand, a function type $T \rightarrow U$ is public only if the return type U is public (otherwise λx:unit. M_{secret} would be public) and the argument type T is tainted (otherwise $\lambda k : \text{PrivKey}\langle\text{Private}\rangle$. let $x = \text{encrypt}\langle\text{Private}\rangle\ k\ M_{\text{secret}}$ in $a_{\text{pub}}!x$ would be public).

Kinding and subtyping for union and intersection types (*)

(Kind And Pub 1)	(Kind And Pub 2)	(Kind And Tnt)
$\dfrac{E \vdash T_1 :: \text{pub} \quad E \vdash T_2}{E \vdash T_1 \wedge T_2 :: \text{pub}}$	$\dfrac{E \vdash T_1 \quad E \vdash T_2 :: \text{pub}}{E \vdash T_1 \wedge T_2 :: \text{pub}}$	$\dfrac{E \vdash T_1 :: \text{tnt} \quad \Gamma \vdash T_2 :: \text{tnt}}{\Gamma \vdash T_1 \wedge T_2 :: \text{tnt}}$
(Kind Or Pub)	(Kind Or Tnt 1)	(Kind Or Tnt 2)
$\dfrac{E \vdash T_1 :: \text{pub} \quad E \vdash T_2 :: \text{pub}}{E \vdash T_1 \vee T_2 :: \text{pub}}$	$\dfrac{E \vdash T_1 :: \text{tnt} \quad E \vdash T_2}{E \vdash T_1 \vee T_2 :: \text{tnt}}$	$\dfrac{E \vdash T_1 \quad E \vdash T_2 :: \text{tnt}}{E \vdash T_1 \vee T_2 :: \text{tnt}}$
(Sub And LB 1)	(Sub And LB 2)	(Sub And Greatest)
$\dfrac{E \vdash T_1 <: U \quad E \vdash T_2}{E \vdash T_1 \wedge T_2 <: U}$	$\dfrac{E \vdash T_1 \quad E \vdash T_2 <: U}{E \vdash T_1 \wedge T_2 <: U}$	$\dfrac{E \vdash T' <: T_1 \quad E \vdash T' <: T_2}{E \vdash T' <: T_1 \wedge T_2}$
(Sub Or Least)	(Sub Or UB 1)	(Sub Or UB 2)
$\dfrac{E \vdash T_1 <: U \quad E \vdash T_2 <: U}{E \vdash T_1 \vee T_2 <: U}$	$\dfrac{E \vdash T <: U_1 \quad E \vdash U_2}{E \vdash T <: U_1 \vee U_2}$	$\dfrac{E \vdash U_1 \quad E \vdash T <: U_2}{E \vdash T <: U_1 \vee U_2}$

The intersection type $T_1 \wedge T_2$ can intuitively be seen as a[3] greatest lower bound of the types T_1 and T_2. Rules (Sub And LB 1) and (Sub And LB 2) ensure that $T_1 \wedge T_2$ is a lower bound: by using reflexivity in the premise we obtain that $T_1 \wedge T_2 <: T_1$ and $T_1 \wedge T_2 <: T_2$. Rule (Sub And Greatest) ensures that $T_1 \wedge T_2$ is greater than any other lower bound: if T' is another lower bound of T_1 and T_2 then T' is a subtype of $T_1 \wedge T_2$. As far as kinding is concerned, the type $T_1 \wedge T_2$ is public if T_1 is public or T_2 is public, and it is tainted if both T_1 and T_2 are tainted.

The union type $T_1 \vee T_2$ intuitively corresponds to a least upper bound of T_1 and T_2. The rules for union types are exactly the dual of the ones for intersection types.

Our type system has no distributivity rules between union and intersection types and the primitive type constructors. Some distributivity rules are derivable from the primitive rules above: for instance we can prove that $T \rightarrow (U_1 \wedge U_2)$ is a subtype of $(T \rightarrow U_1) \wedge (T \rightarrow U_2)$, but not the other way around. In fact adding a subtyping rule in the other direction would be unsound [24], since in our system functions can have side-effects and such distributivity rules would allow circumventing the value restriction on the introduction of intersection types (see §4.4 and §8).

Kinding and subtyping rules for universal types

(Kind Univ*)	(Sub Univ*)
$\dfrac{E, \alpha \vdash T :: k}{E \vdash \forall \alpha. T :: k}$	$\dfrac{E, \alpha \vdash T <: U}{E \vdash \forall \alpha. T <: \forall \alpha. U}$

---

[3] The subtyping relation of RCF is not anti-symmetric, so least and greatest elements are not necessarily unique.

Finally, the rule for subtyping polymorphic types (Sub Univ*) is simple: the type $\forall \alpha.\, T$ is subtype of $\forall \alpha.\, U$ if T is a subtype of U. Similarly, $\forall \alpha.\, T$ has kind k if T has kind k in an environment extended with a binding for α. Note that α can be substituted by any type, so we cannot assume anything about α when checking that $T :: k$ and $T <: U$ respectively.

Kinding and subtyping rules for recursive types

(Kind Rec)	(Sub Pos Rec*)		(Sub Refl*)
$E, \alpha :: k \vdash T :: k$	$E, \alpha \vdash T <: U$ α only occurs positively in T and U		$E \vdash T$
$E \vdash (\mu\alpha.\, T) :: k$	$E \vdash \mu\alpha.\, T <: \mu\alpha.\, U$		$E \vdash T <: T$

The rule (Sub Pos Rec*) for subtyping recursive types is new, and differs significantly from Cardelli's Amber rule [5, 20], which is used by the original RCF:

Cardelli's Amber rule (used by the original RCF)

(Sub Rec)
$E, \alpha <: \alpha' \vdash T <: T'$ $\alpha \neq \alpha'$ $\alpha \notin ftv(T')$ $\alpha' \notin ftv(T)$
$E \vdash \mu\alpha.\, T <: \mu\alpha'.\, T'$

The soundness of the Amber rule (Sub Rec) is hard to prove syntactically [12] – in particular proving the transitivity of subtyping in the presence of the Amber rule requires a complicated inductive argument, which only works for "executable" environments (see [12]), as well as spurious restrictions on the usage of type variables in the rules (Sub Refl*), (Kind And Pub 1), (Kind And Pub 2), (Kind Or Tnt 1), (Kind Or Tnt 2), (Sub And LB 1), (Sub And LB 2), (Sub Or UB 1), (Sub Or UB 2). We use the simpler (Sub Pos Rec*) rule, which is much easier to prove sound and requires no restrictions on the other rules. It resembles (Sub Univ*), our rule for subtyping universal types, with the additional restriction that the recursive variable is not allowed to appear in a contravariant position (such as $\alpha \to T$). While this positivity restriction is crucial for the soundness of the (Sub Pos Rec*) rule, this does not pose any problem in practice, where most of the time only positive recursive types [38, 44] are used. Moreover, this positivity restriction only affects subyping, so programs involving negative occurrences of recursion variables that do not involve subtyping can still be properly type-checked (e.g., we can still type-check the encodings of fixpoint combinators on expressions [12])

4.3   Encoding Types Un and Private in RCF

In RCF [12] the type Un is in fact not primitive. By the (Sub Pub Tnt) rule that relates kinding and subtyping, any type that is both public and tainted is equivalent to Un. Since type unit is both public and tainted, Un is actually encoded as unit.

The (Sub Pub Tnt) rule and kinding for type unit

(Sub Pub Tnt)	(Kind Unit)
$E \vdash T :: \mathsf{pub}$ $E \vdash U :: \mathsf{tnt}$	$E \vdash \diamond$
$E \vdash T <: U$	$E \vdash \mathsf{unit} :: k$

The (Sub Pub Tnt) rule equates many of the types in the system. For instance in RCF all the following types are equivalent: Un, Un $\to$ Un, Un $*$ Un, Un $+$ Un, $\mu\alpha.$ Un, and $\forall\alpha.$ Un. As a consequence it is hard to come up with RCF types that do not share any values with type Un, a property we want for our Private type. Perhaps unintuitively, it is not enough that a type is not public and not tainted to make it disjoint from Un. A final observation is that, in $\text{RCF}_{\wedge\vee}^{\forall}$, in an inconsistent environment ($E \vdash$ false) *all* types are equivalent and all values inhabit all types. This means that Private being disjoint from Un is relative to the formulas in the environment.

Encoding type Private

$$\{C\} \triangleq \{x : \text{unit} \mid C\} \qquad x \notin \textit{free}(C)$$
$$\text{Private}_C \triangleq \{f : \{C\} \to \text{Un} \mid \exists x.\ f = \lambda y : \{C\}.\ \text{assert } C; x\} \qquad \text{Private} \triangleq \text{Private}_{\text{false}}$$

We therefore encode a more general type Private_C, read "private unless C". The values in this type are not known to the attacker, unless the formula C is entailed by the environment. Intuitively, if the attacker would know a value of this type, then he could call it (values of type Private_C have to be functions), which would exercise the assert C and invalidate the safety of the system, unless C can be derived from the formula log. Type Private_C resembles a singleton type, in that it contains only values of a very specific form. We use an existential quantifier over values to ensure that there are infinitely many values of this type. The type Private is obtained as $\text{Private}_{\text{false}}$.

4.4 Typing Values and Expressions

The main judgments of the type system we consider are $E \vdash M : T$, which states that value M has type T, and $E \vdash A : T$, stating that expression A returns a value of type T. These two judgements are mutually-inductively defined, and the most important typing rules are reported below. Most of them are standard, so we focus the explanation only on the rules that are new with respect to [12].

Selected rules for typing values $E \vdash M : T$

(Val Lam)	(Val TLam*)	(Val Refine)
$\dfrac{E, x : T \vdash A : U}{E \vdash \lambda x : T.\ A : (x : T \to U)}$	$\dfrac{E, \alpha \vdash A : T}{E \vdash \Lambda\alpha.\ A : \forall\alpha.\ T}$	$\dfrac{E \vdash M : T \quad E \vdash C\{M/x\}}{E \vdash M : \{x : T \mid C\}}$

(Val And*)	(Val For 1*)	(Val For 2*)
$\dfrac{E \vdash M : T \quad E \vdash M : U}{E \vdash M : T \wedge U}$	$\dfrac{E \vdash M\{\widetilde{T}/\widetilde{\alpha}\} : V}{E \vdash \text{for } \widetilde{\alpha} \text{ in } \widetilde{T}; \widetilde{U}.\ M : V}$	$\dfrac{E \vdash M\{\widetilde{U}/\widetilde{\alpha}\} : V}{E \vdash \text{for } \widetilde{\alpha} \text{ in } \widetilde{T}; \widetilde{U}.\ M : V}$

Rule (Val And*) allows us to give value M an intersection type $T \wedge U$, if we can give M both type T and type U. As discovered by Davies and Pfenning [24] the value restriction is crucial for the soundness of this introduction rule in the presence of side-effects (also see §8). Also, unrelated to the value restriction, this rule is not very useful on its own: since we are in a calculus with typing annotations, it is hard to give one annotated value two different types. For instance, if we want to give the identity function type (Private$\to$Private) $\wedge$ (Un$\to$Un) we need to annotate the argument with type Private (i.e., λx:Private. x) in order to give it type Private$\to$Private, but then we cannot give this value type $Un \rightarrow Un$. Following Pierce [39, 40] and Reynolds [41] we use the for construct to explicitly alternate type annotations. For instance, the identity function of type $(Private \rightarrow Private) \wedge (Un \rightarrow Un)$ can be written as (for α in Private; Un. $\lambda x{:}\alpha.\, x$). By rule (Val For 1*) we can give this value type $Private \rightarrow Private$ if we can give value $\lambda x{:}Private.\, x$ the same type, which is trivial. Similarly, by (Val For 2*) we can give the for value type $Un \rightarrow Un$, so by (Val And*) we can also give it the desired intersection type.

Selected rules for typing expressions $E \vdash A : T$

(Exp Appl)	(Exp Inst*)	(Exp Assert)

$$\frac{E \vdash M : (x : T \rightarrow U) \quad E \vdash N : T}{E \vdash M\ N : U\{N/x\}} \qquad \frac{E \vdash M : \forall \alpha.\, U}{E \vdash M\langle T \rangle : U\{T/\alpha\}} \qquad \frac{E \vdash C}{E \vdash \mathsf{assert}\ C : \mathsf{unit}}$$

(Exp If*)

$$\frac{E \vdash M : T_1 \quad E \vdash N : T_2 \quad \vdash \mathsf{NonDisj}\ T_1\ T_2 \rightsquigarrow C \qquad \quad}{E \vdash \mathsf{if}\ M = N\ \mathsf{as}\ x\ \mathsf{then}\ A\ \mathsf{else}\ B : U}$$
$$E, x : T_1 \wedge T_2, \{x = M \wedge M = N \wedge C\} \vdash A : U \qquad E, \{M \neq N\} \vdash B : U$$

(Exp Case*)

$$\frac{E \vdash M : T_1 \vee T_2 \quad E, x : T_1 \vdash A : U \quad E, x : T_2 \vdash A : U}{E \vdash \mathsf{case}\ x = M : T_1 \vee T_2\ \mathsf{in}\ A : U}$$

(Exp Subsum)

$$\frac{E \vdash A : T \quad E \vdash T <: T'}{E \vdash A : T'}$$

Union Types are introduced by subtyping (T_1 is a subtype of $T_1 \vee T_2$ for any T_2), and eliminated by a case $x = M : T_1 \vee T_2$ in A expression [39] using the (Exp Case*) rule[4]. Given a value M of type $T_1 \vee T_2$, we do not know whether M is of type T_1 or of type T_2, so we have to type-check A under each of these assumptions. This is useful when type-checking code interacting with the attacker. For instance, suppose that a party receives a value encrypted with a public-key that is used by honest parties to encrypt messages of type T (as in the protocol from §2). After decryption, the obtained plaintext is given type $T \vee Un$ since it might come from a honest party as well as from the attacker. We have thus to type-check the remaining code twice, once under the assumption that x is of type T, and once assuming that x is of type Un.

The rule (Exp If*) exploits intersection types for strengthening the type of the values tested for equality in the conditional if $M = N$ as x then A else B. If M is of type T_1 and N is of type T_2, then we type-check A under the assumption that $x = M \wedge M = N$, and x is of type $T_1 \wedge T_2$. This corresponds to a type-cast that is always safe, since the conditional succeeds only if M is syntactically equal to N, in which case the common value has indeed both the type of M and the type of N. This is useful for type-checking the symbolic implementations of digital signatures (see §5.2) and zero-knowledge (see §6). Additionally, if the equality test of the conditional succeeds then the types T_1 and T_2 are not disjoint. However, certain types such as Un and $Private$ have common values only if the environment is inconsistent (i.e., $E \vdash \mathsf{false}$). Therefore, when comparing values of disjoint types it is safe to add false to the environment when type-checking A, which makes checking A always succeed. Intuitively, if T_1 and T_2 are disjoint the

---

[4] As pointed out by Dunfield and Pfenning [28] eliminating union types for expressions that are not in evaluation contexts is unsound in the presence of non-determinism (this is further discussed in §8).

conditional cannot succeed, so the expression A will not be executed. This idea has been applied in [1] for verifying secrecy properties of nonce handshakes, but later disappeared in the more advanced type systems for authorization policies.

Non-disjointness of types (*) $\vdash \mathsf{NonDisj}\ T\ U \rightsquigarrow C$

(ND Private Un)
$$\frac{fv(C) = \emptyset}{\vdash \mathsf{NonDisj}\ \mathsf{Private}_C\ \mathsf{Un} \rightsquigarrow C}$$

(ND True)
$$\frac{}{\vdash \mathsf{NonDisj}\ T_1\ T_2 \rightsquigarrow \mathsf{true}}$$

(ND Sym)
$$\frac{\vdash \mathsf{NonDisj}\ T_2\ T_1 \rightsquigarrow C}{\vdash \mathsf{NonDisj}\ T_1\ T_2 \rightsquigarrow C}$$

(ND Refine)
$$\frac{\vdash \mathsf{NonDisj}\ T_1\ T_2 \rightsquigarrow C}{\vdash \mathsf{NonDisj}\ \{x : T_1 \mid C_1\}\ T_2 \rightsquigarrow C}$$

(ND Rec)
$$\frac{\vdash \mathsf{NonDisj}\ (T\{\alpha/\mu\alpha.\,T\})\ (U\{\beta/\mu\beta.\,U\}) \rightsquigarrow C}{\vdash \mathsf{NonDisj}\ (\mu\alpha.\,T)\ (\mu\beta.\,U) \rightsquigarrow C}$$

(ND Pair)
$$\frac{\vdash \mathsf{NonDisj}\ T_1\ U_1 \rightsquigarrow C_1 \quad \vdash \mathsf{NonDisj}\ T_2\ U_2 \rightsquigarrow C_2}{\vdash \mathsf{NonDisj}\ (T_1 * T_2)\ (U_1 * U_2) \rightsquigarrow C_1 \wedge C_2}$$

(ND Sum)
$$\frac{\vdash \mathsf{NonDisj}\ T_1\ U_1 \rightsquigarrow C_1 \quad \vdash \mathsf{NonDisj}\ T_2\ U_2 \rightsquigarrow C_2}{\vdash \mathsf{NonDisj}\ (T_1 + T_2)\ (U_1 + U_2) \rightsquigarrow (C_1 \vee C_2)}$$

(ND And)
$$\frac{\vdash \mathsf{NonDisj}\ T_1\ U \rightsquigarrow C_1 \quad \vdash \mathsf{NonDisj}\ T_2\ U \rightsquigarrow C_2}{\vdash \mathsf{NonDisj}\ (T_1 \wedge T_2)\ U \rightsquigarrow C_1 \wedge C_2}$$

(ND Or)
$$\frac{\vdash \mathsf{NonDisj}\ T_1\ U \rightsquigarrow C_1 \quad \vdash \mathsf{NonDisj}\ T_2\ U \rightsquigarrow C_2}{\vdash \mathsf{NonDisj}\ (T_1 \vee T_2)\ U \rightsquigarrow C_1 \vee C_2}$$

We take this idea a lot further: we inductively define a ternary relation, which relates two types with a logical formula. If $\vdash \mathsf{NonDisj}\ T_1\ T_2 \rightsquigarrow C$ holds then any environment E in which T_1 and T_2 have a common value, has to entail the condition C (i.e., $E \vdash C$). The base case of this relation is $\vdash \mathsf{NonDisj}\ \mathsf{Private}_C\ \mathsf{Un} \rightsquigarrow C$, in particular $\vdash \mathsf{NonDisj}\ \mathsf{Private}\ \mathsf{Un} \rightsquigarrow \mathsf{false}$. We call two types *provably disjoint* if $\vdash \mathsf{NonDisj}\ T_1\ T_2 \rightsquigarrow C$ for some formula C that logically entails false, so Private and Un are provably disjoint. Intuitively, two provably disjoint types have common values only in an inconsistent environment.

The other inductive rules lift the NonDisj relation to refinement, pair, sum, recursive, union, and intersection types. We explain two of them in terms of provable disjointness. In order to show that two (non-dependent) pair types $(T_1 * T_2)$ and $(U_1 * U_2)$ are provably disjoint, we apply rule (ND Pair) and we need to show that T_1 and U_1 are provably disjoint, or that T_2 and U_2 are provably disjoint (a conjunction is false if at least one of the conjuncts is false). On the other hand, in order to show that two sum types $(T_1 + T_2)$ and $(U_1 + U_2)$ are disjoint using (ND Sum) we need to show both that T_1 and U_1 are disjoint and that T_2 and U_2 are disjoint.

To illustrate the expressivity of this definition we consider a type for binary trees: $\mathsf{tree}\langle\alpha\rangle \triangleq \mu\beta.\,\alpha + (\alpha * \beta * \beta)$. Each node in the tree is either a leaf or has two children, and both kind of nodes store some information of type α. We can show that $\mathsf{tree}\langle\mathsf{Private}\rangle$ and $\mathsf{tree}\langle\mathsf{Un}\rangle$ are provably disjoint. By (ND Rec) we need to show that the unfolded types $\mathsf{Private} + (\mathsf{Private} * \mathsf{tree}\langle\mathsf{Private}\rangle * \mathsf{tree}\langle\mathsf{Private}\rangle)$ and $\mathsf{Un} + (\mathsf{Un} * \mathsf{tree}\langle\mathsf{Un}\rangle * \mathsf{tree}\langle\mathsf{Un}\rangle)$ are disjoint. By (ND Sum) we need to show both that Private and Un are disjoint, which is immediate by (ND Private Un), and that the pair types $(\mathsf{Private} * \mathsf{tree}\langle\mathsf{Private}\rangle * \mathsf{tree}\langle\mathsf{Private}\rangle)$ and $(\mathsf{Un} * \mathsf{tree}\langle\mathsf{Un}\rangle * \mathsf{tree}\langle\mathsf{Un}\rangle)$ are disjoint.

For the latter, by (ND Pair) it suffices to show that the types of the first components of the pair are disjoint, which follows again by (ND Private Un).

We have proved in Coq that our type system enforces robust safety; for details we refer to the long version [7].

5   Implementation of Symbolic Cryptography

In contrast to process calculi for cryptographic protocols [4, 3], $RCF^\forall_{\wedge\vee}$ does not have any built-in construct to model cryptography. Cryptographic primitives are instead encoded using a dynamic sealing mechanism [35], which is based on standard $RCF^\forall_{\wedge\vee}$ constructs. The resulting symbolic cryptographic libraries are type-checked using the regular typing rules. The main advantage is that, adding a new primitive to the library does not involve changes in the calculus or in the soundness proofs: one has just to find a well-typed encoding of the desired cryptographic primitive. In addition, Backes et al. have recently [11] shown that sealing-based libraries for asymmetric cryptography are computationally sound and semantically equivalent to the more traditional Dolev-Yao libraries based on datatype constructors. §5.1 overviews the dynamic sealing mechanism used in [12] to encode symbolic cryptography, while §5.2 and §5.3 show how our expressive type system can be used to improve this encoding and extend the class of supported protocols.

5.1   Dynamic Sealing

The notion of *dynamic sealing* was initially introduced by Morris [35] as a protection mechanism for programs. Later, Sumii and Pierce [43] studied the semantics of dynamic sealing in a λ-calculus, observing a close correspondence with symmetric encryption.

In RCF [12] seals are encoded using pairs, functions, references and lists. A seal is a pair of a *sealing function* and an *unsealing function*, having type:

$$\text{Seal}\,\langle T\rangle = (T \to \text{Un}) * (\text{Un} \to T).$$

The sealing function takes as input a value M of type T and returns a fresh value N of type Un, after adding the pair (M, N) to a secret list that is stored in a reference. The unsealing function takes as input a value N of type Un, scans the list in search of a pair (M, N), and returns M. Only the sealing function and the unsealing function can access this secret list. In RCF, each key-pair is (symbolically) implemented by means of a seal. In the case of public-key cryptography, for instance, the sealing function is used for encrypting, the unsealing function is used for decrypting, and the sealed value N represents the ciphertext.

Let us take a look at the type Seal $\langle T\rangle$. If T is neither public nor tainted, as it is usually the case for *symmetric-key cryptography*, neither the sealing function nor the unsealing function are public, meaning that the symmetric key is kept secret. If T is tainted but not public, as usually the case for *public-key encryption*, the sealing function is public but the unsealing function is not, meaning that the encryption key may be given to the adversary but the decryption key is kept secret. If T is public but not tainted, as typically the case for *digital signatures*, the sealing function is not public and the unsealing function is public, meaning that the signing key is kept secret but the verification key may be given to the adversary.

Although this unified interpretation of cryptography as sealing and unsealing functions is conceptually appealing, it actually exhibits some undesired side-effects when modeling asymmetric cryptography. If the type of a signed message is not public, then the verification key is not public either and cannot be given to the adversary. This is unrealistic, since in most cases verification keys are public even if the message to be signed is not (as in DAA, see §6.1). Moreover, if the type of a message encrypted with a public key is not tainted, then the public key is not public and cannot be given to the adversary. This may be problematic, for instance, when modeling authentication protocols based on public keys as the NSL protocol (see §2), where the type of the encrypted messages is neither public nor tainted.

5.2 Digital Signatures

In this section, we focus on digital signatures and show how union and intersection types can be used to solve the aforementioned problems. The signing key consists of the seal itself and is given type $\mathsf{SigKey}\langle T \rangle \triangleq \mathsf{Seal}\,\langle T \rangle$, as in the original RCF library [12]. The verification key, instead, is encoded as a function that (i) takes the signature x and the signed message t as input; (ii) calls the unsealing function to retrieve the message y bound to x in the secret list; and (iii) returns y if y is equal to t and fails otherwise. In this encoding, the verifier has to know the signed message in order to verify the signature. This is reasonable as, for efficiency reasons, one usually signs a hash of the message as opposed to the message in plain.

Symbolic implementation of signing-verification key pair

```
mkSigPair : ∀α. unit → SigKey⟨α⟩ * VerKey⟨α⟩
mkSigPair = Λα. λu : unit.
    let (seal, unseal) = mkSeal ⟨α⟩ in
    let vk = λx : Un. for β in ⊤; Un. λt : β.
                if t = (unseal x) as z then z else failwith "verification failed"
    in (k, vk)
```

The type $\mathsf{VerKey}\langle T \rangle$ of a verification key is defined as $\mathsf{Un} \to ((x : \top \to \{y : T \mid x = y\}) \wedge (\mathsf{Un} \to \mathsf{Un}))$. The verification key takes the signature of type Un as first argument. The second part of this type is an intersection of two types: The type $x : \top \to \{y : T \mid x = y\}$ is used to type-check honest callers: the signed message x has any type (top type) and the message y returned by the unsealing function has the stronger type T, which means that the unsealing function casts the type of the signed message from $\top$ down to T. This is safe since the sealing function is not public and can only be used to sign messages of type T. The type $\mathsf{Un} \to \mathsf{Un}$ makes $\mathsf{VerKey}\langle T \rangle$ always public[5]. Hence, in contrast to [12], we can reason about protocols where the signing key is used to sign private messages while the verification key is public (e.g., in DAA [18]).

---

[5] A type of the form $\mathsf{Un} \to (T_1 \wedge T_2)$ is public if T_1 or T_2 are public, and in our case $T_2 = \mathsf{Un} \to \mathsf{Un}$ is public.

Finally, we present the typed interface of the functions to create and check signatures:

$$sign : \forall \alpha. \ (x_{sk} : \mathsf{SigKey}\langle \alpha \rangle \rightarrow \alpha \rightarrow \mathsf{Un}) \wedge \mathsf{Un}$$
$$check : \forall \alpha. \ (x_{vk} : \mathsf{VerKey}\langle \alpha \rangle \rightarrow \mathsf{Un} \rightarrow \top \rightarrow \alpha) \wedge \mathsf{Un}$$

We type-check *sign* and *check* twice, to give them intersection types whose right-hand side is Un. While making these functions available to the adversary is not necessary (the attacker can directly use the signing and verification keys to which he has access), this is convenient for the encoding of zero-knowledge we describe in §6 (dishonest verifier cases).

5.3 Public-Key Encryption

For public-key encryption we simply use a seal of type $\mathsf{Seal}\langle T \vee \mathsf{Un} \rangle$, i.e., $\mathsf{PrivKey}\langle T \rangle \triangleq \mathsf{Seal}\langle T \vee \mathsf{Un} \rangle$ and $\mathsf{PubKey}\langle T \rangle \triangleq (T \vee \mathsf{Un}) \rightarrow \mathsf{Un}$. This allows us to obtain the types described in §2.2. In contrast to [12], the encryption key is always public, even if the type T of the encrypted message is not tainted[6].

6   Encoding of Zero-Knowledge

This section describes how we automatically generate the symbolic implementation of non-interactive zero-knowledge proofs, starting from a high-level specification. Intuitively, this implementation resembles an oracle that provides three operations: one for creating zero-knowledge proofs, one for verifying such proofs, and one for obtaining the public values used to create the proofs. Some of the values used to create a zero-knowledge proof are revealed by the proof to the verifier and to any eavesdropper, while the others (which we call witnesses) are kept secret. A zero-knowledge proof does not reveal any information about these witnesses, other than the validity of the statement being proved.

6.1 Illustrative Example: Simplified DAA

We are going to illustrate our technique on a simplified version[7] of the Direct Anonymous Attestation (DAA) protocol [18]. The goal of the DAA protocol is to enable the TPM to sign arbitrary messages and to send them to an entity called the verifier in such a way that the verifier will only learn that a valid TPM signed that message, but without revealing the TPM's identity. The DAA protocol is composed of two sub-protocols: the *join protocol* and the *DAA-signing protocol*. The join protocol allows a TPM to obtain a certificate x_{cert} from an entity called the issuer. This certificate is just a signature on the TPM's secret identifier x_f. The DAA-signing protocol enables a TPM to authenticate a message y_m by proving to the verifier the knowledge of a valid certificate, but without revealing the TPM's identifier or the certificate. In this section, we focus on the DAA-signing protocol and we assume that the TPM has already completed the join

---

[6] A type of the form $(T_1 \vee T_2) \rightarrow \mathsf{Un}$ is public if T_1 or T_2 is tainted, and in our case $T_2 = \mathsf{Un}$ is tainted.

[7] The long version describes the general code generation routine in more detail [7].

protocol and received the certificate from the issuer. In the DAA-signing protocol the TPM sends to the verifier a zero-knowledge proof.

TPM   Verifier

assume $\mathsf{Send}(x_f, y_m)$

$\xrightarrow{\hspace{1cm}\mathsf{zk}_{daa}(x_f, x_{cert}, y_{vki}, y_m)\hspace{1cm}}$

assert $\mathsf{Authenticate}(y_m)$

The TPM proves the knowledge of a certificate x_{cert} of its identifier x_f that can be verified with the verification key y_{vki} of the issuer. Note that although the payload message y_m does not occur in the statement, the proof guarantees non-malleability so an attacker cannot change y_m without redoing the proof. Before sending the zero-knowledge proof, the TPM assumes $\mathsf{Send}(x_f, y_m)$. After verifying the zero-knowledge proof, the verifier asserts $\mathsf{Authenticate}(y_m)$. The authorization policy we consider for the DAA-sign protocol is

$$\text{assume } \forall x_f, x_{cert}, y_m.\ \mathsf{Send}(x_f, y_m) \wedge \mathsf{OkTPM}(x_f) \Rightarrow \mathsf{Authenticate}(y_m)$$

where the predicate $\mathsf{OkTPM}(x_f)$ is assumed by the issuer before signing x_f.

6.2   High-Level Specification

Our high-level specification of non-interactive zero-knowledge proofs is similar in spirit to the symbolic representation of zero-knowledge proofs in a process calculus [10, 8]. For a specification the user needs to provide: (1) variables representing the witnesses and public values of the proof, (2) a Boolean formula over these variables representing the statement of the proof, (3) types for the variables, and, if desired, (4) a promise, i.e., a logical formula that is conveyed by the proof only if the prover is honest.

High-level specification of simplified DAA

```
zkdef daa =
    witness = [x_f : T_vki, x_cert : Un]
    matched = [y_vki : VerKey⟨T_vki⟩]
    public = [y_m : Un]
    statement = [x_f = check⟨T_vki⟩ y_vki x_cert x_f]
    promise = [Send(x_f, y_m)]
where T_vki = {z_f : Private | OkTPM(z_f)}
```

Variables. The variables x_f and x_{cert} stand for witnesses. The value of y_{vki} is matched against the signature verification key of the issuer, which is already known to the verifier of the zero-knowledge proof. The payload message y_m is returned to the verifier of the proof, so it is public.

Statement. The statement conveyed by a zero-knowledge proof is in general a positive Boolean formula over equality checks. In our simplified DAA example this is just $x_f = \mathsf{check}\langle T_{vki}\rangle\ y_{vki}\ x_{cert}\ x_f$.

Types. The user also needs to provide types for the variables. The DAA-sign protocol does not preserve the secrecy of the signed message, so y_m has type Un. On the other hand, the TPM identifier x_f is given a secret and untainted type $T_{vki} = \{z_f : \text{Private} \mid \text{OkTPM}(z_f)\}$. This type ensures that x_f is not known to the attacker and that the predicate $\text{OkTPM}(x_f)$ holds. The verification key of the issuer is used to check signed messages of type T_{vki}, so it is given type $\text{VerKey}\langle T_{vki}\rangle$. Finally the certificate x_{cert} is a signature, so it has type Un. Even though it has type Un, it would break the anonymity of the user to make the certificate a public value, since the verifier could then always distinguish if two consecutive requests come from the same user or not.

Promise. The user can additionally specify a *promise*: an arbitrary authorization logic formula that holds in the typing environment of the prover. If the statement is strong enough to identify the prover as an honest (type-checked) protocol participant (signature proofs of knowledge such as DAA-signing have this property), then the promise can be safely transmitted to the typing environment of the verifier. In the DAA example we have the promise $\text{Send}(x_f, y_m)$, since this predicate holds in the typing environment of a honest TPM.

6.3   Automatic Code Generation

We automatically generate both a typed interface and a symbolic implementation for the oracle corresponding to a zero-knowledge specification.

Generated typed interface for simplified DAA

$\text{create}_{daa} : T_{daa} \vee \text{Un} \to \text{Un}$ $\quad\quad\quad\quad\quad$ $\text{public}_{daa} : \text{Un} \to \text{Un}$

$\text{verify}_{daa} : \text{Un} \to ((y_{vki} : \text{VerKey}\langle T_{vki}\rangle \to U_{daa}) \wedge \text{Un} \to \text{Un})$

where $T_{daa} = y_{vki} : \text{VerKey}\langle T_{vki}\rangle * y_m : \text{Un} * x_f : T_{vki} * x_{cert} : \text{Un} * \{\text{Send}(x_f, y_m)\}$

and $U_{daa} = \{y_m : \text{Un} \mid \exists x_f, x_{cert}. \text{OkTPM}(x_f) \wedge \text{Send}(x_f, y_m)\}$

The *generated interface* for DAA contains three functions that share a hidden seal of type $T_{daa} \vee \text{Un}$. The function create_{daa} is used to create zero-knowledge proofs. It takes as argument a tuple containing values for all variables of the proof, or an argument of type Un if it is called by the adversary. In case a protocol participant calls this function, we check that the values have the specified types. Additionally, we check that the promise $\text{Send}(x_f, y_m)$ holds in the typing environment of the prover. The returned zero-knowledge proof is given type Un so that it can be sent over the public network.

The function public_{daa} is used to read the public values of a proof, so it takes as input the sealed proof of type Un and returns y_m, also at type Un.

The function verify_{daa} is used for verifying zero-knowledge proofs. Because of the second part of the intersection type, this function can be called by the attacker, in which case it returns a value of type Un. When called by a protocol participant, however, it takes as argument a candidate zero-knowledge proof of type Un and the verification key of the issuer with type $\text{VerKey}\langle T_{daa}\rangle$. On successful verification, verify_{daa} returns y_m, the only public variable, but with a stronger type than in public_{daa}. The function guarantees that the formula $\exists x_f, x_{cert}. \text{OkTPM}(x_f) \wedge \text{Send}(x_f, y_m)$ holds, where the witnesses are existentially quantified. The first conjunct, $\text{OkTPM}(x_f)$, guarantees that if verification succeeds then the statement indeed holds, no matter what the origin of the proof is. This predicate is automatically extracted from the return type of the $check\langle T_{vki}\rangle$ function (see §5.2). The second conjunct $\mathsf{Send}(x_f, y_m)$ is the promise of the proof.

The *generated implementation* for this interface creates a fresh seal k_{daa} for values of type $T_{daa} \vee \mathsf{Un}$. The sealing function of k_{daa} is directly used to implement the create$_{daa}$ function. The unsealing function of k_{daa} is used to implement the public$_{daa}$ and verify$_{daa}$ functions. The implementation of public$_{daa}$ is very simple: since the zero-knowledge proof is just a sealed value, public$_{daa}$ unseals it and returns y_m. The witnesses are discarded, and the validity of the statement is not checked.

The implementation of the verify$_{daa}$ function is more interesting. This function takes a candidate zero-knowledge proof z of type Un as input, and a value for the matched variable y_{vki}. Since the type of verify$_{daa}$ contains an intersection type we use a for construct to introduce this intersection type. If the proof is verified by the attacker we can assume that the y_{vki} has type Un and need to type the return value to Un. On the other hand, if the proof is verified by a protocol participant we can assume that y_{vki} has the type $\mathsf{VerKey}\langle T_{vki}\rangle$. In general, it is the strong types of the matched values that allow us to guarantee the strong types of the returned public values, as well as the promise.

Generated symbolic implementation for simplified DAA

```
verify_daa = λz : Un.
    for α in Un; VerKey⟨T_vki⟩. λy'_vki : α.
        let z' = (snd k_daa) z in                              (1)
        case z'' = z' : Un ∨ T_daa in                          (2)
        let (y_vki, y_m, x_f, x_cert, _) = z'' in              (3)
        if y_vki = y'_vki as y''_vki then                      (4)
            if x_f = check⟨T_vki⟩ y''_vki x_cert x_f then y_m  (5)
            else failwith "statement not valid"
        else failwith "y_vki does not match"
```

The generated verify$_{daa}$ function performs the following five steps: (1) it unseals z using "snd k_{daa}" and obtains z'; (2) since z' has a union type, it does case analysis on it, and assigns its value to z''; (3) it splits the tuple z'' into the public values (y_{vki} and y_m) and the witnesses (x_f and x_{cert}). (4) it tests if the matched variable y_{vki} is equal to the argument y'_{vki}, and in case of success assigns the value to the variable y''_{vki} – since y''_{vki} has a stronger type than y'_{vki} and y_{vki} we use this new variable to stand for y_{vki} in the following; (5) it tests if the statement is true by applying the $check\langle T_{vki}\rangle$ function, and checking the result for equality with the value of x_f. In general, this last step is slightly complicated by the fact that the statement can contain conjunctions and disjunctions, so we use decision trees. However, for the DAA example the decision tree has a trivial structure with only one node.

Since the automatically generated implementation of zero-knowledge proofs relies on types and formulas provided by the user, which may both be wrong, the generated implementation is not guaranteed to fulfill its interface. We use our type-checker to check whether this is indeed the case. If type-checking the generated code against its interface succeeds, then this code can be safely used in protocol implementations. Note that because of the for and case constructs the body of verify$_{daa}$ is type-checked four times, corresponding to the following four scenarios: honest prover / honest verifier, honest prover / dishonest verifier, dishonest prover / honest verifier, and dishonest prover / dishonest verifier. In DAA the most interesting case is dishonest prover / honest verifier, when z'' and hence x_f are given type Un, while the result of the signature verification is of type T_{vki}. Since $\vdash$ NonDisj $\{z_f : \mathsf{Private} \mid \mathsf{OkTPM}(z_f)\}$ Un $\rightsquigarrow$ false by rules (ND Refine) and (ND Private Un), false is added to the environment in which y_m is type-checked. The variable y_m has type Un in this environment, but since this environment is inconsistent y_m can also be given type U_{daa}.

7 Implementation

We have implemented a complete tool-chain for $\mathrm{RCF}^{\forall}_{\wedge\vee}$: it includes a type-checker for the type system described in §4, the automatic code generator for zero-knowledge described in §6, an interpreter, and a visual debugger.

The type-checker supports an extended syntax with respect to the one from §3, including: a simple module system, algebraic data types, recursive functions, type definitions, and mutable references. We use first-order logic with equality as the authorization logic and the type-checker invokes the Z3 SMT solver [25] to discharge proof obligations. The type-checker performed very well in our experiments: it type-checks all our symbolic libraries and samples totaling more than 1.5kLOC in around 12 seconds, on a normal laptop.   The type-checker produces an XML log file containing the complete type derivation in case of success, and a partial derivation that leads to the typing error in case of failure. This can be inspected using our visualizer to easily detect and fix flaws in the protocol implementation. The type-checker also performs very limited type inference: it can infer the instantiation of some polymorphic functions from the type of the arguments, however, the user has to provide all the other typing annotations – we would like to improve the amount of type inference in the future (see §9 for a discussion).

The type-checker, the code generator for zero-knowledge, and the interpreter are command-line tools implemented in F#, while the GUIs of the visual debugger and the visualizer for type derivations are specified using WPF (Windows Presentation Foundation). The type-checker consists of around 2.5kLOC, while the whole tool-chain has over 5kLOC. All the tools and samples are available at [7].

8 Related Work on Unions and Intersections

The for construct for explicitly alternating type annotations was introduced by Pierce [39, 40] as a generalization of an idea Reynolds [41] used in Forsythe for giving intersection types to annotated lambda abstractions of the form $\lambda x{:}\tau_1..\tau_n.\,e$. In a Church-style system, however, the for construct does not have a clear operational semantics. Compagnoni [23] gives an operational semantics to function application expressions of the form $((\text{for }\alpha\text{ in }T;U.\ \lambda x{:}V.\,e_1)\ e_2)$ by pushing the application inside the for – i.e., this expression reduces in one step to (for α in $T;U.\ ((\lambda x{:}V.\,e_2)\ e_2))$. It is unclear if this can be generalized to anything other than function applications. Moreover, this reduction rule does not respect the value restriction for the introduction of intersection types (our rule (Val And*) in §4). As discovered by Davies and Pfenning [24] the value restriction on intersection introduction is crucial for soundness in the presence of side-effects. The counterexample they give is in fact very similar to the one used to illustrate the unsoundness of ML, in the absence of the value restriction, due to the interaction of polymorphism with side-effects [33]. Moreover, Davies and Pfenning [24] observed that some standard distributivity laws of subtyping are unsound in a setting with side-effects, since they basically allow one to circumvent the value restriction. We obtain all the benefits of the for construct in $RCF_{\wedge\vee}^{\forall}$, but erase it completely when translating values into Formal-$RCF_{\wedge\vee}^{\forall}$, and use the value restriction on both levels to ensure soundness.

The case construct for eliminating union types was introduced by Pierce [39] as a way to make type-checking more efficient, by asking the programmer to annotate the position in the code where union elimination should occur. Dunfield and Pfenning [28] later pointed out that unrestricted elimination of union types is unsound in the presence of non-determinism. This observation is crucial for us, since our calculus, as opposed to the one studied by Dunfield and Pfenning, is in fact non-deterministic. They propose an evaluation context restriction that recovers soundness, but this is not enough to make type-checking efficient. In recent work, Dunfield [27], shows that carefully transforming programs into let-normal form improves efficiency. This is encouraging, since our expressions are already in let normal form, so we can hope to replace the case construct by a normal let in the future, and still preserve efficient type-checking.

9   Conclusions and Future Work

We have presented a new type system that combines refinement types with union types, intersection types, and polymorphic types. A novelty of the type system is its ability to reason statically about the disjointness of types. This extends the scope of the existing type-based analyses of protocol implementations to important classes of cryptographic protocols that were not covered so far, including protocols based on zero-knowledge proofs. Our type system comes with a mechanized proof of correctness and an efficient implementation [7].

As future work, we plan to investigate the automated generation of concrete cryptographic implementations of zero-knowledge proofs, and thus to complement the generation of symbolic implementations considered in this paper. Also, we intend to apply our framework to analyze implementations of more complex protocols, such as the Civitas electronic voting system [22].

The type-checker we implemented had very good efficiency in our experiments, however, the amount of typing annotations it requires is at the moment quite high. This issue is more pronounced in our symbolic cryptography library, where intersection and union types are pervasive. This is less of a problem in the code that links against these libraries, and in the case of zero-knowledge even the code in the library is automatically generated together with all the necessary annotations. In the future we would like to perform more type inference, maybe leveraging some of the recent progress on type inference for refinement types [42, 34]. The good news is that intersection and union types can be very useful when devising precise type inference algorithms [8, 36].

Acknowledgments. We thank Cédric Fournet, Andy Gordon, Jan Schwinghammer, and Pierre-yves Strub for the constructive discussions. Thorsten Tarrach implemented the original F5 prototype. Stefan Lorenz helped us with the cryptographic implementation of the DAA protocol. Joshua Dunfield and Kim Pecina commented on a draft. Cătălin Hriţcu is supported by a fellowship from Microsoft Research and the International Max Planck Research School for Computer Science. Matteo Maffei is partially supported by the initiative for excellence of the German federal government, by DFG Emmy Noether program, and by MIUR project "SOFT".

References

1. Abadi, M., Blanchet, B.: Secrecy types for asymmetric communication. Theoretical Computer Science 3(298), 387–415 (2003)
2. Abadi, M., Blanchet, B.: Analyzing security protocols with secrecy types and logic programs. Journal of the ACM 52(1), 102–146 (2005)
3. Abadi, M., Fournet, C.: Mobile values, new names, and secure communication. In: Proc. 28th Symposium on Principles of Programming Languages (POPL), pp. 104–115. ACM Press, New York (2001)
4. Abadi, M., Gordon, A.D.: A calculus for cryptographic protocols: The spi calculus. Information and Computation 148(1), 1–70 (1999)
5. Amadio, R.M., Cardelli, L.: Subtyping recursive types. ACM Transactions on Programming Languages and Systems (TOPLAS) 15(4), 575–631 (1993)
6. Backes, M., Grochulla, M.P., Hriţcu, C., Maffei, M.: Achieving security despite compromise using zero-knowledge. In: 22th IEEE Symposium on Computer Security Foundations (CSF 2009). IEEE Computer Society Press, Los Alamitos (July 2009)
7. Backes, M., Hriţcu, C., Maffei, M.: Union and intersection types for secure protocol implementations. Long version, formalization and implementation, http://www.infsec.cs.uni-sb.de/projects/F5/
8. Backes, M., Hriţcu, C., Maffei, M.: Type-checking zero-knowledge. In: 15th ACM Conference on Computer and Communications Security (CCS 2008), pp. 357–370. ACM Press, New York (2008)
9. Backes, M., Maffei, M., Pecina, K.: A security API for distributed social networks. In: 18th Annual Network & Distributed System Security Symposium (NDSS 2011), pp. 35–51. Internet Society, San Diego (2011)
10. Backes, M., Maffei, M., Unruh, D.: Zero-knowledge in the applied pi-calculus and automated verification of the direct anonymous attestation protocol. In: Proc. of 29th IEEE Symposium on Security and Privacy, pp. 202–215. IEEE Computer Society Press, Los Alamitos (2008)
11. Backes, M., Maffei, M., Unruh, D.: Computationally sound verification of source code. In: Proc. 17th ACM Conference on Computer and Communications Security (CCS), pp. 387–398. ACM Press, New York (2010)
12. Bengtson, J., Bhargavan, K., Fournet, C., Gordon, A.D., Maffeis, S.: Refinement types for secure implementations. In: Proc. 21th IEEE Symposium on Computer Security Foundations (CSF), pp. 17–32. IEEE Computer Society Press, Los Alamitos (2008), long version appeared as MSR-TR-2008-118. November 2010 revision that fixes the problems we pointed out is http://research.microsoft.com/en-us/um/people/adg/Publications/MSR-TR-2008-118-SP2.pdf
13. Bhargavan, K., Corin, R., Fournet, C., Zălinescu, E.: Cryptographically verified implementations for TLS. In: 15th ACM Conference on Computer and Communications Security (CCS 2008), pp. 459–468. ACM Press, New York (2008)

14. Bhargavan, K., Fournet, C., Gordon, A.D.: Modular verification of security protocol code by typing. In: Proc. 37th Symposium on Principles of Programming Languages (POPL 2010), pp. 445–456 (2010)
15. Bhargavan, K., Fournet, C., Gordon, A.D., Tse, S.: Verified interoperable implementations of security protocols. In: Proc. 19th IEEE Computer Security Foundations Workshop (CSFW), pp. 139–152. IEEE Computer Society Press, Los Alamitos (2006)
16. Blanchet, B.: An efficient cryptographic protocol verifier based on Prolog rules. In: Proc. 14th IEEE Computer Security Foundations Workshop (CSFW), pp. 82–96. IEEE Computer Society Press, Los Alamitos (2001)
17. Bleichenbacher, D.: Chosen ciphertext attacks against protocols based on the RSA encryption standard PKCS. In: Krawczyk, H. (ed.) CRYPTO 1998. LNCS, vol. 1462, pp. 1–12. Springer, Heidelberg (1998)
18. Brickell, E., Camenisch, J., Chen, L.: Direct anonymous attestation. In: Proc. 11th ACM Conference on Computer and Communications Security, pp. 132–145. ACM Press, New York (2004)
19. Butler, F., Cervesato, I., Jaggard, A.D., Scedrov, A., Walstad, C.: Formal analysis of Kerberos 5. Theoretical Computer Science 367(1), 57–87 (2006)
20. Cardelli, L.: Type systems. In: The Computer Science and Engineering Handbook, pp. 2208–2236 (1997)
21. Chaki, S., Datta, A.: ASPIER: An automated framework for verifying security protocol implementations. Technical report, CMU CyLab (October 2008)
22. Clarkson, M.R., Chong, S., Myers, A.C.: Civitas: A secure voting system. In: Proc. 29th IEEE Symposium on Security and Privacy, pp. 354–368. IEEE Computer Society Press, Los Alamitos (2008)
23. Compagnoni, A.B.: Subject reduction and minimal types for higher order subtyping. Technical Report ECS-LFCS-97-363, LFCS, University of Edinburgh (August 1997)
24. Davies, R., Pfenning, F.: Intersection types and computational effects. In: Proc. International Conference on Functional Programming (ICFP 2000), pp. 198–208 (2000)
25. de Moura, L., Bjørner, N.: Z3: An efficient SMT solver. In: Ramakrishnan, C.R., Rehof, J. (eds.) TACAS 2008. LNCS, vol. 4963, pp. 337–340. Springer, Heidelberg (2008)
26. Denning, D.E., Sacco, G.M.: Timestamps in key distribution protocols. Communications of the ACM 24(8), 533–536 (1981)
27. Dunfield, J.: Untangling typechecking of intersections and unions. In: Workshop on Intersection Types and Related Systems (ITRS) (July 2010)
28. Dunfield, J., Pfenning, F.: Tridirectional typechecking. In: Proc. 31th Symposium on Principles of Programming Languages (POPL 2004), pp. 281–292. ACM Press, New York (2004)
29. Eigner, F.: Type-based verification of electronic voting systems. Master's thesis, Saarland University (2009)
30. Fisher, D.: Millions of .Net Passport accounts put at risk. eWeek (May 2003) (Flaw detected by Muhammad Faisal Rauf Danka)
31. Fournet, C., Gordon, A.D., Maffeis, S.: A type discipline for authorization in distributed systems. In: Proc. 20th IEEE Symposium on Computer Security Foundations (CSF), pp. 31–45. IEEE Computer Society Press, Los Alamitos (2007)
32. Goubault-Larrecq, J., Parrennes, F.: Cryptographic protocol analysis on real C code. In: Cousot, R. (ed.) VMCAI 2005. LNCS, vol. 3385, pp. 363–379. Springer, Heidelberg (2005)
33. Harper, B., Lillibridge, M.: ML with callcc is unsound. Post to TYPES mailing list (July 8, 1991), archived at http://www.seas.upenn.edu/~sweirich/types/archive/1991/msg00034.html
34. Jhala, R., Majumdar, R., Rybalchenko, A.: HMC: Verifying functional programs using abstract interpreters. In: Gopalakrishnan, G., Qadeer, S. (eds.) CAV 2011. LNCS, vol. 6806, pp. 470–485. Springer, Heidelberg (2011), http://arxiv.org/abs/1004.2884v2

35. Morris Jr., J.H.: Protection in programming languages. Communications of the ACM 16(1), 15–21 (1973)
36. Kobayashi, N.: Types and higher-order recursion schemes for verification of higher-order programs. In: Proc. 36th Symposium on Principles of Programming Languages (POPL 2009), pp. 416–428 (2009)
37. Lowe, G.: Breaking and fixing the Needham-Schroeder public-key protocol using FDR. In: Margaria, T., Steffen, B. (eds.) TACAS 1996. LNCS, vol. 1055, pp. 147–166. Springer, Heidelberg (1996)
38. Mendler, N.P.: Inductive types and type constraints in the second-order lambda calculus. Annals of Pure and Applied Logic 51(1-2), 159–172 (1991)
39. Pierce, B.C.: Programming with intersection types, union types, and polymorphism. Technical Report CMU-CS-91-106, Carnegie Mellon University (1991)
40. Pierce, B.C.: Intersection types and bounded polymorphism. Mathematical Structures in Computer Science 7(2), 129–193 (1997)
41. Reynolds, J.C.: Design of the programming language Forsythe. Technical Report CMU-CS-96-146, Carnegie Mellon University (June 1996); Reprinted in O'Hearn, Tennent: ALGOL-like Languages, vol. 1, pp. 173–233. Birkhäuser, Basel (1997)
42. Rondon, P.M., Kawaguchi, M., Jhala, R.: Liquid types. In: Proc. ACM SIGPLAN 2008 Conference on Programming Language Design and Implementation (PLDI 2008), pp. 159–169 (2008)
43. Sumii, E., Pierce, B.C.: A bisimulation for dynamic sealing. Theoretical Computer Science 375(1-3), 169–192 (2007)
44. Urzyczyn, P.: Positive recursive type assignment. In: Hájek, P., Wiedermann, J. (eds.) MFCS 1995. LNCS, vol. 969, pp. 382–391. Springer, Heidelberg (1995)
45. Wagner, D., Schneier, B.: Analysis of the SSL 3.0 protocol. In: Proc. 2nd USENIX Workshop on Electronic Commerce, pp. 29–40 (1996)

Secure Composition of Protocols*

Véronique Cortier

LORIA, CNRS, project Cassis, Nancy, France

Abstract. Security protocols are small distributed programs that are designed to ensure security over untrusted networks such as the Internet. They are notoriously dificult to design and flaws can be found several years after their publication and even their deployment. In particular, they are not securely composable in general: two protocols may be secure when analyzed separately but may cause harmful interactions to each other. We explore how tagging protocols allows to securely compose protocols.

Security protocols are small distributed programs that are designed to ensure security over untrusted networks such as the Internet. Examples of such programs are protocols for e-payment, pay-per-view, authentication or e-voting. They are notoriously dificult to design and flaws can be found several years after their publication and even their deployment.

A recognized way of ensuring a better security level is to analyse security protocols using formal methods, providing rigorous proofs of their security. In this vein, several decision procedures have been developed for checking security properties such as confidentiality or authenticity (e.g. [14,11,2,5,8,16]). These decision procedures have often yield tools that are able to automatically prove security or discovering flaws if any (e.g. [4,3,13,17,15,10]). While automatic tools are successful in analyzing protocols in isolation, they do not perform well when used for analyzing several protocols combined together. We summarize here two approaches (previously presented in [9] and [7]) that show how to securely compose protocols. These results allow to analyze the security of protocols component by component and then deduce directly the security of the combined protocol.

Parallel composition

Many protocols are executed simultaneously over the Internet and they may share some datas such as keys. This is in particular the case of protocols when several versions of the same protocol may be used at the same time (because not everybody uses the most up-to-date version), when several modes are allowed like in IKE, or when protocols make use of public keys. Even if a protocol has

---

* The research leading to these results was performed as part of the ProSecure project which is funding by the European Research Council under the European Union's Seventh Framework Programme (FP7/2007-2013) / ERC grant agreement number 258865.

S. Mödersheim and C. Palamidessi (Eds.): TOSCA 2011, LNCS 6993, pp. 29–32, 2012.

been proved secure against an active attacker that can read, block and create messages, there are absolutely no guarantees that it remains secure when other protocols (possibly variants of it) are executed in parallel in case they share some secret information. Examples of unwanted interactions between protocols can be found in e.g. [12]. To illustrate this discussion, we describe here the toy protocol proposed in [9].

$$P_1 : \quad A \rightarrow B : \{s\}_{\mathsf{pub}(B)} \qquad \begin{array}{ll} P_2 : & A \rightarrow B : \{N_a\}_{\mathsf{pub}(B)} \\ & B \rightarrow A : N_a \end{array}$$

In protocol P_1, the agent A simply sends a secret s encrypted under B's public key. In protocol P_2, the agent sends some fresh nonce to B encrypted under B's public key. The agent B acknowledges A's message by forwarding A's nonce. While P_1 executed alone easily guarantees the secrecy of s, even against active adversaries, the secrecy of s is no more guaranteed when the protocol P_2 is executed. Indeed, an adversary may use the protocol P_2 as an oracle to decrypt any message.

A way to avoid such a bad interaction is to *tag* messages, as proposed e.g. in [1,12,6,5]. Tagging messages consist in adding a protocol identifier in each cyphertext. For example, tagging P_1 and P_2 would result in the two following protocols.

$$P_1' : \quad A \rightarrow B : \{1, s\}_{\mathsf{pub}(B)} \qquad \begin{array}{ll} P_2' : & A \rightarrow B : \{2, N_a\}_{\mathsf{pub}(B)} \\ & B \rightarrow A : N_a \end{array}$$

The main result of [9] demonstrates that such tagged protocols can be safely executed simultaneously, provided that the shared information are either public or are only used for encryption and decryption.

Secure refinement

The situation might be even more complex when protocols are interleaved, one protocol establishing data for the other one and conversely. For example, some protocols run sub-protocols e.g. to establish confidential or authenticated channels. Moreover, protocols usually assume pre-established keys such as long-term symmetric keys or public keys associated with their legitimate owners. Such datas are actually established themselves running other protocols such as key-establishment protocols. Again, there is absolutely no guarantee that a protocol proved secure assuming pre-established keys remains secure independently of the way long-term keys are established. For example, consider the two following protocols.

$$Q_1 : \quad A \rightarrow B : \{k_2\}_{K_1} \qquad Q_2 : \quad A \rightarrow B : k_2, \{s\}_{k_1}$$

Protocol Q_1 establishes a key k_1 between A and B using some long-term key k_2. Protocol Q_2 assumes two pre-established keys k_1 and k_2, reveals k_2 and uses k_1 for transmitting a secret s. The protocol Q_2 alone clearly guarantees the confidentiality of s. However, if Q_1 is used for establishing k_1 in Q_2 then Q_2 is no longer secure. The main result of [7] shows how to securely compose protocols by using distinct cryptographic primitives in each protocol (e.g. Diffie-Helmann for establishing keys in one protocol and standard encryption and signature schemes in the second protocol). If the same primitive needs to be used (e.g. encryption) then tagging protocols again allows to securely combine protocols together.

Acknowledgment. These results have been obtained in joint work with Stéphanie Delaune [9] for and joint work with Stefan Ciobaca for [7].

References

1. Abadi, M., Needham, R.M.: Prudent engineering practice for cryptographic protocols. IEEE Trans. Software Eng. 22(1), 6–15 (1996)
2. Amadio, R., Charatonik, W.: On name generation and set-based analysis in the Dolev-Yao model. In: Brim, L., Jančar, P., Křetínský, M., Kučera, A. (eds.) CONCUR 2002. LNCS, vol. 2421, pp. 499–514. Springer, Heidelberg (2002)
3. Armando, A., Basin, D., Boichut, Y., Chevalier, Y., Compagna, L., Cuellar, J., Drielsma, P.H., Heám, P., Kouchnarenko, O., Mantovani, J., Mödersheim, S., von Oheimb, D., Rusinowitch, M., Santiago, J., Turuani, M., Viganò, L., Vigneron, L.: The Avispa tool for the automated validation of internet security protocols and applications. In: Etessami, K., Rajamani, S.K. (eds.) CAV 2005. LNCS, vol. 3576, pp. 281–285. Springer, Heidelberg (2005)
4. Blanchet, B.: An efficient cryptographic protocol verifier based on Prolog rules. In: Proc. 14th Computer Security Foundations Workshop (CSFW 2001), pp. 82–96. IEEE Comp. Soc. Press, Los Alamitos (2001)
5. Blanchet, B., Podelski, A.: Verification of cryptographic protocols: Tagging enforces termination. In: Gordon, A.D. (ed.) FOSSACS 2003. LNCS, vol. 2620, pp. 136–152. Springer, Heidelberg (2003)
6. Canetti, R., Meadows, C., Syverson, P.F.: Environmental requirements for authentication protocols. In: Okada, M., Babu, C. S., Scedrov, A., Tokuda, H. (eds.) ISSS 2002. LNCS, vol. 2609, pp. 339–355. Springer, Heidelberg (2003)
7. Ciobâcă, Ș., Cortier, V.: Protocol composition for arbitrary primitives. In: Proceedings of the 23rd IEEE Computer Security Foundations Symposium (CSF 2010), Edinburgh, Scotland, UK, pp. 322–336. IEEE Computer Society Press, Los Alamitos (July 2010)
8. Comon-Lundh, H., Cortier, V.: New decidability results for fragments of first-order logic and application to cryptographic protocols. In: Nieuwenhuis, R. (ed.) RTA 2003. LNCS, vol. 2706, pp. 148–164. Springer, Heidelberg (2003)
9. Cortier, V., Delaitre, J., Delaune, S.: Safely composing security protocols. In: Arvind, V., Prasad, S. (eds.) FSTTCS 2007. LNCS, vol. 4855, pp. 352–363. Springer, Heidelberg (2007)
10. Cremers, C.: Scyther - Semantics and Verification of Security Protocols. Ph.D. dissertation, Eindhoven University of Technology (2006)
11. Durgin, N., Lincoln, P., Mitchell, J., Scedrov, A.: Undecidability of bounded security protocols. In: Proc. of the Workshop on Formal Methods and Security Protocols (1999)

12. Kelsey, J., Schneier, B., Wagner, D.: Protocol interactions and the chosen protocol attack. In: Christianson, B., Lomas, M. (eds.) Security Protocols 1997. LNCS, vol. 1361, pp. 91–104. Springer, Heidelberg (1998)
13. Lowe, G.: Casper: A compiler for the analysis of security protocols. In: Proc. 10th Computer Security Foundations Workshop (CSFW 1997). IEEE Comp. Soc. Press, Los Alamitos (1997)
14. Rusinowitch, M., Turuani, M.: Protocol insecurity with finite number of sessions and composed keys is NP-complete. Theoretical Computer Science 299, 451–475 (2003)
15. Schneider, S.: Security properties and CSP. In: Proc. of the Symposium on Security and Privacy, Oakland, pp. 174–187. IEEE Computer Society Press, Los Alamitos (1996)
16. Seidl, H., Verma, K.N.: Flat and one-variable clauses: Complexity of verifying cryptographic protocols with single blind copying. In: Baader, F., Voronkov, A. (eds.) LPAR 2004. LNCS (LNAI), vol. 3452, pp. 79–94. Springer, Heidelberg (2005)
17. Song, D.X.: Athena: A new efficient automatic checker for security protocol analysis. In: Proc. 12th Computer Security Foundations Workshop (CSFW 1999), Mordano, Italy. IEEE Computer Society Press, Los Alamitos (June 1999)

Constructive Cryptography – A New Paradigm for Security Definitions and Proofs[*]

Ueli Maurer

Department of Computer Science
ETH Zurich
CH-8092 Zurich, Switzerland
`maurer@inf.ethz.ch`

Abstract. Constructive cryptography, an application of abstract cryptography proposed by Maurer and Renner, is a new paradigm for defining the security of cryptographic schemes such as symmetric encryption, message authentication codes, public-key encryption, key-agreement protocols, and digital signature schemes, and for proving the security of protocols making use of such schemes. Such a cryptographic scheme can be seen (and defined) as constructing a certain resource (e.g. a channel or key) with certain security properties from another (weaker) such resource. For example, a secure encryption scheme constructs a secure channel from an authenticated channel and a secret key.

The term "construct", which is defined by the use of a simulator, is composable in the sense that a protocol obtained by the composition of several secure constructive steps is itself secure. This is in contrast to both the traditional, game-based security definitions for cryptographic schemes and the attack-based security definitions used in formal-methods based security research, which are generally not composable.

Constructive cryptography allows to take a new look at cryptography and the design of cryptographic protocols. One can give explicit meaning to various types of game-based security notions of confidentiality, integrity, and malleability, one can design key agreement, secure communication, certification, and other protocols in a modular and composable manner, and one can separate the understanding of what cryptography achieves from the technical security definitions and proofs, which is useful for didactic purposes and protocol design.

1 Introduction and Motivation

1.1 Modularity in Constructive Disciplines

A central paradigm in any constructive discipline is the decomposition of a complex system into simpler component systems or modules, which each may consist of yet simpler modules, and so on. This paradigm is useful only if the composition of modules is well-defined and preserves the relevant properties of the

---

[*] This paper is an extended abstract accompanying the author's invited talk at TOSCA 2011. The author is supported by the Swiss National Science Foundation.

S. Mödersheim and C. Palamidessi (Eds.): TOSCA 2011, LNCS 6993, pp. 33–56, 2012.

modules. For example, in software design, the composition operation must preserve correctness of the modules, i.e., correctness should be defined in a way that a system consisting of correct modules is itself correct.

The goal of constructive cryptography is to see cryptography as a constructive discipline, in a well-defined sense. The design of a cryptographic protocol involves several mechanisms (e.g. encryption, message authentication, etc.), each of which is proven secure in isolation (as a module). The security of the composed protocol then follows from a general composition theorem.

However, this approach requires the security of cryptographic schemes to be defined in a suitable manner. Indeed, for the traditional, game-based cryptographic security definitions, as explained below, the composition property is unclear. In contrast, security definitions stated in the proposed constructive manner are intrinsically composable and capture what one really wants to say about a concrete cryptographic system.

1.2   Traditional Security Definitions in Cryptography

In a traditional definition of security of a cryptographic scheme, one usually defines a game that characterizes the capabilities of a (hypothetical) adversary. A cryptographic scheme is defined to be secure if no computationally feasible strategy allows the adversary to win the game with non-negligible probability (or advantage), for reasonable notions of feasible and negligible. The notion of "feasible" is hard-wired into the definition and is defined as some form of polynomial time. Similarly, negligible is defined in a specific manner such that, roughly speaking, feasible times negligible is still negligible. Such definitions are therefore necessarily asymptotic.

For example, the security of a message authentication code (MAC) is defined as follows. Roughly speaking, without access to the secret key, no adversary restricted to feasible computation can win the following game with non-negligible probability. The adversary has access to a MAC-oracle (with the secret key embedded) and can ask for the generation and/or verification of MACs for arbitrary messages. The game is won if the adversary can generate a fresh message (not asked to the oracle before) as well as a correct MAC for it.

While this definition sounds reasonable and strong and naturally captures intuition, one may still ask why it should be the right definition. Indeed, for many cryptographic primitives, several different security definitions have been proposed. For example, a strengthened version of the security of a MAC requires that it even be infeasible to generate another valid MAC for the same message (assuming the MAC scheme is probabilistic). It is generally not clear when such a stronger definition is required.

For encryption, the definitions include security against chosen-plaintext attacks (CPA) or against chosen-ciphertext attacks (CCA), and for different types of distinguishing games. In addition, various integrity definitions for encryption have been defined. Several authors have investigated which combinations of such notions are strong enough in a given context.

1.3 Constructive Cryptography

The question of which definition is adequate should be answered relative to a specification of what is supposed to be achieved by the application of the scheme, under specified assumptions. Hence the constructive approach proposed here.

Constructive cryptography is a new paradigm in which the security definition of cryptographic schemes is radically different. For example, a MAC is defined to be secure if it *constructs* an authenticated communication channel from an insecure communication channel and a secret key, for a well-defined, simulation-based notion of "construct" and for well-defined definitions of an insecure and an authenticated channel[1]. Similarly, a symmetric encryption scheme is defined to be secure if it constructs a secure communication channel from an authenticated communication channel and a secret key.

The general composition theorem (Theorem 1) of this theory implies that the combination of a secure MAC and a secure encryption scheme constructs a secure channel from an insecure channel and two secret keys. By another composition step, the two keys can be constructed from a single secret key using a pseudo-random generator.

The security of public-key cryptosystems, key agreement protocols, and digital signature schemes can be seen similarly in the constructive cryptography paradigm, but this will not be discussed in this paper (but see [21]). The emphasis of this paper is on the general theory, less on the discussion of specific cryptographic schemes, which are discussed in [22,20] and in future papers.

1.4 Outline of the Paper

In Section 2 we discuss the well-known one-time pad from a new perspective, leading to the constructive cryptography viewpoint explained in Section 3. In Section 4 we briefly explain the idea of [18] to introduce abstraction layers in cryptography. In particular, the theory of abstract systems is introduced. In Section 5, the theory of constructive cryptography is explained. Related work is discussed in Section 6, and several research directions that can be addressed in the framework of constructive cryptography are mentioned in the concluding Section 7.

2   Motivating Example: The One-Time Pad

In this section we discuss the one-time pad (OTP), the best-known provably secure cryptosystem, as a motivating example. We recall the traditional (information-theoretic) security proof for OTP-encryption and explain two intrinsic problems with this proof. First, despite the proof, the OTP can be argued

---

[1] While using ideas of the frameworks of Canetti [4] (universal composability, called UC) and of Backes, Pfitzmann and Waidner [24,2] (reactive simulatability), which formalized the so-called "ideal-world real-world" paradigm, constructive cryptography is significantly different, as discussed in Section 6.

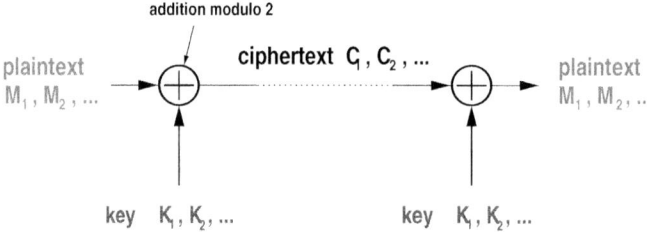

Fig. 1. The one-time pad (OTP) encryption scheme. The plaintext, the key and the ciphertext are bit strings of equal length, say n bits. The key is a uniformly random bit-string that is used only once. Encryption [decryption] consists of XORing (i.e., adding bit-wise modulo 2) the key to the plaintext [ciphertext]. The adversary is assumed to have access to the communication channel (i.e., to the ciphertext) but has no (a priori) information about the key.

to be completely insecure, for two different reasons. Second, the security proof cannot be carried over to a more practical setting where the (long) secret key is replaced by a pseudo-random key generated from a short secret key. Intuitively, an information-theoretic security proof should carry over and become a proof of computational security. The constructive approach to defining security solves both problems of standard security definitions.

2.1   The Traditional Security Proof for the One-Time Pad

The OTP encryption scheme (see Figure 1) can be proved to be information-theoretically secure, i.e., unbreakable even for a computationally unbounded adversary. How can one formulate and prove this claim?

The usual way to argue about the security of OTP-encryption is to show that the plaintext (also called the message) and the ciphertext are statistically independent. This means that the ciphertext gives no information about the plaintext, independent of the available computing power. In other words, if one has to guess the plaintext when given the ciphertext, one can just as well ignore the ciphertext.

Proposition 1. *In one-time pad encryption, the plaintext and the ciphertext are statistically independent (for any plaintext distribution).*

Proof. Let M, C, and K denote random variables corresponding to the plaintext, the ciphertext, and the key, respectively. Because the key K is uniformly distributed, so is the ciphertext C for every choice $M = m$ of the plaintext message. In other words, $\mathsf{P}_{C|M=m}$ is the uniform distribution for all m, and hence so is P_C. Thus

$$\mathsf{P}_{CM}(c, m) \;=\; \mathsf{P}_{C|M}(c, m) \cdot \mathsf{P}_M(m) \;=\; \mathsf{P}_C(c) \cdot \mathsf{P}_M(m),$$

for all m and c, which is the definition of M and C being statistically independent. $\qquad\square$

In the following two subsections we discuss two reasons why this is not really the statement about the OTP one should want to prove.

2.2 Two "Security Problems" of the One-Time Pad

Despite the above security proof, the OTP appears to be very "insecure", at least for two independent reasons.

First, an adversary with access to the communication channel can modify the message in a controlled manner, even though she gets no information about the transmitted message. The adversary can XOR an arbitrary offset δ to the transmitted message, simply by XORing δ to the ciphertext. If OTP-encryption were used in a banking application, an attacker could for instance change the bank account number of a money transfer.

Second, suppose that the OTP is used to encrypt one of the two messages "Yes" and "No" encoded, say, in 8-bit ASCII. Since the two messages have different lengths, the ciphertext leaks complete information about the message, in sharp contradiction to the above claim that the ciphertext is independent of the plaintext message.

What is a reasonable answer to the above two criticisms, apparently suggesting that the security proof for the OTP is useless in practice? The right answer is that we have to declare explicitly what we assume to be available and what we claim to achieve. First, we need to assume that the channel over which the ciphertext is transmitted is an *authenticated* (but not necessarily confidential) channel, preventing an adversary from modifying the ciphertext. Second, we need to state explicitly that the resulting secure channel actually *leaks the message length* (but not more). Then the constructive security proof can be interpreted as stating that OTP-encryption securely constructs a secure length-leaking channel from an authenticated channel and a shared secret key.

2.3 Computational Security: Additive Stream Ciphers

To illustrate the second short-coming of the above security statement (Proposition 1), we consider a variation of OTP-encryption used in practice, where the truly random key is replaced by a keystream sequence that is generated deterministically from a short secret key by a so-called pseudo-random generator. This is called an *additive stream cipher* (see Figure 2).

How should one define the security of such a stream cipher? Obviously, because the entire keystream is generated from a short secret key, the system cannot be information-theoretically secure. One could (theoretically) break the system by trying all possible keys until the correct one is identified as the only key that results in meaningful plaintext after decryption[2]. Hence we must find a way to formulate what it means for this system to be *computationally secure*.

---

[2] This requires a sufficient amount of ciphertext and assumes that the plaintext is redundant, i.e., that one can distinguish between meaningful and meaningless messages.

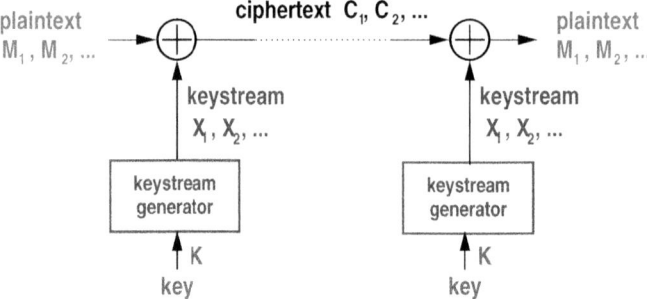

Fig. 2. Additive stream cipher. It is obtained from OTP-encryption by replacing the random key by the output of a pseudo-random generator (also called keystream generator in this context) applied to the secret key K. This system can be used for many consecutive messages if sender and receiver use consecutive portions of the keystream.

Our goal is that the computational security of the additive stream cipher follows from the (information-theoretic) security proof of the OTP and the assumption that the keystream generator is a cryptographically secure pseudo-random generator. What we need are two things: a computational version of "securely construct" and a composition theorem that allows to combine such statements. Here the two statements are that a pseudo-random generator (computationally) securely constructs a long secret key from a short secret key, and the previously explained constructive statement for the OTP.

3   Explaining the Security of the One-Time Pad in Constructive Cryptography

3.1   The Basic Approach

In the constructive cryptography approach, a cryptographic mechanism (e.g. the one-time pad) is interpreted as a method for constructing a certain *ideal resource* from a certain *real resource*. This is in the spirit of [4,24,2]. One argues that an adversary could, in an ideal world where the ideal resource is available, achieve anything that he could achieve in the real world where the real resource is given. This argument involves, as a thought experiment, a simulator system which transforms the ideal resource into the real-world system consisting of the real resource and the protocol engines (called converters).

This paradigm will be explained at an abstract level in Section 5. In the following we discuss the one-time pad example. What will be important to note is that we consider two types of systems: resources and converters.

3.2   The One-Time Pad Example

We need to define the real resource and the ideal resource for the one-time pad example. We refer to Figure 3.

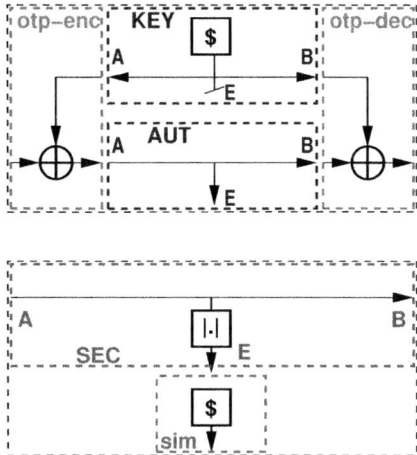

Fig. 3. The one-time pad (OTP) as an example of the constructive cryptography approach. The OTP constructs a secure channel SEC (the ideal resource) from an authenticated channel AUT and a secret key KEY (the real resource). There exists a simulator system sim which, when attached to interface E of the ideal resource SEC, makes it equivalent to the real resource with the protocol engines otp-enc and otp-dec attached. Equation (1) is an alternative (algebraic) way of describing the systems and stating their equivalence.

The ideal resource is a secure channel (see Figure 3, bottom), denoted as SEC (or also as $A \bullet\!\!-\!\!\!\longrightarrow\!\! \bullet B$ in the so-called $\bullet$-calculus; see [21,22]). A secure channel SEC (for sending a single message from A to B) is a system with three interfaces, for a sender A, a receiver B, and an adversary E. SEC takes an input (from some message space) at interface A, outputs the message at interface B, and outputs the length of the message (indicated by $|\cdot|$) at interface E.

Systems like SEC, AUT, otp-enc, and those discussed below can be made precise in any suitable language, but this is beyond the scope of this paper. As mathematical objects, they are random systems (see [14] or [17]). One also has to specify aspects like whether the adversary E has the capability of deleting a message, and whether the channel allows to send only one or several consecutive messages. For simplicity, the reader can think of our channels as allowing the transmission of a single message, but the claims also hold for channels allowing to send several messages.

The real resource (see Figure 3, top) consists of an authenticated channel, denoted as AUT (or also as $A \bullet\!\!\longrightarrow B$, see [21,22]), and, in parallel, a shared secret key, denoted as KEY (or also as $A \bullet\!\!=\!\!\!=\!\! \bullet B$). This system can be written as AUT‖KEY[3]. In contrast to a secure channel SEC, an authenticated channel AUT

---

[3] The parallel composition for resources, denoted ‖ is neither commutative nor (necessarily) associative. It is postulated in an abstract sense in Section 4, and it must

is one in which E can also learn the message sent by A but, like for a secure channel, E cannot modify the message output to B.

The protocol specifies protocol engines (later called *converter systems*) for A and B, namely otp-enc and otp-dec, respectively, which they attach to the system AUT‖KEY, resulting in a system we can write as

$$\text{otp-dec}^{B}\ \text{otp-enc}^{A}\ (\text{KEY‖AUT}).$$

Here the superscripts (e.g. B in otp-dec^{B}) specifies that the converter otp-dec is attached to interface B of the resource system AUT‖KEY (see Section 4).

How can we argue that OTP encryption constructs a (length-leaking) secure channel? After all, in the real world (i.e., when OTP encryption is used) the adversary receives something, namely the ciphertext, while she receives nothing in the ideal world. How can we resolve this apparent problem?

3.3   The Simulator

Since the ciphertext is statistically independent of the message, we can argue that the adversary is not better off when the ideal resource SEC is available compared to when OTP encryption is used. If the ideal resource were used, he could *simulate* the ciphertext (he would receive in the real world, see Figure 3, top) by himself. More precisely, if a simulator sim generating a random ciphertext (of appropriate length[4]) is attached to the adversary interface of the ideal system, then the resulting system (see Figure 3, bottom) is equivalent (i.e., identical) to the system in the real world (OTP encryption). Written as an equation of systems, we have

$$\text{otp-dec}^{B}\ \text{otp-enc}^{A}\ (\text{KEY‖AUT})\ \equiv\ \text{sim}^{E}\ \text{SEC}. \qquad (1)$$

(see the top and bottom systems in Figure 3). Here equivalent means that the entire input-output behavior is exactly the same. In other words, both systems (at the top and the bottom of Figure 3) behave identically. Each system takes an input at interface A, outputs this message at interface B, and outputs a random string of the same length at interface E. Equivalent behavior means that the two systems behave identically if plugged into any possible environment or application. This means that from the adversary's viewpoint, the ideal world is just as good as the real world because anything that could happen in the real world could identically happen in the ideal world. We remark that this simulation paradigm has a deeper justification in the abstract cryptography framework [18], where simulators are not part of a security definition but only part of the *proof* of a security statement.

---

be defined concretely for a specific instantiation of the system concept. Here is is understood naturally as the asynchronous parallel composition.

[4] The length must be given as an input to the simulator, hence it must be "leaked" by the secure channel.

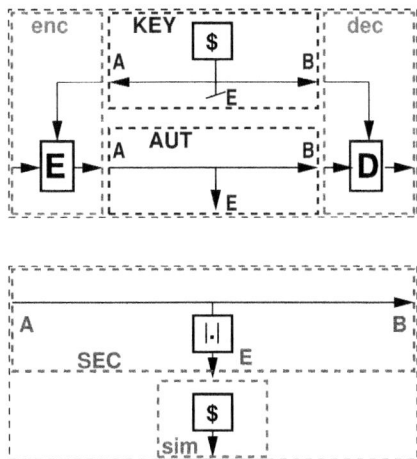

Fig. 4. Explaining symmetric encryption in constructive cryptography. The only change compared to the one-time pad example is that the two protocol systems (later called converters) otp-enc and otp-dec are replaced by enc and dec which implement the encryption algorithm E and decryption algorithm D, respectively. Equation (1) is replaced by (2).

3.4 Computational Security

It is well-known that the one-time pad, and any other information-theoretically secure encryption scheme, is impractical because, roughly speaking, the key must be as long as the total message length to be sent[5]. In practice one therefore strives for security (only) against computationally bounded adversaries, which is called *computational security*. Computational hardness is usually phrased in an asymptotic sense, and the bound on the adversary's computing power is usually assumed to be polynomial in the security parameter[6].

Figure 4 shows a setting where the OTP encryption scheme is replaced by a computationally secure encryption scheme, for example a secure stream cipher as shown in Figure 2. One can use the same simulator for the ideal system (generating a random ciphertext of appropriate length). However, the real resource with encryption/decryption and the ideal resource with simulator are not identical anymore. All we want to argue is that they are *essentially similar* (or, alternatively stated, very close) for an adversary with bounded computing power. More generally, we want to argue that they behave essentially identically in any realistic application context, where realistic means that only feasible computations occur. Written as an equation of systems, the requirement can be stated as

---

[5] This is true if no additional source of information (e.g. a satellite with noisy channels to the parties) is available [13].

[6] However, as explained in [18], this is not essential; what is relevant is a composition property of the feasibility notion.

$$\mathsf{dec}^{\mathrm{B}}\,\mathsf{enc}^{\mathrm{A}}\,(\mathsf{KEY}\|\mathsf{AUT})\quad\approx\quad\mathsf{sim}^{\mathrm{E}}\,\mathsf{SEC}, \tag{2}$$

where the notion of system being approximately equivalent needs to be defined.

3.5   Distinguishers and Computational Indistinguishability

The notion of two systems S and T "being similar" or "behaving essentially identically" in any context is captured by the concept of a *distinguisher*. A distinguisher D for two systems of the same type is a system (or algorithm) that can access ("play with") a system of this type and outputs a bit. The distinguisher's advantage is the difference of probability of outputting 1 in the two cases, where D is connected to S and where D is connected to T, respectively.

Two systems S and T are ε-similar (or ε-close) if no distinguisher (in a certain class of distinguishers) has a distinguishing advantage of more than ε. If we consider the class of all *feasible* (e.g. polynomial time) distinguishers and ε is very small (negligible), then this means that in any computationally efficient environment or application (which can be considered as the distinguisher) the two systems behave essentially the same. The probability that a difference can be observed is at most ε.

This leads to a constructive security definition of an encryption scheme; it is secure if it *constructs*, in the sense of computational indistinguishability (eq. (2)), a secure channel from an authenticated channel and a secret key.

3.6   One-Time Pad Encryption over an Insecure Channel

While, as explained above, encryption is naturally used over an authenticated channel, one may ask what happens when it is used over an insecure channel. Indeed, some protocols (e.g. SSL) can be seen as first transforming an insecure channel into a confidential channel (without or with limited authenticity) and then using a MAC to transform the confidential channel into a secure channel (see Section 5.2). Such a confidential channel is characterized by some form of malleability (see [22]).

Specifically, it is quite easy to see that if one uses OTP encryption over an insecure (rather than authenticated) channel, then the resulting channel is an XOR-malleable channel allowing the adversary E to XOR an arbitrary offset δ to the transmitted message. However, the message remains confidential (except for its length), and the adversary cannot modify the message in any other way. For example, he can not swap the first and the second half of the message (even though it might seem that swapping the ciphertext halves might result in swapping the plaintext halves).

4   An Abstract Theory of Systems

This section is based on abstract cryptography [18] and we refer to that paper for more details.

4.1   Abstraction in Cryptography

Before we explain constructive cryptography at a general abstract level, we first recall the discussion in [18] (also presented in [15]) of the role of abstraction in cryptography.

In every mathematical discipline one tries to identify the key concepts and to formalize them in an abstract manner. Abstraction means to eliminate irrelevant details from consideration, thereby focusing only on the relevant aspects of a problem or context. The purpose of abstraction is to provide, at the same time, simpler definitions, higher generality of results, simpler proofs, improved elegance, better didactic suitability, and, perhaps most importantly, new insights.

In many contexts, the highest achievable level of abstraction, once identified, appears natural and stable. For example, the natural mathematical concepts of a relation, a function, a graph, a group, a field, or a vector space capture exactly, in a minimal manner, the relevant notions. In contrast, in cryptography definitions, theorems, and proofs are generally highly technical and have substantial complexity due to the technical artifacts of the particular model (e.g. defining the computational model via Turing machines and communication via tapes, using asymptotic definitions of systems and protocols, defining efficiency as polynomial-time, using a particular adversarial model, etc.).

In view of this, it seems desirable to state cryptographic definitions in an abstract manner and to leave the technical aspects to a lower level of abstraction. This allows for simplicity (e.g. non-asymptotic definitions and proofs) and generality (e.g. simultaneous treatment of different security notions, like information-theoretic and computational).

4.2   Levels of Abstraction: Bottom-Up vs. Top-Down

The traditional approach in theoretical computer science, and more specifically in complexity theory and cryptography, is bottom-up. One first defines (at a low level) a computational model (e.g. a Turing machine or a circuit), based on which one defines the concept of an algorithm for the model and a communication model (e.g. based on tapes). One then defines a complexity notion for an algorithm (e.g. the number of steps), and then a notion of efficiency (e.g. polynomial in some parameter(s), in an asymptotic sense). Finally, based on all these notions, one defines the security of a cryptosystem, typically as the infeasibility for the adversary to win a specific game.

The paradigm shift proposed in [18] is to use a top-down approach. In order to state definitions and develop a theory, one starts from the other end, the highest possible level of abstraction, and proceeds downwards, introducing in each new lower level only the minimal necessary specializations of that level necessary for expressing what one wants to capture.

It is important to point out that theorems proved at a certain (high) level of abstraction are completely precise (as they are mathematical theorems). This is true without instantiations of the lower levels, which is exactly the point of abstraction. The definitions and theorems are inherited by the lower levels, provided (of course) that the lower levels satisfy the postulated properties or axioms of the higher levels. It is hence strictly more desirable to prove theorems at higher levels of abstraction; nothing is lost by doing this[7].

This paper deals only with high levels of abstraction. Modeling systems at a concrete level (with potentially tedious details), except for the examples given, is left to other papers (e.g. [22,20]).

4.3 Resources and Converters

At the highest level of abstraction, a *system* is an abstract object with *interfaces* by which it interacts with its environment and with other systems. Interfaces are labeled with elements of a label set. Two systems can be composed into a single system by connecting one interface from each system.

Specific types of systems, for example discrete systems as defined in the random system framework [14], are defined at the next lower level of abstraction (see [18]).

In this paper we consider only two special types of systems: resource systems and converter systems. In the statements we make about systems composed of resources and converters, we also consider distinguishers as a third type of system.

An $\mathcal{I}$-*resource system* (or simply $\mathcal{I}$-*resource*), usually denoted by capital letters (e.g. R or S) or by a symbol like SEC in the examples discussed earlier, is a system with interface label set $\mathcal{I}$ (e.g. $\mathcal{I} = \{1, \ldots, n\}$ or $\mathcal{I} = \{A, B, E\}$). Typically (but not only) one can think of each interface being accessible to one party. A *converter system* (or simply converter), usually denoted by a Greek letter (e.g. α or π) or by a symbol like otp-enc, is a system with two interfaces, where one interface is designated as the *outside* interface and the other as the *inside* interface[8]. The inside interface of a converter α can be connected to interface $i \in \mathcal{I}$ of a resource system R; the outside interface of α serves as the new interface i of the combined system, which is again a resource system and is denoted $\alpha^i R$[9].

4.4 Cryptographic Algebras

We now formalize the notions introduced above.

Definition 1. A *cryptographic algebra* $\langle \Phi, \Sigma \rangle$ for an interface set $\mathcal{I}$ consists of a set Φ of $\mathcal{I}$-resources with a parallel composition operation $\|$,[10] a set Σ of

---

[7] For example, in algebra one proves theorems about groups, without having to mention examples of groups, and the point of doing so is that such a theorem applies to *every* group, i.e., every structure satisfying the group axioms.

[8] One can think of such a system as a protocol engine converting or transforming an interface of a resource into an interface with a different behavior.

[9] A system composed of a resource and converters has a star-shaped topology, with a resource in the center and a (possibly empty) chain of converter systems attached to each interface. The resulting system is again a resource with the same interface set.

[10] For every $i \in \mathcal{I}$, the i-interface of $R\|S$ can be thought of as consisting of the two i-interfaces of R and S merged into a single interface, by some addressing mechanism that is not (yet) of interest at this level of abstraction.

converters, and a mapping $\Sigma \times \Phi \times \mathcal{I} \mapsto \Phi$ defining the resource obtained when converter α is attached to interface i of resource R, denoted as $\alpha^i R$, such that

(i) Converter application at different interfaces commutes:

$$\alpha^i \beta^j R = \beta^j \alpha^i R$$

for all $i \neq j$, $R \in \Phi$, and $\alpha, \beta \in \Sigma$.

(ii) Attaching no converter is defined as a special *neutral* converter $1 \in \Sigma$ satisfying $1^i R = R$ for all $i \in \mathcal{I}$ and $R \in \Phi$.

The commutativity condition of the above definition is a special case of composition-order independence [18], the statement that the order in which systems are composed does not matter[11].

One can naturally define serial and parallel composition operations on the converter set Σ as follows. Serial composition: $\alpha\beta$ (or $\alpha \circ \beta$) is defined by

$$(\alpha\beta)^i R := \alpha^i \beta^i R$$

for all i and R. This composition operation is associative because function composition is: $(\alpha\beta)\gamma = \alpha(\beta\gamma)$. Note that $1\alpha = \alpha 1 = \alpha$. Parallel composition: $\alpha\|\beta$ is defined by

$$(\alpha\|\beta)^i (R\|S) := \alpha^i R \,\|\, \beta^i S$$

for all i and $R, S \in \Phi$[12].

We also consider a pseudo-metric[13] on the space Φ of resources to measure the similarity or dissimilarity of resources. As discussed in Section 4.5, the metric is usually defined as the best distinguishing advantage for a certain class of distinguishers, but it is useful to consider an abstract pseudo-metric. Two special and natural properties of a pseudo-metric are captured in the following definition. They state that the pseudo-metric is non-expanding in the sense that $d(R, S)$ does not increase if one puts a resource T in parallel to R and S,[14] or if one connects a converter to the same interface of R and S.

Definition 2. A pseudo-metric d on Φ is *compatible* with the cryptographic algebra $\langle \Phi, \Sigma \rangle$ if

$$d(R\|R', S\|S') \leq d(R, S) + d(R', S') \tag{3}$$

for all $R, R', S, S' \in \Phi$, and

$$d(\alpha^i R, \alpha^i S) \leq d(R, S) \tag{4}$$

for all $i \in \mathcal{I}$, $R, S \in \Phi$ and $\alpha \in \Sigma$.

---

[11] This is what one has in mind when drawing a figure of a system composed of subsystems connected by lines, as the drawing does not preserve information about the order in which the various parts were drawn.

[12] Note that $(\alpha\|\beta)^i T$ need not be explicitly defined if T is not of a the form $T = R\|S$.

[13] A pseudo-metric on a set S is a function $d : S \times S \to \mathbf{R}^+$ such that $d(a, a) = 0$, $d(a, b) = d(b, a)$, and $d(a, c) \leq d(a, b) + d(b, c)$.

[14] Note that (3) is equivalent to $d(R\|T, S\|T) \leq d(R, S)$ and $d(T\|R, T\|S) \leq d(R, S)$.

4.5 Distinguisher-Based Pseudo-Metrics

A distinguisher D (for n-interface resources) can be defined as a system with $n+1$ interfaces, where n interfaces connect to the interfaces of a resource R and the other (outside) interface outputs a bit.

The typical pseudo-metrics in cryptography are distinguisher-based metrics, i.e., the distance between two resource systems is the best advantage a distinguisher in a certain class $\mathcal{D}$ of distinguishers can achieve:

$$d(R, S) = \Delta^{\mathcal{D}}(R, S) := \sup_{D \in \mathcal{D}} \Delta^D(R, S),$$

where $\Delta^D(R, S)$ is the advantage of D in distinguishing R and S.

The class $\mathcal{D}$ is, for example, either the set of *all* distinguishers (information-theoretic security) or the set of all *feasible* distinguishers (computational security). In the first case, one can distinguish between perfect security (the distance is 0) or statistical security (the distance is very small).

A distinguisher D emulating (internally) a converter $\alpha \in \Sigma$ at interface i induces a new distinguisher, denoted $D\alpha^i$, defined by

$$\Delta^{D\alpha^i}(R, S) = \Delta^D(\alpha^i R, \alpha^i S).$$

Similarly, a distinguisher D emulating a resource $T \in \Phi$ in parallel induces a new distinguisher, denoted $D[\cdot\|T]$, defined by

$$\Delta^{D[\cdot\|T]}(R, S) = \Delta^D(R\|T, S\|T).$$

$D[T\|\cdot]$ is defined analogously.

An important property of a distinguisher class $\mathcal{D}$ is that it is closed under the emulation of a converter, in the sense that $\mathcal{D}\Sigma^i \subseteq \mathcal{D}$, where $\mathcal{D}\Sigma^i = \{D\alpha^i | D \in \mathcal{D}, \alpha \in \Sigma\}$. In other words, a converter can be absorbed into a distinguisher without extending the distinguisher class: For $D \in \mathcal{D}$ and $\alpha \in \Sigma$, we also have $D\alpha^i \in \mathcal{D}$.

Similarly, $\mathcal{D}$ should also be closed under emulation of a resource, in the sense that $\mathcal{D}[\cdot\|\Phi] \subseteq \mathcal{D}$ and $\mathcal{D}[\Phi\|\cdot] \subseteq \mathcal{D}$, where for example $\mathcal{D}[\Phi\|\cdot] = \{D[T\|\cdot] : D \in \mathcal{D}, T \in \Phi\}$.

Lemma 1. *For a distinguisher class $\mathcal{D}$ for resources in Φ, the pseudo-metric $\Delta^{\mathcal{D}}$ is compatible with the cryptographic algebra $\langle \Phi, \Sigma \rangle$ if*

$$\mathcal{D}\Sigma^i \subseteq \mathcal{D}, \qquad \mathcal{D}[\cdot\|\Phi] \subseteq \mathcal{D}, \qquad and \qquad \mathcal{D}[\Phi\|\cdot] \subseteq \mathcal{D}.$$

Proof. Since $\mathcal{D}\alpha^i \subseteq \mathcal{D}\Sigma^i \subseteq \mathcal{D}$ we have

$$\Delta^{\mathcal{D}}(\alpha^i R, \alpha^i S) = \Delta^{\mathcal{D}\alpha^i}(R, S) \leq \Delta^{\mathcal{D}}(R, S),$$

which is (4). Similarly, since $\mathcal{D}[\cdot\|T] \subseteq \mathcal{D}[\cdot\|\Phi] \subseteq \mathcal{D}$ we have

$$\Delta^{\mathcal{D}}(R\|T, S\|T) = \Delta^{\mathcal{D}[\cdot\|T]}(R, S) \leq \Delta^{\mathcal{D}}(R, S).$$

As mentioned, this inequality together with the dual inequality $\Delta^{\mathcal{D}}(T\|R, T\|S) \leq \Delta^{\mathcal{D}}(R, S)$ implies (3). $\square$

If one considers the class of feasible distinguishers and converters, then one needs a feasibility notion for which the conditions of Lemma 1 are satisfied. Since one can repeatedly absorb converters into the class, the class needs to be defined asymptotically. For example, polynomial-time notions of feasibility, if properly defined, have this composition property. In fact, this can, in retrospect, be seen as a reason for working with polynomial-time notions in cryptography and complexity theory. However, as we have illustrated (see also [18]), an abstract treatment is possible, is simpler, and implies the corresponding statements for any composable feasibility notion, not just (a specific form of) polynomial-time.

In such an asymptotic definition of feasibility, the systems are actually asymptotic families of systems (indexed by some parameter) and the distance is a function of the parameter rather then a number. This view is compatible with the abstract view presented above. One can define a negligibility notion, which is a subset of the functions $\mathbf{N} \to \mathbf{R}^+$, containing the constant 0-function, and closed under multiplication with a feasible function. We do not expand further on these lower-level issues and refer to [18].

5 Constructive Cryptography for the Alice-Bob-Eve Setting

A standard cryptographic setup consists of two honest parties, Alice and Bob, connected by a certain communication resource (e.g., an insecure channel) that may be partially controlled by an adversary, Eve. This setup corresponds to a special case of abstract cryptography [18], where the interface set is $\mathcal{I} = \{A, B, E\}$, where A and B are assumed to be honest and E is assumed to be the adversary, and where one considers single resources rather than resource sets (called specification in [18]). The term *constructive cryptography* [16] here refers to the application of abstract cryptography to defining classical cryptographic primitives in a constructive way. We refer also to [22,19].

5.1 Defining "Secure Construction"

In the following, we consider resources with interface set $\mathcal{I} = \{A, B, E\}$, where E is the adversary interface. We will define what it means to "securely construct" a resource S from a resource R using converters π_1 for A and π_2 for B. Recall the discussion in Section 3.

Since the party E is only introduced as a thought experiment to define security, it can not be assumed to be present. A resource can be modeled as having two modes, one mode when E is not present and one mode when E is present and makes potential use of its assumed power. There are several ways to model such a two-mode resource. A natural one is to assume a special converter $\perp$ which, when attached to the E-interface, puts the resource into the "no adversary" mode. In other words, the two modes of a resource R are $\perp^E R$ and R (where, in the latter, E has direct access to R).

Concretely, the converter $\perp$ can for example be thought of as shielding the interface to the outside (i.e., to a distinguisher) and setting some kind of flag at its inside interface which tells the resource to behave in a certain restricted mode (corresponding to E not being present). A resource could for example be (but does not have to be) modeled as taking as an initial input a "cheating bit" c at interface E. If the bit is set to $c = 1$, then the interface provides additional functionality (like allowing E to read and/or modify a message) compared to the case $c = 0$, which corresponds to E not being present. This can be interpreted as follows: An adversary E sets the bit to 1 in order to acquire additional power. In this view, $\perp$ is a converter which sets $c = 0$ (at the inside interface) and shields the outside interface. For example, an insecure channel can be modeled by specifying that if $c = 0$, then the message(s) input by A are delivered to B, whereas if $c = 1$, then E receives a message sent by A and can replace it by an arbitrary message, which is delivered to B. Similarly, a secure channel with deletion feature can be modeled by specifying that if $c = 0$, then the message(s) input by A are delivered to B, whereas if $c = 1$, then E learns the message length and can input a bit indicating whether the message should be delivered to B or deleted.

The two modes must be considered separately, resulting in two conditions which can be called availability (E not present) and security (E present).

Definition 3. Consider a cryptographic algebra $\langle \Phi, \Sigma \rangle$ for interface set $\mathcal{I} = \{A, B, E\}$ and a pseudo-metric d on Φ. For resources R and S we say that protocol (π_1, π_2) for $\pi_1, \pi_2 \in \Sigma$ *(securely) constructs* S from R, within ε, denoted

$$R \xrightarrow{(\pi_1, \pi_2, \varepsilon)} S,$$

if the following two conditions (availability and security) are satisfied:

1. $d(\pi_1^A \pi_2^B \perp^E R, \perp^E S) \leq \varepsilon$

2. $\exists \sigma \in \Sigma : \quad d(\pi_1^A \pi_2^B R, \sigma^E S) \leq \varepsilon.$

In the one-time pad example (Section 3), only the second condition (security) was discussed. The first condition (availability) was not mentioned, but of course it is necessary, and indeed satisfied for encryption (in particular the one-time pad) as explained in Section 3. Otherwise a secure channel (with deletion feature for E) could be constructed from a communication channel that never delivers a message to B, which obviously would not make sense. Here we do not discuss the first condition further.

5.2   Composability

A notion of "construction" must be composable to be useful. For example, if a certain scheme constructs a secret key from an authenticated communication channel (e.g. a key agreement protocol like a variant of the Diffie-Hellman protocol [9]), then composing such key generation with encryption (and another authenticated channel) should construct a secure channel. Similarly, since a secure MAC constructs an authenticated channel from a secret key and an insecure channel, and encryption constructs a secure channel from an authenticated channel and (another) secret key, the combination of MAC and encryption should construct a secure channel from an insecure channel and two secret keys (see [22]). This corresponds to the well-known encrypt-then-MAC paradigm. Note that the order (encrypt-then-MAC) in which converters are applied to the message is reversed compared to the order in which transformations are applied. We refer to [22] for a discussion of this and of the dual MAC-then-encrypt paradigm.

The above are two examples of serial composability. We also need parallel composability, as described in the following theorem. Composability was defined abstractly in [18], and here we consider a special case.

Theorem 1. *The construction notion $R \xrightarrow{(\pi_1,\pi_2,\varepsilon)} S$ as defined in Definition 3 is generally composable if the pseudo-metric d is compatible with the cryptographic algebra, i.e., we have:*

(i) $\quad R \xrightarrow{(\pi_1,\pi_2,\varepsilon)} S \ \wedge \ S \xrightarrow{(\pi_1',\pi_2',\varepsilon')} T \quad \Longrightarrow \quad R \xrightarrow{(\pi_1'\pi_1,\pi_2'\pi_2,\varepsilon+\varepsilon')} T;$

(ii) $\quad R \xrightarrow{(\pi_1,\pi_2,\varepsilon)} S \ \wedge \ R' \xrightarrow{(\pi_1',\pi_2',\varepsilon')} S' \quad \Longrightarrow \quad R\|R' \xrightarrow{(\pi_1'\|\pi_1,\pi_2'\|\pi_2,\varepsilon+\varepsilon')} S\|S';$

(iii) $\quad R \xrightarrow{(1,1,0)} R.$

Conditions 2 and 3 together imply

$$R \xrightarrow{(\pi_1,\pi_2,\varepsilon)} S \quad \Longrightarrow \quad R\|T \xrightarrow{(\pi_1\|1,\pi_2\|1,\varepsilon)} S\|T,$$

which can be interpreted as *context-insensitivity* in the sense that resources (e.g. T) available in parallel (a context) does not invalidate a construction statement. (The analogous statement with T on the left side also holds.) Note that, for example, if Φ and Σ are the sets of feasibly implementable resources and converters, respectively, then the context-insensitivity does not hold with respect to, say, a factoring oracle T (if factoring is computationally hard). But such a T would not be in Φ.

Proof. The theorem makes six statements that can be proved independently: For each of (i) to (iii) we have to prove conditions 1 and 2 of Definition 3. Here we only prove one of these statements.

To prove condition 2 claimed by (i), assume that $R \xrightarrow{(\pi_1,\pi_2,\varepsilon)} S$ and $S \xrightarrow{(\pi_1',\pi_2',\varepsilon')} T$ are satisfied. By definition, this implies that

$$d(\pi_1^A \pi_2^B R, \ \sigma^E S) \le \varepsilon$$

for some $\sigma \in \Sigma$, as well as

$$d(\pi_1'^A \pi_2'^B S, \ \sigma'^E T) \le \varepsilon'$$

for some $\sigma' \in \Sigma$. We need to prove that there exists a simulator $\hat{\sigma}$ such that

$$d((\pi_1'\pi_1)^A(\pi_2'\pi_2)^B R, \ \hat{\sigma}^E T) \ \le \ \varepsilon + \varepsilon'. \tag{5}$$

We prove that this holds for $\hat{\sigma} = \sigma\sigma'$. Commutativity of converter application at different interfaces implies

$$(\pi_1'\pi_1)^A (\pi_2'\pi_2)^B R \;=\; \pi_1'^A \pi_1^A \pi_2'^B \pi_2^B R \;=\; \pi_1'^A \pi_2'^B \pi_1^A \pi_2^B R.$$

Using (4), namely the compatibility of d, we obtain

$$
\begin{aligned}
d((\pi_1'\pi_1)^A (\pi_2'\pi_2)^B R, \; \pi_1'^A \pi_2'^B \sigma^E S) &= d(\pi_1'^A \pi_2'^B \pi_1^A \pi_2^B R, \; \pi_1'^A \pi_2'^B \sigma^E S) \\
&\leq d(\pi_1^A \pi_2^B R, \; \sigma^E S) \\
&\leq \varepsilon.
\end{aligned}
$$

Using (4) we also obtain

$$d(\sigma^E \pi_1'^A \pi_2'^B S, \; \sigma^E \sigma'^E T) \;\leq\; d(\pi_1'^A \pi_2'^B S, \; \sigma'^E T) \;\leq\; \varepsilon'.$$

Using $\sigma^E \pi_1'^A \pi_2'^B S = \pi_1'^A \pi_2'^B \sigma^E S$ (commutativity) and $\hat{\sigma} = \sigma\sigma'$,[15] we thus have

$$d(\pi_1'^A \pi_2'^B \sigma^E S, \; \hat{\sigma}^E T) \;\leq\; \varepsilon'.$$

The triangle inequality now yields (5):

$$
\begin{aligned}
&d((\pi_1'\pi_1)^A (\pi_2'\pi_2)^B R, \; \hat{\sigma}^E T) \\
&\leq\; d((\pi_1'\pi_1)^A (\pi_2'\pi_2)^B R, \; \pi_1'^A \pi_2'^B \sigma^E S) + d(\pi_1'^A \pi_2'^B \sigma^E S, \; \hat{\sigma}^E T) \\
&\leq\; \varepsilon + \varepsilon'. \qquad\qquad\qquad\qquad\qquad\qquad\qquad\qquad\qquad\qquad\qquad\square
\end{aligned}
$$

We note that this proof of composition holds in complete generality, independently of how one defines technical aspects at lower layers. It would, for example, even hold for systems connected via an analog communication mechanism, and it holds for any composable notion of feasibility and any model of computation.

6   History and Related Work

The idea that cryptographic schemes can be described as transformations of channel security properties, in a constructive sense, was first proposed in the author's lecture notes in the early 90's and was published in [21]. This approach to explaining cryptography, and protocols combining the use of several cryptographic schemes, as channel transformations, also making trust assumptions explicit, has been called the •-calculus (see for example [21,22,23]). Constructive cryptography as discussed here can be seen as defining the semantics of transformations in the •-calculus, which was originally used with only an intuitive semantics, mainly for didactic purposes. We do not elaborate further on the •-calculus.

The so-called "ideal-world real-world" paradigm in cryptography emerged in the context of secure multi-party computation which was (and is) understood

---

[15] Note that the order of composing protocols and simulators is different. The reason can be seen by drawing a figure.

as the emulation of an (ideal) trusted party that computes a certain function or specification, in a real world where only communication channels are available to the parties. It was introduced formally in the frameworks of Canetti [4] (universal composability, called UC) and of Backes, Pfitzmann and Waidner [24,2] (reactive simulatability), based on the simulation paradigm.

In these frameworks, the basic idea is to consider an ideal system (often called a functionality) capturing the goal one wants to securely realize, when given a complete asynchronous network and possibly a set-up, using a protocol specifying what the honest parties have to do. The definition of what it means to "securely realize" involves an adversary who can corrupt certain parties, and captures the idea that whatever the adversary can achieve in the real world he could also achieve in the ideal world. This is made precise by means of a so-called *simulator*, an ingenious concept introduced by Goldwasser, Micali, and Rackoff [10] to define zero-knowledge protocols.

The frameworks [4,24,2] are technically quite specific and have several drawbacks and limitations explained in the abstract cryptography framework [18]. This framework gives a new, direct semantics to the "ideal-world real-world" paradigm based on the concept of a resource isomorphism. In this theory, simulators are only a proof technique, not part of the (security) definition. Actually, in this framework there is not necessarily a central adversary, and simulators are local (as opposed to monolithic).

Constructive cryptography was developed in parallel with abstract cryptography [18], which is joint work with Renato Renner, from which we borrow substantially, including the use of the abstract theory of systems. Constructive cryptography can be seen both as a fragment and as an application of abstract cryptography. Basic ideas of constructive cryptography were also described in [19].

In view of the "ideal-world real-world" paradigm, constructive cryptography appears natural. Nevertheless, previous works on the security of cryptographic schemes work with game-based definitions. We refer to [20] for a discussion of the game-based approach in view of constructive cryptography. Some papers have defined ideal functionalities for certain secure communication primitives. Shoup [25] investigated functionalities for secure key exchange. Bellare et al. [3] propose a modular approach to designing authentication and key exchange protocols, but their approach mixes the game-based and the "ideal-world real-world" approach. This is also true for [6]. Canetti and Krawczyk [7] propose ideal functionalities in the UC-framework for key exchange and secure channels, but their approach is quite technical and involves apparently unnecessary artifacts (e.g. a so-called non-information oracle). These works, and many more, can now be reexamined in the spirit of constructive cryptography.

Many works that define ideal functionalities to explain traditional cryptography actually define functionalities for the cryptographic schemes rather than the channels or keys. For example, Canetti [5] defines an ideal functionality for a digital signature scheme. In constructive cryptography, this appears surprising, as a digital signature scheme corresponds to a pair of *converters*, not a *resource*.

This illustrates that constructive cryptography, while using ideas of previous frameworks, is intrinsically different, in addition to being phrased at a more abstract and general level.

There exists a vast literature on applying formal methods to the design and the analysis of security protocols, and some of them deal with the composition of protocols (e.g., see [8,11,12,23,26] and the references therein). It is beyond the scope of this extended abstract to give a detailed comparison between these approaches and our approach, but we mention a few intrinsic differences.

The most important difference between works in the formal-methods community and the cryptography community is in the *kind* of (mathematical) statement one makes, not in the manner how these statements and the proofs are formalized. We explain three major aspects in which the statements made in the two approaches differ.

First, security is often defined as the absence of a certain class of *attacks*, i.e., the inexistence of a trace in the class of considered attack traces. A major question is whether the class of attack traces captures all relevant attacks. More precisely, the question is what the absence of attack traces of a certain type really means. For example, it should allow one to conclude the security of a protocol that makes use of the given protocol as a subprotocol. We refer to [11] for a discussion of work on protocol composition. In contrast, security in constructive cryptography is defined by the specification of the ideal resource, which characterizes completely what a certain entity (e.g. the adversary E) can do. The notion of attack does not exist in this view, as everything relevant is said by the resource specification. As a consequence, in constructive cryptography, composition follows by a general composition theorem, that is, by design of the kind of statement one makes.

Second, most works applying formal methods make use of a specific idealized model of cryptography, typically the Dolev-Yao model, which abstracts away many relevant aspects. For example, it does not capture that the message length could leak. We refer to [1] for a more detailed discussion of what statements derived for the Dolev-Yao model can actually mean.

Third, realistic statements in cryptography are generally of a probability-theoretic nature, for example stating a bound on the probability that the adversary can break a system or on the advantage in distinguishing two systems. Most works on formal methods do not consider probabilities.

Work based on formal methods comes with the promise of being completely rigorous. Of course, the precision of security statements is important, no matter what kind of statement one makes, and formal methods of various types can provide tools to achieve precision and proof automation. But rigor and precision does not require a statement to be made in a particular formal language. We point out that in this paper, only the statements of Sections 4 and 5 are rigorous, while Sections 2 and 3 are intentionally stated in a less formal language. However, discrete systems and their composition can be formalized in the language of random systems [14] (see also [17]). An interesting open question is how formal methods can be applied to derive statements in constructive cryptography.

On the other hand, since in our approach protocols can be decomposed into elementary steps that are quite easy to prove, the security proof of a complex protocol can actually be simple enough that it may not be necessary to apply formal methods to capture a statement and its proof. We believe that precision and simplicity are not contradictory and that one should always strive for simplicity, without sacrificing rigor.

7   Conclusions and Future Work

Based on [18], we have considered the common cryptographic setting with two honest parties Alice and Bob and an adversary Eve. We have proposed to model cryptography in this setting as a constructive discipline in which resources (e.g. channels) are constructed from resources (e.g. channels and keys), by a cryptographic scheme that corresponds to a pair of converters (constituting the protocol engines) for Alice and Bob.

While the constructive approach could in principle also be phrased in an existing framework such as the UC-framework [4],[16] we present our theory at an abstract level where only the relevant aspects need to be considered, resulting in simplicity and minimality of the arguments. For example, a feasibility notion must, abstractly speaking, only be such that the feasible distinguisher class is closed under emulation of feasible resources and converters. It is possible, but not necessary, to define feasibility as some form of polynomial-time. Asymptotics, Turing machines, and other artifacts that are an integral part of any conventional security definition in cryptography, are not necessary at this abstract level, without loss of precision.

Our approach illustrates the importance of distinguishing between two system types, converters and resources. Cryptographic schemes correspond to converters, not resources. For example, in our view, secrecy is an attribute of a channel, not necessarily a property of an encryption scheme. The (often considered) security goal of achieving secrecy and authenticity means to construct a resource (channel) with these two attributes, not to design an encryption scheme that has two properties which can be called secrecy and integrity. This construction can be divided into two composable steps (see [22]), in two alternative ways: authenticate-then-encrypt and encrypt-the-authenticate.

Constructive cryptography makes precise the intuitive high-level understanding of what cryptography and cryptographic protocols achieve (e.g. constructing a secure channel), separating it from rather involved mathematical security definitions and proofs. One can understand cryptography without understanding security definitions. This separation of concerns suggests a new approach in teaching where the high-level understanding of cryptography can be treated precisely, without need for understanding cryptographic definitions (e.g. simulators), in a

---

[16] Note that abstract cryptography [18] is more general and can *not* be phrased in the UC-framework, as it not only considers a single (central) adversary but models more generally parties with conflicting goals.

general self-contained course on information security, while security definitions and proofs can be treated in a specialized course on cryptography.

Many relevant topics could not be discussed in this paper and are deferred to subsequent papers. Three of them are addressed below.

First, symmetric encryption is the only cryptographic primitive that was actually explained in this paper as a constructive step. Other cryptographic primitives such as message authentication codes, public-key encryption, key-agreement protocols, and digital signature schemes, can also be described as constructive steps, in the spirit described in [21], leading to constructive security definitions for these schemes.

Second, the previous game-based security definitions can be explained in the context of constructive cryptography, giving them a (constructive) semantics. Usually one of the known game-based definitions, if lifted to a more abstract level where one does not necessarily have to talk about asymptotics, polynomial-time, etc., is equivalent to a given constructive security definition. For the case of symmetric encryption, the relation between constructive and game-based definitions is investigated in [20].

Third, we can now design a complete protocol constructing a secure communication channel between two entities A and B from a secret key shared by them and an insecure network (which is a resource involving many entities, including A and B). In addition to the two constructive steps of applying message authentication and encryption (see [22]), the roles of addresses (sender and receiver) and of sequence numbers and/or nonces must also be made explicit as constructive steps. For a protocol designed in this manner, attacks (e.g. replay attacks, reflection attacks, etc.) sometimes successful against conventionally designed protocols, can be excluded by design and need therefore not even be considered. In a certain sense, the constructive paradigm is type-safe, avoiding unexpected effects when different protocol components are combined. Future protocol suites for key management, secure communication, certification, etc., can be designed (and hence be proven secure) in the constructive cryptography paradigm.

Acknowledgements. Constructive cryptography was developed in parallel with abstract cryptography [18]. The collaboration with Renato Renner was essential. I have had numerous very helpful discussions and an on-going collaboration with Björn Tackmann who also provided continuous motivation. Many current and former group members have provided useful feedback in the context of the courses I taught at ETH, and with several colleagues I have had many useful discussions. These people include Divesh Aggarwal, Kfir Barhum, David Basin, Sandro Coretti, Grégory Demay, Martin Hirt, Dennis Hofheinz, Thomas Holenstein, Christoph Lucas, Sebastian Mödersheim, Krzysztof Pietrzak, Bartosz Przydatek, Dominik Raub, Pavel Raykov, Christoph Sprenger, Stefano Tessaro, Zuzana Trubini(-Beerliova), Luca Viganò, Stefan Wolf, and Vassilis Zikas.

References

1. Backes, M., Hofheinz, D., Unruh, D.: CoSP: A general framework for computational soundness proofs. In: ACM Conference on Computer and Communications Security, pp. 66–78 (2009)
2. Backes, M., Pfitzmann, B., Waidner, M.: A general composition theorem for secure reactive systems. In: Naor, M. (ed.) TCC 2004. LNCS, vol. 2951, pp. 336–354. Springer, Heidelberg (2004)
3. Bellare, M., Canetti, R., Krawczyk, H.: A modular approach to the design and analysis of authentication and key exchange protocols. In: Proc. 30th Annual Symposium on the Theory of Computing (STOC), pp. 419–428. ACM, New York (1998)
4. Canetti, R.: Universally composable security: A new paradigm for cryptographic protocols. In: FOCS, pp. 136–145 (2001)
5. Canetti, R.: Universally composable signature, certification, and authentication. In: 17th IEEE Computer Security Foundations Workshop (CSF 2004), p. 219 (2004)
6. Canetti, R., Krawczyk, H.: Analysis of key-exchange protocols and their use for building secure channels. In: Pfitzmann, B. (ed.) EUROCRYPT 2001. LNCS, vol. 2045, pp. 453–474. Springer, Heidelberg (2001)
7. Canetti, R., Krawczyk, H.: Universally composable notions of key exchange and secure channels. In: Knudsen, L. (ed.) EUROCRYPT 2002. LNCS, vol. 2332, pp. 337–351. Springer, Heidelberg (2002)
8. Cortier, V., Delaune, S.: Safely composing security protocols. Formal Methods in System Design 34(1), 1–36 (2009)
9. Diffie, W., Hellman, M.E.: New directions in cryptography. IEEE Transactions on Information Theory 22, 644–654 (1976)
10. Goldwasser, S., Micali, S., Rackoff, C.: The knowledge complexity of interactive proof systems. SIAM J. Comput. 18(1), 186–208 (1989)
11. Gross, T., Mödersheim, S.: Vertical protocol composition. In: 24th IEEE Computer Security Foundations Workshop (CSF 2011) (to appear, 2011)
12. Guttman, J.D., Thayer, F.J.: Protocol Independence through Disjoint Encryption. In: Computer Security Foundations Workshop, pp. 24–34 (2000)
13. Maurer, U.: Secret key agreement by public discussion from common information. IEEE Transactions on Information Theory 39(3), 733–742 (1993)
14. Maurer, U.: Indistinguishability of random systems. In: Knudsen, L.R. (ed.) EUROCRYPT 2002. LNCS, vol. 2332, pp. 110–132. Springer, Heidelberg (2002)
15. Maurer, U.: Abstraction in cryptography. In: Halevi, S. (ed.) CRYPTO 2009. LNCS, vol. 5677, p. 465. Springer, Heidelberg (2009)
16. Maurer, U.: Constructive cryptography - a primer. In: Sion, R. (ed.) FC 2010. LNCS, vol. 6052, p. 1. Springer, Heidelberg (2010)
17. Maurer, U., Pietrzak, K., Renner, R.: Indistinguishability amplification. In: Menezes, A. (ed.) CRYPTO 2007. LNCS, vol. 4622, pp. 130–149. Springer, Heidelberg (2007)
18. Maurer, U., Renner, R.: Abstract cryptography. In: The Second Symposium in Innovations in Computer Science, ICS 2011, pp. 1–21. Tsinghua University Press, Beijing (January 2011)
19. Maurer, U., Renner, R., Wolf, S.: Unbreakable keys from random noise. In: Tuyls, P., et al. (eds.) Security with Noisy Data, pp. 21–44. Springer, Heidelberg (2007)
20. Maurer, U., Rüedlinger, A., Tackmann, B.: Confidentiality and integrity revisited (manuscript in preparation)

21. Maurer, U., Schmid, P.E.: A calculus for security bootstrapping in distributed systems. Journal of Computer Security 4(1), 55–80 (1996); appeared also In: Gollmann, D. (ed.) ESORICS 1994. LNCS, vol. 875, pp. 175–192. Springer, Heidelberg (1994)
22. Maurer, U., Tackmann, B.: On the soundness of authenticate-then-encrypt. In: ACM Conference on Computer and Communications Security, pp. 505–515 (2010)
23. Mödersheim, S., Viganò, L.: Secure pseudonymous channels. In: Backes, M., Ning, P. (eds.) ESORICS 2009. LNCS, vol. 5789, pp. 337–354. Springer, Heidelberg (2009)
24. Pfitzmann, B., Waidner, M.: Composition and integrity preservation of secure reactive systems. In: ACM Conference on Computer and Communications Security, pp. 245–254 (2000)
25. Shoup, V.: On formal models for secure key exchange. IBM Research report, no. RZ 3120 (April 1999)
26. Sprenger, C., Basin, D.A.: Developing security protocols by refinement. In: ACM Conference on Computer and Communications Security, pp. 361–374 (2010)

G2C: Cryptographic Protocols
from Goal-Driven Specifications

Michael Backes[1,2], Matteo Maffei[1], Kim Pecina[1], and Raphael M. Reischuk[1]

[1] Saarland University, Saarbrücken, Germany
[2] Max Planck Institute for Software Systems (MPI-SWS)

Abstract. We present G2C, a goal-driven specification language for distributed applications. This language offers support for the declarative specification of functionality goals and security properties. The former comprise the parties, their inputs, and the goal of the communication protocol. The latter comprise secrecy, access control, and anonymity requirements. A key feature of our language is that it abstracts away from *how* the intended functionality is achieved, but instead lets the system designer concentrate on *which* functional features and security properties should be achieved. Our framework provides a compilation method for transforming G2C specifications into symbolic cryptographic protocols, which are shown to be optimal. We provide a technique to automatically verify the correctness and security of these protocols using ProVerif, a state-of-the-art automated theorem-prover for cryptographic protocols. We have implemented a G2C compiler to demonstrate the feasibility of our approach.

1 Introduction

Designing cryptographic protocols is tremendously difficult and error-prone. Protocol designers struggle to keep pace with the variety of possible security vulnerabilities, which have affected early authentication protocols such as the Needham-Schroeder protocol [19,31], carefully designed de facto standards like SSL and PKCS [46,8], and even widely deployed products such as Microsoft Passport [21] and Kerberos [11]. The task of designing cryptographic protocols is made more and more challenging by the dimension and complexity of modern distributed architectures (e.g., collaborative platforms, content sharing applications, social networks) and the number of security properties that have to be simultaneously fulfilled (e.g., user anonymity, access control, secrecy, and authentication). There are only few suitable guidelines [3] or automated tools [36,14,47,14,22,6,40] to assist system designers and, at present, the development of cryptographic protocols is mostly carried out by relying on common practice and on the creativity and experience of designers, rather than on rigorous and formal design techniques.

Recent research has started to address this problem by providing techniques to compile high-level protocol specifications into concrete cryptographic protocols [6,22,40] or to strengthen existing cryptographic protocols and make them resistant to sophisticated threat models [4]. These approaches, however, take as

S. Mödersheim and C. Palamidessi (Eds.): TOSCA 2011, LNCS 6993, pp. 57–77, 2012.
© Springer-Verlag Berlin Heidelberg 2012

input a detailed specification of the structural aspects of the protocol: one has to describe in depth which messages are exchanged between which participants and, in some cases, even which cryptographic primitives are used. In general, these techniques require expert knowledge in current security research and, arguably, they are hardly accessible to system designers. Ideally, designers should be required to solely state in a simple, yet precise, manner *which* functionality should be realized and *which* security properties should be guaranteed, without necessarily having to think *how* this can be achieved.

1.1   Contributions

Inspired by the increasingly popular approach of declarative networking [30,29,48,34] — a high-level programming paradigm to conveniently describe and implement distributed systems — we propose G2C, a concise, *goal-driven specification language* for distributed applications. G2C allows the designer to specify the functionality of the protocol and the desired security properties (secrecy, access control, and anonymity) without specifying the actual communication patterns or the cryptographic infrastructure, in the spirit of "say what you want, not how to do it." Only the following information has to be specified: the protocol input (given facts like information from some customers), the desired protocol functionality (the survey institute obtains a statistical analysis of the customer's review) and the desired security properties (the customers' review should not leak out and customers should stay anonymous).

We present a *compilation technique* from G2C specifications into Dolev-Yao-style protocols expressed in the applied π-calculus [1]. This compilation is achieved using a combination of standard public-key encryptions and signatures, and, if necessary to achieve anonymity properties, broadcast encryptions [20,9,10] and ring signatures [38,26,12]. Our compiler first generates several candidate protocols and then automatically selects the protocol that minimizes the structural complexity.

We finally present an *automated validation technique* to check the correctness and the security of the synthesized cryptographic protocols using ProVerif [7], a state-of-the-art theorem prover based on Horn-clause resolution that yields security proofs for an unbounded number of protocol sessions. Our compiler embeds ProVerif annotations in the synthesized applied π-calculus code. These annotations allow for the validation of functional correctness, secrecy, and access control. The compiler additionally generates ProVerif bi-processes that capture the intended anonymity properties. In general, this translation validation approach has the advantage that even if we apply drastic optimizations, or completely reimplement the transformation, we do not need to redo any proofs. While a direct proof of correctness of the translation would provide stronger guarantees for any generated protocol implementation without relying on any validator, this far-from-trivial proof would need to be redone every time the transformation is changed, e.g., to apply optimizations or to consider additional security properties. We believe that the added benefits of having such a direct proof are greatly

outweighed by the amount of work necessary to create it and keep it up-to-date
as the transformation evolves.

1.2   Related Work

In declarative network systems, which our approach is inspired by, such as
P2/Overlog [30], NDlog [29], SeNDlog [48], the actions for each network node
have to be specified. Similarly, in process calculi [32,1,2], it is necessary to specify both source and destination as well as the content of network messages. This
holds true also for the number of languages for the specification of multiparty
sessions that have been proposed in the last years [17,16,6,22]. In all these approaches, protocol designers have to specify concrete actions for each principal.
As shown in the figure below, our approach provides a higher level of abstraction
that lets the designer focus on *what* goals should be achieved, without specifying
how this can be done, i.e., omitting the protocol details.

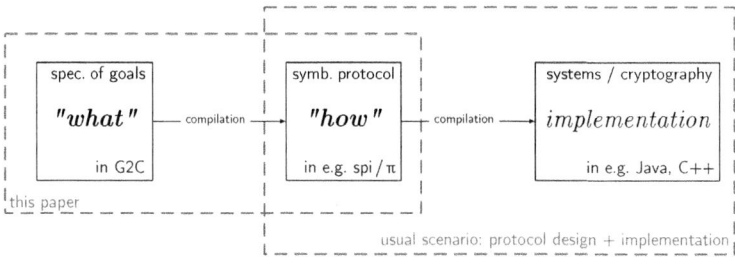

Fig. 1. Positioning of our work. While existing approaches concentrate on designing
and reasoning about symbolic protocols and corresponding implementations, we provide a more abstract layer for the specification functionality goals and security properties, together with a compilation procedure to symbolic protocols.

A data model [5] that resembles the model we use in G2C has been used to
specify the HIPAA privacy rule [43], which regulates the transmission of protected health information by hospitals, doctors, insurance companies, etc. These
privacy provisions, stated in terms of logical formulae, can be expressed in our
language. Moreover, our framework is fine-grained enough to support both roles
and groups of principals. In the HIPAA data model, each statement is dedicated
to a single principal. In contrast, our framework allows statements to represent
information of several principals (e.g., the result of the statistical analysis of
customers' reviews). Jif [33] is a version of Java that incorporates a type system
for the enforcement of secure information flow; Jif/Split [14] is an extension of
Jif that automatically partitions programs to run securely on a distributed system. Fabric [28] is an extension of Jif/Split that allows new nodes to join the
system and supports consistent, distributed computations over shared persistent
data. Jif/Split and Fabric deal with confidentiality and integrity, but they do not

address anonymity. AURA [27] is a typed language for authorization and audit that includes mechanically verified proofs of the decidability. AuraConf [44] is an extension of Aura that deals with confidentiality properties. In contrast to our approach, neither Aura nor AuraConf focus on the automated generation of cryptographic protocols and do not address anonymity properties. An approach in the area of trust-negotiation protocols [13] is close to our approach of minimizing the cost of a DAG, i.e., minimizing the amount of necessary prerequisites in order to achieve a given goal.

Translation validation [37] is an accepted technique for detecting compiler bugs and preventing incorrect code from being run. Since the validator is usually developed independently from the compiler and uses very different algorithms, translation validation significantly increases the confidence of the user in the compilation process. The validator can use a variety of techniques, ranging from program analysis and symbolic execution [35,42] to model checking and theorem proving [37]. We use ProVerif to validate the results of our compilation.

1.3   Outline

The remainder of this paper is organized as follows. For the sake of exposition, Section 2 introduces our framework by means of an illustrative example, Section 3 presents the compilation to symbolic protocols. Section 4 explains how anonymity is achieved and verified. Finally, Section 5 concludes.

2   Illustrative Example

The language G2C is best explained by means of an illustrative example of a goal-driven G2C specification. (We refer to Appendix A for a formal grammar of the G2C syntax.) In this example, information about different topics is collected from a set of customers (collection phase). This information is evaluated, i.e., using some statistic analyses by a manager (evaluation phase), and then sent to a survey institute that can publish the final document (publication phase). Among other functional goals and security constraints, the goal of this protocol is to ensure (1) anonymity of the customers who initially have some private or confidential information and (2) anonymity of the manager who evaluates the collected information. In this case, the final document can only be signed by a member of a pool of trustworthy managers, but the survey institute shall not know who the responsible manager is who actually signed the document.

Principals. The G2C specification for such a protocol defines a set of principals $\mathcal{P}$ occurring in the system. Each principal is assigned one or more tags $t_i \in \mathcal{T}$. By default, each principal $p \in \mathcal{P}$ is implicitly tagged by a tag with his own name p, i.e., the set of tags $\mathcal{T}$ is implicitly extended to comprise $\mathcal{P}$ if necessary.

For this example, there are some customers tagged `customer`, and some managers tagged `manager`, and the survey institute tagged `government`:

```
Principals:
  cust1 : customer
  cust2 : customer
  ...
  mng1  : manager
  mng2  : manager
  ...
  surveyinstitute : government
```

Tags. Both principals and statements (see below) are tagged. These tags can be related via a partial-order relation, a *tag lattice* with a least element `public`, which provides an access control mechanism for statements: principal p tagged t_p may only access statements tagged $t_s \leq t_p$. Intuitively, the higher the position of a tag $t_s \in \mathcal{T}$ in the lattice, the more confidential are the statements tagged by t_s. The usage of tags allows us to build upon several role-based access control mechanisms [18,45,39]. The presented example does not use an explicitly specified lattice, only the implicit relation $\forall t \in \mathcal{T}.\,\texttt{public} \leq t$.

Statements. The specification defines a set $\mathcal{S}$ of statements that occur in the system. Statements can be considered as place-holders for the actual values in a protocol run. At specification time, these values are irrelevant in the sense that they do not affect the protocol construction. For this reason, we symbolically abstract values as statements. The syntax of a statement specification is of the form `s : t`, where $s \in \mathcal{S}$ and $t \in \mathcal{T}$. Arguments can be constants (lowercase strings and numbers), variables (strings beginning with an uppercase letter) or wildcards (*). The tags on the right-hand side of the colon can be either constants or variables that are bound in the argument list of the specified statement.

```
Statements:
  document(2011) : manager or government
  info(*)        : customer or manager
  manager_pwd()  : manager
```

The statements in this case are: `document(2011)`, which represents the final document that is created by the managers for the year 2011. It is accessible for all principals that are tagged `manager` or `government`. The statements called `info(topic)` contain the information that is collected in the collection phase for a specific topic. These statements are accessible for customers and managers. They can be parameterized to specify which particular information the statement contains. The statement `manager_pwd()` is a password that is necessary to compute and trustworthily sign the document. Its content is only accessible for those principals that are tagged `manager`.

Inputs. Initially, each principal $p \in \mathcal{P}$ has some input statement $s \in \mathcal{S}$ to the system. These inputs are captured in the input section. The syntax is `s @ p`.

In our example, the customers have information about certain topics, and all managers have the manager password.

```
Input:
  info(*)           @ $PRINCIPALS_TAGGED(customer)
  manager_pwd()     @ $PRINCIPALS_TAGGED(manager)
```

The G2C language supports some syntactic sugar. The input specification expression s @ $PRINCIPALS_TAGGED(t) is evaluated to a list of input specifications s @ p_1, s @ p_2, ..., where $p_i \in \mathcal{P}$ are the principals that are declared to have tag t. Statements may be parameterized by constants and wildcards.

Functional goals. A *functional* goal of the protocol is to make the document available to the customers. The goal section states these goals by listing statements at principals. It is syntactically similar to the input section.

```
Goals:
  document(2011)         @ surveyinstitute
```

Rules. In order to enforce the stated functional goals, a set of computation rules $\mathcal{R}$ has to be specified. In the section for rules, computations are abstractly specified using arbitrary function symbols like create_document. The intuition behind rules is that anyone can compute the head of a rule (in this case the statement document) whenever all computation arguments are available (in this case the manager password and the information about the topics).

```
Rules:
  document(2011)  :- create_document[
                     info(topic1), info(topic2), ...,
                     manager_pwd()
                     ]
```

More formally, a computation rule $r \in \mathcal{R}$ is a variant of a Horn clause of the form $h :- f[b_1, \ldots, b_n]$. The *head* h of r is a statement possibly parameterized by constants or by variables. The right-hand side of the rule operator :- contains the *body* of r. The body comprises a function symbol f and a list of comma separated statements b_i. These statements can be parameterized by constants and variables. The variables must be bound as parameters of h. We stress that, for the reason of abstraction, the specification does not take the semantics for the specified function symbols into account. Any principal p can compute h whenever p knows *all* statements b_i. For each rule, our compiler automatically derives the set of principals that can apply that rule.

Anonymity. The *security* goals supported by G2C are secrecy and access control (as specified by the statement tags) and anonymity. The latter is captured in the anonymity section. An anonymity specification is a tuple $(s, \mathcal{A}, \mathcal{F})$. The first component $s \in \mathcal{S}$ is a statement. The second component $\mathcal{A} \subseteq \mathcal{P}$, the *among-set*, is a set of principals that shall be anonymous among each other. The third component $\mathcal{F} \subseteq \mathcal{P}$, the *for-set*, is a set of principals that shall not be able to distinguish who in the among set is involved in the computation of s. This notion of anonymity is similar to the concept of k-anonymity [41,15], which states the impossibility to determine who among k users is active. Our definition is more fine-grained in that it specifies the action with respect to which the user should stay anonymous and also the intended distinguishers (implicitly, the for-set additionally includes external observers eavesdropping the communication).

```
Anonymity:
  document(2011) among { cust1,cust2,... } for { surveyinstitute }
  document(2011) among { mng1,mng2,... }  for { cust1,cust2,... }
  document(2011) among { mng1,mng2,... }  for { surveyinstitute }
```

Intuitively, the first of the above specifications means that in the final document, all customers shall be anonymous *among* each other *for* the survey institute. This implies that the survey institute shall not be able to distinguish whether cust1 or whether cust2 was involved in the final document. The second and third specifications demand that the managers be anonymous for the customers and the survey institute, respectively. In other words, neither a customer, nor the survey institute shall learn who the actual manager is that has created and signed the document.

3 Compilation to Symbolic Protocols

In the first step (Section 3.1), an intermediate representation of the specification, a so called data flow graph, is generated. This graph is constructed based on the specified goals, the input patterns, and the corresponding computation rules. The access control specifications for the declared statements are also considered in order to prevent the graph from growing too fast. In the second step (Section 3.2), the data flow graph is condensed in that optimal nodes and edges are selected with respect to the overall communication complexity the final protocol would have. In the third step (Section 3.3), the paths of the condensed graph are translated into a cryptographic protocol expressed in the applied π-calculus.

3.1 Intermediate Representation as Data Flow Graphs

This section formally defines data flow graphs. Data flow graphs serve as an intermediate representation of the protocol specification where nodes represent knowledge of principals, and edges represent the flow of knowledge between principals (i.e., the communication patterns). This data structure provides all necessary information for generating a cryptographic protocol in a symbolic calculus. Data flow graphs are constructed by an iterative bottom-up procedure, which is best explained using the illustrative example of Section 2.

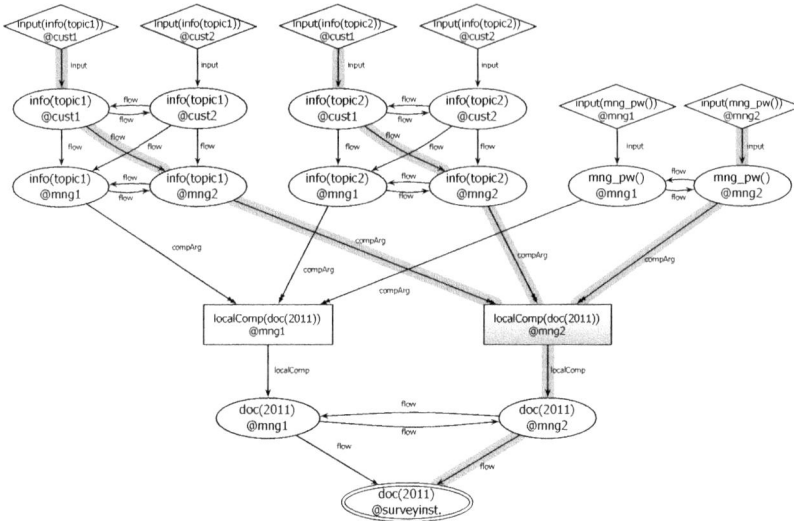

Fig. 2. Data flow graph for the example of Section 2. For the sake of readability, the graph contains only two customers, two managers, and only information about two topics; some statements are abbreviated; the costs for edges and computations are omitted. An optimal selection of edges is colored in gray (cf. Section 3.2).

Example graph. The data flow graph for the example of Section 2 is illustrated in Figure 2. Data flow graphs are constructed in a bottom-up manner, starting with the specified *goal nodes* (doubly circled), which are added to an exploration queue of nodes that have to be explored further. For each node from the queue, the following three exploration steps are performed:

(1) Possible flows from other *knowledge nodes* (round shape) are considered in case the access control specifications permit these flows. In the example, there are flows from the managers' knowledge nodes, document(2011)@mng1 and document(2011)@mng2. These knowledge nodes, if not existent yet, are created within this first step and then added to the exploration queue.

(2) If the statement of the currently explored node is an instantiation of the head statement of a computation rule, a new *computation node* (rectangular shape) is created and added to the queue. Moreover, the inputs for such a computation, again knowledge nodes, are created and added to the queue. In the example above, the computation nodes are localComp(document(2011)@mng1) and localComp(document(2011)@mng2). The inputs to those computation nodes are knowledge nodes representing information about certain topics and the manager password.

(3) The statement of the currently explored node is matched against the input patterns that are provided in the specification. If an instantiation of an input pattern matches the node statement, a new *input node* (diamond shape) is created. This node is not added to the queue as it is not explored further.

Due to this bottom-up construction, and to the immediate instantiations of variables, nodes with neither preceding computation node nor input node might be added to the queue. Therefore, in the end, subgraphs that have no input node as ancestors are removed from the graph.

The edges of the data flow graph express possible *communication structures* of the synthesized protocol. Edges labeled *flow* connect two knowledge nodes that consist of the same statement, but at different principals. These edges correspond to messages that are sent in the synthesized cryptographic protocol. Edges labeled *localComp*, *compArg*, or *input* are virtual edges — they do not represent actual network messages.

Data flow graphs, formally. A data flow graph consists of a set of nodes $\mathcal{N}$ and a set of edges $\mathcal{E}$. The nodes are split into three disjoint sets: *input* nodes $\mathcal{N}_i \subseteq \{\text{input}(S@P)\}_{S \in \mathcal{S}, P \in \mathcal{P}}$, *knowledge* nodes $\mathcal{N}_k \subseteq \{S@P\}_{S \in \mathcal{S}, P \in \mathcal{P}}$, and *computation* nodes $\mathcal{N}_c \subseteq \{\text{localComp}(S@P)\}_{S \in \mathcal{S}, P \in \mathcal{P}}$. A subset of the knowledge nodes $\mathcal{N}_{goal} \subseteq \mathcal{N}_k$ is called *goals*. The set of edges is split into the disjoint sets of input edges $\mathcal{E}_i$, flow edges $\mathcal{E}_f$, computation argument edges $\mathcal{E}_a$ and computation result edges $\mathcal{E}_r$.

Nodes. A data flow graph for a given specification is the smallest graph satisfying the following rules. The numbers refer to the aforementioned explorations.

$$\frac{\text{input}(S^*@P) \in \text{SPEC} \qquad S \lessapprox S^*}{\text{input}(S@P) \in \mathcal{N}_i} \; \text{NInput}^{(3)} \qquad\qquad \frac{\text{input}(S@P) \in \mathcal{N}_i}{(S@P) \in \mathcal{N}_k} \; \text{NKnowInput}^{(3)}$$

$$\frac{\text{rule}(S^* \leftarrow f(S_1^*, \ldots, S_n^*)) \in \text{SPEC}}{\forall i.\,(S_i@P) \in \mathcal{N}_k \qquad \langle S, S_1, \ldots, S_n \rangle \lessapprox_{\mathcal{R}} S^* \leftarrow f(S_1^*, \ldots, S_n^*)}{\text{localComp}(S@P) \in \mathcal{N}_c} \; \text{NComputation}^{(2)}$$

$$\frac{\text{goal}(S@P) \in \text{SPEC}}{(S@P) \in \mathcal{N}_{goal}} \; \text{NGoal}^{(init)} \qquad\qquad \frac{\text{localComp}(S@P) \in \mathcal{N}_c}{(S@P) \in \mathcal{N}_k} \; \text{NKnowComp}^{(2)}$$

$$\frac{(S@P') \in \mathcal{N}_k \qquad \text{may\_access}(P, S)}{(S@P) \in \mathcal{N}_k} \; \text{NKnowFlow}^{(1)}$$

NInput introduces input nodes for instantiated statements $S@P$ that match an input pattern $S^*@P$ from the specification. $S \lessapprox S^*$ denotes that S is a statement instantiation of S^*, i.e., wildcards $*$ and variables in S^* are consistently instantiated, and $\lessapprox_{\mathcal{R}}$ denotes a rule instantiation The details of the instantiation procedure are described in the long version [23]. We stress that the instantiation in NInput is minimal in the sense that only those statements are generated that are necessary to reach the goals (this prevents the graph from growing more than required). Hypotheses of the form $X \in \text{SPEC}$ assume X to occur in the G2C specification. NKnowInput creates knowledge nodes from input nodes. NComputation creates computation nodes for existing knowledge nodes $S_i@P$ and a computation rule occurring in the specification. NGoal directly introduces goal nodes from the specification. NKnowComp creates knowledge nodes from computation nodes. NKnowFlow creates knowledge nodes from existing knowledge nodes if the access control specification permits this step, i.e., the premise may_access(P, S) holds.

Edges. We define the edges $\mathcal{E}$ as the smallest set satisfying the following rules:

$$\frac{n_i = \text{input}(S@P) \in \mathcal{N}_i \qquad n_k = (S@P) \in \mathcal{N}_k}{(n_i, n_k) \in \mathcal{E}_i} \ \text{EInput}^{(3)}$$

$$\frac{n_1 = (S@P_1) \in \mathcal{N}_k \qquad n_2 = (S@P_2) \in \mathcal{N}_k}{(n_1, n_2) \in \mathcal{E}_f} \ \text{EFlow}^{(1)}$$

$$\frac{n_k = (S@P) \in \mathcal{N}_k \qquad n_c = \text{localComp}(S'@P) \in \mathcal{N}_c}{\text{rule}(S^* \leftarrow f(S_1^*, \ldots, S_n^*)) \in \text{SPEC} \qquad S' \overset{\triangle}{\sim} S^* \qquad \exists i : S \overset{\triangle}{\sim} S_i^*}{(n_k, n_c) \in \mathcal{E}_a} \ \text{ECompArg}^{(2)}$$

$$\frac{n_c = \text{localComp}(S@P) \in \mathcal{N}_c \qquad n_k = (S@P) \in \mathcal{N}_k}{(n_c, n_k) \in \mathcal{E}_r} \ \text{ECompRes}^{(2)}$$

Given an input node and a knowledge node, EINPUT creates an input edge (labeled *input*). EFLOW creates flow edges between knowledge nodes (labeled *flow*). Computation argument edges (labeled *compArg*) from knowledge node n_k to computation node n_c are introduced by ECOMPARG in case the statement of n_k is a valid instantiation of an argument of the computation rule contained in n_c. The knowledge node representing the result of a computation is connected via ECOMPRES.

We stress that data flow graphs are finite since there are only finitely many statements, finitely many principals, and finitely many constants.

3.2 Condensed Data Flow Graphs – Selection of the Protocol Skeleton

The idea behind condensing a data flow graph is to find a minimal subset $E \subseteq \mathcal{E}$ of edges, such that all goal nodes are *active* in E. Informally, a knowledge node n_k is active if at least one direct predecessor of n_k is active, a computation node n_c is active if all predecessors of n_c are active, input nodes are always active. In Figure 2, both computation nodes localComp(document(2011)@mng1) and localComp(document(2011)@mng2) are active since all necessary inputs are available and hence, all predecessor knowledge nodes are active. For the same reason, the goal node document(2011)@surveyinstitute is active as well. The *selected* subset of edges is depicted with a gray background. There are several other subsets of edges that make the goal node active. For example, principal cust2 could also give his inputs; or principal mng1 could provide the password.

Besides the condition that, in the final synthesized protocol, all goal nodes must be active, we require that the final protocol be minimal, i.e., the message complexity of the final protocol must not exceed the complexity of the synthesized protocol that has lowest complexity. This minimal subset of edges is referred to as *protocol skeleton* or *condensed data flow graph*. It constitutes the communication structure of the synthesized protocol.

Message complexity. In order to optimize the communication and computation complexity of synthesized protocols, we show a measure of the complexity for sent messages and for computed statements. Computing the minimal number of messages sent around the network requires to take reuse of computed information into account. The problem can be formulated as the task of finding a spanning tree, an acyclic subset of the edges from the data flow graph, such that all goal nodes can be computed with minimal cost. This problem is a classical planning problem [25], mostly investigated by the AI community.

The precise optimization problem $MinMsgCplx(\mathcal{G})$ is defined as follows. Given a directed acyclic flow graph $\mathcal{G} = (\mathcal{N}, \mathcal{E})$ in which the nodes are split into two disjoint sets: $\mathcal{N} = \mathcal{N}_k \cup \mathcal{N}_{ci}$ with $\mathcal{N}_{goal} \subseteq \mathcal{N}_k$ and $\mathcal{N}_{ci} = \mathcal{N}_c \cup \mathcal{N}_i$. Intuitively, a node $n \in \mathcal{N}_k$ depends on only one of its predecessor nodes, whereas $n \in \mathcal{N}_{ci}$ depends on all predecessor nodes. Each edge $e \in \mathcal{E} \subseteq \mathcal{N} \times \mathcal{N}$ is assigned a cost $c(e) \in \mathbb{N}$. The goal is to compute a *valid* set $E \subseteq \mathcal{E}$ such that $\sum_{e \in E} c(e)$ is minimal. A set $E \subseteq \mathcal{E} \subseteq \mathcal{N} \times \mathcal{N}$ is valid (i.e., it fulfills the *graph constraints*) if

1. $\forall n \in \mathcal{N}_{goal} : n$ is active in E.
2. $\forall n \in \mathcal{N}_k$ active in E, $\exists m \in \mathcal{N} : (m, n) \in E$.
3. $\forall n \in \mathcal{N}_{ci}$ active in E, $\forall m \in \mathcal{N} : (m, n) \in \mathcal{E} \Rightarrow (m, n) \in E$.

where $n \in \mathcal{N}$ is *active* in E whenever $\exists m \in \mathcal{N}$ with $(n, m) \in E$ or $(m, n) \in E$.

Define the decision problem $MsgCplx(\mathcal{G}, c^*)$ that asks whether there is a subset of edges $E \subseteq \mathcal{E}$ satisfying $\sum_{e \in E} c(e) \leq c^*$.

Theorem 1. *MsgCplx is $\mathcal{NP}$-complete.*

We refer to Appendix B for the proof.

Graph constraints in SAT. In order to select nodes and edges, thereby enforcing the graph constraints, the data flow graph is translated into a satisfiability problem with clauses in disjunctive normal form. Each variable v_e of the SAT problem represents an edge $e \in \mathcal{E}$. Iff in a satisfying assignment of variables, variable v_e is true, then e is selected. From all satisfying assignments of variables, the assignment that minimizes $\sum_{e \in \mathcal{E}} e \cdot c(e)$ is eventually chosen as communication structure for the final protocol. Our framework uses a state-of-the-art constraint solver, *Gecode* [24], in order to obtain an optimal solution.

The translation of the graph constraints corresponds closely to the above definition of valid edge sets. For demonstration issues, we assume only two incoming edges and two outgoing edges per node. (1) For goal nodes with incoming edges i_1 and i_2, we post the constraint

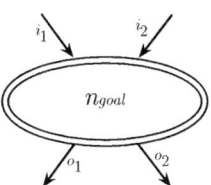

$$i_1 \vee i_2$$

since at least one of i_1 and i_2 must be active in order to activate n_{goal}. The outgoing edges are not necessary to activate n_{goal}.

(2) The incoming edges of a knowledge node n_k shall only be active if at least one of the outgoing edges is active. For each outgoing edge o_j, we post the constraint

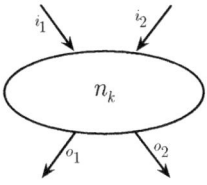

$$o_j \rightarrow (i_1 \vee i_2)$$

which represents the clause $\bar{o}_j \vee i_1 \vee i_2$.

(3) The scenario for computation nodes is slightly more complex. For a computation node n_c to be active, *all* incoming edges, hence all direct predecessors of n_c must be active. For each outgoing edge o_j, we post the constraint

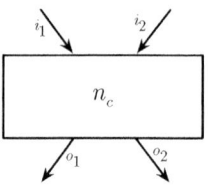

$$o_j \rightarrow (i_1 \wedge i_2)$$

which is equivalent to the formula $\bar{o}_j \vee (i_1 \wedge i_2)$. This formula is translated to two clauses $\bar{o}_j \vee i_1$ and $\bar{o}_j \vee i_2$.

Cycles. Consider goal nodes u and v that are connected via two flow edges (u, v) and (v, u). The constraints for knowledge nodes are satisfied if both theses edges are active. Such cycles, of course, do not solve the problem of activating goal nodes. In order to prevent these cycles in the SAT instance, we post more constraints: Given knowledge node n_k with incoming flow edge i, for each outgoing flow edge o, we add the constraint $i \rightarrow \bar{o}$, which corresponds to the clause $\bar{i} \vee \bar{o}$. This prevents node n_k from acting as "knowledge forwarding" node. Edges from input nodes are not considered, nor are edges from computation nodes.

3.3 Synthesizing Cryptographic Protocols for the Applied π-Calculus

We now detail the translation from a condensed data flow graph into a cryptographic protocol in the applied π-calculus [1]. We build a process for every principal P involved in the protocol. The final protocol consists of the parallel execution of all principal processes, i.e., all principals run concurrently. We assume all principals to be semi-honest, i.e., principals follow the protocol properly, but are curious in that they attempt to learn additional information.

First, we describe the translation of the specified functional goals (together with their annotations for the ProVerif validation) and the security properties. Second, we show how the obtained processes can be modified in order to validate the desired anonymity requirements in ProVerif.

* An *input* with corresponding input node input(s@p) is expressed in the process of principal p as a restriction of a fresh name s. This captures the intuition that, initially, the statement s is only known to principal p. Moreover, the event event s is raised, which states that the input has taken place. Events will be used later in order to show that a computation can only take place if all proper inputs are available.
* A *computation* at node localComp(s@p) with function symbol f and arguments arg1,arg2,... is translated for the process of principal p into a constructor application f(arg1,arg2,...). Every such application is followed by the event event s in order to track that computation.
* A *goal* with corresponding goal node s@p raises the event event s. This is necessary to verify the reachability property of functional goals (see below).

For the purpose of validation, we insert correspondence queries for each computation: every computation h :- func[b$_1$,...,b$_\ell$] in the G2C specification is translated into a ProVerif query of the form query ev:h ==> ev:b_1 & ... & ev:b_ℓ. to validate the functional goals of our protocols. Since event h and the corresponding symbolic term must be preceded by all the events b_1 to b_ℓ along with the corresponding symbolic terms, such queries ensure that all computations are executed only with the expected inputs. For each goal s@p, we insert a query of the form query ev:s. If ProVerif successfully validates all queries, then all computations are well-formed and all goal nodes are reachable.

Flow edges are the only edges that are explicitly modeled in the symbolic protocol. These flows represent the actual communication over a public network. Loosely speaking, the sender first signs the message to ensure its integrity and then encrypts the resulting signature for the recipient to protect the statement's confidentiality. If the G2C specification includes anonymity requirements, then the implementation of the flow edges relies on more sophisticated cryptographic primitives, as detailed in the next section. For the validation of secrecy for statements, we use ProVerif's standard secrecy queries.

4 Anonymity

Anonymity is a security property that reasons about *knowledge* that principals have or do not have. Intuitively, a principal p is anonymous while performing some action α if no other principal p' has any knowledge about that action. If p' has the knowledge that action α took place, but if p' is not able to determine which principal from a set $\mathcal{A}$ of principals actually performed that action, then we say that p is anonymous in action α *among $\mathcal{A}$ for p'*. If any subset of principals $\mathcal{F}$ is not able to distinguish individual principals from $\mathcal{A}$ in action α, we say that principal p is anonymous in α among $\mathcal{A}$ for $\mathcal{F}$. In the following, we call $\mathcal{A}$ the *among*-set and we call $\mathcal{F}$ the *for*-set.

4.1 Anonymity as Symmetric Paths in the Graph

Intuitively, the anonymity requirement $(s, \mathcal{A}, \mathcal{F})$ is fulfilled if for each pair of principals p, p' in $\mathcal{A}$, there exist two subgraphs, both leading to goal s, which are equal up to the identities of p and p'. More precisely, if p is active in goal s, i.e., p contributes to the goal nodes with statement s, then for each other principal $p' \in \mathcal{A}$, there must be another subgraph, such that, after replacing all principals not in the among-set, nor in the for-set by a special symbol $\natural$, and after replacing the two compared principals p and p' by a special symbol $\bullet$, the corresponding subgraphs are equal.

For a more formal definition, let $\mathcal{N}_{goal(s)}$ be the set of goal nodes in which statement s occurs. Let G be a minimal subgraph such that all goal nodes are active (as described in Section 3.2). For all goal nodes $n \in \mathcal{N}_{goal(s)}$, for all $p, p' \in \mathcal{A}$ with $p \neq p'$, we check that one of the following cases is satisfied:

1. p is inactive in n, i.e., for all edges $e_i = (u, v) \in G$ that are (not necessarily direct) ancestor edges of n, we have $prin(u) \neq p \neq prin(v)$, where $prin(s@p) = p$ is the principal for node $(s@p)$.

2. p is active in n and there exists a subgraph G' in which p' is active so that for $q_i \in \mathcal{P} \setminus (\mathcal{A} \cup \mathcal{F})$ the following subgraphs are equal:

$$G\left\{\sharp/_{q_1}\right\} \cdots \left\{\sharp/_{q_\ell}\right\} \left\{\bullet/_p\right\} = G'\left\{\sharp/_{q_1}\right\} \cdots \left\{\sharp/_{q_\ell}\right\} \left\{\bullet/_{p'}\right\}$$

The substitution $G\{^a/_b\}$ replaces all occurrences of b in G by a. This affects statements and principals.

Example. Consider the examples depicted on the right. There are two ways of achieving the goal Z. If $\mathcal{A} = \{A, B\}$, we require that the subgraphs G and G' be equal up to the identities of A and B. For the first example, this requires among others that principals C and D do not occur in $\mathcal{F}$: they know whether they were involved in the protocol. In this case, the substitution σ replaces all occurrences of C and D by $\sharp$ before the subgraphs are compared. For the second example, as both A and B occur in $\mathcal{A}$, σ replaces only the occurrences of A and B by $\bullet$. This means that (although only A occurs in both G and G'), the resulting subgraphs are equal.

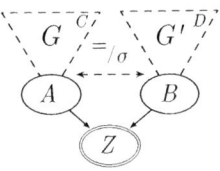

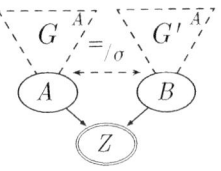

4.2   Cryptographic Primitives for Anonymity

Digital signatures and encryption schemes preserve the integrity and the privacy of data, respectively. In general however, these primitives do not suffice to enforce anonymity requirements. For instance, a digital signature immediately reveals the signer's identity and a ciphertext may reveal the intended recipient. We address these issues by deploying *ring signatures* [38,26,12] and *broadcast encryptions* [20,9,10].

A ring signature preserves the integrity of the signed message but the signer remains anonymous within a chosen group of people. More formally, the signer first decides on the ring he will use. A ring is an arbitrary group of people including the principal himself. He collects the (public) verification keys of all ring members and his own signing key. The resulting ring signature reveals only the fact that one person in the ring signed the message but does not reveal the actual signer. Ring signatures are thus a salient tool to protect the anonymity of principals in the among-set when sending messages to principals in the for-set (referred to as *forward anonymity* in the following). More formally, given an anonymity specification $(s, \mathcal{A}, \mathcal{F})$, whenever communication takes place between a principal p_A in $\mathcal{A}$ and a principal p_F in $\mathcal{F}$, p_A uses a ring signature where the ring consists of all principals from $\mathcal{A}$. We model ring signatures in the applied π-calculus with the constructor $\mathtt{rnsign}(\mathtt{m},\mathtt{sk}_1,\mathtt{vk}_2,\ldots,\mathtt{vk}_n)$ where $(\mathtt{vk}_i,\mathtt{sk}_i)$ denotes the i-th ring member verification key/signing key pair. The ring signature verification $\mathtt{rncheck}(\mathtt{s},\mathtt{vk}_1,\mathtt{vk}_2,\ldots,\mathtt{vk}_n)$ succeeds and returns $\mathtt{m}$ if and only if $\mathtt{s} = \mathtt{rnsign}(\mathtt{m},\mathtt{sk}_1,\mathtt{vk}_2,\ldots,\mathtt{vk}_n)$. Here, the first principal signs the message. However, by extending the destructor reduction rules to handle permutations, we allow the actual signer to occur on arbitrary position.

Dually, we use broadcast encryption schemes to protect the anonymity of principals within the among-set when receiving messages from principals within the for-set (*backward anonymity*). More precisely, given an anonymity specification $(s, \mathcal{A}, \mathcal{F})$, when a principal $p_F \in \mathcal{F}$ communicates a message to a principal $p_A \in \mathcal{A}$, then p_F is required to use a broadcast encryption involving the public encryption keys of all principals in $\mathcal{A}$. This encryption ensures that the ciphertext is addressed to the correct set of principals and that the same plaintext is broadcast to all those principals. One might be tempted to simply require principals in the for-set to issue one encryption for each member of the among-set. A corrupted sender, however, could send only one encryption for a single principal in the among-set thus exploiting a termination channel. Alternatively, the sender could send different messages to different principals and then determine the active principal's identity by scrutinizing the output of a computation. In principle, it is also possible to use zero-knowledge proofs to counter the aforementioned attacks. However, broadcast encryptions entail a significantly lower computational overhead while achieving the same goal: the sender only creates one single ciphertext and the decryption will reveal if that ciphertext was indeed addressed to the proper group of people. For instance, the broadcast encryption scheme by Boneh et al. [9] requires that the encryption keys of all among-set members be available: we model broadcast encryptions with the constructor $bnenc(m, ek_1, ek_2, \ldots, ek_n)$ where (ek_i, dk_i) denotes the i-th principal's encryption key/decryption key pair. The decryption $bndec(e, ek_1, dk_2, \ldots, ek_n)$ succeeds and returns m if and only if $e = bnenc(m, ek_1, ek_2, \ldots, ek_n)$. As seen for ring signatures, the destructor is applicable independently of the position of the party decrypting the ciphertext.

We finally remark that both ring signatures and broadcast encryptions are very efficient cryptographic schemes.

Example. Let us exemplify the notions of forward and backward anonymity on the anonymity specification from Section 2:

```
Anonymity:
    document(2011) among { cust1, cust2 } for { surveyinstitute }
    document(2011) among { mng1, mng2 }  for { cust1, cust2 }
    document(2011) among { mng1, mng2 }  for { surveyinstitute }
```

For the first specification, as the customers never directly communicate with the survey institute, we do not take special precautions: we assume that only principals listed in the for-set are corrupted and thus the managers do not reveal the identity of the customers. Hence, the privacy offered by encryption schemes is sufficient to conceal the identity of the originator of a message.

The second specification requires the customers to use a broadcast encryption (backward anonymity): the manager will receive the input directly from the customers who should not be able to distinguish one manager from another. The simplified applied π-calculus code looks as follows:

```
Customer 1:
    ... new topic1;    (* input *)
    out(c, b2enc(sign(topic1,sk_cust1),ek_mng1,ek_mng2)); ...

Manager 2:
    ... in(c, esv_topic1);    (* signed-then-encrypted *)
    let sv_topic1 = b2dec(esv_topic1,ek_mng1,dk_mng2) in
    let  v_topic1 = check(sv_topic1,vk_cust1) in ...
```

Since the customer is not required to remain anonymous for the managers, it is sufficient for him to use a digital signature rather than a computationally more involved ring signature.

The third specification demands that the survey institute does not learn which manager collected the customer data (forward anonymity); the active manager uses a ring signature where the ring comprises all managers:

```
Manager 2:
    ... let document = create_document(topic1,topic2,manager_pwd) in
    out(c, enc(r2sign(document,vk_mng1,sk_mng2),ek_surveyinst)); ...

Survey Institute:
    ... in(c, esv_document);    (* signed-then-encrypted *)
    let sv_document = dec(esv_document,dk_surveyinst) in
    let  v_document = r2check(sv_document,vk_mng1,vk_mng2) in ...
```

4.3   Verification of Anonymity in the Synthesized Protocol

To verify the given anonymity specification, we use ProVerif's so-called *choice operator*. Intuitively, this operator allows us to model two processes that are structurally equal but differ only in certain terms. The resulting process is called a bi-process. We check that the attacker cannot distinguish the two executions in such a bi-process. Therefore, we let all the principals in $\mathcal{F}$ be corrupted, i.e., we let them release all their secrets and let them take no further action. The attacker can thus act arbitrarily on behalf of those principals. We then pick two principals I, J from $\mathcal{A}$ and construct a bi-process where one choice corresponds to I's code and the other corresponds to J's code. The graph generation algorithm ensures that the two processes are structurally equal (cf. Section 4.1) and that they can be cast into a bi-process. As we verify an equivalence relation, for each anonymity specification, we only consider a chain of relations and use transitivity to obtain observational equivalence among all pairs of principals in $\mathcal{A}$.

Example. Let us consider again the above example: the two managers must remain anonymous for the survey institute. Thus, we cast both managers into a bi-process. The left process corresponds to manager 1 interacting in the protocol and the right process corresponds to manager 2 giving input to the survey institute. As the survey institute occurs in $\mathcal{F}$, we assume it to behave arbitrarily, and we hence let the attacker impersonate the survey institute.

```
Manager 1+2:
  let document = create_document(topic1,topic2,manager_pwd) in
  out(c, enc(r2sign(document,choice[sk_mng1,vk_mng1],
                              choice[vk_mng2,sk_mng2]),ek_surveyinst));

Survey Institute:
  out(c, (vk_surveyinst,sk_surveyinst));
  out(c, (ek_surveyinst,dk_surveyinst)).
```

5 Conclusions and Future Work

We have presented a novel high-level goal-driven specification language, called G2C, that offers support for the declarative specification of functionality goals and security properties. We have presented an automated compilation technique for transforming G2C specifications into corresponding cryptographic protocols, using a combination of public-key encryption, digital signatures, broadcast encryption, and ring signatures. The specified functionality goals as well as the secrecy and anonymity properties are automatically validated using ProVerif.

Drawing on ideas from the vast amount of existing work on authentication and authorization we plan to incorporate further features such as delegation and revocation mechanisms, which are notoriously difficult to combine with privacy and anonymity properties. This extension will naturally involve the usage of more sophisticated cryptographic primitives, such as zero-knowledge proofs. We additionally intend to consider further security properties, such as differential privacy.

References

1. Abadi, M., Fournet, C.: Mobile Values, New Names, and Secure Communication. In: POPL 2001 (2001)
2. Abadi, M., Gordon, A.D.: A Calculus for Cryptographic Protocols: The Spi Calculus. In: CCS 1997. ACM, New York (1997)
3. Abadi, M., Needham, R.: Prudent engineering practice for cryptographic protocols. IEEE Trans. Softw. Eng. 22(1) (1996)
4. Backes, M., Grochulla, M.P., Hriţcu, C., Maffei, M.: Achieving security despite compromise using zero-knowledge. In: CSF 2009. IEEE, Los Alamitos (2009)
5. Barth, A., Datta, A., Mitchell, J.C., Nissenbaum, H.: Privacy and Contextual Integrity: Framework and Applications. In: SP 2006. IEEE, Los Alamitos (2006)
6. Bhargavan, K., Corin, R., Deniélou, P.-M., Fournet, C., Leifer, J.J.: Cryptographic protocol synthesis and verification for multiparty sessions. In: CSF 2009. IEEE, Los Alamitos (2009)
7. Blanchet, B.: An efficient cryptographic protocol verifier based on Prolog rules. In: CSFW 2001 (2001)
8. Bleichenbacher, D.: Chosen ciphertext attacks against protocols based on the RSA encryption standard PKCS. In: Krawczyk, H. (ed.) CRYPTO 1998. LNCS, vol. 1462, pp. 1–12. Springer, Heidelberg (1998)
9. Boneh, D., Gentry, C., Waters, B.: Collusion resistant broadcast encryption with short ciphertexts and private keys. In: Shoup, V. (ed.) CRYPTO 2005. LNCS, vol. 3621, pp. 258–275. Springer, Heidelberg (2005)

10. Boneh, D., Waters, B.: A fully collusion resistant broadcast, trace, and revoke system. In: CCS 2006. ACM, New York (2006)
11. Butler, F., Cervesato, I., Jaggard, A.D., Scedrov, A., Walstad, C.: Formal analysis of Kerberos 5. Theoretical Computer Science, 367(1) (2006)
12. Chandran, N., Groth, J., Sahai, A.: Ring signatures of sub-linear size without random oracles. In: Arge, L., Cachin, C., Jurdziński, T., Tarlecki, A. (eds.) ICALP 2007. LNCS, vol. 4596, pp. 423–434. Springer, Heidelberg (2007)
13. Chen, W., Clarke, L., Kurose, J., Towsley, D.: Optimizing cost-sensitive trust-negotiation protocols. In: INFOCOM 2005, pp. 1431–1442. IEEE, Los Alamitos (2005)
14. Chong, S., Liu, J., Myers, A.C., Qi, X., Vikram, K., Zheng, L., Zheng, X.: Secure web applications via automatic partitioning. SIGOPS Operating System Review 41 (2007)
15. Ciriani, V., De Capitani di Vimercati, S., Foresti, S., Samarati, P.: k-Anonymity. Secure Data Management in Decentralized Systems 33 (2007)
16. Corin, R., Deniélou, P.-M.: A protocol compiler for secure sessions in ml. In: Barthe, G., Fournet, C. (eds.) TGC 2007. LNCS, vol. 4912, pp. 276–293. Springer, Heidelberg (2008)
17. Corin, R., Deniélou, P.-M., Fournet, C., Bhargavan, K., Leifer, J.: Secure implementations for typed session abstractions. In: CSF 2007 (2007)
18. Denning, D.E.: A Lattice Model of Secure Information Flow. Communications of the ACM 19(5) (1976)
19. Denning, D.E., Sacco, G.M.: Timestamps in key distribution protocols. Communications of the ACM 24(8) (1981)
20. Fiat, A., Naor, M.: Broadcast encryption. In: Stinson, D.R. (ed.) CRYPTO 1993. LNCS, vol. 773, pp. 480–491. Springer, Heidelberg (1994)
21. Fisher, D.: Millions of .Net Passport accounts put at risk. eWeek (2003)
22. Fournet, C., Guernic, G.L., Rezk, T.: A security-preserving compiler for distributed programs: From information-flow policies to cryptographic mechanisms. In: CCS 2009. ACM, New York (2009)
23. G2C website (2011), http://www.infsec.cs.uni-saarland.de/~reischuk/g2c/
24. Gecode: generic constraint development environment (2011), http://www.gecode.org
25. Ghallab, M., Nau, D., Traverso, P.: Automated Planning: Theory and Practice. Morgan Kaufmann, San Francisco (2004)
26. Herranz, J.: Identity-based ring signatures from RSA. Theoretical Computer Science 389 (2007)
27. Jia, L., Vaughan, J.A., Mazurak, K., Zhao, J., Zarko, L., Schorr, J., Zdancewic, S.: AURA: A Programming Language for Authorization and Audit. In: ICFP 2008, ACM, New York (2008)
28. Liu, J., George, M.D., Vikram, K., Qi, X., Waye, L., Myers, A.C.: Fabric: A platform for secure distributed computation and storage. In: SOSP 2009. ACM, New York (2009)
29. Loo, B.T., Condie, T., Garofalakis, M., Gay, D.E., Hellerstein, J.M., Maniatis, P., Ramakrishnan, R., Roscoe, T., Stoica, I.: Declarative Networking: Language, Execution and Optimization. In: SIGMOD 2006. ACM, New York (2006)
30. Loo, B.T., Condie, T., Hellerstein, J.M., Maniatis, P., Roscoe, T., Stoica, I.: Implementing Declarative Overlays. In: Herbert, A., Birman, K.P. (eds.) SOSP 2005. ACM, New York (2005)

31. Lowe, G.: Breaking and fixing the Needham-Schroeder public-key protocol using FDR. In: Margaria, T., Steffen, B. (eds.) TACAS 1996. LNCS, vol. 1055, pp. 147–166. Springer, Heidelberg (1996)
32. Milner, R.: Communicating and Mobile Systems: The Pi-Calculus. Cambridge University Press, Cambridge (1999)
33. Myers, A., Liskov, B.: Protecting privacy using the decentralized label model. ACM Transactions on Software Engineering and Methodology (2000)
34. Navarro, J.A., Rybalchenko, A.: Operational semantics for declarative networking. In: Gill, A., Swift, T. (eds.) PADL 2009. LNCS, vol. 5418, pp. 76–90. Springer, Heidelberg (2008)
35. Necula, G.C.: Translation validation for an optimizing compiler. ACM SIGPLAN Notices 35(5) (2000)
36. Ocenasek, P., Sveda, M.: An approach to automated design of security protocols. In: ICMLS 2006 (2006)
37. Pnueli, A., Siegel, M., Singerman, E.: Translation validation. In: Steffen, B. (ed.) TACAS 1998. LNCS, vol. 1384, pp. 151–166. Springer, Heidelberg (1998)
38. Rivest, R.L., Shamir, A., Tauman, Y.: How to leak a secret. Communications of the ACM 22(22) (2001)
39. Sabelfeld, A., Myers, A.C.: Language-Based Information Flow Security. IEEE Journal on Selected Area in Communications 21(1) (2003)
40. Sprenger, C., Basin, D.: Developing security protocols by refinement. In: CCS 2010. ACM, New York (2010)
41. Sweeney, L.: k-anonymity: a model for protecting privacy. International Journal on Uncertainty, Fuzziness and Knowledge-based Systems 10(5) (2002)
42. Tristan, J.-B., Leroy, X.: Formal verification of translation validators: A case study on instruction scheduling optimizations. In: POPL 1908. ACM, New York (2008)
43. US Depart. of Health & Human Services. The Health Insurance Portability and Accountability Act of 1996 Privacy Rule (2009), http://www.hhs.gov/ocr/privacy
44. Vaughan, J.A.: A confidentiality extension to the Aura programming language. In: TLDI 2011. ACM, New York (2011)
45. Volpano, D., Smith, G., Irvine, C.: A Sound Type System for Secure Flow Analysis. Journal of Computer Security 4(2-3) (1996)
46. Wagner, D., Schneier, B.: Analysis of the SSL 3.0 protocol. In: EC 1996 (1996)
47. Xue, H., Zhang, H., Qing, S.: A schema of automated design security protocols. In: CISW 2007 (2007)
48. Zhou, W., Mao, Y., Loo, B.T., Abadi, M.: Unified Declarative Platform for Secure Networked Information Systems. In: ICDE 2009. IEEE, Los Alamitos (2009)

A   Syntax of G2C

		Terms
$\mathcal{P}$ ::= $\mathcal{C}$		Principal
$\mathcal{T}$ ::= $\mathcal{C}$		Tag
$\mathcal{S}$ ::= $\mathcal{C}$ '(' $arglist$ ')'		Statement
$\mathcal{K}$ ::= $\mathcal{S}$ '@' $\mathcal{P}$		Knowledge
arg ::= $\mathcal{C}$ | $\mathcal{V}$ | '$*$'		Argument
$arglist$ ::= [$arglist$ ','] arg		Argument list
$tagvarlist$ ::= [$tagvarlist$ 'or'] arg		Tags/variable list
$plist$ ::= [$plist$ ','] $\mathcal{P}$		Principal list
$statlist$ ::= [$statlist$ ','] $\mathcal{S}$		Statement list
$knowlist$ ::= [$knowlist$ 'or'] $\mathcal{K}$		Knowledge list

		Expressions
$princ$ ::= [$princ$] $\mathcal{P}$ ':' $\mathcal{T}$		Principals
$stats$ ::= [$conf$] $\mathcal{S}$ ':' $tagvarlist$		Statements
$tags$ ::= [$tags$] $\mathcal{T}$ '<' $\mathcal{T}$		Tags
$\mid$ [$tags$ '<'] $\mathcal{T}$ '<' $\mathcal{T}$		
$\mid$ [$tags$ '<'] $\mathcal{T}$ '<' $\mathcal{T}$ '<' $\mathcal{T}$		
$rules$ ::= [$rules$] $\mathcal{S}$ ':-' $\mathcal{C}$ '[' $statlist$ ']'		Rules
$input$ ::= [$input$] $\mathcal{K}$		Input
$goals$ ::= [$goals$] $\mathcal{K}$		Goals

		Specification
$spec$ ::= 'Principals:' $princ$		Specification
'Input:' $input$		
'Rules:' $rules$		
'Goals:' $goals$		
'Tags:' $tags$		
'Statements:' $stats$		

Fig. 3. Formal grammar for the specification language G2C

A formal grammar for the syntax of G2C is shown in Figure 3. Optional parts are enclosed in square brackets [·], literal character sequences are enclosed in single quotes '·', choice is denoted by · | ·. We assume $\mathcal{C}$ to be constants (strings consisting of $\{a, \ldots, z, 0, \ldots, 9\}$) and $\mathcal{V}$ to be variables (strings consisting of $\{a, \ldots, z\}$, beginning with a capital letter).

We call a specification *syntactically well-formed* iff all of the following hold.

1. The argument lists of rules do not contain wildcards.
2. Rules are safe: the argument lists of head statements of rules do not contain unbound variables, i.e., all variables are bound in the body statements.
3. Rules do not introduce constants, i.e., all constants occurring in the head statement must also occur in the body statements.
4. The argument lists of input statements contain only constants and wildcards.
5. The argument lists of goal statements contain only constants.
6. The arity n of a statement $s(s_1, \ldots, s_n) \in \mathcal{S}$ is the same for all occurrences of s.
7. All principals $P \in \mathcal{P}$ are declared in the section *Principals*.

We call a specification *consistent* if the following holds for all $P \in \mathcal{P}, S, S_i \in \mathcal{S}$:

1. input($S@P$) $\Rightarrow$ may_access(P, S)
2. goal($S@P$) $\Rightarrow$ may_access(P, S)
3. $(S \leftarrow f[S_1, \ldots, S_n]) \in \mathcal{R} \Rightarrow \forall i \neq j : S_i \neq S_j$
4. $((S \leftarrow f[S_1, \ldots, S_n]) \in \mathcal{R} \wedge \forall i : \text{may\_access}(P, S_i)) \Rightarrow \text{may\_access}(P, S)$

The intuition behind the last requirement is that whenever there exists a rule $r \in \mathcal{R}$ for which P knows all necessary arguments, then P can compute the function value of r and hence the specification should permit the access to the computed value.

B Proof for Theorem 1

Proof. $MsgCplx \in \mathcal{NP}$ since any $E \subseteq \mathcal{E}$ with $\sum_{e \in E} c(e) \leq c^*$ serves as poly-length witness, verifiable by a poly-time bounded Turing machine.

The remainder of the proof is a poly-time Karp reduction from 3-SAT. Let a 3-SAT formula F in conjunctive normal form (CNF) with r variables and m clauses be given:

$$F = \bigwedge_{i \in \{1, \ldots, m\}} K_i \quad \text{where } K_i = x_{i_1}^{\alpha_{i_1}} \vee x_{i_2}^{\alpha_{i_2}} \vee x_{i_3}^{\alpha_{i_3}}$$

The superscript $\alpha_{i_j} \in \{+, -\}$ denotes whether variable x_{i_j} occurs positive or negated.

Construct the graph $\mathcal{G}_F$ as follows (see Figure 4 for illustration). For each variable $x_i \in \{x_1, \ldots, x_r\}$ introduce two nodes $x_i, \overline{x_i} \in \mathcal{N}_k$ and a node $v_i \in \mathcal{N}_k$ with edges $(x_i, v_i), (\overline{x_i}, v_i) \in \mathcal{E}$. Introduce another node $v \in \mathcal{N}_c$ that has an incoming edge from every node v_i. For each clause K_i introduce a node $k_i \in \mathcal{N}_k$ with corresponding nodes $x_{i_j} \in \mathcal{N}_k$ for the literals of K_i. Add the edges (x_{i_j}, k_i) for $i \in \{1, \ldots, m\}$ and $j \in \{1, 2, 3\}$. Finally, create a node $c \in \mathcal{N}_c$ that has incoming edges from v and all k_i. According to F, whenever a variable x_i appears in a clause K_j, an edge from either x_i or $\overline{x_i}$ is drawn to the corresponding literal of K_j (see the two dashed edges as examples). Note that there is exactly one incoming edge for each literal.

All edges ending in variable nodes $x_1, \overline{x_1}, x_2, \ldots, \overline{x_r}$ have a cost of 1, all other edges have cost 0.

In order to satisfy node v, for each variable x_i either the positive or the negative variant has to be selected. This gives a cost of exactly r. If the formula F is satisfiable, then any satisfying assignment will have the same cost r, since any variable x_i has a fixed assignment to either true or false. On the other hand, if F is not satisfiable, then there is at least one clause K_i for which a dotted edge is missing. This edge would satisfy the clause, incrementing the total cost to at least $r + 1$.

Finally, we have that F is satisfiable iff $\mathcal{G}_F$ has cost r.

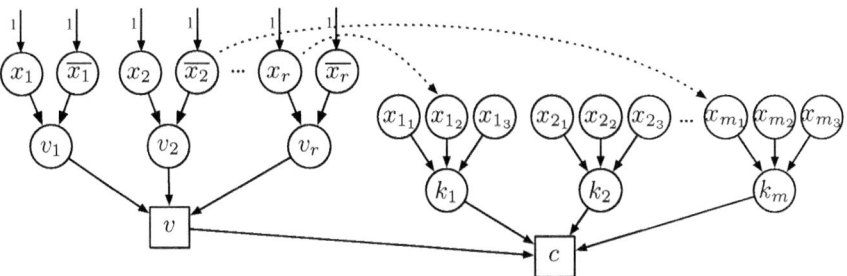

Fig. 4. Graph $\mathcal{G}_F$ constructed from 3-SAT instance

Modeling Long-Term Signature Validation for Resolution of Dispute

Moez Ben MBarka[1,2], Francine Krief[2], and Olivier Ly[2]

[1] Cryptolog International, Paris, France
moez.benmbarka@cryptolog.com
[2] LaBRI, University of Bordeaux 1, 33400 Talence, France
{krief,ly}@labri.fr

Abstract. This paper considers the case where a dispute occurs between a verifier and a signer about the validity of a digital signature. In non-repudiation services such dispute may occur long after the signature creation and approval. We present a security model for digital signature validation with the notion of dispute. The first contribution of this paper is the definition of the semantics of a Resolution of Dispute Rule (RDR) in the scope of this model. The second contribution is a calculus for reasoning about the validation of digital signatures at a particular date which may be in the past (so-called long-term signature validation). This calculus is then used to implement the RDR. The usefulness of the calculus is demonstrated through modeling Evidence Record Syntax (ERS), one of the main protocols used in practice for long-term signature validation.

Keywords: long-term signature validation, resolution of dispute, formal calculus, Public Key Infrastructure.

1   Introduction

A digital signature is a piece of digital data that can be used to guarantee integrity, authenticity, and non-repudiation in electronic communications. It is nowadays based on public key cryptography. To see how it works, suppose that a signer Bob wants to sign a message that will be verified by Alice. Bob computes the hash of the message and then encrypts the output using his private key. Alice can then verify the signature using Bob's public key. This mathematical verification allows to prove the integrity of the message and the binding between the message and a public key. Authenticity and non repudiation come from verifying the binding between this public key and the signer using public key certificates. In the widely used X.509-based PKI model (PKIX [1]), this binding is signed by a Certification Authority (CA) which is trusted to verify the identity of the certificate's owner (called certificate's subject) before signing the certificate. The certificate's owner may be another CA (certification authority certificate) or an entity which is not a CA (end entity certificate). Various circumstances (e.g. key compromise) may cause a certificate to become invalid prior to its expiration. Under such circumstances, the CA needs to revoke the certificate [1,2].

S. Mödersheim and C. Palamidessi (Eds.): TOSCA 2011, LNCS 6993, pp. 78–97, 2012.

1.1   Statement of the Problem

Digital signatures are gradually acquiring legal equivalence of handwritten signatures promoting their use to secure business and commercial digital communications. Nowadays digital signature schemes and the infrastructure within which they operate have time limitations which may be due to some inner expiration dates (e.g. the expiration of a certificate) or to the fact that the underlying cryptographic security relies on the presumed computational difficulty of certain theoretic problems (e.g. integer factorization) [3]. This situation is disturbing considering that there are many cases such as government records where the signatures are required by civil laws to be kept valid for a long period of time.

We address this issue by modeling long-term signature validation in the scope of a dispute between the typical actors: a verifier (Alice) who claims the validity of the signature at some date (possibly in the past) and a signer (Bob) who denies this claim. Imagine for a moment a judge trying to resolve a dispute between Alice and Bob in the year 2030. To prove their point, the parties invoke several records that were digitally signed by them in the year 2005. The judge needs to decide if the evidence presented is admissible in court. We use our model to define the semantics of a resolution of dispute rule that can be used by the judge to take a decision about the validity of the presented digital signatures.

1.2   Related Work

Long-Term Validation. It is already known that time-stamp services can be used to maintain digital document (in particular digital signatures) integrity and authenticity. The time-stamp is a digital attestation signed by a trusted third party, called Time-Stamping Authority (TSA), that a submitted document has been presented to the TSA at a certain time. For a document m, the time-stamp is a signature where the signer is a TSA and the signed message includes the pair $(T, h(m)))$ such as T is the current time retrieved from a reliable source of time and h is a cryptographic hash function.

Many technical frameworks for long-term signatures validation are defined in the literature [4,5,6,7,8] and are mainly based on time-stamping: the signature is time-stamped indicating that it was created at a moment before a subsequent key or algorithm compromise; this time-stamp is refreshed before the used algorithms or keys become compromised, ensuring its validity through the years. Most of these techniques rely on the use of Evidence Record Syntax (ERS) [8]. ERS uses a chain of time-stamps to prove the existence of some digital data at a certain date. Each time-stamp may protect a single data object or to a group of objects using a hash tree where only the root of the tree is time-stamped. ERS defines two renewal algorithms: the simple and the complex renewal methods. In the case of the simple renewal, only the last generated time-stamp has to be time-stamped again. In this scenario, it is not necessary to access the initially archived data objects themselves, since the algorithms used for the previous time-stamps are recognized as being still reliable. The simple renewal method is not sufficient when the hash functions used in the previous time-stamps become insecure. In this scenario, not only the initial time-stamps but also the initial data have to be time-stamped again using newer algorithms.

PKI Calculus. In [9], Maurer presented the pioneer deterministic calculus for PKI. The calculus is based on four statements (authenticity, trust, certificate, recommendation) and two inference rules. Starting from an initial set of statements (called Alice's initial view), Alice uses the inference rules to derive new statements. In this model, Alice can use a certificate issued by a CA X for a user Bob if and only if she can derive the following statements: she has a certificate signed by X for Bob, she knows X's public key and believes that it is authentic and she trusts X to correctly authenticate the owner of a public key. The objective of Alice is to derive these statements from her initial view using the inference rules. Later, many authors [10,11] revisited this model to add additional concepts such as time, certificate expiration and revocation.

Signature Validity Models. In [12], the authors surveyed three validity models for digital signatures:

1. Shell model: in this model, the signature is always validated at the current date. The signature becomes invalid once the signer certificate gets expired.
2. Modified shell model: The signature is validated at the signing date and not at the verification date. Therefore, the expiration or revocation of the signer certificate does not affect the signature validity.
3. Chain model: in addition to the signing date, this model takes into account the issuance date of each certificate in the certificate validation chain. Not only, the expiration of the signer certificate does not affect the signature validity but also the signature remains valid even if an intermediate CA is revoked before the signing date.

The natural conclusions from these models are that:

- the shell model is only suitable for authentication services where the validity of the signature is required for short term.
- the modified shell and the chain models have the fundamental property: if a digital signature is valid at the signing date, it remains valid forever. Therefore, these models are suitable for long-term validation.

1.3   Motivations and Organization of the Paper

While many long-term signature validation frameworks [4,5,6] and standards [8,7] are currently in use in practice, to the best of our knowledge, there is no formal model showing that they provide the evidences they claim. These frameworks miss formal definitions of long-term validation semantics. Defining such semantics is necessary to have a formal calculus. This is the first contribution of this paper. On the other hand, Maurer's calculus and its extensions showed above can be used to reason about public key authenticity but miss many features required to deal with long-term validation. The second contribution is the proposition of a formal calculus which captures these features (Figure 1).

Feature	our calculus	Maurer's calculus and extensions
Authenticity and revocation	yes	yes
Time aware signature validation	yes	no
Algorithm security	yes	no
Proof of existence	yes	no

Fig. 1. Our calculus vs previous calculus based on Maurer's model

The rest of the paper is organized as follows: Section 2 presents a simple security model for digital signature validation. Section 3 defines the resolution of dispute in the scope of this model. Section 4 presents our calculus which is used to implement the Resolution of Dispute Rule in Section 5. Section 6 uses the calculus to model ERS. Finally, Section 7 concludes the paper.

2 Security Model and Notations

In our model, a digital signature is denoted $Sig(X, m, sa, sv)$ where X identifies the signer, m is the signed message, sa identifies the signature algorithm, and sv is the signature value computed on m using sa and the private key corresponding to X's public key. The integrity and authenticity come from the cryptographic properties of the signature algorithm sa (namely, existential unforgeability against chosen message attacks [13]). A signature is said "cryptographically valid" if and only if sv verifies with X's public key on the message m using the signature algorithm sa. Non-repudiation relies on the authenticity of the signer's public key that can be derived from the certificate. The most widely PKI trust model is a hierarchy of CAs. In this model, the validation of a certificate at some date T consists in building and validating a certificate path from a trusted CA (called trust anchor) to the certificate to validate. Below, we combine the certificate validation algorithm defined in PKIX [1] with the cryptographic verification to define a Signature Validation Function (SVF). In the model, we accept SVF as the mean to prove integrity, authenticity and non-repudiation.

Definition 1 (Signature Validation Function (SVF)). SVF *takes as input the following: a signature* $Sig(X, m, sa, sv)$, *a set of trust anchors* $\mathcal{K}$, *a set of validation objects* $\mathcal{O}$, *and a date* T. *The function returns a pair* $(status, \mathcal{P})$ *such that status = true if and only if:*

- *the signature is cryptographically valid.*
- *there exists a sequence of certificates* $Cert_1, \ldots, Cert_n$ *in* $\mathcal{O}$ *such that:*
  - $\forall i \in [1, n-1]$, $Cert_i$'s *subject is* $Cert_{i+1}$'s *issuer and* $Cert_i$ *is a certification authority certificate.*
  - $Cert_1$ *is issued by a trust anchor in* $\mathcal{K}$.
  - $Cert_n$ *is an end entity certificate and is issued to* X.
  - $\forall i \in [1, n]$, $Cert_i$ *is valid at* T *and there exists a revocation object* $Rev_i \in \mathcal{O}$ *signed by* $Cert_i$'s *issuer indicating that* $Cert_i$ *is not revoked at* T.

- $\forall i \in [1, n]$, the signatures in $Cert_i$ and Rev_i are cryptographically valid.

If $status = true$ then the signature is said "valid" at T and $\mathcal{P}$ is the sequence $\{Cert_1, Rev_1, \ldots, Cert_n, Rev_n\}$. Otherwise, the signature said is "invalid" at T.

The function above requires a set of trust anchors that the verifier trusts without prior verification. In addition, the verifier needs to trust some assumptions about the security of the used algorithms. This yields a particular set that we will call Initial View of Trust ($\mathcal{IVT}$):

Definition 2 (Initial View of Trust ($\mathcal{IVT}(T)$)). $\mathcal{IVT}(T)$ is composed of the following:

- a set of trust anchors $\mathcal{K} = \{TA_1, \ldots, TA_n\}$ such that $\forall i \in [1, n]$, TA_i is a CA identified by a certification authority certificate.
- a set of algorithm trust assertions $\mathcal{A} = \{(a_1, T_{a_1}), \ldots, (a_k, T_{a_k})\}$, such that $\forall i \in [1, k], a_i$ is a cryptographic hash function or a signature algorithm considered secure until at least the date T_{a_i}.

The semantics of "secure" depends on the nature of the cryptographic algorithm. In our model, we will say that an algorithm is secure until at least T if it is commonly believed that the scientific knowledge and computing power will not allow to break the security properties of the algorithm until at least T.

3   Resolution of Dispute

In the model, Bob uses his private key to sign some digital data and Alice verifies the signature using Bob's public key. For instance, consider a scenario where Bob signs a contract with Alice to pay monthly some amount of money. If in the future, Bob's certificate is revoked, he may claim that he never signed the contract and stop paying Alice. This leads to a dispute situation: on one hand, Alice claims the validity of a signature and that this signature has been created at a date in the past (before revocation); on the other hand, Bob denies these claims. First, we define the dispute. Next, we define the resolution of dispute.

Definition 3 (Dispute). If Alice (A) claims at a date $T \geq T_d$ that a signature $Sig(B, m, sa, sv)$ is signed by Bob (B) and is valid at T_d; and if Bob denies any of these claims, we say that Alice is in a dispute $\mathsf{Dispute}(A, B, S, T_d)$ with Bob. T_d is called the dispute date and T the resolution date.

Both Alice and Bob rely on a third party, called the Judge, to resolve the dispute. The Judge can resolve the dispute using a Resolution of Dispute Rule (RDR) at T based on validation objects (certificates, CRLs...) provided by Alice:

Definition 4 (Resolution of Dispute Rule). If a dispute $\mathsf{Dispute}(A, B, S, T_d)$ occurs between Alice and Bob at T, the Judge executes the RDR. The RDR takes as input the following: the signature S, a set of validation objects $\mathcal{O}$ provided by Alice, $\mathcal{IVT}(T)$, the dispute date T_d, and the resolution date T. It outputs a pair

$(status, \mathcal{P})$ such that $status \in \{true, false\}$ and $\mathcal{P} \subseteq \{S\} \cup \mathcal{O} \cup \mathcal{IVT}(T)$. If $status = true$, the Judge rules in favor of Alice. Otherwise, he rules in favor of Bob. In addition, if $status = true$ then $\mathcal{P} \neq \emptyset$ is the proof of the validity of the claims of Alice and is called the judgment proof.   ○

3.1   Threat Model

The Judge is trusted to honestly run the RDR and honestly output the result. However, any of the other actors can run the RDR and thus verify the output. Indeed, the Judge can be seen as a procedure (e.g. enforced by a court) whose output can be verified by other actors.

$\mathcal{IVT}$ is a public set trusted by all actors. This assumes that no attacker has significantly more computing power or cryptanalytic knowledge than what is widely known. $\mathcal{IVT}$ may naturally be updated to take account of new algorithms and authorities. We will assume that any update to $\mathcal{IVT}$ does not remove or reduce the validity interval of any algorithm or authority in the previous $\mathcal{IVT}$.

Finally, a traditional assumption in a PKI context is that honest involved authorities (namely TSAs and CAs) act honestly. In particular, we assume that the CAs conform to their Certification Policies (CP) that describe certificate issuance and revocation rules. We assume that the CPs of all involved CAs guarantee at least the following: a certificate can be revoked but not suspended and a signer can not access the signing key before the issuance date of her certificate. We will also assume that all honest CAs provide instant revocation for all honestly issued certificates during their validity intervals: there is no delay between effective compromise and the publication of the revocation information. We are aware that in the real world there is an inevitable delay between the compromise and the revocation. For the sake of simplicity, this delay will be first ignored but will be discussed later.

3.2   RDR Semantics

The objective of RDR is to build proofs of the validity of Alice's claims at the resolution date. If such proofs can be built in a verifiable way, the Judge rules in favor of Alice, otherwise, he rules in favor of Bob. Note that the latter case does not mean that Alice's claims are provably false, but only that these claims can not be proven using the provided inputs. We start by defining two properties that must be satisfied by the RDR. The first requirement is Correctness. This means that if the Judge rules in favor of Alice then her claims are correct. Naturally, we use the modified shell model: the signature is validated at the signing date.

Property 1 (Correctness). Given the the signature $S_d = Sig(B, m, sa, sv)$ and the Dispute(A, B, S_d, T_d); if RDR$(S_d, \mathcal{O}, \mathcal{IVT}(T), T_d, T)$ outputs *true* then S_d is created at a date $T_s \leq T_d$ and is valid at T_s ○

The second consideration is that a digital signature can not be repudiated. In other words, If a signature is accepted valid at some date is should remain valid forever: if a Judge rules in favor of the validity of a signature at a date T_d, he would rule in favor of the validity of the signature at any date after the date for which he has a proof of the existence and unforgeability of the signature.

Property 2 (Eternal Validity). Given the signature $S_d = Sig(B, m, sa, sv)$ and the dispute $\mathsf{Dispute}(A, B, S_d, T_d)$; if $\mathsf{RDR}(S_d, \mathcal{O}, \mathcal{IVT}(T), T_d, T)$ outputs *true* and S_d is proven to exist at T_s and uses an algorithm trusted to be secure until at least T_s such that $T_s \leq T_d$, then $\mathsf{RDR}(S_d, \mathcal{O}, \mathcal{IVT}(T), T_d', T)$ outputs *true* $\forall\ T_d' \geq T_s$. 　　　　○

Now let go to the definition of the RDR semantics:

Definition 5 (RDR Semantics). *Given the signature $S_d = Sig(B, m, sa, sv)$, the set of the validation objects $\mathcal{O}$ provided by Alice and the $\mathsf{Dispute}(A, B, S_d, T_d)$; $\mathsf{RDR}(S_d, \mathcal{O}, \mathcal{IVT}(T), T_d, T)$ outputs true if and only if there exists a date $T_s \leq T_d$ such that the Judge can prove that all the following statements are valid at T:*

1. *there exists a date $T_x \geq T_s$ such that $\mathsf{SVF}(S_d, \mathcal{K}, \mathcal{O}, T_x) = (true, \mathcal{P})$.*
2. *each validation object V in $\mathcal{P}$ exists at a date $T_V \leq T_x$ and uses an algorithm trusted to be secure until at least T_V.*
3. *S_d exists at T_s and uses an algorithm trusted to be secure until at least T_s.* ○

Proposition 1. *The RDR Semantics has both the Correctness and Eternal Validity properties.*

Proof.

– Correctness:The first part of the correctness is obvious: since S_d exists at T_s, then S_d is created at a date $T_s' \leq T_s \leq T_d$. It remains to prove that S_d is valid at T_s'. Let us denote $\mathcal{IVT}(T) = (\mathcal{K}, \mathcal{A})$ and $\mathcal{P} = \{Cert_1, Rev_1, \ldots, Cert_n, Rev_n\}$ the sequence of certificates and revocation objects returned by SVF at T_x and $\{CA_0, \ldots, CA_{n-1}\}$ the set of CAs such that $\forall i \in [1, n-1]$, CA_i is the CA identified in $Cert_i$, and CA_0 is the trust anchor from $\mathcal{K}$ that issued $Cert_1$. $\forall i$, we will denote $[T_{b_i}, T_{e_i}]$ the validity interval of $Cert_i$. First, we show by induction that $\forall i \in [1, n]$, $Cert_i$ and Rev_i are honestly generated.
  - for $i = 1$, $Cert_1$ and Rev_1 are honestly generated by CA_0 because they are created, using a secure algorithm, by a trust anchor which can not be compromised.
  - assume that $Cert_i$ and Rev_i are honestly generated. If $Cert_{i+1}$ or Rev_{i+1} is not honestly generated but forged (say by Alice), then Alice needs to access to the signing key (because $Cert_{i+1}$ and Rev_{i+1} are created at date before T_x using a secure algorithm). So, we have two cases:
    * The private key of CA_i is compromised (anyone including Alice may have access to this private key). So, Rev_i is also forged (because it indicates that $Cert_i$ is not revoked at T_x).
    * CA_i is not an honest CA. So $Cert_i$ is forged.
  Then, either $Cert_i$ or Rev_i is forged which contradicts the induction hypothesis. Hence, $Cert_{i+1}$ and Rev_{i+1} are honestly generated. Thus, $\forall i \in [1, n]$, $Cert_i$ and Rev_i are honestly generated by honest CAs.

On the other hand, a private key is not issued before the certificate issuance date. Since the creation of the signature at T'_s needs the private key (the signature algorithm is secure at $T'_s \leq T_s$), this gives $T'_s \in [T_{b_n}, T_d]$ and therefore $\forall i \in [1, n]$, $T'_s \in [T_{b_i}, T_{e_i}]$. Since $Cert_i$ is not revoked at T_x, then it is not revoked at any date in $[T_{b_i}, T_x]$ (a certificate can not be suspended) and in particular at T'_s. In addition, since $\forall i \in [1, n]$, $Cert_i$ is honestly issued by an honest CA, there exists a revocation object Rev'_i issued by CA_{i-1} that indicates that $Cert_i$ is not revoked at T'_s. Thus, the sequence $\mathcal{P}' = \{Cert_1, Rev'_1, \ldots, Cert_n = B, Rev'_n\}$ verifies the conditions of SVF and then $SVF(S, \mathcal{K}, \mathcal{P}', T'_s)$ outputs *true*. Hence, the Correctness property. □

– Eternal validity:If it happens that S_d is proven to exist at T_s and uses an algorithm trusted to be secure until at least T_s and $\mathsf{RDR}(S_d, \mathcal{O}, \mathcal{IVT}(T), T_{d_1}, T)$ outputs *true* such that $T_{d_1} \geq T_s$, then there exists a date $T_x \geq T_s$ which verifies the first statements and a set of n dates $T_{VO_1} \ldots T_{VO_n}$ which verify the second statements. We can use the same dates for any date $T_{d_2} \geq T_s$ such that $\mathsf{RDR}(S_d, \mathcal{O}, \mathcal{IVT}(T), T_{d_2}, T)$ outputs also *true*. □

3.3   Discussions

Role of Bob. Bob is not involved in the semantics above. One may think that this is unfair towards Bob. Due to the Correctness property, if it happens that the Judge rules in favor of Alice although Bob is not the actual signer, then this means that Bob's private key has been compromised before the date T_s but the revocation information was not yet published at T_x. This can not happen in the considered model as we assumed instant revocation. However, in the real world, there is always an inevitable delay between the effective compromise and the publication of the revocation information [14]. Therefore, it is important to wait some period of time after the signing date before considering the signature valid. This period (called caution period) is the estimated time duration required to process and publish the last revocation information. The value of the caution period must be established in agreement between all actors.

Using a Caution Period C. To consider a caution period, we need to update the Correctness property: the validity of the signature must be established at the signing date shifted (in the future) by the caution period:

Property 3 (Correctness with caution period). Given $S_d = Sig(B, m, sa, sv)$, a caution period C, and $\mathsf{Dispute}(A, B, S_d, T_d)$; if $\mathsf{RDR}(S_d, \mathcal{O}, \mathcal{IVT}(T), T_d, T)$ outputs *true* then S_d is created at a date $T_s \leq T_d$ and is valid at $T_s + C$.   ○

We also need to update the RDR semantics. The first statement in Definition 5 needs to be updated to the following: there exists a date $T_x \geq T_s + C$ such that $\mathsf{SVF}(S_d, \mathcal{K}, \mathcal{O}, T_x) = (true, P)$. For the sake of simplicity, the rest of the document will use the semantics without caution period.

4   Calculus for Long-Term Signature Validation

This section defines a formal calculus modeling the resolution of dispute. It uses a simplified subset of the sequent logic syntax which provides a formal setting to reason about logical truth based on deduction using inference rules. The formulas are a set of statements indicating trust relationship. Axioms are a set of particular statements, called Judge's Initial View, accepted as trustworthy by the Judge prior to deriving any judgments. In contrast with classical sequent calculus, values assigned to formulas are not *true* and *false*, but *valid* and *invalid*. For instance, an *invalid* formula is not necessary *false* but indicates that the Judge does not trust the statement inferred from this formula.

4.1   Statements

The statements use date instants T ($now()$ will denote the current date) and date intervals (e.g. $I = [T_b, T_e]$). All validation objects considered below are signed objects. In general, a validation object may be denoted V or $V(sa)$ where sa is the signature algorithm used to sign V. We will consider two types of statements:

Validation Object Statements. A validation object statement indicates that the Judge holds a validation object:

- $Sig(X, m, sa, sv)$ denotes that the Judge holds a signature signed by X. The signature value sv is computed on m using the signature algorithm sa.
- $EECert(X, Y, I, sa)$ denotes that the Judge holds an end entity certificate for Y's public key signed by X using sa. The certificate is valid in I.
- $CACert(X, Y, I, sa)$ denotes that the Judge holds a CA's certificate for Y's public key signed by X using sa. The certificate is valid in I.
- $NRev(X, Y, I, sa)$ denotes that the Judge holds an evidence signed by X using sa and indicating that Y's key is not revoked in I.
- $TSP(X, h(m), T_{tsp}, sa)$ denotes that the Judge holds a time-stamp signed by X at T_{tsp} using the signature algorithm sa on the hash of m using the cryptographic hash function h.

Assertion Statements. An assertion statement indicates that the Judge believes that an assertion is trustworthy:

- $CAAut(X, I)$ denotes that the Judge believes that X is a CA and that X's public key is authentic in I.
- $Aut(X, I)$ denotes that the Judge believes that X is an entity which is not a CA and that X's public key is authentic in I.
- $POE(V, T_{poe})$ denotes that the Judge believes in the existence of the validation object V at T_{poe}.
- $POI(V(sa), T_{poe})$ denotes that the Judge believes in the existence of the validation object $V(sa)$ at T_{poe} and that $V(sa)$ has not been forged.
- $Algo(a, T_a)$ denotes that the Judge believes that the algorithm a is trusted to be secure until at least T_a.

4.2   Initial View Construction

The Initial View IV is the set of initial statements considered trustworthy.

Definition 6 (Initial View Construction). *Given the trust anchors* $\mathcal{K} = \{Cert_1, \ldots, Cert_n\}$, *the algorithm assertions* $\mathcal{A} = \{(a_1, T_{a_1}), \ldots, (a_p, T_{a_p})\}$, *the signed validation objects* $\mathcal{O} = \{V_1, \ldots, V_k\}$ *and the signature* $S = Sig(B, m, sa, sv)$; *the initial view* $IV = IV(\mathcal{K}, \mathcal{A}, \mathcal{O}, S)$ *is constructed as follows:*

1. *initialize* IV *with the empty set.*
2. *if* S *is cryptographically valid, add* S *to* IV.
3. $\forall i \in [1, k]$, *if the signature in* V_i *is cryptographically valid, add* V_i *to* IV.
4. *For each certificate* $Cert_i$ *in* $\mathcal{K}$, *add* $CAAut(X_i, I_{X_i})$ *to* IV *such that* X_i *is the subject of the certificate* $Cert_i$ *and* I_{X_i} *is its validity interval.*
5. *For each pair* (a_i, T_{a_i}) *in* $\mathcal{A}$, *add* $Algo(a_i, T_{a_i})$ *to* IV. $\quad\quad\quad\quad\quad\quad\circ$

4.3   Inference Rules

In our model, we will consider the following inference rules:

Authenticity of public keys. Informally, Y is authentic if and only if the Judge holds a certificate for Y signed by X believed to be authentic and owned by a CA. Besides, the Judge must hold a revocation signed by X indicating that Y is not revoked. Finally, the judge must hold a POI for any used object. If Y is a CA, the Judge derives $CAAut$, otherwise, he derives Aut. $\forall T \in I = I_1 \cap I_2 \cap I_3 = [T_1, T_2]$:

$$\frac{CAAut(X, I_1) \quad\quad POI(CACert(X, Y, I_2, sa_2), T) \quad\quad POI(NRev(X, Y, I_3, sa_3), T)}{CAAut(Y, [T, T_2])} \tag{1}$$

$$\frac{CAAut(X, I_1) \quad\quad POI(EECert(X, Y, I_2, sa_2), T) \quad\quad POI(NRev(X, Y, I_3, sa_3), T)}{Aut(Y, [T, T_2])} \tag{2}$$

Immediate proof of existence. Informally, if the Judge holds a validation object V, then he holds a proof of existence of this object at the current date.

$$\frac{V}{POE(V, now())} \tag{3}$$

Proof of existence based on time-stamps. In our model, this is the only way to derive a proof of existence of an object at a date in the past. $\forall T \in I_X$:

$$\frac{POI(TSP(X, h(V), T_{TSP}, sa_{tsp}), T) \quad\quad Aut(X, I_X)}{POE(h(V), T_{TSP})} \tag{4}$$

Indirect proof of existence

Theorem 1. *If $m = h(d)$ is proven to exist at T_1 where d is a message proven to exist at a date $T \geq T_1$ and h is a preimage-resistant hash function secure until at least a date $T_h \geq T$, then d is indirectly proven to exist at T_1.*

The proof is straightforward and is relative to the resistance to preimage of the cryptographic hash function h [15]. Indeed, this guarantees that, given m, until the date T_h it is hard to find a message d' such that $m = h(d')$. This means that d exists at T_1. This gives the following inference rule: $\forall T_1 \leq T \leq T_h$:

$$\frac{POE(h(V), T_1) \qquad POE(V, T) \qquad Algo(h, T_h)}{POE(V, T_1)} \tag{5}$$

Proof of integrity. Informally, this rule means that if a signed object exists at T and the signature algorithm is trusted until at least $T_{sa} \geq T$, then the object exists at T and has not been forged at T. $\forall T \leq T_{sa}$:

$$\frac{POE(V(sa), T) \qquad Algo(sa, T_{sa})}{POI(V(sa), T)} \tag{6}$$

Eternal proof of integrity. Informally, this rule means that if a signed object has not been forged at T_0, then the signed object has not been forged for any later date. $\forall T \geq T_0$:

$$\frac{POI(V(sa), T_0)}{POI(V(sa), T)} \tag{7}$$

4.4   Statement Validity

Definition 7. *Given an initial view IV, a statement G is said valid at T if and only if $G \in IV$ or G can be derived at T by using the inference rules.*   ○

Definition 8 (Derivation tree and derivation proof). *Given an initial view IV and a statement G valid at T, the derivations used to derive G from IV can be represented by a tree rooted by G, where the leaves are statements from IV and each non-leaf node is derived from its children using one inference rule. This tree is called the derivation tree of G at T. The set of leaf nodes is called derivation proof of G at T and is denoted $P(IV, G, T)$.*   ○

Note that there may be several derivation trees for the same G, IV, and T which may yield different derivation proofs. A derivation proof is only unique given a particular derivation tree. Intuitively, a proof $\mathcal{P}$ is a minimal subset of IV that can allow the derivation of G at T using the same tree (or possibly another tree).

5 Implementing the Resolution of Dispute Rule

This section uses the calculus defined above to implement the RDR semantics. First we define an additional assertion statement: $Res_{A,B}(Sig(B, m, sa, sv), T)$ denotes that the Judge believes in the validity of Alice's claims for the dispute $\mathsf{Dispute}(A, B, Sig(B, m, sa, sv), T)$. The RDR semantics can be written using the following inference rule: $\forall T \geq T_s$ such that $T_s \leq T_{B_2}$:

$$\frac{POI(Sig(B, m, sa, sv), T_s) \qquad Aut(B, [T_{B_1}, T_{B_2}])}{Res_{A,B}(Sig(B, m, sa, sv), T)} \tag{8}$$

Definition 9 (Resolution of Dispute Rule). *Given* $\mathcal{IVT}(T) = (\mathcal{K}, \mathcal{A})$, *the signature* $S_d = Sig(B, m, sa, sv)$, *the set of the validation objects* $\mathcal{O}$ *provided by Alice and the* $\mathsf{Dispute}(A, B, S_d, T_d)$; $\mathsf{RDR}(S_d, \mathcal{O}, \mathcal{IVT}(T), T_d, T)$ *outputs true if and only if the statement* $Res_{A,B}(S_d, T_d)$ *is valid at* T *with the initial view* $IV = IV(\mathcal{K}, \mathcal{A}, \mathcal{O}, S_d)$. *In addition, if the Judge rules in favor of Alice, then* $P(IV, Res_{A,B}(S_d, T_d), T)$ *is a judgment proof.*   ○

Proposition 2 (Correctness). *Given a dispute* $\mathsf{Dispute}(A, B, S_d, T_d)$; *the Judge rules in favor of Alice at* T *according to Definition 5 if and only if he rules in favor of Alice at* T *according to Definition 9.*

The proof is depicted in Appendix A. This proposition will allow us to define some properties of the judgment proof using the calculus.

5.1 Expiration of the Judgment Proof

Since derivations are deterministic, if the derivation of $Res_{A,B}(S_d, T_d)$ from IV yields the derivation proof $\mathcal{P}$ then $Res_{A,B}(S_d, T_d)$ can always be derived from $\mathcal{P}$ at T by building the same derivation tree. Therefore, replaying the RDR at the same judgment date using as input the judgment proof gives the same result. An important question is the following: if Alice comes later with this proof, will the Judge also rule in her favor? Each statement in the proof has an expiration date. For instance, certificate, revocation and authenticity statements have a validity interval from which we have the expiration date. An algorithm trust statement has also an expiration date which is the expiration date of the algorithm.

Definition 10 (Expiration date of a proof). *Given a judgment proof* $\mathcal{P}_p$ *obtained at a date* T_p, *let us denote* $E_1 \ldots E_n$ *the expiration dates extracted from the statements in* $\mathcal{P}$. *The expiration date of* $\mathcal{P}$ *is denoted* $E(\mathcal{P})$ *and is defined by the following date:*

$$E(\mathcal{P}) = min\{E_i, E_i > T_p\}_{1 \geq i \geq n}$$

○

Proposition 3. *Given a proof* $\mathcal{P}_p$ *obtained at* T_p *for* $\mathsf{Dispute}(A, B, S_d, T_d)$; *if at* $T \in [T_P, E(\mathcal{P}_p)]$, *Alice provides* $\mathcal{O}$ *such that* $\mathcal{P}_p \subseteq IV(\mathcal{IVT}(T), \mathcal{O}, S_d)$, *then the Judge will rule in favor of Alice for* $\mathsf{Dispute}(A, B, S_d, T)$ *at* T. *In addition, if* $T_d < T_p$, *the Judge will rule in favor of Alice for* $\mathsf{Dispute}(A, B, S_d, T_d)$ *at* T.

The proof is depicted in Appendix B. Therefore, Alice has interest to archive the validation objects in $\mathcal{P}_p$. During $[T_p, E(\mathcal{P}_p)]$, favorable judgments are guaranteed to Alice provided she comes with these objects. Note that this works because we assumed that any update to $\mathcal{IVT}$ guarantees that any assertion statement derived from $\mathcal{IVT}(T_p)$ can be derived from any later $\mathcal{IVT}(T)$. If Alice needs favorable judgments beyond $E(\mathcal{P}_p)$, she needs to renew this proof. The proposition below is the foundation of renewal algorithms that will be showed in the next section.

Proposition 4. *Given a proof* $\mathcal{P}_p$ *obtained at* T_p *for* Dispute(A, B, S_d, T_d); *let us denote* $\{V_1 \ldots V_n\}$ *the subset of validation objects in* $\mathcal{P}_p$. *If at* T, *Alice provides* $\mathcal{O}$ *such that* $\mathcal{P}_p \subseteq IV(\mathcal{IVT}(T), \mathcal{O}, S_d)$ *and that the Judge can derive* $\{POE(V_1, T_{poe}) \ldots POE(V_n, T_{poe})\}$ *where* $T_{poe} \in [T_p, E(\mathcal{P}_p)]$, *then the Judge will rule in favor of Alice for the* Dispute(A, B, S_d, T_{poe}) *at* T. *In addition, if* $T_d < T_p$, *the Judge will rule in favor of Alice for the* Dispute(A, B, S_d, T_d) *at* T.

This is a corollary of Proposition 3 and the proof is omitted.

Example. We consider the Dispute$(A, B, S_d, now())$ where $S_d = Sig(B, m, sa, sv)$. The RDR is executed at $now()$ with the following: $\{S_d, \quad EECert(X, B, I_b, sa), \quad NRev(X, B, I_{rb}, sa)\}$. We will use $\mathcal{IVT}(now()) = (\{CAAut(X, I_x)\}, \{Algo(sa, T_{sa})\})$. We assume: $I_{rb} = [T_1, T_2]$ and $now() \in I_{rb} \subset I_b \subset I_x$ and T_{sa} is greater than the upper bound of I_x. First we build IV (assuming that all objects have cryptographically valid signatures): $\{Sig(B, m, sa, sv), EECert(X, B, I_b, sa), NRev(X, B, I_{rb}, sa), Algo(sa, T_{sa}), CAAut(X, I_x, sa)\}$. From this IV, we can build the proof tree depicted in Figure 2. Leaf $POIs$ are derived by successive application of Rules (3) and (6).

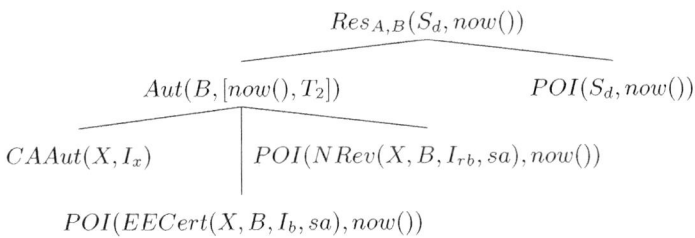

Fig. 2. Resolution proof tree

The judgment proof is: $\mathcal{P} = \{S_d, Aut(X, I_x), EECert(X, B, I_b, sa), NRev(X, B, I_{rb}, sa), Algo(sa, T_{sa})\}$. This proof expires at $E(\mathcal{P}) = T_2$.

6   Using the Calculus in the Real World

One of the motivations of this work is to propose a calculus that can be used to model several frameworks [4, 5, 6] used in practice for long-term signature validation. Most of theses frameworks rely on the use of ERS [8]. In this section, we will model the use of ERS to renew the validity of a signature beyond the expiration date of a judgment proof. For this purpose, we will model the following operations: ERS creation, simple renewal and complex renewals.

ERS Creation. Prior to create an ERS, Alice should ensure that she has appropriate validation data to have a favorable judgment at the current date for $Dispute(A, B, S_d, now())$. With our calculus, this means that executing RDR at $now()$ outputs a proof $\mathcal{P}_0$. The objective of Alice is to continuously renew this proof to guarantee favorable judgments for the dispute $Dispute(A, B, S_d, T_0)$ where T_0 is as close as possible to the current date. For this purpose, Alice needs to create an ERS as soon as possible (before the date $E(\mathcal{P}_0)$).

ERS creation consists in requesting a time-stamp on the validation objects used to validate the signature. In our calculus, this means requesting time-stamps for the validation objects $\{V_1 \ldots V_n\}$ in $\mathcal{P}_0$. Let us denote $ERS_0 = \{TSP_0 \ldots TSP_n\}$ the obtained time-stamps using the authority X_0, the cryptographic function h_0 and the signature algorithm sa_0.

Now, how ERS_0 can allow to have a favorable judgment after $E(\mathcal{P}_0)$? At $T > E(\mathcal{P}_0)$, in addition to the validation objects $V_1 \ldots V_n$, Alice needs to come with the set ERS_0 and the validation data that allow the Judge to derive $Aut(X_0, I_{X_0})$ at T. In this case, the Judge can derive at T, the statements $POE(V_i, T_0)$ for any $i \in [1, n]$ using the tree in Figure 3. Note that this requires that h_0 and sa_0 are trusted at T. Thus, he will rule in favor of Alice for $Dispute(A, B, S_d, T_0)$ (Proposition 4) with a judgment proof $\mathcal{P}_1$. During the interval $[T, E(\mathcal{P}_1)]$, $\mathcal{P}_1$ guarantees favor judgments for Alice for $Dispute(A, B, S_d, T_0)$. To go beyond $E(\mathcal{P}_1)$, Alice needs to continuously execute the renewal algorithms.

Simple Renewal. The simple renewal applies to the last time-stamps. i.e. the preceding time-stamps are time-stamped again together with complementary validation objects if needed. In our model, the simple renewal consists in requesting new time-stamps (ERS_1) for the time-stamps in ERS_0 and any validation object used to derive $Aut(X_0, I_{X_0})$. This renewal must occur at $T_1 < E(\mathcal{P}_1)$.

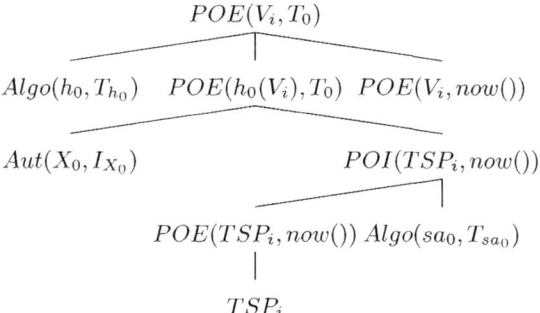

Fig. 3. Derivation of $POE(V_i, T_0)$ after ERS creation $(T = now())$

Now, how ERS_1 allows the Judge to rule in favor of Alice after $E(\mathcal{P}_1)$? Let denote X_1, sa_1 and h_1 respectively the TSA, the signature algorithm and the cryptographic hash function used at T_1. To have favorable judgments at a date $T > E(\mathcal{P}_1)$, Alice needs to provide $\{V_1 \ldots V_n\}$, ERS_0, ERS_1 and the validation objects that allow to derive $Aut(X_1, I_{X_1})$ at T. From ERS_1 and the derivation proof of $Aut(X_1, I_{X_1})$, the Judge can derive $POE(TSP(X_0, h_0(V_i), T_0, sa_0), T_1)$ for any $i \in [1, n]$ in the same way as in Figure 3. Also, since ERS_1 includes time-stamps on the validation objects used to derive the authenticity of X_0, this allows to derive $Aut(X_0, I_{X_0})$ at T. From that, the Judge can derive $POE(V_i, T_0)$ for any $i \in [1, n]$ and therefore he will rule in favor of Alice (Proposition 4) using a proof $\mathcal{P}_2$. Note again that this requires that h_0, h_1, and sa_1 are trusted at T. $\mathcal{P}_2$ guarantees favorable judgments to Alice until the date $E(\mathcal{P}_2)$. Before this date, Alice needs to run again the simple renewal algorithm.

Recursive simple renewals may allow Alice to postpone the expiration of the judgment proof. Naturally, Alice should use state of art algorithms and authorities at each renewal to be able to validate the last time-stamps. However, recursive simple renewals can not allow "eternal" validity. Indeed, for all the proofs $\mathcal{P}_i$ obtained after k simple renewals, $Algo(h_j, T_{h_j}) \in \mathcal{P}_i$, $\forall j \leq i$ (where h_j is the hash function used for the jth simple renewal). Thus, for all the proofs $\mathcal{P}_i$ we have $E(\mathcal{P}_i) < min\{T_{h_j}, j \leq i\}$. We can fairly assume that, at each renewal, Alice uses an up to date hash function such that $T_{h_{j+1}} \geq T_{h_j} \forall j$. Therefore, T_{h_0} represents the maximum date for which Alice can have favorable judgments by recursive simple renewals. To have favorable judgments beyond this date, Alice needs to execute the complex renewal.

Complex Renewal. This renewal is performed when the probability of hash function compromise is foreseen. Not only time-stamps are re-timestamped but also data objects protected by the time-stamps. In our model, the need to execute this renewal occurs when the expiration date of a judgment proof $\mathcal{P}_{k+1}$ obtained after the kth simple renewal becomes close to the lowest expiration date (say T_{h_0}) of the hash functions used in the previous simple renewals. The renewal must be executed at a date $T_{k+1} < E(\mathcal{P}_{k+1})$. It consists in creating a new ERS on: $\{V_1, \ldots, V_n\}$, ERS_k and the objects used at T_{k+1} to derive $Aut(X_k, I_{X_k})$ where X_k is the TSA used for the kth simple renewal.

Now, how the complex renewal allows the Judge to rule in favor of Alice at a date $T > T_{h_0}$? Let us denote h_{k+1}, X_{k+1} and ERS_{k+1} respectively the hash function, the TSA and the set of obtained time-stamps. At T, Alice needs to come with the validation objects in $\mathcal{P}_{k+1}$, ERS_{k+1} and the objects that allow to derive $Aut(X_{k+1}, I_{X_{k+1}})$. Since the complex renewal is also a simple renewal, it allows to derive $POE(TSP(X_0, h_0(V_i), T_0, sa_0), T_1)$ for any i in $[1, n]$ and $Aut(X_0, I_{X_0})$ at T. In addition, ERS_{k+1} includes a time-stamp on the object V_i which allows to derive $POE(V_i, T_{k+1})$ for any i in $[1, n]$. From that, $POE(V_i, T_0)$ can be derived at T for any $i \in [1, n]$. Thus, the Judge will rule in favor of Alice at T (Proposition 4) with a proof $\mathcal{P}_{k+2}$. If Alice needs favorable judgments after $E(\mathcal{P}_{k+2})$, she needs to continue to execute the simple renewal. Again, once the expiration date of a proof becomes close to the expiration of the hash functions used with a previous ERS, the complex renewal should be performed.

7   Conclusion and Future Work

We presented a security model for digital signature validation with the notion of dispute about the validity of a signature. The first contribution of this paper is the definition of the semantics of a resolution of dispute rule. The second contribution is a new calculus for reasoning about the validation of digital signatures at a particular date which may be in the past. The usefulness of our calculus is demonstrated through modeling ERS, one of the main techniques used in practice. The calculus allowed to model at which date the renewal becomes necessary, which data must be archived and how the renewal allows to have a favorable judgment after the expiration of the last proof.

One of the main components of the model is $\mathcal{IVT}$. The hypothesis that all actors trust a common set of trust anchors and algorithms seems very strong. If we can establish such agreement in a non-repudiable way, one may ask why this same way is not used to implement the resolution of dispute. On the other hand, this agreement requires that Bob agrees on the content of $\mathcal{IVT}$ at the signing date. We may assume that this $\mathcal{IVT}$ is part of the signed message which proves Bob's commitment. However, because we need to continuously update $\mathcal{IVT}$, we need Bob's commitment for each new $\mathcal{IVT}$. Bob's collaboration is then necessary for long-term validation which may be refused by Bob. In real world, this issue is resolved by the use of a third trusted party. The origin of this trust is usually legal frameworks [3, 16, 17] to which all other actors refer in case of dispute.

An interesting future work is the definition of other semantics for RDR. Ideally, in the scope of long-term validation, completely honest behaviors should not be an assumption. A potential interesting work is to capture other PKI models with potential malicious actors. This suggests the extension of the calculus to a model based on confidence valuation similar to the probabilistic model proposed by Maurer [9]. This will allow to define an evaluation metric for the judgment proofs based on the confidence levels of the statements composing the proofs. The Judge would select the proof with the highest confidence level and rule in favor of Alice provided this level goes beyond a determined threshold.

Acknowledgment. The authors would like to thank the anonymous reviewers for their valuable comments.

References

1. Cooper, D., Santesson, S., Farrell, S., Boeyen, S., Housley, R., Polk, W.: Public key infrastructure: Certificate and CRL profile, IETF, Tech. Rep. RFC 5280 (2008)
2. Aarnes, A.: Public key certificate revocation schemes, Ph.D. dissertation, Norwegian University of Science (2000)
3. ETSI, Algorithms and parameters for secure electronic signatures; part 1: Hash functions and asymmetric algorithms, Tech. Rep. ETSI TS 102 176-1 V2.0.0 (2007)

4. Jerman Blaič. A., Klobučar, T., Jerman, B.D.: Long-term trusted preservation service using service interaction protocol and evidence records. Comput. Stand. Interfaces 29 (2007)
5. Huhnlein, D., Korte, U., Langer, L., Wiesmaier, A.: A comprehensive reference architecture for trustworthy long-term archiving of sensitive data. In: Third International Conference on New Technologies, Mobility and Security (2009)
6. Troncoso, C., De Cock, D., Preneel, B.: Improving secure long-term archival of digitally signed documents. In: Proceedings of the 4th ACM International Workshop on Storage Security and Survivability, pp. 27–36. ACM, New York (2008)
7. ETSI, CMS Advanced Electronic Signatures, Tech. Rep. ETSI TS 101 733 (2008)
8. Gondrom, T., Brandner, R., Pordesch, U.: Evidence Record Syntax (ERS), Tech. Rep. RFC4998 (2007)
9. Maurer, U.M.: Modelling a public-key infrastructure. In: Martella, G., Kurth, H., Montolivo, E., Hwang, J. (eds.) ESORICS 1996. LNCS, vol. 1146, pp. 325–350. Springer, Heidelberg (1996)
10. Marchesini, J., Smith, S.: Modeling public key infrastructures in the real world. In: Chadwick, D., Zhao, G. (eds.) EuroPKI 2005. LNCS, vol. 3545, pp. 118–134. Springer, Heidelberg (2005)
11. Bicakci, K., Crispo, B., Tanenbaum, A.S.: How to incorporate revocation status information into the trust metrics for public-key certification. In: Proceedings of the 2005 ACM Symposium on Applied Computing, pp. 1594–1598. ACM, New York (2005)
12. Baier, H., Karatsiolis, V.: Validity models of electronic signatures and their enforcement in practice. In: Martinelli, F., Preneel, B. (eds.) EuroPKI 2009. LNCS, vol. 6391, pp. 255–270. Springer, Heidelberg (2010)
13. Goldwasser, S., Micali, S., Rivest, R.L.: A digital signature scheme secure against adaptive chosen-message attacks. SIAM Journal on Computing 17, 281–308 (1988)
14. Walleck, D., Li, Y., Xu, S.: Empirical analysis of certificate revocation lists. In: Atluri, V. (ed.) DAS 2008. LNCS, vol. 5094, pp. 159–174. Springer, Heidelberg (2008)
15. Menezes, A.J., van Oorschot, P.C., Vanstone, S.A.: Handbook of Applied Cryptography. Discrete Mathematics and Its Applications. CRC Press, Boca Raton (1997)
16. FNISA, Annexe B1 - règles et recommandations concernant le choix et le dimensionnement des mécanismes cryptographique, French Network and Information Security Agency, Tech. Rep. Version 1.20 du (janvier 26, 2010)
17. ETSI, Provision of harmonized trust service provider status information, Tech. Rep. ETSI TS 102 231 V3.1.2 (2009)

A   Proof of Proposition 2

Let us first assume that the Judge rules in favor of Alice according to Definition 5. We want to prove that with the same inputs, the Judge will rule in favor of Alice according to Definition 9. Definition 5 means that there exists a date $T_s \leq T_d$ such that the three statements of the definition are satisfied at T.

1. The first statement means that there exists a date $T_x \geq T_s$ such that $\mathsf{SVF}(S_d, \mathcal{K}, \mathcal{O}, T_x) = (true, P)$, where P is a sequence of certificates and revocation objects. Let us denote this sequence by:

$$P = \begin{pmatrix} CACert(X_0, X_1, I_1, sa_1), NRev(X_0, X_1, I_1', sa_1') \\ \dots \\ CACert(X_{n-2}, X_{n-1}, I_{n-1}, sa_{n-1}), NRev(X_{n-2}, X_{n-1}, I_{n-1}', sa_{n-1}') \\ EECert(X_{n-1}, X_n, I_n, sa_n), NRev(X_{n-1}, X_n, I_n', sa_n') \end{pmatrix}$$

From the definition of SVF, we have the following:

- X_0 is a trust anchor from $\mathcal{K}$. Therefore, there exits an interval I_0 such that $T_x \in I_0$ and $CAAut(X_0, I_0) \in IV$.
- the last certificate is issued to Bob ($X_n = B$).
- the signatures in S_d, the certificates and revocation objects in P are cryptographically valid. Therefore, $\{S_d, P\} \subset IV$.
- all certificates and revocation objects in P are valid at T_x. Therefore, $\forall i \in [1, n], T_x$ is included in I_i and I_i'.

2. The second statement means that any validation object in P exists at a date earlier than T_x and that at this date the signature algorithm used to protect the object is trusted to be secure. This gives us the following:

- $\forall i \in [0, n-2]$, there exists a date $T_i \leq T_x$ (respectively a date $T_i' \leq T_x$) such that $POE(CACert(X_i, X_{i+1}, I_{i+1}, sa_{i+1}), T_i)$ (respectively $POE(NRev(X_i, X_{i+1}, I_{i+1}', sa_{i+1}'), T_i'))$ can be derived at T.
- There exists a date $T_n \leq T_x$ (respectively a date $T_n' \leq T_x$) such that $POE(EECert(X_{n-1}, X_n, I_n, sa_n), T_n)$ (respectively $POE(NRev(X_{n-1}, X_n, I_n', sa_n'), T_n'))$ can be derived at T.
- $\forall i \in [1, n]$, there exists a date $T_{sa_i} \geq T_i$ such that (sa_i, T_{sa_i}) is in $\mathcal{A}$ and then $Algo(sa_i, T_{sa_i}) \in IV$.

With theses POE and $Algo$ statements, the Judge can derive the following statements using Rule (6) to have a POI with a date earlier than T_x then Rule (7) to have a POI with T_x:

- $\forall i \in [0, n-2]$: $POI(CACert(X_i, X_{i+1}, I_{i+1}, sa_{i+1}), T_x)$ and $POI(NRev(X_i, X_{i+1}, I_{i+1}', sa_{i+1}'), T_x)$
- $POI(EECert(X_{n-1}, X_n, I_n, sa_n), T_x)$
- $POI(NRev(X_{n-1}, X_n, I_n', sa_n'), T_x)$

Now, we will show that, with the previous statements, the Judge can derive $Aut(B, I_B)$ such that I_B is an interval that contains the date T_x. First, let us prove by induction the following: $\forall i \in [1, n-1]$, there exists an interval I_i'' such that $T_x \in I_i''$ and the statement $CAAut(X_i, I_i'')$ is valid at T:

- for $i = 1$, $CAAut(X_1, I_1'')$ can be derived with the following such that $T_x \in I_1''$ (Rule (1)):

$$\frac{CAAut(X_0, I_0) \qquad POI(CACert(X_0, X_1, I_1, sa_1), T_x)}{CAAut(X_1, I_1'')} \frac{POI(NRev(X_0, X_1, I_1', sa_1'), T_x)}{}$$

This works because we showed that $CAAut(X_0, I_0) \in IV$, and T_x is included in all the intervals I_i and I_i'.

– Now we assume that there exists an interval I_i'' such that $T_x \in I_i''$ and $CAAut(X_i, I_i'')$ is valid at T. The application of Rule (1) gives $CAAut(X_{i+1}, I_{i+1}'')$ such that $T_x \in I_{i+1}''$:

$$\frac{CAAut(X_i, I_i'') \quad POI(CACert(X_i, X_{i+1}, I_{i+1}, sa_{i+1}), T_x)}{POI(NRev(X_i, X_{i+1}, I_{i+1}', sa_{i+1}'), T_x)} \over CAAut(X_{i+1}, I_{i+1}'')$$

Therefore, there exists an interval I_{n-1}'' such that $T_x \in I_{n-1}''$ and $CAAut(X_{n-1}, I_{n-1}'')$ is valid at T. Now, we use Rule (2) to derive $Aut(B, I_B)$ such that $T_x \in I_B$:

$$\frac{CAAut(X_{n-1}, I_{n-1}'') \quad POI(EECert(X_{n-1}, X_n, I_n, sa_n), T_x)}{POI(NRev(X_{n-1}, X_n, I_n', sa_n'), T_x)} \over Aut(X_n = B, I_n'' = I_B)$$

3. The last statement in Definition 5 gives the following: $POE(S_d, T_s)$ is valid at T and there exists a date $T_{sa} \geq T_s$ such that (sa, T_{sa}) is in $\mathcal{A}$ and then in $Algo(sa, T_{sa}) \in IV$. Therefore, Rule (6) allows to derive $POI(S_d, T_s)$.

In conclusion, we showed that the Judge can derive the statements $POI(S_d, T_s)$ and $Aut(B, I_B = [T_{B_1}, T_{B_2}])$ at T where $T_d \geq T_s$ and $T_s \leq T_{B_2}$ (because $T_s \leq T_x$ and $T_x \in I_B$). Then, Rule (8) allows to derive $Res_{A,B}(S_d, T_d)$ at T. Therefore, the Judge will rule in favor of Alice according to Definition 9. $\quad\square$

The other part of the proof is similar and is omitted.

B   Proof of Proposition 3

We want to prove that Alice will have a favorable judgment at any date $T \in [T_P, E(\mathcal{P}_p)]$ provided she comes with the objects $\mathcal{O}$ such that $\mathcal{P}_p \subseteq IV = IV(\mathcal{IVT}(T), \mathcal{O}, S_d)$. If the Judge rules in favor of Alice at T_p, this means that $Res_{A,B}(S_d, T_d)$ can be derived at T_p from $\mathcal{P}_p$. Then, there exist an interval $I_B = [T_{B_1}, T_{B_2}]$ and a date T_s verifying $T_s \leq T_{B_2}$ and $T_s \leq T_d$ such that the statements $POI(S_d, T_s)$ and $Aut(B, I_B)$ can be derived at T_p. $Aut(B, I_B)$ means that the Judge believes at T_p that B's key is authentic within the interval I_B. Let us extract the expiration dates from the statements in $\mathcal{P}_p$ and order them chronologically in the following dates $E_1...E_k$. With T_p, this gives us $k + 2$ intervals. Within each interval, the validity status of all statements in $\mathcal{P}_p$ are constant. Therefore, the validity status of any Aut and $CAAut$ is constant within each interval. We consider the date $E_j = E(\mathcal{P}) = min\{E_i, E_i > T_p\}_{1 \geq i \geq k}$. Since $Aut(B, I_B)$ can be derived at T_p from $\mathcal{P}_p$, then $Aut(B, I_B)$ can be derived at any date $T \in [T_p, E(\mathcal{P}_p)]$. In addition, since S_d and $Algo(sa, T_{sa})$ are in $\mathcal{P}_p$, then Rule (3) gives $POE(S_d, T)$ and Rule (6) gives $POI(S_d, T)$ ($T \leq E(\mathcal{P}_p) \leq T_{sa}$). Finally, Rule (8) gives $Res_{A,B}(S_d, T)$ ($T \leq E(\mathcal{P}_p) \leq T_{B_2}$). Therefore, the Judge will rule in favor of Alice at T for the dispute Dispute(A, B, S_d, T).

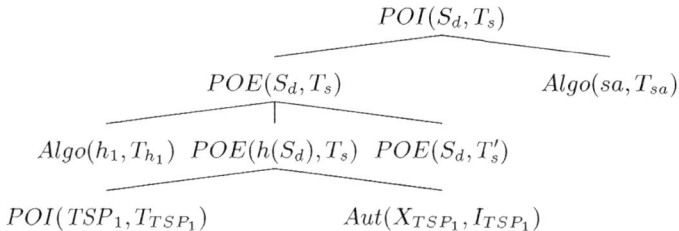

Fig. 4. Derivation of $POI(S_d, T_s)$ at T_p ($T_s \leq T'_s \leq T_{h_1}$ and $T_{TSP_1} \in I_{TSP_1}$)

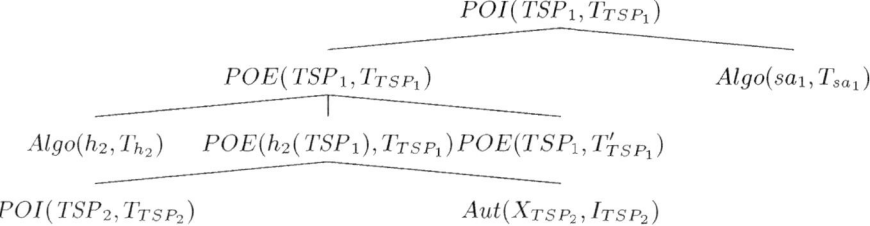

Fig. 5. Derivation of $POI(TSP_1, T_{TSP_1})$ at T_p

Now, we consider the case $T_d < T_p$. This means that at T_p, the Judge derived a POI for S_d with a date in the past ($T_s \leq T_d < T_p$). The only way is using Rule (4) with a time-stamp $TSP_1 = TSP(X_{TSP_1}, h_1(S_d), T_s, sa_1)$ as in Figure 4. First, using the same reasoning as above for $Aut(B, I_B)$, $Aut(X_{TSP_1}, I_{TSP_1})$ can be derived at any date $T \in [T_p, E(\mathcal{P}_p)]$. Second, we have two cases:

- If $T_{TSP_1} = T_p$, then $[T_p, E(\mathcal{P}_p)] \subset I_{TSP_1}$ and therefore $T \in I_{TSP_1}$. Thus, $POI(S_d, T_s)$ can be derived at T with the derivation tree in Figure 4 using T instead of T_{TSP_1} and T'_s (recall that $T \leq E(\mathcal{P}_p) \leq T_{h_1}$).
- If $T_{TSP_1} < T_p$, then the Judge derived at T_p a POI statement for TSP_1 with a date $T_{TSP_1} < T_p$. The only way is using Rule (4) with $TSP_2 = TSP(X_{TSP_2}, h_2(TSP_1), T_{TSP_1}, sa_2)$ (Figure 5). We have again two cases:
  - If $T_{TSP_2} = T_p$, then $POI(TSP_1, T_{TSP_1})$ can be derived at T using $T_{TSP_2} = T'_{TSP_1} = T$ and thus, $POI(S_d, T_s)$ can be derived at T.
  - If $T_{TSP_2} < T_p$, then $POI(TSP_2, T_{TSP_2})$ was derived at T_p using Rule 4 with a time-stamp $TSP_3 = TSP(X_{TSA_3}, h_3(TSP_2), T_{TSP_2}, sa_3)$.
  Recursively, we end with a time-stamp TSP_n such that $T_{TSP_n} = T_p$ and then $POI(TSP_{n-1}, T), \ldots, POI(TSP_1, T)$ can be derived at T which allows to derive $POI(S_d, T_s)$ at T.

Therefore, in both cases $POI(S_d, T_s)$ can be derived at T. This allows the Judge to derive $Res_{A,B}(S_d, T_d)$ at T and then to rule in favor of Alice at T for the dispute $\mathsf{Dispute}(A, B, S_d, T_d)$.   □

Formal Analysis of Privacy for Anonymous Location Based Services

Morten Dahl[1], Stéphanie Delaune[2], and Graham Steel[2]

[1] Department of Computer Science, Aalborg University
[2] LSV, ENS Cachan & CNRS & INRIA Saclay Île-de-France

Abstract. We propose a framework for formal analysis of privacy in location based services such as anonymous electronic toll collection. We give a formal definition of privacy, and apply it to the VPriv scheme for vehicular services. We analyse the resulting model using the ProVerif tool, concluding that our privacy property holds only if certain conditions are met by the implementation. Our analysis includes some novel features such as the formal modelling of privacy for a protocol that relies on interactive zero-knowledge proofs of knowledge and list permutations.

1 Introduction

The sophistication and quantity of embedded devices in modern vehicles is growing rapidly. Ad-hoc wireless networking is envisioned as one of the next big steps, with various car-to-infrastructure and car-to-car communication applications planned [12,14]. Many of these applications are location-based, and providing the precise position of the vehicle is essential to the quality of the service provided. As these applications are deployed, privacy concerns naturally emerge.

Some of the location-based services already in widespread use today, such as RFID tag based electronic toll collection systems, offer little privacy protection to drivers [16]. By using the same fixed identifying tag whenever they have to pay a toll fee, it becomes trivial to later trace the routes of any driver given the database of payments. Little is gained by using a fixed random tag instead of a real-world identifier such as the license plate. Although the tolling database may not be publicly available, the privacy of drivers is still at risk of exploitation from within the toll company.

The more widespread employment of such systems, combined with the possibility of moving them to the emerging general framework for network communication, increases the need for privacy oriented systems. In this paper, we bring the privacy analysis of location-based services into the world of formal methods, leveraging previous work on privacy for vehicular mix-zones [10], electronic voting [11,15], and RFID tags [3,8]. In particular, we concentrate on VPriv [7], a proposed scheme for building location-based services using zero-knowledge techniques, designed to ensure that the paths of drivers are not revealed to the service providers, while nonetheless preventing drivers from reporting fake paths. We use the formal notion of indistinguishability to formalise privacy and carry out the

S. Mödersheim and C. Palamidessi (Eds.): TOSCA 2011, LNCS 6993, pp. 98–112, 2012.

analysis with the aid of the protocol analysis tool ProVerif [5]. In particular, we will use a notion of trace equivalence, after explaining why the more usual notion of observational equivalence is not suitable in this setting. To the best of our knowledge this is the first use of the tool for analysing a protocol that relies on interactive zero-knowledge proofs of knowledge. Note that contrary to non-interactive ones that can be abstracted by means of an appropriate equational theory (see *e.g.* [4]), interactive proofs cannot since the interactions between the participants reveal some information that has to be considered when we carry out the privacy analysis.

2   The VPriv Scheme

In this section we introduce the VPriv scheme [7], a protocol that offers a variety of location-based vehicular services such as "pay-as-you-go" insurance, electronic toll collection, etc. Its goal is to both protect the privacy of drivers whilst ensuring that they cannot cheat service providers by, for instance, paying a lower price.

2.1   Description

The participants are a set of users with vehicles and a service provider. We assume that time is split into periods. The following three phases detailed below are executed in order by each vehicle during each period. At the start of a period, the vehicle generates fresh random tags for the period and registers commitments to encrypted versions of these with the service provider (registration phase). Then, whenever the vehicle must emit a message containing an identifier during the period it will choose a new tag from its set of fresh tags. The tags are emitted in clear and the service provider records all tags v emitted by all vehicles together with the emission location l and a timestamp t, building a database containing a mixture of tuples (v, t, l) (driving phase). Finally, at the end of a period, each user initiates a protocol with the service provider in order to compute and settle the payable debts (reconciliation phase).

In the following, $[M]_d$ denotes a commitment to message M that can only be revealed with opening key d. Moreover, it is assumed to be a homomorphic commitment scheme, thus we have that:

$$[M_1]_{d_1} \cdot [M_2]_{d_2} = [M_1 + M_2]_{d_1 + d_2}.$$

We further use $f_k(M)$ to denote a deterministic one-way function f that is parametrized by a key k. Note that knowing $f_k(M)$ and k does not allow one to retrieve M but only to compute a new encryption matching $f_k(M)$.

Phase 1 - Registration. Each vehicle generates a set V of fresh tags $v_1, \ldots, v_n$ and a set of fresh keys $k^1, \ldots, k^s$ for f. It furthermore generates opening keys $dk^1, \ldots, dk^s$ and $dv_1^1, \ldots, dv_n^s$. It then forms s *round packages*

$$\mathcal{V} \to \mathcal{S}: \ r^i = \left(id, i, [k^i]_{dk^i}, [f_{k^i}(v_1)]_{dv_1^i}, \ldots, [f_{k^i}(v_n)]_{dv_n^i} \right)$$

consisting of the *round number* $i \in [1; s]$, a commitment to the *round key* k^i, and commitments to encryptions of the vehicle's tags under the round key. The vehicle sends the round packages to the server together with a fixed identifier id for the user, such as the vehicle's license plate.

Phase 2 - Driving. Each vehicle emits its tags $v_1, \ldots, v_n$ in random order along its route. The server records these tags along with the location l where it was emitted and a timestamp t.

Phase 3 - Reconciliation. The server starts the reconciliation phase by sending the list W of all m tags w_j in its database together with their associated cost c_j, *i.e.* W contains all tags emitted by all vehicles during the period. Then the vehicle computes C as the sum of the costs of its own tags contained in W and sends this back to the server

$$\mathcal{S} \rightarrow \mathcal{V} : W = \Big[(w_1, c_1), \ldots, (w_m, c_m)\Big]$$
$$\mathcal{V} \rightarrow \mathcal{S} : id, C$$

The remaining part of the protocol consists of several rounds. For each round i, the vehicle generates opening keys $dc_1^i, \ldots, dc_m^i$. Then, it processes all pairs in W by encrypting the tag w_j under its round key k^i and committing to the associated cost c_j using opening key dc_j^i. It permutes the pairs using a random permutation σ^i and sends the resulting list U^i to $\mathcal{S}$ together with its identifier. Then, the server decides to either verify that U^i is indeed the correct processing of W under k^i and $dc_1^i, \ldots, dc_m^i$ or to verify that the user has correctly calculated the cost C. In the former case it sends $b^i = 0$ to the vehicle and in the latter case $b^i = 1$.

$$\mathcal{V} \rightarrow \mathcal{S} : id, U^i = \Big[\big(f_{k^i}(w_{\sigma^i(1)}), [c_{\sigma^i(1)}]_{dc_1^i}\big), \ldots, \big(f_{k^i}(w_{\sigma^i(m)}), [c_{\sigma^i(m)}]_{dc_m^i}\big)\Big]$$
$$\mathcal{S} \rightarrow \mathcal{V} : b^i$$
$$\mathcal{V} \rightarrow \mathcal{S} : \begin{cases} id, dk^i, dc_1^i, \ldots, dc_m^i & \text{if } b^i = 0 \\ id, dv_1^i, \ldots, dv_n^i, D^i & \text{if } b^i = 1 \end{cases}$$

If $b^i = 0$ the server receives $dk^i, dc_1^i, \ldots, dc_m^i$ from the vehicle. It can then obtain k^i from r^i and verify that U^i correctly follows from W. If $b^i = 1$ the server receives $dv_1^i, \ldots, dv_n^i$ to open the commitments in r^i to obtain the encrypted version of the vehicle's tags $f_{k^i}(v_1), \ldots, f_{k^i}(v_n)$. Knowing these it can pick out the pairs from U^i belonging to the vehicle (by the deterministic nature of f_{k^i}). It multiplies the cost commitments from these together and verifies that they indeed open to C under opening key D^i that is provided by the vehicle.

If the above mentioned checks pass for every round then the server accepts, the client is billed, and a new period begins. It can be argued that the probability of a cheating vehicle convincing the server of a false cost is 2^{-s}. This probability can hence be made arbitrarily low by choosing a large enough number of rounds.

Spot checks. Note that there is no mechanism in the protocol described above that prevents vehicles from cheating by not emitting the tags they have committed to in order to reduce the price they have to pay. To address this the protocol suggests random spot checks. A spot check consists of an enforcement device that secretly collects identifying data about passing vehicles at locations where they are supposed to emit tags, for instance by taking a photograph of the license plate. This way it will obtain a database DB of tuples (id, v, l, t) each with an identity id, a tag v, a location l and a timestamp t. Before the reconciliation phase the server will ask the vehicle about its identity id, challenge it with $\{(l, t) \mid (id, v, l, t) \in DB\}$, and *e.g.* fine the user if it fails to provide matching tags or the provided tags are not in the server's database. Since the location of the spot checks are assumed to be unknown to the vehicles, it can be argued that they do not know when they can safely avoid emitting a (valid) tag and hence must always do so when they are supposed to. Note that some privacy is leaked due to the spot checks; it is argued that this is at an acceptable level.

2.2   Privacy

The privacy definition for the VPriv scheme as stated in [7] asks that the privacy guarantees from the system are the same as those of a system in which the server, instead of storing tuples (v, t, l), stores only tag-free path points (t, l). In other words, from the server's point of view, the tags might just as well be uncorrelated and random. This definition accounts for the fact that some privacy leaks are unavoidable and should not be blamed on the system. For instance, if one somehow learns that only a single vehicle was on a certain road at a particular time, then that vehicle's tags can of course be linked to the tags emitted along the road at that time.

3   Formal Model

The process calculus used as input to the ProVerif tool is a variant of the applied pi calculus [1], a process calculus for formally modelling concurrent systems and their interactions. We here recall the basic ideas and concepts of this calculus that are needed for our analysis.

3.1   Messages

To describe messages, we start with a set of *names* used to identify communication channels and other atomic data, a set of *variables* $x, y, \ldots$ and a signature Σ formed by a finite set of *function symbols* $\mathsf{f}, \mathsf{g}, \ldots$ each with an associated arity. Function symbols are distinguished into two categories: *constructors* and *destructors*. We use standard notation for function application, *i.e.* $\mathsf{f}(M_1, \ldots, M_n)$. Constructors are used for building messages. Destructors represent primitives for taking messages apart and can visibly succeed or fail (while constructors always succeed). Messages $M, N, \ldots$ are obtained by repeated application of constructors on names and variables whereas a term evaluation D can also use destructors. The semantics of a destructor g of arity n is given by a set of rewrite rules of the form $g(M_1, \ldots, M_n) \rightarrow M_0$ where $M_0, \ldots, M_n$ are messages that only contain constructors and variables. Given a term evaluation D, we write $D \Downarrow M$ when D can be reduced to M by applying some destructor rules.

In the following, we consider constructors to model commitments and the one-way function f. Since there is no destructor associated to f we have only one destructor whose semantics is given by the following rule:

$$\text{open}(\text{com}(x, y), y) \rightarrow x.$$

The applied pi calculus is quite general: it allows us, for instance, to model the homomorphism property of the commitment scheme by means of an equational theory containing, among others, the equation

$$\text{com}(x_1, y_1) \times \text{com}(x_2, y_2) = \text{com}(x_1 + x_2, y_1 + y_2).$$

However, since ProVerif will not be able to reason with this equation, we will remove the homomorphic property in Section 5 and instead consider a simplified version of the protocol with no costs.

3.2   Processes

Processes are built from the grammar described below, where M is a message, D is a term evaluation, n and c are names, x is a variable, and i is a positive integer.

$P, Q, R ::=$	processes
0	null process
$P \mid Q$	parallel composition
$!P$	replication
new $n; P$	name restriction
let $M = D$ in P else Q	term evaluation
in$(c, M); P$	message input
out$(c, M); P$	message output
phase $i; P$	phase separation

The process "let $M = D$ in P else Q" tries to evaluate D; if this succeeds and if the resulting message matches the term M then the variables in M are bound and P is executed; if not then Q is executed. As explained in [5], the process phase $i; P$ indicates the beginning of phase i. Intuitively, the process first executes phase 0, that is, it executes all instructions not under phase $i \geq 1$. Then, when changing from phase i to phase $i + 1$, all processes that have not reached a phase $i' \geq i+1$ instruction are discarded and the instructions under phase $i+1$ are executed. The rest of the syntax is quite standard. To ease the presentation we will use tuples of messages, denoted by parentheses, while keeping the reduction rules for these tuples implicit. We will omit "else Q" when Q is 0. In the remainder of the paper, we use the more intuitive notation "if $M = N$ then P else Q" instead of "let $M = N$ in P else Q".

An *evaluation context* C is a process with a hole, built from $[\_]$, $C \mid P$, $P \mid C$ and new $n; C$. We obtain $C[P]$ as the result of filling the hole in C with P. A process P is *closed* if all its variables are bound through an input or a let construction.

The vehicle process. To illustrate the calculus used throughout this paper, we give in Figure 1 a partial description of the vehicle process. It follows the description given in the previous section but is simplified in several aspects to keep this illustrative example as simple as possible. A more accurate model is described in Section 5.

Here we consider the case where a vehicle only has two tags v_1 and v_2, and where the reconciliation phase consists of only one round. We assume that during the driving phase the vehicle will visit only two locations and that the vehicle is spot checked at the second location. The vehicle receives a list of tags of size three (in reality, the length of the list is not known *a priori*), and instead of applying a random permutation, we only encode one particular permutation.

$\mathsf{Vehicle}(id, l_1, l_2) \overset{\text{def}}{=}$
  phase 1; (* *registration phase* *)
  new v_1; new v_2;
  new k; new dk; new dv_1; new dv_2;
  $\mathsf{out}(c, (id, \mathsf{com}(k, dk), \mathsf{com}(\mathsf{f}(v_1, k), dv_1), \mathsf{com}(\mathsf{f}(v_2, k), dv_2)))$;
  phase 2; (* *driving phase* *)
  $\mathsf{out}(c, (l_1, v_1))$; $\mathsf{out}(c, (l_2, v_2, id))$;
  phase 3; (* *reconciliation phase* *)
  $\mathsf{in}(c, (x_1, x_2, x_3))$;
  $\mathsf{out}(c, (id, \mathsf{f}(x_2, k), \mathsf{f}(x_1, k), \mathsf{f}(x_3, k)))$;
  $\mathsf{in}(c, y)$;
  if $y = \mathsf{false}$ then $\mathsf{out}(c, (id, dk))$ else $\mathsf{out}(c, (id, dv_1, dv_2))$

Fig. 1. Illustrative vehicle process

The operational semantics of processes is essentially defined by two relations, namely *structural equivalence* and *reduction*. Structural equivalence, denoted by $\equiv$, is the smallest equivalence relation on processes that is closed under application of evaluation contexts and standard rules such as associativity and commutativity of the parallel operator. Moreover, in order to deal with the phase construct, we have also the following rules (see [6]):

$$\text{new } n; \text{phase } i; P \equiv \text{phase } i; \text{new } n \; ; P$$
$$\text{phase } i; (P \mid Q) \equiv \text{phase } i; P \mid \text{phase } i; Q$$
$$\text{phase } i; \text{phase } i'; P \equiv \text{phase } i'; P \quad \text{if } i < i'$$

Reduction at phase i, denoted by $\to_i$, is the smallest relation closed under structural equivalence and application of evaluation contexts such that:

RED I/O   phase i; $(\text{out}(c, M).Q \mid \text{in}(c, N).P) \to_i$ phase i; $(Q \mid P\sigma)$

RED FUN 1   phase i; let $N = D$ in P else $Q \to_i$ phase i; $P\sigma$ if $D \Downarrow M$

RED FUN 2   phase i; let $N = D$ in P else $Q \to_i$ phase i; Q
$\qquad\qquad\qquad\qquad\qquad\qquad$ if there is no M such that $D \Downarrow M$

REPL   phase i; $!P \to_i$ phase i; $(P \mid !P)$

where σ is the substitution defined on the variables that occur in N and such that $M = N\sigma$. In case such a substitution does not exist, the resulting process will be $Q \mid \text{in}(c, N).P$ for the RED I/O rule and Q for the RED FUN 1 rule. We denote $\to = \bigcup_{i \geq 0} \to_i$ and we write $\to^*$ for the reflexive and transitive closure of reduction.

4   Privacy for Interactive Zero-Knowledge Protocols

We will define privacy using indistinguishability, which in turn will be formalized by a notion of equivalence. Equivalences have already been used to model privacy properties in formal analysis for *e.g.* vehicular mix-zones [10] and electronic voting [11,15]. The precise notion used is often *observational equivalence* but as we will explain, it happens that this notion is too strong to analyse interactive zero-knowledge protocols. So, we will rely on *trace equivalence* to formalize our notion of privacy in Section 4.2. However, the only equivalence relation supported by ProVerif is a stronger notion called *diff-equivalence*, and thus we explain in Section 4.3 how to use this tool to analyse trace equivalence-based properties.

4.1   Equivalences

One equivalence notion for formalizing indistinguishability is observational equivalence [17]. Here we write $P \Downarrow_c$ when P can send an observable message on the channel c; that is, when $P \to^* C[\text{phase } i; \text{out}(c, M); Q]$ for some evaluation context C that does not bind c, some message M, some process Q, and some integer i.

Definition 1 (Observational equivalence). *Observational equivalence, denoted $\sim_o$, is the largest symmetric relation $\mathcal{R}$ on closed processes P and Q such that $P\,\mathcal{R}\,Q$ implies:*

1. *if $P \Downarrow_c$ then $Q \Downarrow_c$;*
2. *if $P \to P'$ then there exists Q' such that $Q \to^* Q'$ and $P'\,\mathcal{R}\,Q'$;*
3. *$C[P]\,\mathcal{R}\,C[Q]$ for all evaluation contexts C.*

Intuitively, a context may represent an attacker, and two processes are observationally equivalent if they cannot be distinguished by any attacker at any step: every output step in an execution of process P must have an indistinguishable equivalent output step in the execution of process Q. If not then there exists a context that 'breaks' the equivalence.

In the case of privacy for the VPriv protocol, we will see that this notion is too strong (see the discussion in Section 4.2). Instead, we will use the notion of *trace equivalence* (also called *testing equivalence* in some other contexts [2]).

Definition 2 (Trace equivalence). Trace equivalence $\sim_t$ *is the largest symmetric relation on closed processes P and Q such that for all evaluation contexts C we have $C[P]\Downarrow_c$ if and only if $C[Q]\Downarrow_c$.*

This is a strictly weaker notion than observational equivalence (see *e.g.* [9]) but intuitively it captures the equivalence upon which we can *a priori* hope to base our privacy property, as we explain below.

4.2 Formal Definition of Privacy

In our formal privacy definition we will assume that we have at least two honest vehicles called A and B. As we are interested in studying privacy guarantees for A, the process V_A for this vehicle will consist of all three phases of the protocol (registration, driving, and reconciliation). We assume that vehicle A has three tags, one of which is emitted at one of the two locations $route_{left}$ and $route_{right}$, one which is 'leaked', *i.e.* given to the server along with the vehicle's identity to model the spot-check procedure, and one which is not emitted. On the other hand, vehicle B is only needed to counterbalance the effect of the tag emitted by A at a *route* location. Thus, we will consider a vehicle B that only executes its driving phase, denoted V_B^{dri} in the equivalence below, by emitting its tag at the *route* not visited by vehicle A.

We say that privacy holds if the following equivalence holds:

$$C_T\big[\,V_A(route_{left}) \mid V_B^{dri}(route_{right})\,\big]$$
$$\sim_t$$
$$C_T\big[\,V_A(route_{right}) \mid V_B^{dri}(route_{left})\,\big]$$

where C_T is an evaluation context modelling additional assumptions that may have to be made for the privacy property to hold (*e.g.* that the server is curious but otherwise assumed to be honest and following the protocol, or the existence of a trusted third party helping vehicles ensure that the list of tags received from the server contains tags from both vehicles). The next section presents the analysis we have performed, including the definition of the vehicles processes and the different contexts C_T within which we have performed the analysis.

Note that observational equivalence would be too strong for this property to hold. This is due to the interactive zero-knowledge subprotocol that occurs in the reconciliation phase. Consider the two slightly different processes $V_A(route_{left})$ and $V_A(route_{right})$ in our privacy definition and assume that the two processes have reached the reconciliation phase. At this point, the server will send a list of tags to vehicle A. Then one of the two processes, say the former one, will commit to a permuted list. To mimic this step, the latter process has also to commit to a permuted list. However, no matter what list it commits to, this list will not mimic the former process' list for either $b = 0$ or $b = 1$ because of the slight difference between them. In other words, the choice of a list to mimic the former process depends on the challenge bit b that has not yet been received from the server. Thus observational equivalence is impossible to achieve. However, moving from observation equivalence to trace equivalence allows us to choose the mimic trace only after the challenge bit has been learned. Intuitively, this captures privacy: if an attacker observes a trace of registration, tag emission and reconciliation, and then guesses that vehicle A took a particular route, then there is an equivalent trace where vehicle A takes a different route. The fact that we cannot specify the equivalent trace until we have seen the whole of the first trace does not seem to lead to any loss of privacy. In fact, from the definition of zero-knowledge protocols in the computational model [13, §4] we see that the protocol is actually designed to support only trace equivalence and furthermore, that soundness contradicts observational equivalence.

4.3   Checking Privacy with ProVerif

The basic idea behind equivalence checking in ProVerif is to overlap the two processes that are supposedly equivalent, thereby forming a *biprocess* B. To achieve this, the syntax of ProVerif contains a *choice*$[M, M']$ operator which allows us to model a pair of processes that have the same structure and differ only in the choice of terms. Given a biprocess B, the process $P = fst(B)$ is obtained by replacing all occurrences of *choice*$[M, M']$ in B with M. Similarly, $Q = snd(B)$ is obtained by replacing *choice*$[M, M']$ with M'. When ProVerif is able to conclude positively on B, this implies that $P \approx_o Q$. However, ProVerif checks a stronger equivalence than observational equivalence and hence it fails on some simple examples of processes that are equivalent, but whose equivalence cannot be simulated by the moves of a single biprocess.

We will use two transformations in order to use ProVerif to check the trace equivalence defining our privacy property. The first arises from recent work which shows how to use ProVerif to prove observational equivalence for a wider class of processes [11]. Additionally, we also transform our biprocess B into another biprocess B' that preserves the traces of each underlying process, *i.e.* $fst(B)$ and $fst(B')$ will produce the same traces, and likewise for $snd(B)$ and $snd(B')$. This ensures that our transformation preserves trace equivalence. In our case study this transformation consists of guessing b in advance and deadlocking the process if it later turns out that the guess was wrong.

5   Privacy Analysis

The purpose of our analysis is to investigate the privacy guarantees provided for an honest user in the VPriv protocol. We do not attempt to analyse whether users can cheat the server nor whether the server will accuse an honest user of cheating.

Section 5.1 contains a description of the simplifications we had to make in order to carry through the analysis in ProVerif. In Section 5.2 we describe our formal model of the VPriv protocol using the applied pi calculus from the previous section. We give the results of our analysis in Section 5.3.

5.1   Simplifications

The following simplifications were necessary in order to carry through the analysis in ProVerif.

Removing Costs. In the extreme case where a unique price is used for every tag, the system cannot protect the privacy of users. It seems reasonable however, to assume that the information leaked by costs will in practice not affect the privacy of users. Forcing a uniform cost for every tag seems to be the only solution if we want to carry out our analysis with ProVerif. Furthermore, while we could model the homomorphic commitment scheme and its arithmetic properties by means of an equational theory, we know that ProVerif will not be able to deal with it properly in that it will not terminate. Thus, we remove prices and costs and proceed with a simplified version of the VPriv protocol. This change only affects the reconciliation phase where the list W sent by the server is now simply

$$\mathcal{S} \to \mathcal{V} : W = \left[w_1, \dots, w_m \right]$$

and the round subprotocol as described in Figure 2.

$$\mathcal{V} \to \mathcal{S} : id, U^i = \left[f_{k^i}(w_{\sigma^i(1)}), \dots, f_{k^i}(w_{\sigma^i(m)}) \right]$$
$$\mathcal{S} \to \mathcal{V} : b^i$$
$$\mathcal{V} \to \mathcal{S} : \begin{cases} id, dk^i & \text{if } b^i = 0 \\ id, dv_1^i, \dots, dv_n^i & \text{if } b^i = 1 \end{cases}$$

Fig. 2. Reconciliation round protocol without cost

Fixing the length of W. It turns out that privacy can be violated if the list of tags sent by the server is blindly accepted by the vehicles without any scrutiny. Some sanity conditions must be fulfilled in order to guarantee privacy. Furthermore, implementing these sanity checks together with the random permutation would lead us to consider a complex model that ProVerif is not able to handle. So instead, we fix *a priori* the length of the list expected by the vehicle to a size of three. This will allow us to easily encode the sanity checks and the random permutation, and despite its simplicity, still allow us to discover a number of issues to which attention should be paid when implementing the protocol. Note that with the sanity conditions discovered we can argue that fixing the length to three does not weaken the attacker.

5.2   Analysis Model

The model is represented by the biprocess B_S defined in Figure 3. In the following we show only the main details of this process and refer the interested reader to the full model available at http://www.cs.aau.dk/~dahl/vpriv/.

$$B_S(id^A, v_1^A, v_2^A, v_3^A, v_1^B, v_l, v_r) \stackrel{\text{def}}{=}$$
$$\text{new } pc;$$
$$\quad \text{phase } 2; B_{\text{dri}}$$
$$\quad | \text{ phase } 3; B_{\text{BB}}$$
$$\quad | \text{ ! new } k, dk, dv_1, dv_2, dv_3 \left(\text{phase } 1; V_{\text{reg}}; \text{phase } 3; V_{\text{rec}}^{b=0}\right)$$
$$\quad | \text{ ! new } k, dk, dv_1, dv_2, dv_3 \left(\text{phase } 1; V_{\text{reg}}; \text{phase } 3; V_{\text{rec}}^{b=1}\right)$$

Fig. 3. System biprocess

The system B_S consist of five parts: B_{dri}, V_{reg}, $V_{\text{rec}}^{b=0}$, $V_{\text{rec}}^{b=1}$, and B_{BB}. The first four of these together make up the behaviour of vehicle A and vehicle B. Using the choice operator the emitter biprocess B_{dri} outputs the tags of both vehicles while V_{reg} and the two V_{rec} are responsible for performing registration and reconciliation, respectively, for vehicle A. By splitting up vehicle A in this way we accurately model an unbounded number of reconciliation rounds while only emitting tags once. The bulletin board B_{BB} is responsible for performing sanity checks on W. It receives a list of tags on a public channel and forwards the list to the V_{rec} biprocesses on the private channel pc an unbounded number of times if the checks succeed. Note that to avoid trivial false attacks, any checks against v_1^A and v_1^B must use the choice operator and hence the bulletin board is a biprocess. Finally, we use ProVerif's phases to orchestrate the processes so that they follow the order dictated by the protocol.

As discussed in Section 4, in order to establish the equivalence between the two cases, the selection of permutation for U^i depends upon the bit b^i that will be send by the server. We have two separate reconciliation processes $V_{\text{rec}}^{b=0}$ and $V_{\text{rec}}^{b=1}$ to model this. They guess that $b = 0$ and $b = 1$ will be sent, respectively, and permute accordingly. If the guess was correct the process proceeds as dictated by the protocol, otherwise it comes to a deadlock. Formally, let process P_{xyz} be defined by

$$P_{xyz} = \text{in}(s_1, \cdot); \text{out}\left(c, \left(id^A, f(w_x, k), f(w_y, k), f(w_z, k)\right)\right); \text{out}(s_2, \cdot); 0$$

which outputs the encrypted tags w_1, w_2 and w_3 permuted according to xyz. The initial input on s_1 is used to ensure that only a single permutation is selected and the final output on s_2 to indicate that the output was completed. The $\cdot$ stands for any name never used after it is bound. Using this process we then define $V_{\text{rec}}^{b=0}$ as shown in Figure 4 and $V_{\text{rec}}^{b=1}$ as shown in Figure 5. We note that because of the diff-equivalence that ProVerif is actually checking (see Section 4.3) it will only try to match the permutations at the same syntactical position. This means that we have to specify to ProVerif how permutations should be matched. For $V_{rec}^{b=0}$ we can choose the same permutation in the two cases and hence no further modelling is needed and $V_{rec}^{b=0}$ is actually just a process. However, this is not true for $V_{rec}^{b=1}$ where we have to move the processes P_{xyz} around depending on which case we are in. We do this using the choice operator and hence $V_{rec}^{b=1}$ is a biprocess. Let v_l be the tag emitted at $route_{left}$ and v_r the tag emitted at $route_{right}$. We have then chosen to arrange the permutations based on $w_1 = v_l$ and $w_3 = v_r$ and hence need to enforce this in the bulletin board.

$$V_{rec}^{b=0}(id^A, pc, k, dk) \overset{\text{def}}{=}$$
$$\text{new } s_1, s_2;$$
$$\text{in}(pc, (w_1, w_2, w_3));$$
$$\text{out}(s_1, \cdot); 0$$
$$| P_{123} | P_{132} | P_{213} | P_{231} | P_{312} | P_{321}$$
$$| \text{in}(s_2, \cdot); \text{in}(c, b); \text{ if } b = 0 \text{ then out}(c, (id^A, dk))$$

Fig. 4. Reconciliation process for $b = 0$

$$V_{rec}^{b=1}(id^A, pc, k, dv_1, dv_2, dv_3) \overset{\text{def}}{=}$$
$$\text{new } s_1, s_2;$$
$$\text{in}(pc, (w_1, w_2, w_3));$$
$$\text{out}(s_1, \cdot); 0$$
$$| P_{123} | P_{132} | P_{213} | P_{231} | P_{312} | P_{321}$$
$$| \text{in}(s_2, \cdot); \text{in}(c, b); \text{ if } b = 1 \text{ then out}(c, (id^A, dv_1, dv_2, dv_3))$$

Fig. 5. Reconciliation process for $b = 1$

5.3 Analysis Results

Unsurprisingly, it turns out that we have no privacy if W only contains tags of a single vehicle. It is necessary to ensure that the tags of both of the two honest vehicles are included in W, *i.e.* that W contains at least v_1^A (the tag emitted by vehicle A at its *route* location), and v_1^B (the tag emitted by the vehicle B at its *route* location). Actually, this is not sufficient since the server can still break privacy by sending a list with duplicates. An attack using this trick was reported by ProVerif.

With the above model P_S we performed several analyses by varying the sanity checks performed by the bulletin board. For the simplest case *without any checks* on W an attack is reported where arbitrary values are sent for $w_1 = w_2$ and w_3. This is a false attack caused by the way we match permutations in $V_{rec}^{b=1}$. We can investigate the need for checks by removing all $V_{rec}^{b=1}$. Then a real attack is reported: by sending arbitrary values for w_1 and w_2 and $w_3 = v_l$ the server can tell the cases apart when it sends $b = 0$.

In the case with W subject to *inclusion checks only* the attacker is allowed to choose w_2 but must send $w_1 = v_l$ (i.e. whichever tag was emitted in the left location) and $w_3 = v_r$ (whichever tag was emitted on the right). An attack is found when $w_2 = v_l$ by a comparison of the encrypted elements of U^i.

Finally, for the case with W subject to *inclusion checks and no duplicates* ProVerif is unable to conclude when *no duplicates* is interpreted as $w_2 \neq v_l \wedge w_2 \neq v_r$. However, if we interpret this as $w_2 = v_2^A \vee w_2 = v_3^A$, i.e. rather than using an arbitrary tag not equal to v_l or v_r, the attacker must specifically use one of the unused registered tags, ProVerif is able to prove the equivalence and thus the privacy property for our model.

5.4   Evaluation

We evaluate first the VPriv protocol, then our analysis. Results on the privacy-preserving properties of the protocol are largely positive, at least in our abstract model. We discovered only privacy breaches that are possible for an active attacker who can tamper with the list, not for an 'honest but curious' attacker who merely inspects the protocol trace. We proposed some checks that could be made on the list W to thwart even an active attacker. The check for no duplicates is easy enough for a single vehicle to apply, but the check that the list really contains the tags of other vehicles is less easy and may require a trusted third party.

Turning to our analysis, it should be clear that a reasonable amount of work was required to develop an abstract model suitable for ProVerif whilst preserving the features of the protocol. However, it was not our aim to formalise the protocol just to exemplify the use of ProVerif but rather to push the boundaries of the tool in terms of protocol features. As such we have succeeded in identifying several features that a future version of the tool might handle better, namely lists, permutations, and homomorphic encryption schemes.

6   Conclusion

We have presented a privacy analysis of the VPriv scheme for anonymous location-based vehicular services. We have shown how a notion of trace equivalence captures the privacy notion the protocol is intended to provide, and have formally verified this property, albeit for an abstract model of the protocol. During our analysis we uncovered a number of areas where special attention needs to be paid when implementing such a protocol. We also introduced novel features into formal privacy modelling such as random list permutations and reasoning about interactive zero-knowledge protocols.

In future work we plan to investigate proofs of soundness for abstractions in the context of privacy properties, and apply our method to other privacy-enhancing protocols. In particular, it would be interesting to investigate a more general approach to reasoning about zero-knowledge protocols using the ProVerif tool set.

References

1. Abadi, M., Fournet, C.: Mobile values, new names, and secure communication. In: Proc. 28th ACM Symposium on Principles of Programming Languages (POPL 2001), pp. 104–115. ACM Press, New York (2001)
2. Abadi, M., Gordon, A.: A calculus for cryptographic protocols: The spi calculus. In: Proc. 4th ACM Conference on Computer and Communications Security, Zurich, Switzerland, pp. 36–47. ACM Press, New York (1997)
3. Arapinis, M., Chothia, T., Ritter, E., Ryan, M.: Analysing unlinkability and anonymity using the applied pi calculus. In: Proc. 23rd IEEE Computer Security Foundations Symposium (CSF 2010), pp. 107–121. IEEE Computer Society Press, Los Alamitos (2010)
4. Backes, M., Maffei, M., Unruh, D.: Zero-knowledge in the applied pi-calculus and automated verification of the direct anonymous attestation protocol. In: Proc. Symposium on Security and Privacy (S&P 2008), pp. 202–215. IEEE Computer Society Press, Los Alamitos (2008)
5. Blanchet, B.: Cryptographic Protocol Verifier User Manual (2004), http://www.di.ens.fr/~blanchet/crypto/proverif-manual.ps.gz
6. Blanchet, B., Abadi, M., Fournet, C.: Automated verification of selected equivalences for security protocols. Journal of Logic and Algebraic Programming 75(1), 3–51 (2008)
7. Blumberg, A.J., Balakrishnan, H., Popa, R.: VPriv: Protecting privacy in location-based vehicular services. In: Proc. 18th Usenix Security Symposium (2009)
8. Bruso, M., Chatzikokolakis, K., den Hartog, J.: Formal verification of privacy for RFID systems. In: Proc. 23rd IEEE Computer Security Foundations Symposium (CSF 2010). IEEE Computer Society Press, Los Alamitos (2010)
9. Cortier, V., Delaune, S.: A method for proving observational equivalence. In: Proc. 22nd IEEE Computer Security Foundations Symposium (CSF 2009), Port Jefferson, NY, USA, pp. 266–276. IEEE Computer Society Press, Los Alamitos (2009)
10. Dahl, M., Delaune, S., Steel, G.: Formal analysis of privacy for vehicular mix-zones. In: Gritzalis, D., Preneel, B., Theoharidou, M. (eds.) ESORICS 2010. LNCS, vol. 6345, pp. 55–70. Springer, Heidelberg (2010)
11. Delaune, S., Ryan, M.D., Smyth, B.: Automatic verification of privacy properties in the applied pi-calculus. In: Proc. 2nd Joint iTrust and PST Conferences on Privacy, Trust Management and Security (IFIPTM 2008). IFIP Conference Proceedings, vol. 263, pp. 263–278. Springer, Heidelberg (2008)
12. Dikaiakos, M.D., Iqbal, S., Nadeem, T., Iftode, L.: VITP: an information transfer protocol for vehicular computing. In: Proc. 2nd International Workshop on Vehicular Ad Hoc Networks (VANET 2005), pp. 30–39 (2005)
13. Goldreich, O.: The Foundations of Cryptography, vol. 1. Cambridge University Press, Cambridge (2001)
14. IEEE. IEEE standard. IEEE Trial-Use Standard for Wireless Access in Vehicular Environments – Security Services for Applications and Management Messages, approved (June 8, 2006)

15. Kremer, S., Ryan, M.D.: Analysis of an electronic voting protocol in the applied pi-calculus. In: Sagiv, M. (ed.) ESOP 2005. LNCS, vol. 3444, pp. 186–200. Springer, Heidelberg (2005)
16. Lawson, N.: Highway to hell: Hacking toll systems. Presentation at Blackhat (2008), slides
    `http://rdist.root.org/2008/08/07/fastrak-talk-summary-and-slides/`
17. Milner, R.: A Calculus of Communication Systems. LNCS, vol. 92. Springer, Heidelberg (1980)

Formal Analysis of the EMV Protocol Suite

Joeri de Ruiter and Erik Poll

Digital Security Group
Institute for Computing and Information Science (ICIS)
Radboud University Nijmegen

Abstract. This paper presents a formal model of the EMV (Europay-MasterCard-Visa) protocol suite in F# and its analysis using the protocol verification tool ProVerif [5] in combination with FS2PV [4].

The formalisation covers all the major options of the EMV protocol suite, including all card authentication mechanisms and both on- and offline transactions. Some configuration parameters have to be fixed to allow any security analysis; here we follow the configuration of Dutch EMV banking cards, but the model could easily be adapted to other configurations.

As far as we know this is the first comprehensive formal description of EMV. The convenience and expressivity of F# proved to be a crucial advantage to make the formalisation of something as complex as EMV feasible. Even though the EMV specs amount to over 700 pages, our formal model is only 370 lines of code.

Formal analysis of our model with ProVerif is still possible, though this requires some care. Our formal analysis does not reveal any new weaknesses of the EMV protocol suite, but it does reveal all the known weaknesses, as a formal analysis of course should.

1 Introduction

EMV is the world's leading standard for payments with Integrated Circuit Cards (ICCs), i.e. bank or credit cards that incorporate a smartcard chip. The initiative for EMV was taken by Europay, MasterCard and Visa in the 1990s. Currently the EMV standard is maintained by EMVCo, a company jointly owned by MasterCard, Visa, American Express, and JCB. According to EMVCo, the number of EMV cards in use reached 1 billion in 2010. In Europe, the UK has already completed migration to EMV, and the rest of Western Europe is following suit as part of the Single Euro Payment Area (SEPA).

The EMV specifications[1] consist of four books [8,9,10,11], amounting to over 700 pages. These books do not define a single protocol, but a highly configurable tool-kit for payment protocols. For instance, it allows a choice between:

- three *Card Authentication Methods*: SDA, DDA, and CDA, discussed in more detail in Section 2;

---

[1] Publicly available from http://www.emvco.com

S. Mödersheim and C. Palamidessi (Eds.): TOSCA 2011, LNCS 6993, pp. 113–129, 2012.

- five *Cardholder Verification Methods*: none, signature, online PIN, offline unencrypted PIN, and offline encrypted PIN;
- on- and off-line transactions.

Moreover, many of these options are again parameterised, as explained in Section 2, possibly using proprietary data and formats. All these options and parameterisations make the EMV standard very difficult to comprehend, and a formal model to analyse the security implications all the more valuable.

Some weaknesses of certain EMV configurations are widely known and apparently accepted – at least by some issuers. For example, SDA cards can be cloned, and these clones can be used for offline transactions. The DDA mechanism that prevents such cloning authenticates the card but not the subsequent transaction, which led to a further improvement in the form of the CDA mechanism. More recently, a weakness in some configurations of EMV was discovered whereby a payment terminal can be fooled into thinking a payment was confirmed with PIN, when in reality it is not [12].

The rest of this paper is organised as follows. The EMV standard is explained in sections 2 and 3: Section 2 explains the fundamental concepts and terminology used in the standard, and then Section 3 describes the EMV protocols. Section 4 describes our formal F# model of EMV. Finally Section 5 discusses the security requirements for this formal model which have been verified using ProVerif.

2   EMV Fundamentals

This section explains the basic building blocks of EMV and some central concepts and terminology, and some of our notation.

In the EMV protocol several entities can be identified. First we have the customer, who is in possession of his EMV-compliant banking card, issued by his bank. The customer can use the card to perform a transaction at a merchant. The merchant has a terminal that can communicate with the customer's card. The terminal can also communicate over a secure channel with the bank, who has to authorise and perform the actual transaction. The terminal is trusted to provide the customer with secure input (a keypad that is trusted to enter the PIN code) and output (a display that is trusted to show transaction details).

Key Infrastructure. The essence of the key set-up in EMV is as follows:

- Every card has a unique symmetric key MK_{AC} that it shares with the issuer, derived from the issuer's master key MK_I. Using this key a session key SK_{AC} can be computed, based on the transaction counter.
- The issuer has a public-private key pair (P_I, S_I), and the terminal knows this public key P_I.
- Cards that support asymmetric crypto also have a public-private key pair (P_{IC}, S_{IC}).

This key setup is the basis of trust between the different parties.

This set-up provides cards with 2 mechanisms to prove authenticity of data:

1. All EMV cards can put MACs on messages, using the shared symmetric key with the issuing bank. The issuer can check these MACs, to verify authenticity of the messages, but the terminal cannot.
2. Cards that support asymmetric crypto can also digitally sign data to prove their authenticity to the terminal, as well as to the issuer.

We write H for hashing, encrypt for encrypting, and sign for signing.

Card Authentication Mechanisms (CAMs). The EMV standard defines three card authentication mechanisms: SDA, DDA, and CDA.

- In *SDA (Static Data Authentication)* the card provides some digitally signed data (including e.g. the card number and expiry date) to the terminal to authenticate itself. This allows the terminal to check the authenticity of this data, since it knows the issuer's public key, but does not rule out cloning.
- *DDA (Dynamic Data Authentication)* cards can do asymmetric crypto[2] and have a public/private key pair. DDA then involves a challenge-response mechanism, where the card proves its authenticity by signing a challenge chosen by the terminal using a private asymmetric key. Unlike SDA, this does rule out cloning.

  After the authentication of the card, DDA does not tie the subsequent transaction to that card. In other words, the terminal cannot verify that the transaction was actually carried out by the card.
- *CDA (Combined Data Authentication)* repairs this deficiency of DDA. With CDA the card digitally signs all important transaction data, not only authenticating the card, but also authenticating the transaction.

The data that is authenticated with SDA, referred to in the standard as *Static Data to be Authenticated*, is also authenticated with DDA or CDA. For these authentication methods a hash over the data is included in the certificate containing the public key of the card. In this sense DDA and CDA subsume SDA.

DOLs. An important concept in the EMV specification is that of *Data Object List*, or *DOL*. A DOL specifies a list of data elements, and the format of such a list. Example data elements are the card's *Application Transaction Counter (ATC)*, the transaction amount, the currency, the country code, and card- or terminal-chosen nonces.

An EMV card supplies several DOLs to the terminal. Different DOLs specify which data the card expects as inputs in some protocol step (and then also the format that this data has to be in) or which data the card will provide as (signed) output in some protocol step. This is explained in more detail in Section 3.

The use of these DOLs make EMV highly parameterisable. The choices for DOLs are of crucial importance for the overall security, as they control which

---

[2] This makes SDA cards cheaper than DDA cards, which seems to be SDA's raison d'être.

data gets signed or MACed, and hence no security analysis is possible without making some assumptions on the DOLs. Our model makes some assumptions on DOLs based on what we observed in Dutch bank and credit cards.

3 An EMV Protocol Session

An EMV protocol session can roughly be divided into four steps:

1. *initialisation*: selection of the application on the smartcard and reading of some data;
2. (optionally) *data authentication*, by means of SDA, DDA, or CDA;
3. (optionally) *cardholder verification*, by means of PIN or signature;
4. the actual *transaction*.

Each of these steps is described in more detail below. Here we use the usual semi-formal Alice-Bob style for security protocols, where square brackets indicate optional (parts of) messages. The card is here denoted by C, and the terminal by T.

3.1 Initialisation

In the first phase of the EMV session, the terminal obtains basic information about the card (such as card number and expiry date) and the information about the features the card supports and their configurations. This is information the terminal needs for the subsequent steps in the EMV session.

Optionally, the card may require some information from the terminal before providing this information, as specified in the first response.

> T → C: SELECT_APPLICATION
> C → T: [PDOL]
> T → C: GET_PROCESSING_OPTIONS [(data specified by the PDOL)]
> C → T: (AIP, AFL)
>   Repeat for all records in the AFL:
> T → C: READ_RECORD (i)
> C → T: (Contents of record i)

The protocol starts by selecting the payment application. In response to the selection, the card optionally provides a *Processing Options Data Object List (PDOL)*. The PDOL specifies which data, if any, the card wants from the terminal; this could for instance include the Terminal Country Code or the amount. Note that none of this data is authenticated.

The card then provides its *Application Interchange Profile (AIP)* and the *Application File Locator (AFL)*. The AIP consists of two bytes indicating the supported features (SDA/DDA/CDA/Cardholder verification/Issuer authentication) and whether terminal risk management should be performed.

The AFL is a list identifying the files to be used in the transaction. For each file it is indicated whether it is included in the offline data authentication; if so, the contents of this file is authenticated as part of the card authentication later.

The following files are mandatory:

– *Application Expiry Date*,
– *Application Primary Account Number (PAN)*,
– *Card Risk Management Data Object List 1 (CDOL1)*, and
– *Card Risk Management Data Object List 2 (CDOL2)*.

For cards that support SDA the *Signed Static Application Data (SSAD)* is also mandatory.

Note that none of the data provided by the card or by the terminal is authenticated at this stage. The process of card authentication, discussed below, will authenticate some of the data provided by the card.

3.2   Card Authentication

As already mentioned, there are three data authentication methods. The AIP tells the terminal which methods the cards supports, and the terminal should then choose the 'highest' method that both the card and itself support.

SDA. On cards that support SDA, the *Signed Static Application Data (SSAD)* is the signed hash of the concatenation of the files indicated by the AFL, optionally followed by the value of the AIP. Whether the AIP is included is indicated by the optional *Static Data Authentication Tag List*, which can be specified in a record. For SDA no additional communication is needed, since the data needed to verify the SSAD was already retrieved in the initialisation phase.

DDA. For DDA some additional communication is needed. DDA consists of two steps.

First, the certificate containing the card's public key is checked. This certificate also contains the hash of the concatenation of the files indicated by the AFL, so this authenticates the same static data that is authenticated with SDA.

Second, a challenge-response protocol is performed. For the challenge an `INTERNAL_AUTHENTICATE` message is sent to the card. The argument of this message is the data specified by the *Dynamic Data Authentication Data Object List (DDOL)*. The DDOL can be supplied by the card, otherwise a default DDOL should be present in the terminal. The DDOL always has to contain at least a terminal-generated nonce.

The *Signed Dynamic Application Data (SDAD)* is the signed *ICC Dynamic Data* and hash of the ICC Dynamic Data and data specified by the DDOL. The ICC Dynamic Data contains at least a time-variant parameter, e.g. a nonce or a transaction counter. On the bank and credit cards we studied, the DDOL only specified a terminal-generated nonce, and the ICC Dynamic Data only consisted of a card-generated nonce.

$$\text{T} \rightarrow \text{C: INTERNAL\_AUTHENTICATE(data specified by DDOL)}$$
$$\text{C} \rightarrow \text{T: sign}_{S_{IC}}(\text{ ICC Dynamic Data,}$$
$$\text{H(ICC Dynamic Data, data specified by DDOL) })$$

CDA. Card authentication using CDA does not require additional messages, but is combined with the actual transaction. As with DDA, the Static Data to be Authenticated is authenticated using the certificate for the public key of the card.

With CDA, the Signed Dynamic Application Data (SDAD) is a signature on a card-generated nonce, the CID, the cryptogram, the *Transaction Data Hash Code (TDHC)* and a terminal-generated nonce (specified by the CDOL1 and CDOL2):

$$\text{SDAD} = \text{sign}_{S_{IC}}(\text{ nonce}_{IC}, \text{CID}, \text{AC}, \text{TDHC},$$
$$\text{H}(\text{nonce}_{IC}, \text{CID}, \text{AC}, \text{TDHC}, \text{nonce}_{Terminal})).$$

Here the TDHC is a hash of the elements specified by the PDOL, the elements specified by the CDOL1, the elements specified by the CDOL2 (in case of the second GENERATE_AC command) and the elements returned by the card in the response.

3.3   Cardholder Verification

Cardholder verification can be done in several ways: by a PIN, a handwritten signature, or it can simply not be done. The process to decide which *Cardholder Verification Method (CVM)* is used – if any – is quite involved. The card provides the terminal with its list of CVM Rules, that specify under which conditions which CVMs are acceptable, in order of decreasing preference. The terminal then chooses the CVM to be used. In all Dutch banking cards we inspected, the CVM List is included in the Static Data to be Authenticated.

If cardholder verification is done by means of a PIN, there are three options:

– online PIN, in which case the bank checks the PIN;
– offline plaintext PIN, in which case the chip checks the PIN, and the PIN is transmitted to the chip in the clear;
– offline encrypted PIN, in which case the chip checks the PIN, and the PIN is encrypted before it is sent to the card.

Note that the card is only involved in cardholder verification in case of offline – plaintext or encrypted – PIN, as detailed below. Encrypting the PIN requires a card that supports asymmetric crypto. Online PIN verification is performed using a different protocol between the terminal and the bank. In this case the card is not involved in the cardholder verification.

Offline Plaintext PIN Verification. With plaintext PIN verification the PIN code is sent in plain to the card, which in its turn will return an unauthenticated response indicating whether the PIN was correct or how many failed PIN attempts there are left before the card blocks.

T → C: VERIFY(pin)
C → T: Success/ (PIN_failed, tries_left) / Failed

Offline Enciphered PIN Verification. If the verification is done using the encrypted PIN, the terminal first requests a nonce from the card. Using the public key of the card, the terminal encrypts the PIN together with the nonce and some random padding created by the terminal. The result of the verification is then returned unauthenticated to the terminal.

T → C: GET_CHALLENGE
C → T: nonce$_{IC}$
T → C: VERIFY(encrypt$_{P_{IC}}$(pin, nonce$_{IC}$, random_padding))
C → T: Success/ (PIN_failed, tries_left) / Failed

3.4   The Transaction

In the final step of an EMV session, after the optional card authentication and card holder verification, the actual transaction is performed. Transactions can be offline or online. The terminal chooses which it wants to use, but the card may refuse to do a transaction offline and force the terminal to do an online transaction instead.

For a transaction the card generates one or two cryptograms: one in the case of an offline transaction, and two in the case of an online transaction.

- In an offline transaction the card provides a proof to the terminal that a transaction took place by means of a *Transaction Certificate (TC)*, which the terminal sends to the issuer later.
- In an online transaction the card first provides an *Authorisation Request Cryptogram (ARQC)* which the terminal forwards to the issuer for approval. If the card receives approval, the card then provides a Transaction Certificate (TC) as proof that the transaction has been completed.

In both on- and offline transactions the card can also choose to refuse or abort the transaction, in which case an *Application Authentication Cryptogram (AAC)* is provided instead of TC or ARQC.

Below we first discuss the different types of cryptograms, before we describe the protocol steps for off- and online transactions.

Cryptograms. Using the GENERATE_AC command, the terminal can ask the card to compute one of the types of cryptograms mentioned above, i.e. TC, ARQC or AAC.

Arguments of the GENERATE_AC command tell the card which type of cryptograms to produce and whether CDA has to be used. Additional arguments that have to be supplied by the terminal are specified by CDOL1 and CDOL2. CDA is only performed on TC or ARQC messages, and not on AAC messages.

The response always contains

- the Cryptogram Information Data (CID),
- the Application Transaction Counter (ATC) and
- an Application Cryptogram (AC) or proprietary cryptogram.

Optionally, the response may contain

- the Issuer Application Data (IAD),
- other proprietary data,

– the Signed Dynamic Application Data (SDAD), namely if CDA is requested and the type of the response message is not AAC.

The cryptogram returned by the card can either be in the format specified in the EMV standard, or in a proprietary format. Since we do not know how the cryptogram is computed on the Dutch banking cards, we follow the recommendations from the EMV specification. Here a MAC is computed using the symmetric key SK_{AC}, which is shared between the card and the issuer, on a minimum set of recommended data elements. The recommended minimum set of elements to be included in the AC is specified in Book 2, Section 8.1.1. It consists of the amount, terminal country, terminal verification results, currency, date, transaction type, terminal nonce, AIP and ATC. The AIP and ATC are data provided by the card, the other elements are provided by the terminal in the CDOL1 and CDOL2.

Additionally, if CDA is used, the card also returns the SDAD over the response using its private key P_{IC} so that the terminal can check the authenticity of the complete message.

Both CDOL1 and CDOL2 always include a terminal-generated nonce. A CDOL might request a *Transaction Certificate Hash*, which is a hash on the elements in the *Transaction Certificate Data Object List (TDOL)*. The TDOL might be provided by the card, or a default by the terminal can be used.

If no CDA is performed, the response to a GENERATE_AC command consists of the CID, the ATC, the AC and optionally the IAD. When performing CDA, the AC is replaced by the SDAD.

The GENERATE_AC command starts with a parameter indicating the type of AC that is requested. The boolean parameter cda_requested specifies whether a CDA signature is requested.

T → C: GENERATE_AC (TC, cda_requested, data specified by the CDOL1)

C → T: TC = (CID, ATC, MAC, [IAD])

where $MAC = MAC_{SK_{IC}}$(amount, terminal country, terminal verification results, currency, date, transaction type, terminal nonce, AIP, ATC).

The card may refuse to do the transaction offline, and generate an ARQC cryptogram instead of the requested TC, forcing the terminal to go online.

In an online transaction the EXTERNAL_AUTHENTICATE command is used to pass the issuer's response to the ARQC back to the card. Alternatively, this response can be passed as a parameter of the next GENERATE_AC command.

4   Formalisation in F#

The complete formal model for card and terminal can be found online.[3] The issuer is not yet considered in the model. For the security properties considered in Section 5 we do not need the issuer.

We assume that the channel between the card and terminal is public, i.e. a man-in-the-middle can intercept and modify all communication. Since the cards are provided by the bank, we assume that there are no dishonest cards. The terminal is assumed to have secure input and output with the customer.

---

[3] Available from http://www.cs.ru.nl/~joeri/

Card and Terminal Configuration Options. For both card and terminal the model includes a number of boolean parameters that describe their configuration parameters. For the card these parameters include

- sda, dda, cda: three booleans that define which card authentication mechanisms are supported;[4]
- force_online: a boolean that determines whether the card will force the transaction to go online if the terminal starts an offline transaction.

For the terminal these parameters include

- pin_enabled: can the terminal check pin codes?
- online_enabled: is the transaction forced online by the terminal?

When analysing the model we have the choice between fixing certain values of these parameters, or leaving them open. Advantage of the second approach is that properties of multiple configurations can be verified in one go. Disadvantage is that the model may be too complicated for ProVerif to verify (within a reasonable response time), in which case some of these parameters should be fixed. For a bank issuing a specific type of card, it would be fine to fix all the parameters for the card; still, one should then consider all the possible terminal behaviours this card might encounter.

In our model, after the data has been read, the terminal optionally performs card authentication and cardholder verification, and then, for a fresh card-generated nonce and new value of the transaction counter, it provides at most two cryptograms as requested by the terminal and described in Section 3: (either just a TC or AAC, or an ARQC followed by a TC, or an ARQC followed by an AAC).

DOLs

Although our model leaves many configuration options for card and terminal open, as described above, the values of the DOLs have to be fixed and hard-coded in the model. Given that the DOLs determine which data is signed or MACed in various protocol steps, we cannot expect to do any security analysis without at least making some minimal assumptions.

The DOLs in our model are based on what we observed on Dutch bank and credit cards:

- PDOL: the empty list
- DDOL: $(\text{nonce}_{Terminal})$
- CDOL1: $(\text{amount, CVM Results, nonce}_{Terminal})$, where the *CVM Results (Cardholder Verification Method Results)* contains the result of the cardholder verification.
- CDOL2: $(\text{nonce}_{Terminal})$
- TDOL: not used

---

[4] The EMV specs apparently allow cards to support more than one card authentication mechanism, though this seems strange. Actual cards we observed always provide just one, namely SDA or DDA.

These are not the precise DOLs of the bank cards we looked at, but rather subsets (or sub-lists) of them. For readability we omitted some of the data elements. For the properties we wanted to verify, omitting these data elements is safe: if with the DOLs above it is impossible to fake messages, then for DOLs with more data elements – which would result in the inclusion of *more* data elements in digital signatures, (signed) hashes, or MACs, it is still impossible to fake messages.

Adding Events to Express Security Requirements. To express interesting security properties, our formal model is augmented with *events* that mark important steps in the protocol by different participants. Without these, all that can be verified are confidentiality properties, as these are 'built-in' to ProVerif.

Events added to the model are

- `CardVerifyPIN(success)`: a failed or successful verification of the PIN code by the card.
- `TerminalVerifyPIN(success)`: a failed or successful verification of the PIN code by the terminal.
- `CardTransactionInit(atc,sda,dda,cda,pan)`: the card starting an EMV session.
- `TerminalSDA(success, pan)`, `TerminalDDA(success, pan)`, `TerminalCDA(success,atc,ac_type)`, and `TerminalCDA2(success,atc,ac_type)`: a failed or successful data authentication by the terminal.
- `TerminalTransactionFinish(sda,dda,cda,pan,atc,success)`:the terminal completing a transaction.
- `CardTransactionFinish(sda,dda,cda,pan,atc,success)`: similarly, the card completing a transaction.

Here `success`, `sda`, `dda`, `cda`, are boolean parameters to indicate success or failure and describe the card authentication mechanism used, while `atc` and `pan` are integer parameters for the card's Application Transaction Counter and Primary Account Number.

Translation to ProVerif. Using the FS2PV tool [4], our F# model can be translated to a model in the applied pi calculus, which can then be analysed using the ProVerif tool [5], as discussed in the next section. The model grows substantially in size with this translation: whereas the F# model is 370 lines of code, the resulting ProVerif model is 2527 lines of code. The increase in size is caused by the many if-statements in the F# model – which result in duplications of large fragments of code in the applied pi calculus – and the (convenient) use of functions in F#.

In fact, initially we tried to formalise the EMV protocol in the applied pi calculus, but we gave up as the model became too complex to oversee.

5   Security Requirements

For the resulting ProVerif model we have verified three types of properties: sanity checks, secrecy requirements, and, most interestingly of all, integrity and authenticity requirements.

The F# code models a card that performs a single transaction. For most security properties we want to consider cards performing multiple transactions. For this we have to edit the generated ProVerif code, by simply adding ! for repetition in the right place.

Sanity Checks. A silly mistake in the formal model could cause a deadlock, in some or all the branches of the protocol, preventing these branches from ever being completed, and then making some security properties for these branches trivially true. To detect this, we have checked that all events are triggered, so it is possible to reach all events and hence perform all possible variations of the protocol.

Confidentiality. The confidentiality requirements for EMV are the usual ones, namely confidentiality of the private asymmetric keys and the shared symmetric keys.

Integrity and Authenticity. To check for integrity and authenticity we make use of two types of ProVerif queries. First we use the type

```
ev:Event1() ==> ev:Event2()
```

This query checks if event Event1 was executed, then event Event2 was executed.
    The second type of query to verify is

```
evinj:Event1() ==> evinj:Event2()
```

In this case, for every execution of event Event1 there exists a distinct executed event Event2.

Card authentication. If the terminal successfully performs a card authentication, it should be the highest card authentication method supported by both the card and the terminal, to rule out forced fall-back, e.g. from DDA to SDA. To check this, we verified the following two queries:

```
ev:TerminalSDA(True(),pan) ==>
ev:CardTransactionInit(atc,True(),False(),False(),pan)
```

and

```
ev:TerminalDDA(True(),pan) ==>
ev:CardTransactionInit(atc,sda,True(),False(),pan)
```

The PAN is unique for each card, so these queries express that if a terminal successfully performs SDA or DDA this was the highest supported card authentication method. Both queries are evaluated to true by ProVerif for multiple transactions per card, so no fallback can be forced.
    The particular EMV configuration that we model, based on our observations of Dutch banking cards, is of importance here. The only reason that rollbacks of the card authentication method are not possible is that the AIP, which contains

the data authentication methods that are supported by the card, is included in the data that is authenticated as part of SDA, DDA and CDA[5].

To prevent replay, we also want the card to participate in each data authentication. This is checked by using so-called injectivity in the queries:

```
evinj:TerminalSDA(True(),pan) ==>
evinj:CardTransactionInit(atc,sda,dda,cda,pan)
```

and

```
evinj:TerminalDDA(True(),pan) ==>
evinj:CardTransactionInit(atc,sda,dda,cda,pan)
```

These queries state that if a terminal completes an authentication, the corresponding card (with that PAN) is in fact involved.

ProVerif was not able to prove the first query when considering multiple sessions per card. However, with a single transaction per card the query evaluates to false. If this query does not hold with a single session per card, it will also not hold with multiple sessions per card. This result is as expected, as SDA allows replays. The second query could again be proved for multiple sessions per card. This query evaluated to true, as the challenge-response mechanism used in DDA does not allow replays.

Customer authentication. If the customer is authenticated using his PIN code, the terminal and card should agree on whether the PIN was accepted or not. To check this the following query is used:

```
evinj:TerminalVerifyPIN(True()) ==> evinj:CardVerifyPIN(True())
```

ProVerif tells that this query is false. The root cause is that the response of the card to an attempted (offline) PIN verification is not authenticated, so a man-in-the-middle attack could fake it. This weakness is exploited in the attack by Murdoch et al. [12].

Transaction authenticity. If a transaction is successfully completed by the terminal, the corresponding card should also agree on having the transaction completed successfully. This is checked using the following query:

```
evinj:TerminalTransactionFinish(sda,dda,cda,pan,atc,True())
==>
evinj:CardTransactionFinish(sda2,dda2,cda2,pan,atc,True())
```

Not surprisingly, this query evaluates to false, as both SDA and DDA do not authenticate the transaction in any way that the terminal can verify.

When using CDA, the card and terminal should agree on the result of the transaction, i.e. if CDA is successful performed and the transaction is concluded

---

[5] Not including this AIP in the data that is authenticated is allowed by the EMV specs, but obviously a bad choice, and one that the specs could warn against, or even disallow.

with a TC message at the terminal side, the card should also successfully have completed the transaction. This is checked using the following queries:

```
evinj:TerminalCDA(True(),atc,DataTC()) ==>
evinj:CardTransactionFinish(sda,dda,cda,pan,atc,True())
```

and

```
evinj:TerminalCDA2(True(),atc,DataTC()) ==>
evinj:CardTransactionFinish(sda,dda,cda,pan,atc,True())
```

For both queries the result is true for cards with multiple transactions. Using CDA thus guarantees that both the card and terminal agree on successful transactions.

Experiences using ProVerif. We ran ProVerif on a machine with an Intel Core i5-M540 processor at 2.53 GHz and 4GB of RAM memory. The running times for the final model range from 5 seconds for the sanity checks to around 5 minutes for the more complex queries.

When constructing the model, usually ProVerif could verify the properties we were interested in a few minutes. Occasionally, it would take hours. To reduce the time needed to verify, we removed types from the functions used and tried to reduce the number of if-statements. Small changes in the F# model could result in quite different ProVerif code. For example using a boolean condition b in an if-statement resulted at one point in ProVerif not being able to compute the result within hours. Changing the condition to $b = true$ resulted in code being verified by ProVerif within minutes.

6   Including the Issuer

When extending the model with the issuer we can check not only whether the card and terminal agree on the details of the transaction, but also whether the issuer agrees. This is for example interesting for online transactions, where the terminal relies on the response by the issuer in accepting or denying the transaction. In an extension of the previously discussed model we included the issuer in the code for the terminal, as we assume the communication between the terminal and the issuer to be secure. Since we did not know how the MACs in the cryptograms are actually computed we used the recommended minimum set of elements to be included as specified in the EMV standard [9, Page 88]. These included elements are amount, terminal country, Terminal Verification Results, currency, date, transaction type, terminal generated nonce, Application Interchange Profile and Application Transaction Counter. Notice that the type of the cryptogram is not included in this set of data elements. This resulted in a new weakness found by ProVerif in our model. If a transaction is declined by the card by sending an AAC to the terminal, a man-in-the-middle could change the type of the message to a TC. This would result in the terminal and issuer accepting the transaction, tough the card denied the transaction. This attack does not work if CDA is used, as changing the message type would invalidate the signature on the message. This is a theoretical weakness, as we do not know how the banks implemented the actual Dconstruction of the cryptograms.

7   Conclusions

We have presented a first formal model of the EMV protocol suite and demonstrated that it can be analysed using ProVerif in combination with FS2PV.

Our model covers all the important options for card and terminal, including all card authentication methods (SDA, DDA, CDA) and transaction types (on- and offline). For some of the configuration parameters, the so-called DOLs, minimal assumptions are hard-coded in the model; these can easily be changed, but analysis of EMV without making assumptions about the DOLs is clearly impossible.

Given the size complexity of the EMV specifications, the formal model is surprisingly small. The model still fits on 5 pages. The use of F# as modelling language was crucial to keep the formalisation tractable. Our initial attempts to model EMV in applied pi calculus failed, and the use of if-statements and function in F# were a huge improvement to keep the model comprehensible. Indeed, whereas the F# is 370 lines, the generated ProVerif code by FS2PV is 2527 lines. Admittedly, a handwritten ProVerif model might be smaller, but this comes at the cost of readability.

Of course, our model abstracts from some of the low-level details that are in the 700-odd pages EMV specs, e.g. about byte- and bit-level encodings of data. Such abstraction seems crucial to keep an overview and understand the standard as a whole. The EMV specs make very little attempt at providing useful levels of abstractions, apart from use of a standard Tag-Length-Value (TLV) encoding.

We had to come up with the security requirements to verify ourselves, as these are at best very implicit in the official specs. We expected this might be hard, but the rather generic security requirement – that after a transaction all parties agree on all that transaction's parameters – captures the essential security requirement in an intuitive and easy way.

Our formal analysis reveals all the known weaknesses and limitations in the security of the EMV protocol suite, e.g. the possibilities

- to use cloned SDA cards for offline transactions,
- to fake transactions with DDA cards used offline, and
- to fool a terminal into thinking a PIN was correctly entered [12].

Moreover, these problems *inevitably* come to light when trying to establish the very generic security requirement that whenever a transaction is completed, all parties agree on the transaction's parameters (incl. whether it was with/without PIN, off- or online, on the amount, and on the card authentication mechanism used).

The most recent attack published on EMV is a man-in-the-middle attack that forces a rollback to unencrypted offline PIN, which then allows the plaincode PIN code to be observed [2]. (In this attack the CVM list provided by the card is modified; suprisingly, this attack may be possible even when the CVM list is signed, which it typically is, i.e. when the terminal can tell the CVM list has been modified.) This attack does not come up in our analysis, because our model excludes the complex process by which the terminal decides which Cardholder Verification Method to use, and simply always does offline unencrypted PIN.

Given the complexity of the EMV specifications, and the bewildering range of options and parameters, we hope that our formal model can be a useful tool in evaluating the security of different EMV configurations – or of other protocols, such as EMV-CAP [7], that have been defined on top of EMV.

Related Work. Even though the EMV specifications are public, and obviously very important, there has been surprisingly little public scrutiny of them. Possibly the large size of the specifications, or the fact that they cannot be analysed without fixing some of the configurations and parameters, have discouraged people. A brief overview of EMV is given in [6], but this mainly discusses the cryptographic primitives and the PKI, and does not go into details about the actual protocol. EMV security is analysed in [13], but with the view to using it for internet payments.

Researchers at the university of Cambridge have been studying EMV for quite some time [1], e.g. investigating the possibility of relay attacks, the security of the EMV API in HSMs (Hardware Security Modules), and discovering a weakness in EMV configurations of some UK banks [12]. They also reverse-engineered and investigated EMV-CAP, a proprietary MasterCard protocol for internet banking and online payments that builds on EMV [7].

Future Work. We still want to extend our model to include the issuer. Instead of using ProVerif in combination with FS2PV, we also want to experiment with verification using F7 [3]. This avoids the translation from F# to ProVerif, and might produce better and more predictable response times in verification.

Our F# models are executable. By supplying the right helper functions to deal with the low level details of smartcard communication, it should be possible to interact with real cards and terminals (i.e. have the F# terminal model interact with real EMV smartcards, and – using special but readily available hardware to provide a smartcard interface to a laptop – have the F# card model card interact with a real EMV terminal). This would provide the strongest possible guarantee that our formalisation is indeed correct, as well as a highly trustworthy terminal implementation.

Finally, it would also be interesting to see if the F# models would be useful for (model-based) testing of terminals and cards, or for security code reviews.

Acknowledgements. Thanks to Karthikeyan Bhargavan and Andy Gordon for producing a patch for FS2PV. This work is supported by the European Commission, through the ICT programme under contract ICT-2007-216676 ECRYPT II, and the Netherlands Organisation for Scientific Research (NWO).

References

1. Adida, B., Bond, M., Clulow, J., Lin, A., Murdoch, S., Anderson, R., Rivest, R.: Phish and chips: Traditional and new recipes for attacking EMV. In: Christianson, B., Crispo, B., Malcolm, J.A., Roe, M. (eds.) Security Protocols. LNCS, vol. 5087, pp. 40–48. Springer, Heidelberg (2009)
2. Barisani, A., Bianco, D., Laurie, A., Franken, Z.: Chip & PIN is definitely broken. Presentation at CanSecWest Applied Security Conference, Vancouver (2011), slides `http://dev.inversepath.com/download/emv/emv_2011.pdf`
3. Bhargavan, K., Fournet, C., Gordon, A.: Modular verification of security protocol code by typing. ACM SIGPLAN Notices 45(1), 445–456 (2010)
4. Bhargavan, K., Fournet, C., Tse, S.: Verified interoperable implementations of security protocols. In: Computer Security Foundations Workshop (CSFW), pp. 139–152. IEEE, Los Alamitos (2006)
5. Blanchet, B.: An efficient cryptographic protocol verifier based on Prolog rules. In: Computer Security Foundations Workshop (CSFW), pp. 82–96. IEEE, Los Alamitos (2001)
6. de Soete, M., Ward, M.: EMV. In: van Tilborg, H. (ed.) Encyclopedia of Cryptography and Security, pp. 197–202. Springer, Heidelberg (2005)
7. Drimer, S., Murdoch, S., Anderson, R.: Optimised to fail: Card readers for online banking. In: Dingledine, R., Golle, P. (eds.) FC 2009. LNCS, vol. 5628, pp. 184–200. Springer, Heidelberg (2009)
8. EMVCo. EMV– Integrated Circuit Card Specifications for Payment Systems, Book 1: Application Independent ICC to Terminal Interface Requirements (2008)
9. EMVCo. EMV– Integrated Circuit Card Specifications for Payment Systems, Book 2: Security and Key Management (2008)
10. EMVCo. EMV– Integrated Circuit Card Specifications for Payment Systems, Book 3: Application Specification (2008)
11. EMVCo. EMV– Integrated Circuit Card Specifications for Payment Systems, Book 4: Cardholder, Attendant, and Acquirer Interface Requirements (2008)
12. Murdoch, S., Drimer, S., Anderson, R., Bond, M.: Chip and PIN is Broken. In: Symposium on Security and Privacy, pp. 433–446. IEEE, Los Alamitos (2010)
13. Van Herreweghen, E., Wille, U.: Risks and potentials of using EMV for internet payments. In: Proceedings of the 1st USENIX Workshop on Smartcard Technology, USENIX Association (1999)

Glossary

- AAC - Application Authentication Cryptogram
- AC - Application Cryptogram, which can be an AAC, ARCQ, or TC
- AFL - Application File Locator; identifies files on the card, and indicates whether their content is included in the SSAD
- AIP - Application Interchange Profile; indicates which authentication options the card supports
- ARQC - Authorisation Request Cryptogram
- ATC - Application Transaction Counter
- CAM - Card Authentication Method
- CVM - Cardholder Verification Method

- CDA - Combined Data Authentication
- CDOL - Card Risk Management DOL
- CID - Cryptogram Information Data; indicates the type of the cryptogram and the actions to be performed by the terminal
- DDA - Dynamic Data Authentication
- DDOL - Dynamic Data Authentication DOL
- DOL - Data Object List
- IAD - Issuer Application Data; proprietary data to be sent to the issuer
- MAC - Message Authentication Code
- PAN - Primay Account Number
- PDOL - Processing Options DOL
- SDA - Static Data Authentication
- SSAD - Signed Static Application Data; used in SDA
- SDAD - Signed Dynamic Application Data; used in DDA and CDA
- TC - Transaction Certificate
- TDHC - Transaction Data Hash Code; used in CDA
- TDOL - Transaction Certificate DOL

Security Goals and Protocol Transformations[*]

Joshua D. Guttman

Worcester Polytechnic Institute

Abstract. Cryptographic protocol designers work incrementally. Having achieved some goals for confidentiality and authentication in a protocol Π_1, they transform it to a richer Π_2 to achieve new goals.

But do the original goals still hold? More precisely, if a goal formula Γ holds whenever Π_1 runs against an adversary, does a translation of Γ hold whenever Π_2 runs against it?

We prove that a transformation preserves goal formulas if a labeled transition system for analyzing Π_1 simulates a portion of an LTS for analyzing Π_2, while preserving progress in that portion.

Thus, we examine the process of analyzing a protocol Π. We use LTSs that describe *our* activity when *analyzing Π*, not that of the principals *executing Π*. Each analysis step considers—for an observed message reception—what earlier transmissions would explain it. The LTS then contains a transition from a fragmentary execution containing the reception to a richer one containing an explaining transmission. The strand space protocol analysis tool CPSA generates some of the LTSs used.

1 Introduction

Protocol design is an art of reuse. A few basic patterns for achieving authentication and confidentiality—despite actively malicious parties—are frequently adapted to new contexts. Designers combine these patterns, piggy-backing values on top of them, to solve many problems. The transformations modify message structure; add new transmissions or receptions on a given role; and add entirely new roles. Constructing protocols may be difficult, particularly for interactions involving more than two participants: Some data values may be shared among subsets of the participants, while remaining hidden from the other participants. Designers use existing protocols as heuristics for parts of the protocol, welding the parts cleverly together, so that the transformed protocol preserves the goals achieved by the components, while achieving additional goals.

Our goal here is not to make this cleverness unnecessary, but to explain it semantically. Thm. 2 justifies inferring that a transformed protocol satisfies some security goals, when the source protocol did. Although a logical result about models of protocol behavior and the formulas they satisfy, it is a corollary of a logic-free theorem (Thm. 1). The latter concerns only fragments of protocol executions (called *skeletons*), the information-preserving maps (*homomorphisms*) between them, and some labeled transition systems. These LTSs formalize the

---

[*] Supported by the National Science Foundation under grant CNS-0952287.

S. Mödersheim and C. Palamidessi (Eds.): TOSCA 2011, LNCS 6993, pp. 130–147, 2012.

activity of protocol analysis. Reifying the protocol analysis activity into LTSs, and explaining relations between protocols using them, are new in this paper.

Although these results help us avoid verifying the transformed protocol directly, they also have a deeper value. They suggest design principles for incremental construction of protocols. We expect future work to lead to *syntactic* conditions that imply that a transformation preserves security goals. Protocol design, now a hit-or-miss activity requiring experience and ingenuity, could become a more predictable and possibly tool-supported process.

Structure of this paper. Section 2 introduces two protocols, with two transformations between them, motivating a definition of transformation (Def. 2). Section 3 analyzes these protocols, illustrating how a transformation can preserve the activity of protocol analysis. Section 4 axiomatizes these analysis activities, representing them as labeled transition systems. A simulation-plus-progress relation on LTSs ensures that a transformation does not create counterexamples to security goals (Section 5). Section 6 defines classical first order languages $\mathcal{L}(\Pi)$, and defines security goal translations. We lift Thm. 1 to satisfaction of goals (Thm. 2) in Section 7, and comment on related and future work.

Strand Spaces. We work within the strand space theory [18]. A **strand** is the sequence of message transmissions and message receptions executed by a single principal in a single protocol session. Transmission and reception events jointly are **nodes**. We will write strands, either horizontally or vertically, as sequences of bullets connected by double arrows: $\bullet \Rightarrow \bullet$. (See [18, Sec. 2.4].)

A **protocol** Π consists of a finite set of strands, called the **roles** of the protocol, possibly annotated with some trust assumptions that we will not need here. We give each Π a "listener" role, consisting of a single node receiving a message t, which can witness for the disclosure of t. An **instance** of a role $\rho \in \Pi$ results from choosing values from some reasonable algebra $\mathfrak{M}$ of messages for ρ's parameters. We formalize this choice by applying a substitution α to ρ, where a substitution α means a homomorphism from $\mathfrak{M}$ to itself. The strand $\alpha(\rho)$ is the sequence of transmissions and receptions in which each message in ρ is instantiated according to α. That is, each parameter x appearing in ρ is replaced by $\alpha(x)$. Each strand $\alpha(\rho)$ is a **regular** behavior of some principal in Π, i.e. a local session in which the principal complies with Π. (See [18, Sec. 2.5].)

A fragmentary execution, called a **skeleton**, consists of a number of regular strands of Π, or their initial segments. A skeleton $\mathbb{A}$ consists of its regular nodes, equipped with (i) a partial ordering $\preceq_{\mathbb{A}}$, akin to the Lamport causal ordering [22]; (ii) some assumptions unique($\mathbb{A}$) about freshly chosen values; and (iii) some assumptions non($\mathbb{A}$) about uncompromised long term keys. (See [18, Def. 3.1].)

A skeleton $\mathbb{A}$ is **realized** if, whenever n is a reception node in $\mathbb{A}$, an adversary can obtain or construct its message t, without violating the assumptions unique($\mathbb{A}$) and non($\mathbb{A}$). No value assumed freshly chosen should equal a guessed or independently chosen value. No long term key assumed uncompromised should be used by the adversary. (See [18, Defs. 3.2–4].) A realized skeleton is a full execution. When node n receives t, then the adversary obtains t, or can derive it using transmissions prior to n in the partial ordering $\preceq_{\mathbb{A}}$.

Any skeleton $\mathbb{A}$ represents a set of realized skeletons $\mathbb{B}$. These are the executions in which at least the transmissions and receptions in $\mathbb{A}$ have occurred, possibly made more specific by a substitution α, and node ordering extends $\preceq_{\mathbb{A}}$. Moreover, the assumptions $\alpha(\mathsf{unique}(\mathbb{A}))$ and $\alpha(\mathsf{non}(\mathbb{A}))$—i.e. the images of $\mathsf{unique}(\mathbb{A})$ and $\mathsf{non}(\mathbb{A})$ under α—must be satisfied.

Definition 1. The concatenation of two messages t_0 and t_1 is $t_0 \hat{\ } t_1$, and the (asymmetric) encryption of t using the public encryption key of B is $\{\!|t|\!\}_{\mathsf{pk}(B)}$.

The ith node along a strand s, starting from 1, is $s \downarrow i$.

We write $t_0 \sqsubseteq t_1$ to mean that message t_0 is an **ingredient** in t_1, i.e. that t_0 is a subterm of t_1 considering plaintexts but not the keys used to prepare encryptions. That is, $\sqsubseteq$ is the smallest reflexive transitive relation such that $t_0 \sqsubseteq \{\!|t_0|\!\}_K$; $t_0 \sqsubseteq t_0 \hat{\ } t_1$, and $t_1 \sqsubseteq t_0 \hat{\ } t_1$. The key K used in an encryption $\{\!|t_0|\!\}_K$ is not an ingredient of it, however, unless it was an ingredient of t_0 (contrary to good practice). For instance, $N_b \sqsubseteq \{\!|N_b \hat{\ } B|\!\}_{\mathsf{pk}(A)}$, but $\mathsf{pk}(A) \not\sqsubseteq \{\!|N_b \hat{\ } B|\!\}_{\mathsf{pk}(A)}$.

A message t_0 **originates at** a node n iff n is a transmission node, $t_0 \sqsubseteq \mathsf{msg}(n)$, and for all m such that $m \Rightarrow^+ n$, $t_0 \not\sqsubseteq \mathsf{msg}(m)$. Thus, t_0 originates at n when it was transmitted as an ingredient, but was neither transmitted nor received earlier on the same strand.

If $\rho \in \Pi$ is a role of protocol Π, then $\mathsf{instances}(\rho)$ is the set of instances of ρ, i.e. the set $\{\alpha(\rho) \colon \alpha$ is a substitution$\}$. The (larger) set of strands that agree with a member of $\mathsf{instances}(\rho)$ on the first i nodes is defined: $\mathsf{instances}(\rho|_i) = \{s \colon \exists r \in \mathsf{instances}(\rho) . \forall j \leq i . s \downarrow j = r \downarrow j\}$. So $\mathsf{instances}(\rho|_i)$ contains a strand if it is indistinguishable from a run of ρ while only i events have occurred. If $r \in \mathsf{instances}(\rho)$ agrees with s up to i, then r is an $\mathsf{instances}(\rho|_i)$-**witness for** s.

2   Some Protocol Transformations

The Protocol HD. HD, one of the simplest possible authentication protocols, is a half-duplex, authentication-only subprotocol of Needham-Schroeder [24]. It is shown in Fig. 1. HD gives the initiator an authentication guarantee that the responder has participated; it gives the responder no guarantee. HD does not establish any shared secret. The top half of the figure shows the initiator role, first transmitting the encrypted message for B and then receiving the freed nonce N. The bottom half shows the responder role, first receiving the encrypted message and then freeing and transmitting N'. A regular strand of HD is any instance of either one of these roles, using any values for the parameters N, B, N', B'. We do not show the listener role in this or other protocol diagrams, since it is always present, and simply passively receives a message t.

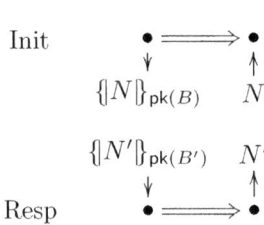

Init

$\{\!|N|\!\}_{\mathsf{pk}(B)}$ N

$\{\!|N'|\!\}_{\mathsf{pk}(B')}$ N'

Resp

Fig. 1. Protocol HD

A skeleton $\mathbb{A}$ over HD contains any number of these regular strands, and selects sets of freshness and non-compromise assumptions $\mathsf{unique}(\mathbb{A})$ and $\mathsf{non}(\mathbb{A})$. $\mathbb{A}$ is realized if an adversary can synthesize the message received on each reception node, using messages transmitted earlier relative to $\preceq_\mathbb{A}$, without violating the assumptions unique($\mathbb{A}$) and non($\mathbb{A}$).

The Yes-or-No Protocol. The Yes-or-No Protocol YN allows a Questioner to ask a question, to which the Answerer gives a private, authenticated reply; YN is constructed by two transformations of HD. In YN, the question and answer should each remain secret. Indeed, the protocol should prevent even an adversary who has guessed the question from determining what answer was given. The Questioner authenticates the Answerer as supplying an answer. The Questioner chooses two random nonces, and encrypts them, together with the question. The Answerer releases the first of the two nonces to indicate a *yes*, and the second to indicate a *no*. No adversary learns anything, since whichever nonce was released, the questioner was equally likely to have used it in the other position.

The protocol has four roles (Fig. 2). One describes the behavior of a Questioner receiving an affirmative answer. The second describes the behavior of a Questioner receiving a negative answer. The remaining two describe the behavior of an Answerer providing an affirmative and respectively negative answer.

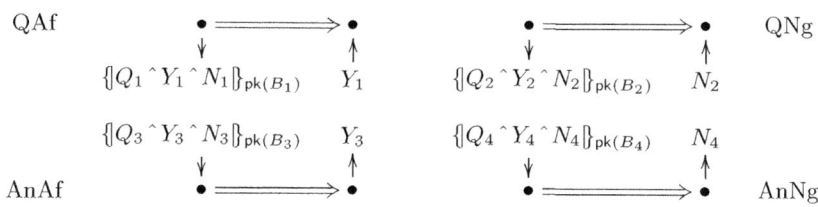

Fig. 2. The Yes-or-No Protocol YN

We can view either half of this diagram as a transformation of the protocol HD. We first rename the nonces N, N' of HD to the affirmative nonces Y_1, Y_3, to view the left half in this way. We would rename N, N' to the negative nonces N_2, N_4 for the right half. Before formalizing the transformations, we formalize these renamings as substitutions (homomorphisms) on the message algebra $\mathfrak{M}$. The renamings, yielding respectively the protocols $\alpha_1(\mathsf{HD})$ and $\alpha_2(\mathsf{HD})$, are:

$$\alpha_1 = [N \mapsto Y_1, \ N' \mapsto Y_3, \ B \mapsto B_1, \ B' \mapsto B_3] \quad \text{and}$$
$$\alpha_2 = [N \mapsto N_2, \ N' \mapsto N_4, \ B \mapsto B_2, \ B' \mapsto B_4]$$

We could alternatively incorporate substitutions such as α_1, α_2 into the transformations themselves, but at the cost of complicating the already subtle Def. 2.

Protocol Transformations. By a *protocol transformation* from a source protocol Π_1 to a target protocol Π_2, we mean a map from nodes on roles of Π_1 to nodes on roles of Π_2. The images of nodes of a single role $\rho_1 \in \Pi_1$ all lie along a single role $\rho_2 \in \Pi_2$, so we formalize this with two components: one which selects the correct ρ_2, and another which is a function g that maps the index of a node on ρ_1 to the index of its image along ρ_2. Thus:

F_1: $\alpha_1(\mathsf{HD}) \to \mathsf{YN}$ sends Init to the Questioner's Affirmative role QAf. The first node of Init—the transmission node—is associated with the first node of QAf, and the second nodes are associated. F_1 sends Resp to the Answerer's Affirmative role AnAf, preserving node indices.

So $F_1(\mathrm{Init}) = (\mathsf{QAf}, \mathsf{Id})$ and $F_1(\mathrm{Resp}) = (\mathsf{AnAf}, \mathsf{Id})$.

F_2: $\alpha_2(\mathsf{HD}) \to \mathsf{YN}$ acts similarly, with negative target roles. It sends Init to the Questioner's Negative role QNg. It sends Resp to the Answerer's Negative role AnNg. In both, F_2 preserves node indices, so $F_2(\mathrm{Init}) = (\mathsf{QNg}, \mathsf{Id})$, and $F_2(\mathrm{Resp}) = (\mathsf{AnNg}, \mathsf{Id})$.

These node index functions g are the identity Id, but other transformations use non-identity gs. For instance, if one principal in YN sent a message before the messages shown, which the other received before the messages shown, then we would alter F_1, F_2 to use $\lambda i \, . \, i + 1$ to increment each node index.

Our examples have several properties. The node index mapping functions are order-preserving, and the transformations also preserve the direction of the nodes (transmission vs. reception). The transmission node n of the HD initiator originates the value N and this value—as renamed by α_1—also originates on $F_1(n)$ (see Def. 1). The reception node m of the HD responder receives $N \sqsubseteq \mathsf{msg}(m)$, and we also have $\alpha_1(N) \sqsubseteq \mathsf{msg}(F_1(m))$. Thus, F_1 preserves the originated values and the ingredients of nodes. Similarly, F_2 preserves these properties of $\alpha_2(N)$.

These properties, with one other, define a protocol transformation. This last property is vacuously true of F_1, F_2. It concerns branching, as for instance, in a transformation $F: \mathsf{YN} \to \Pi$, QAf and QNg branch after a first node in common. It says that the result in the target Π should not commit to either branch until the source behaviors have committed by diverging from each other.

Definition 2 (Transformation). *Suppose F maps each role $\rho_1 \in \Pi_1$ to a pair ρ_2, g, where $\rho_2 \in \Pi_2$ and $g: \mathbb{N}^+ \to \mathbb{N}^+$. F is a* protocol transformation *iff:*

1. *g is order-preserving and $g(\mathsf{length}(\rho_1)) \leq \mathsf{length}(\rho_2)$;*
2. *$\rho_1 \downarrow i$ is a transmission (or resp. reception) node iff $\rho_2 \downarrow g(i)$ is;*
3. *Whenever $x \sqsubseteq \mathsf{msg}(\rho_1 \downarrow i)$, there exists a $j \leq g(i)$ such that $x \sqsubseteq \mathsf{msg}(\rho_2 \downarrow j)$;*
4. *Whenever x originates on $\rho_1 \downarrow i$, for some $j \leq g(i)$, x originates on $\rho_2 \downarrow j$;*
5. *Suppose that ρ_1 and $\sigma_1 \in \Pi_1$ have a common instance up to i, i.e. $\alpha(\rho_1) \in \mathsf{instances}(\sigma_1|_i)$. Let $F(\sigma_1) = \sigma_2, h$. Then we have $g(j) = h(j)$ for all $j \leq i$. Moreover, $\alpha(\rho_2) \in \mathsf{instances}(\sigma_2|_{h(i)})$.*

3   Security Analysis of **HD** and **YN**

Security analysis aims to find what must have happened—or must not have happened—if a certain situation has arisen. In the case of HD, the relevant analysis considers what must have happened, when there has been a local session of the initiator role. If its nonce N was freshly chosen, and B's private decryption key was uncompromised, what can we be sure has happened?

CPSA [26] is a software tool to answer such questions. It starts with an object representing the situation—namely a skeleton $\mathbb{A}$ (cf. p. 132)—and generates enriched skeletons to represent all the complete executions compatible with the starting point $\mathbb{A}$. In each step it takes, CPSA locates an *unsolved test*, some reception node that cannot be explained by adversary activity, given the regular (non-adversarial) activity currently present in the skeleton. For each alternate piece of regular activity that could help explain the current skeleton, CPSA constructs an enriched skeleton; the search branches to explore those enrichments. When every reception node is explained, and the skeleton is realized, CPSA has found a leaf in the search ("a shape").

CPSA implements a labeled transition system. The nodes are skeletons. There is a transition $\mathbb{A} \overset{\ell}{\rightsquigarrow} \mathbb{B}_i$ if $\mathbb{B}_i$ is one of the alternate enrichments that explains a test ℓ unsolved in $\mathbb{A}$. All of the $\mathbb{B}_i$ that provide alternate solutions to ℓ are successors of $\mathbb{A}$ with the same label ℓ. A label ℓ indicates some unexplained behavior in $\mathbb{A}$ that prevents it from being realized; each $\mathbb{B}_i$ offers a different potential way to fix ℓ. Given a protocol Π, security analysis for authentication and confidentiality goals involving the situation $\mathbb{A}_0$ consists of exploring the portion of the LTS for Π accessible from $\mathbb{A}_0$.

Analyzing HD. In HD, the relevant starting skeleton is $\mathbb{A}_0$, shown on the left in Fig. 3, where the assumptions—that N was freshly chosen and B's decryption key is uncompromised—are shown in the caption. CPSA identifies the lower reception node as unexplained, given the assumptions: how did N escape from the encryption $\{\!|N|\!\}_{\mathsf{pk}(B)}$? It can be solved in only one way, namely, a responder strand can extract N and retransmit it as shown. The result of this step, $\mathbb{A}_1$, is now realized, i.e. fully explained.

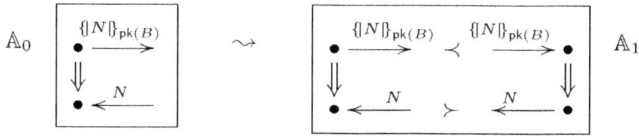

Fig. 3. Goal met by HD, with $\mathsf{unique} = \{N\}, \mathsf{non} = \{\mathsf{pk}(B)^{-1}\}$

Since every realized skeleton that enriches $\mathbb{A}_0$ must solve this test, it must be an enrichment of $\mathbb{A}_1$. In every situation in which an initiator has acted as in $\mathbb{A}_0$, a responder has had a corresponding local session. This is A's authentication guarantee, telling A that B has participated in the session.

Transforming our Analysis under F_1, F_2. Each transformation $F \colon \Pi_1 \mapsto \Pi_2$ determines a map that lifts any skeleton $\mathbb{A}$ of the protocol Π_1 to a corresponding skeleton $F(\mathbb{A})$ of Π_2. In particular, suppose $\mathbb{A}$ contains the first j nodes of a strand s, and s is an instance of a role $\rho_1 \in \Pi_1$. Thus, for some substitution β, $s = \beta(\rho_1)$. When $F(\rho_1) = (\rho_2, g)$, then $F(\mathbb{A})$ should contain the first

$g(j)$ nodes of a strand $F(s)$. It should be an instance of $\rho_2 \in \Pi_2$. Specifically $F(s) = \beta'(\rho_2)$, where β' agrees with β on all the parameters appearing in the first j nodes of ρ_1. The remaining parameters of ρ_2 are assigned new values, chosen to be distinct from any of the other values selected for $F(\mathbb{A})$. Since β' depends on all of $\mathbb{A}$, it would be more accurate to write $F_\mathbb{A}(s)$ rather than $F(s)$, although we will not do so.

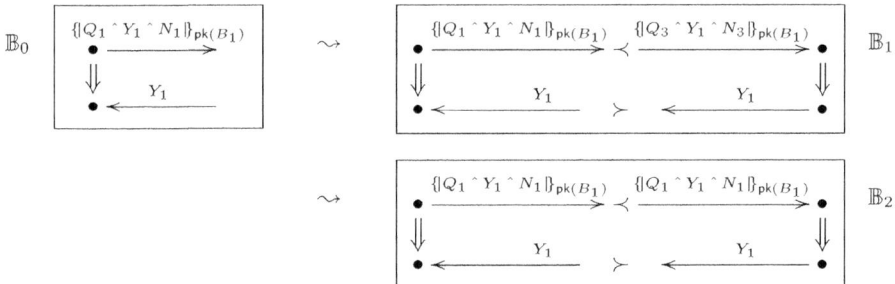

Fig. 4. A goal met by YN, with unique $= \{Y_1\}$, non $= \{\mathsf{pk}(B_1)^{-1}\}$

If we apply first α_1 and then F_1 mechanically to Fig. 3, we obtain the upper two skeletons in Fig. 4. In $\mathbb{B}_0$, the lower node, which is the image of the unsolved test node of $\mathbb{A}_0$, is itself an unsolved test node. Moreover, the new strand in $\mathbb{B}_1$ is the image of the one solution in HD. However, $\mathbb{B}_1$ is not realized. There is only one way to complete the search for a realized skeleton, namely to identify corresponding parameters in the questioner and answerer strands of $\mathbb{B}_1$, setting $Q_3 = Q_1$ and $N_3 = N_1$. The result is $\mathbb{B}_2$.

CPSA generates $\mathbb{B}_2$ from $\mathbb{B}_0$ in one step, which factors through $\mathbb{B}_1$: To realize $\mathbb{B}_0$, one must add the information present in $\mathbb{B}_1$, and also the additional information that $Q_3 = Q_1$ and $N_3 = N_1$. In any YN scenario in which $\mathbb{B}_0$ has occurred, the information in $\mathbb{B}_1$ also holds. Thus, the security analysis of HD has given us sound conclusions about YN. We now formalize this relation.

4   What Is Protocol Analysis?

In our examples, we started with skeletons $\mathbb{A}_0, \mathbb{B}_0$. They were not large enough to be realized, i.e. to be executions that could really happen without any extra regular behavior. We then enriched them to the realized skeletons $\mathbb{A}_1, \mathbb{B}_2$.

Homomorphisms. These enrichments are examples of *homomorphisms* among skeletons [18, Def. 3.6]. A *homomorphism* $H: \mathbb{A} \to \mathbb{B}$ between skeletons of Π transforms messages in a structure-respecting way, mapping transmission nodes to transmission nodes and reception nodes to reception nodes. A homomorphism must preserve the ordering relations of the source, and it must preserve its freshness and non-compromise assumptions. It is an *information-preserving map*.

Homomorphisms determine a preorder, not a partial order, since $\mathbb{A} \xrightarrow{H} \mathbb{B} \xrightarrow{J} \mathbb{A}$ does not imply that $J \circ H$ is an isomorphism. However, if H, J map distinct nodes of their sources injectively to distinct nodes of their targets, then $J \circ H$ is an isomorphism (under reasonable assumptions about the algebra of messages). Thus, these *node-injective* homomorphisms $H \colon \mathbb{A} \rightarrowtail_{ni} \mathbb{B}$ determine a partial order $\leq_{ni}$ on skeletons to within isomorphism.

Lemma 1 ([18, Lemma 3.11]). $\leq_{ni}$ *is a well-founded partial order. Indeed, for every $\mathbb{B}$, there are only finitely many non-isomorphic $\mathbb{A}$ such that $\mathbb{A} \leq_{ni} \mathbb{B}$.*

Protocol analysis: A search through $\rightarrow$. Protocol analysis is a search through part of the preorder $\rightarrow$. Skeletons $\mathbb{A}_0$ determine starting points for the search; protocol analysis then seeks realized skeletons $\mathbb{C}$ such that $\mathbb{A} \rightarrow \mathbb{C}$. CPSA computes a set of representative realized skeletons we call *shapes*. Within the set of all realized $\mathbb{B}$ such that $\mathbb{A} \rightarrow \mathbb{B}$, the shapes are the *minimal* ones in the node-injective ordering $\leq_{ni}$ [13]. CPSA's test-and-solution steps form a labeled transition system, where $\mathbb{A}_0 \xrightarrow{\ell} \mathbb{A}_1$ means that $\mathbb{A}_0$ has an unsolved test described by the label ℓ, and $\mathbb{A}_1$ contains one solution to this test. Figs. 3 and 4 give examples of test-and-solution steps. The LTS $\rightsquigarrow$ is a subrelation of $\rightarrow$.

Indeed, most of the search process works in the partial order $\leq_{ni}$. Although CPSA's implementation is somewhat different, its search could be separated into two phases. After an initial non-node-injective step, all of its test-solving could take place in the node-injective ordering (see [18, Thm. 6.5]).

Core Idea of this Paper. If $F \colon \Pi_1 \mapsto \Pi_2$, the portion of the LTS for Π_1 accessible from $\mathbb{A}_0$ may *simulate* the portion of the LTS for Π_2 accessible from the Π_2 skeleton $F(\mathbb{A}_0)$. Since the labels on the two transition systems may differ, in finding the successful simulation, we freely choose a *relabeling function* Δ mapping Π_1 labels to Π_2 labels. A simulation using Δ *progresses* iff, whenever a Π_1 skeleton $\mathbb{A}$ can take some ℓ-transition, the Π_2 skeleton $F(\mathbb{A})$ can take some $\Delta(\ell)$ transition. If for some Δ, we have a simulation that progresses, then F preserves all security goals concerning the starting situation $\mathbb{A}_0$.

We axiomatize the crucial properties of test-and-solution LTSs, rather than defining one as a function of Π. This has two advantages. First, we can establish goal preservation using finite, often very small, LTSs. Second, particularly for Π_2, we can use a finer LTS (as in Fig. 4) or a coarser one than CPSA would generate.

Definition 3. *Let S be a set of skeletons, and* dead $\in \Lambda$. *A ternary relation $\cdot \rightsquigarrow \cdot \subseteq S \times \Lambda \times S$ is a* test-and-solution lts *or* TLTS *for S, Λ iff:*

1. *If $\mathbb{A} \in S$, then: there exists a $\mathbb{B}$ such that $\mathbb{A} \rightsquigarrow \mathbb{B}$ iff $\mathbb{A}$ is not realized;*
2. *If $\mathbb{A} \xrightarrow{\ell} \mathbb{B}$, then:*
   (a) If $\ell =$ dead, then $\mathbb{A} = \mathbb{B}$ and there is no realized $\mathbb{C}$ such that $\mathbb{A} \rightarrow \mathbb{C}$;
   (b) If $\ell \neq$ dead, then $\mathbb{A} \leq_{ni} \mathbb{B}$ and $\mathbb{B} \not\leq_{ni} \mathbb{A}$;
   (c) For every homomorphism $J \colon \mathbb{A} \rightarrow \mathbb{C}$ from $\mathbb{A}$ to a realized $\mathbb{C}$, there exists some $\mathbb{B}'$ such that $\mathbb{A} \xrightarrow{\ell} \mathbb{B}'$, and $J = K \circ H$, where $\mathbb{A} \xrightarrow{H} \mathbb{B}' \xrightarrow{K} \mathbb{C}$.

Let $S(\rightsquigarrow) = \{\mathbb{A} \colon \exists \mathbb{B} . \mathbb{A} \rightsquigarrow \mathbb{B}\} \cup \{\mathbb{B} \colon \exists \mathbb{A} . \mathbb{A} \rightsquigarrow \mathbb{B}\}$.

Our TLTSs have the finite image property, i.e. $\{\mathbb{B}: \mathbb{A} \overset{\ell}{\rightsquigarrow} \mathbb{B}\}$ is finite for all $\mathbb{A}, \ell$. The non-dead labels in our applications are triples c, E, n_1, where c is a value received in a new, unexplained form in the node n_1. "Unexplained" because in n_1 c is not contained within a set of encryptions E. We call E an "escape set," since c has escaped from the protection of the encryptions E before reaching n_1.

In Fig. 3, c is the nonce N. E is the singleton set $\{\,\{\!|N|\!\}_{\mathsf{pk}(B)}\,\}$, which is the one form in which N has been seen. The node n_1 is the lower (reception) node of $\mathbb{A}_0$, in which N is suddenly received outside of its encrypted form in E.

For both steps in Fig. 4, c is the nonce Y_1, and E is the singleton set $\{\,\{\!|Q_1 \,\hat{}\, Y_1 \,\hat{}\, N_1|\!\}_{\mathsf{pk}(B_1)}\,\}$, which is the one form in which N_b has been seen prior to the test nodes n_1. In the first step, the test node n_1 is the lower (reception) node of $\mathbb{B}_0$, in which Y_1 is suddenly received outside of its encrypted form in E. In the second step, the test node n_1 is the upper right (reception) node in $\mathbb{B}_1$, in which Y_1 is received packaged with the (possibly distinct) values Q_3, N_3. The protocol provides no way to perform this repackaging if $Q_3 \neq Q_1$ or $N_3 \neq N_1$, so the only possible explanation is to equate them. Non-singleton Es arise naturally in protocols that use a nonce repeatedly, for successive authentication steps.

Lemma 2. *Suppose that* $\cdot \overset{\cdot}{\rightsquigarrow} \cdot$ *is a* TLTS, *and* $\mathbb{A} \in S(\rightsquigarrow)$. *If* $\mathbb{A} \rightarrow_{ni} \mathbb{C}$ *where* $\mathbb{C}$ *is realized, then there exists a realized* $\mathbb{B}$ *such that* $\mathbb{A} \rightsquigarrow * \mathbb{B}$ *and* $\mathbb{B} \rightarrow_{ni} \mathbb{C}$.

This lemma is an instance of Thm. 1, and can be proved by specializing its proof.

Homomorphisms and Transformations. Homomorphisms are preserved by protocol transformations (Def. 2). Writing $\mathsf{Skel}(\Pi_i)$ for the set of skeletons over Π_i, $F: \Pi_1 \to \Pi_2$ determines an *image* operation $\mathsf{Skel}(\Pi_1) \to \mathsf{Skel}(\Pi_2)$. The *image* operation supplies new values for Π_2 role parameters that do not appear in their Π_1 preimages, using some convention. We write $F(\mathbb{A})$ for $\mathbb{A}$'s image.

Lemma 3 ([17]). *Suppose that* $F: \Pi_1 \to \Pi_2$ *is a protocol transformation.*

1. *If* $H: \mathbb{A} \rightarrowtail \mathbb{B}$, *for* $\mathbb{A}, \mathbb{B} \in \mathsf{Skel}(\Pi_1)$, *there is a unique* $F(H): F(\mathbb{A}) \rightarrowtail F(\mathbb{B})$ *that commutes with the* image *operation.*
2. *If* $G: F(\mathbb{A}) \rightarrowtail F(\mathbb{B})$ *is any homomorphism between skeletons of this form, then* $G = F(H)$ *for some* $H: \mathbb{A} \rightarrowtail \mathbb{B}$.
3. *If* $\mathbb{D} \in \mathsf{Skel}(\Pi_2)$, *then* $\{\mathbb{A}: F(A) \leq_{ni} \mathbb{D}\}$ *has a* $\leq_{ni}$-*maximum in* $\mathsf{Skel}(\Pi_1)$.

5   The Preservation Theorem

Preserving protocol goals is about TLTSs for the two protocols. Assume a relabeling function $\Delta: \Lambda(\Pi_1) \to \Lambda(\Pi_2)$. The $\mathsf{Skel}(\Pi_1)$ argument determines what parameters in $\mathbb{A}$ to avoid, when choosing new role parameters.

Definition 4.   *1. F, Δ preserve progress for* $\rightsquigarrow_1$ *and* $\rightsquigarrow_2$ *iff: (a)* $\ell = $ dead *iff* $\Delta(\ell) = $ dead, *and (b) for every* $\ell \in \Lambda$, $\mathbb{A} \overset{\ell}{\rightsquigarrow}_1$ *implies* $F(\mathbb{A}) \overset{\Delta(\ell)}{\rightsquigarrow}_2$.
2. *Lts* $\rightsquigarrow_1$ *simulates* $\rightsquigarrow_2$ *under* F, Δ *iff: whenever* $F(\mathbb{A}) \overset{\ell'}{\rightsquigarrow}_2 \mathbb{B}'$ *and* $\ell' = \Delta(\ell)$, *then there exists a* $\mathbb{B}$ *s.t.* $\mathbb{B}' = F(\mathbb{B})$ *and* $\mathbb{A} \overset{\ell}{\rightsquigarrow}_1 \mathbb{B}$.

If F, Δ preserve progress, $\mathbb{A} \in S(\rightsquigarrow_1)$ implies $F(\mathbb{A}) \in S(\rightsquigarrow_2)$. There may be many $\ell' \in \Lambda(\Pi_2)$ outside $\mathrm{ran}(\Delta)$, for instance the second step in Fig. 4. In F_1, F_2, Δ is determined directly from F_i; in other cases, $\Delta(\ell)$ can use a larger escape set E than the naïve choice suggested by F.

Theorem 1. *Let* $F \colon \Pi_1 \to \Pi_2$, *and* $\Delta \colon \Lambda(\Pi_1) \to \Lambda(\Pi_2)$. *Let* $\rightsquigarrow_1$ *and* $\rightsquigarrow_2$ *be* TLTSs *with* $\mathbb{A} \in S(\rightsquigarrow_1) \subseteq \mathsf{Skel}(\Pi_1)$ *and* $S(\rightsquigarrow_2) \subseteq \mathsf{Skel}(\Pi_2)$. *Suppose that:*

1. *F, Δ preserve progress for $\rightsquigarrow_1$ and $\rightsquigarrow_2$;*
2. *$\rightsquigarrow_1$ simulates $\rightsquigarrow_2$ under F, Δ.*

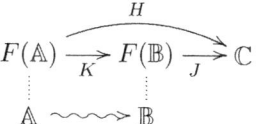

For every Π_2-realized $\mathbb{C}$, if $H \colon F(\mathbb{A}) \!\to_{ni}\! \mathbb{C}$, there is a Π_1-realized $\mathbb{B}$ such that $\mathbb{A} \rightsquigarrow_1 * \mathbb{B}$, and the accompanying diagram commutes.

Proof. We use induction on the set $\{\mathbb{D} \colon F(\mathbb{A}) \leq_{ni} \mathbb{D} \leq_{ni} \mathbb{C}\}$, since by Lemma 1, there are only finitely many non-isomorphic $\mathbb{D} \leq_{ni} \mathbb{C}$, and thus only finitely many s.t. $F(\mathbb{A}) \leq_{ni} \mathbb{D} \leq_{ni} \mathbb{C}$.

$\mathbb{A}$ **dead:** If $\mathbb{A} \overset{\mathrm{dead}}{\rightsquigarrow_1}$, then by progress, $F(\mathbb{A}) \overset{\mathrm{dead}}{\rightsquigarrow_2}$ contrary to Def. 3, Clause 2a.

$\mathbb{A}$ **realized:** If $\mathbb{A}$ is realized, it is the desired $\mathbb{B}$, with $K = \mathsf{Id}_{F(\mathbb{A})}$ and $J = H$.

Otherwise, for some $\ell \neq \mathrm{dead}$, $\mathbb{A} \overset{\ell}{\rightsquigarrow_1}$. By progress, $F(\mathbb{A}) \overset{\Delta(\ell)}{\rightsquigarrow_2}$. By Def. 3, Cl. 2c, H factors through some member of $\{\mathbb{E} \colon F(\mathbb{A}) \overset{\Delta(\ell)}{\rightsquigarrow_2} \mathbb{E}\}$, say $\mathbb{E}_0$. By simulation, $\mathbb{E}_0 = F(\mathbb{A}')$ for some $\mathbb{A}'$ with $\mathbb{A} \overset{\ell}{\rightsquigarrow_1} \mathbb{A}'$. By Defn. 3, Cl. 2b, $F(\mathbb{A}) \leq_{ni} F(\mathbb{A}')$ but $F(\mathbb{A}') \not\leq_{ni} F(\mathbb{A})$.

Hence, the following proper inclusion eliminates an isomorphism class:

$$\{\mathbb{D} \colon F(\mathbb{A}') \leq_{ni} \mathbb{D} \leq_{ni} \mathbb{C}\} \subsetneq \{\mathbb{D} \colon F(\mathbb{A}) \leq_{ni} \mathbb{D} \leq_{ni} \mathbb{C}\};$$

i.e. the cardinality (modulo isomorphism) is reduced. Thus, we can apply the induction hypothesis to $\mathbb{A}'$ in place of $\mathbb{A}$.   □

Lemma 2 is the special case of Thm. 1 in which F, Δ are the identity functions.

Although Thm. 1 is not about logical formulas, it has a corollary about security goal formulas for Π_1. If the Π_2-realized $\mathbb{C}$ is a *counterexample* to a Π_1 goal formula, then the Π_1-realized $\mathbb{B}$ will also be a counterexample to that goal.

6   The Language $\mathcal{L}(\Pi)$ of a Protocol Π

$\mathcal{L}(\Pi)$ is a classical first order language with equality [16][1]. A formula

$$\forall \overline{x} . (\phi \quad \supset \quad \exists \overline{y} . \psi_1 \vee \ldots \vee \psi_j) \tag{1}$$

is a *security goal* if (i) ϕ and each ψ_i is a conjunction of atomic formulas, (ii) $\overline{x}$ and $\overline{y}$ are disjoint lists of variables, and (iii) all variables free in any ψ_i but not

---

[1] Although the syntax is simplified from [16], $\mathcal{L}(\Pi)$'s expressiveness is unchanged.

in ϕ is free in $\overline{y}$. Null and unary disjunctions ($j = 0$ or $j = 1$) are permitted, where the null disjunction $\bot$ is the constantly false formula.

Since $\mathcal{L}(\Pi)$ says nothing about the structure of Π's messages, it can express goals that are preserved when message structure is transformed. It describes nodes by their role, their index along the role, and the role's parameters.

$\mathcal{L}(\Pi)$ contains function symbols $\mathrm{pk}(a)$, $\mathrm{sk}(a)$, and $\mathrm{inv}(a)$, for a's public encryption key; a's private signature key; and the inverse member of a key pair.

Example 1: $\mathcal{L}(\mathbf{HD})$. $\mathcal{L}(\mathrm{HD})$ shares some vocabulary with the other $\mathcal{L}(\Pi)$:

$$\mathrm{Prec}(m, n) \qquad \mathrm{Unq}(v) \qquad \mathrm{UnqAt}(n, v) \qquad \mathrm{Non}(v)$$

expressing node precedence; unique origination of v; unique origination of v at the node n; and non-origination of v. Its protocol-specific relations are:

$$\begin{array}{ccccc}
\mathrm{AtPos1}(s, n) & \mathrm{AtPos2}(s, n) & \mathrm{Init}(s) & \mathrm{Resp}(s) & \mathrm{Lsn}(s) \\
\mathrm{Peer}(s, b) & \mathrm{Self}(s, b) & \mathrm{Nonce}(s, v) & \mathrm{Hear}(s, v) &
\end{array}$$

The predicates $\mathrm{AtPos1}$ and $\mathrm{AtPos2}$ say that a node n lies at the first or second position (resp.) on strand s. Init and Resp say that a strand s is an initiator or responder strand (resp.). $\mathrm{Lsn}(s)$ says that s is a listener strand, a purely receptive strand that can witness that a value is disclosed. Peer says that s's name parameter is b, if s is an initiator strand. This name refers to s's intended partner. Self says that s's name parameter is b, if s is a responder strand. This name refers to the active party in this strand, the owner of the decryption key. We use Nonce to say that v is the nonce in either type of strand s. Hear says that s has received the value v, if s is a listener strand. The skeleton $\mathbb{A}_0$ of Fig. 3 *satisfies* the formula $\Phi_0 =$

$$\begin{array}{c}
\mathrm{Init}(s) \wedge \mathrm{AtPos1}(s, n) \wedge \mathrm{AtPos2}(s, m) \wedge \mathrm{Peer}(s, b) \\
\wedge \mathrm{Nonce}(s, v) \wedge \mathrm{Non}(\mathrm{inv}(\mathrm{pk}(b))) \wedge \mathrm{UnqAt}(n, v),
\end{array}$$

when we assign s to the initiator strand shown; assign n and m to its first and second nodes resp.; assign b to the name B; and assign v to nonce N. If $\Phi_1 =$

$$\begin{array}{c}
\mathrm{Resp}(s') \wedge \mathrm{AtPos1}(s', n') \wedge \mathrm{AtPos2}(s', m') \wedge \mathrm{Self}(s', b) \\
\wedge \mathrm{Nonce}(s', v) \wedge \mathrm{Prec}(n, n') \wedge \mathrm{Prec}(m', m),
\end{array}$$

then $\mathbb{A}_1$ satisfies $\Phi_0 \wedge \Phi_1$, when we (additionally) assign s' to the responder strand shown, and n', m' to its first and second nodes resp. The variables b, v are *not* primed in Φ_1, expressing the agreement of the initiator and responder strands on these parameters. So $\Phi_0 \supset \Phi_1$ is an authentication goal.

Although HD does not achieve any confidentiality goal, we would express it with a null conclusion, and with the Lsn and Hear predicates in the hypothesis. Letting $\bot$ be the vacuously false null disjunction:

$$\begin{array}{c}
(\ \mathrm{Init}(s) \wedge \mathrm{AtPos1}(s, n) \wedge \mathrm{Peer}(s, b) \\
\mathrm{Nonce}(s, v) \wedge \mathrm{Non}(\mathrm{inv}(\mathrm{pk}(b))) \wedge \mathrm{UnqAt}(n, v) \\
\mathrm{Lsn}(s') \wedge \mathrm{AtPos1}(s', n') \wedge \mathrm{Hear}(n', b)\ ) \quad \supset \bot
\end{array}$$

would express the secrecy of b.

$\mathcal{L}(\Pi)$ **in General.** In the previous paragraphs, we created an intuitive relation between a particular protocol Π and the predicates of its language. To do the same thing more generally, we will use a table τ.

The table τ should associate a distinct one place predicate with each role. For HD, τ mapped the initiator role to the Init predicate and the responder role to Resp. These are the *role predicates*. We also have τ associate each pair of a role and parameter of that role to a two place predicate. For HD, τ mapped the initiator role and the parameter N to the predicate Nonce; it also maps the responder role and N' to Nonce. These are the *parameter predicates*. We require (i) role predicates and parameter predicates are disjoint, and (ii) τ maps different parameters of the same role to different parameter predicates. For precision, we could write $\mathcal{L}_\tau(\Pi)$ for the language determined by a particular choice of τ, but the choice of τ makes no semantically relevant difference in security goals.

We add k position predicates $\texttt{AtPos1}(s, n)$, ..., $\texttt{AtPos}k(s, n)$, where k is the length of the longest role in Π. $\mathcal{L}(\Pi)$ contains these position predicates, the shared predicates $\texttt{Prec}, \texttt{Unq}, \texttt{UnqAt}, \texttt{Non}$, and the predicates in the range of τ.

Classical Semantics of $\mathcal{L}(\Pi)$. Fix a message algebra $\mathfrak{M}$. Each skeleton $\mathbb{A}$ for Π determines a model for $\mathcal{L}(\Pi)$ where the domain contains the messages in $\mathfrak{M}$ together with the strands and nodes of $\mathbb{A}$. Given an assignment η mapping free variables to values in the domain, the value $\eta(v)$ of any term v, involving variables and functions symbols such as pk, etc., is determined by η and $\mathfrak{M}$. The satisfaction conditions for the predicates are:

$\mathbb{A} \models_\eta \texttt{Prec}(n, n')$ iff $\eta(n) \prec_\mathbb{A} \eta(n')$;

$\mathbb{A} \models_\eta \texttt{Non}(v)$ iff $\eta(v) \in \mathsf{non}_\mathbb{A}$;

$\mathbb{A} \models_\eta \texttt{Uniq}(v)$ iff $\eta(v) \in \mathsf{unique}_\mathbb{A}$;

$\mathbb{A} \models_\eta \texttt{UniqAt}(n, a)$ iff $\eta(v) \in \mathsf{unique}_\mathbb{A}$ and $\eta(v)$ originates at $\eta(n)$ in $\mathbb{A}$;

$\mathbb{A} \models_\eta \texttt{AtPos}k(s, n)$ iff $\eta(n) \in \mathsf{nodes}_\mathbb{A}$ and $\eta(n) = \eta(s) \downarrow k$;

$\mathbb{A} \models_\eta \texttt{RolePred}(s)$ iff for some $j > 0$, $\mathsf{nodes}_\mathbb{A}$ contains exactly j nodes of $\eta(s)$, and $\eta(s) \in \mathsf{instances}(\rho|_j)$, where $\tau(\rho)$ is $\texttt{RolePred}$;

$\mathbb{A} \models_\eta \texttt{ParamPred}(s, v)$ iff for some $j > 0$, $\mathsf{nodes}_\mathbb{A}$ contains exactly j nodes of $\eta(s)$, and $\eta(s) \in \mathsf{instances}(\rho|_j)$, and for every $\mathsf{instances}(\rho|_j)$-witness $\alpha(\rho)$ for $\eta(s)$ has $\alpha(a) = \eta(v)$, where $\tau(\rho, a)$ is $\texttt{ParamPred}$.

The definition ensures that $\mathbb{A} \models_\eta \phi[s]$ is never sensitive to the part of $\eta(s)$ outside $\mathbb{A}$. As in Def. 2, Clause 5, $\mathcal{L}(\Pi)$ is insensitive to not-yet-executed branch points.

This definition also justifies our claims about Φ_0 and $\Phi_0 \wedge \Phi_1$ above. Φ_0 is satisfied in both $\mathbb{A}_0$ and $\mathbb{A}_1$. Indeed, because Φ_0 is a conjunction of atoms, it will be satisfied in *every* homomorphic image of $\mathbb{A}_0$. Specifically, if $H : \mathbb{A}_0 \rightarrow \mathbb{C}$, then composing H with the variable assignment η, we have $\mathbb{C} \models_{H \circ \eta} \Phi_0$. Moreover, this is exact: If $\mathbb{C} \models_\theta \Phi_0$, then for some $H : \mathbb{A}_0 \rightarrow \mathbb{C}$, $\theta = H \circ \eta$.

Definition 5. $\mathbb{A}, \eta$ *is a Φ-characteristic pair iff (i) $\mathbb{A} \models_\eta \Phi$ and (ii), for all $\mathbb{B}, \theta$, if $\mathbb{B} \models_\theta \Phi$ implies $\exists! H . H : \mathbb{A} \rightarrow \mathbb{B}$ and for all $x \in \mathsf{fv}(\Phi)$, $\theta(x) = (H \circ \eta)(x)$.*

$\mathbb{A}$ is a Φ-characteristic skeleton iff some $\mathbb{A}, \eta$ is a Φ-characteristic pair.

We write $\mathbb{A}, \eta = \mathsf{cp}(\Phi)$ for the characteristic pair and $\mathbb{A} = \mathsf{cs}(\Phi)$ for the characteristic skeleton, when they exist, since they are unique to within isomorphism.

$\mathbb{A}_0$ is the characteristic skeleton of Φ_0, i.e. $\mathbb{A}_0 = \mathsf{cs}(\Phi_0)$, and $\mathbb{A}_1 = \mathsf{cs}(\Phi_0 \wedge \Phi_1)$. In Fig. 3, since every $H \colon \mathbb{A}_0 \to \mathbb{C}$ to a realized skeleton factors through $\mathbb{A}_0 \leadsto \mathbb{A}_1$, we have demonstrated the goal $\Gamma_1 =$

$$\forall s, n, m, b, v \, . \, (\Phi_0 \supset \exists s', n', m' \, . \, \Phi_1). \tag{2}$$

Role-Specific Formulas. A variable s appearing in a role predicate in ϕ, or as the first argument to a position predicate or a role parameter predicate, is called a *strand variable* in ϕ. A variable n appearing as the second argument to a role position predicate, or either argument to an order predicate, or the first argument to an UnqAt predicate, is called a *node variable*.

A conjunction of atoms ϕ is *role specific* if strand and node variables are disjoint; every strand variable appears in exactly one role predicate; and every node variable appears in exactly one position predicate. Φ_0 and $\Phi_0 \wedge \Phi_1$ are role specific, but Φ_1 alone is not. Node variables m, n occur in no position predicate in Φ_1. By associativity and commutativity, a role specific ϕ can be rewritten so every leftmost subformula is role specific. That is, ϕ is equivalent to $\phi_0 \wedge \psi_1$ where ϕ_0 is role specific, and if ϕ_0 is a conjunction $\phi_1 \wedge \psi_1$, then ϕ_1 satisfies the same property recursively. This holds because the role predicate for s can precede position and parameter predicates for it, and the position predicate for n can precede Pred and UnqAt predicates for it. As in [16, Thm. 5.2]:

Lemma 4. *If ϕ is role specific, the characteristic skeleton $\mathsf{cs}(\phi)$ is defined.*

If Γ is a goal formula as in Eqn. (1), then we say that Γ is role specific if ϕ is, and each of the conjunctions $\phi \wedge \psi_i$ is, where $1 \le i \le j$.

Example 2: $\mathcal{L}(\mathsf{YN})$. The language $\mathcal{L}(\mathsf{YN})$, like $\mathcal{L}(\mathsf{HD})$, has the position predicates $\mathtt{AtPos1}(s, n)$ and $\mathtt{AtPos2}(s, n)$. It has five role predicates, namely $\mathtt{QAf}(s)$, $\mathtt{QNg}(s)$, $\mathtt{AnAf}(s)$, $\mathtt{AnNg}(s)$, and $\mathtt{Lsn}(s)$. Again expressing an intended peer via $\mathtt{Peer}(s, b)$, and an actual identity via $\mathtt{Self}(s, b)$, we have five parameter predicates:

$$\mathtt{Quest}(s, q), \quad \mathtt{YesVal}(s, v), \quad \mathtt{NoVal}(s, v), \quad \mathtt{Peer}(s, b), \quad \mathtt{Self}(s, b).$$

Protocol Transformations and Language Translations. Each $F \colon \Pi_1 \to \Pi_2$ determines a translation $Tr_F(\cdot)$ between role specific goal formulas of $\mathcal{L}(\Pi_1)$ and $\mathcal{L}(\Pi_2)$. We translate conjunctions by translating each conjunct. Let $F(\rho_1) = (\rho_2, g)$. The order and assumption predicates are translated verbatim. For the remaining predicates, we use the tables τ_1 and τ_2.

$\mathtt{RolePred1}(s)$: If $\mathtt{RolePred1}$ is $\tau_1(\rho_1)$, translate it to $\tau_2(\rho_2)$.

$\mathtt{PosPred}i(s, n)$: Because the formula is role specific, there is a single conjunct $\mathtt{RolePred1}(s)$ with the same s. If $\mathtt{RolePred1}$ is $\tau_1(\rho_1)$, then letting the index $j = g(i)$, the result is $\mathtt{PosPred}j(s, n)$.

$\mathtt{ParamName1}(s, t)$: Again, there is a single conjunct $\mathtt{RolePred1}(s)$ with this s, by role specificity. Let $\mathtt{RolePred1}$ be $\tau_1(\rho_1)$, and $\mathtt{ParamName1}$ be $\tau_1(\rho_1, a)$. Select the predicate $\mathtt{ParamName2}$ to be $\tau_2(\rho_2, a)$.

If either (i) a does not appear in ρ_2, or (ii) for all parameters a of ρ_1, $\mathtt{ParamName1}$ is not $\tau_1(\rho_1, a)$, then the result is vacuously true: $s = s \wedge t = t$.

If $\phi \wedge \psi_i$ is role specific, $Tr_F^\phi(\psi)$ translates ψ_i the same way, using conjuncts of ϕ to provide the specification of the roles. We have ensured that $\mathsf{fv}(Tr_F(\phi)) = \mathsf{fv}(\phi)$ and $\mathsf{fv}(Tr_F^\phi(\psi)) = \mathsf{fv}(\psi)$. So, let $Tr_F(\forall \overline{x} . (\phi \supset \exists \overline{y} . \psi_1 \vee \ldots \vee \psi_k))$ be

$$\forall \overline{x} . (Tr_F(\phi) \supset \exists \overline{y} . Tr_F^\phi(\psi_1) \vee \ldots \vee Tr_F^\phi(\psi_k)). \tag{3}$$

For the goal formula Γ_1 describing Fig. 3, $Tr_{F_1}(\Gamma_1)$ is:

$$\forall s, n, m, b, v . \quad (\mathtt{QAf}(s) \ \wedge \ \mathtt{AtPos1}(s, n) \ \wedge \ \mathtt{AtPos2}(s, m) \ \wedge \quad \mathtt{Peer}(s, b)$$
$$\wedge \ \mathtt{Non}(\mathsf{inv}(\mathsf{pk}(b))) \wedge \ \mathtt{YesVal}(s, v) \ \wedge \ \mathtt{UnqAt}(n, v)$$
$$\supset \exists s', n', m' . \ \mathtt{AnAf}(s') \wedge \ \mathtt{AtPos1}(s', n') \ \wedge \mathtt{AtPos2}(s', m') \ \wedge \quad \mathtt{Self}(s', b)$$
$$\wedge \ \mathtt{YesVal}(s', v) \ \wedge \quad \mathtt{Prec}(n, n') \ \wedge \mathtt{Prec}(m', m)).$$

If η is an variable assignment taking values in $\mathbb{A}$, define $\overline{\eta}$ to be the corresponding assignment taking values in $F(\mathbb{A})$. In particular, $\overline{\eta}$ agrees with η for variables whose value is a message. For variables whose value is a strand or node, we have $\overline{\eta}(v) = F(\eta(v))$, so that $\overline{\eta}$ is the composition of η with the "image" map from $\mathbb{A}$ to $F(\mathbb{A})$.

Lemma 5.   *1. If $\mathbb{A} \models_\eta \phi$, then $F(\mathbb{A}) \models_{\overline{\eta}} Tr_F(\phi)$.*
2. If $\mathbb{A} \models_\eta \phi \wedge \psi$, then $F(\mathbb{A}) \models_{\overline{\eta}} Tr_F^\phi(\psi)$.
3. If $\mathbb{B} \models_\theta Tr_F(\phi)$ and $\mathsf{cp}(\phi) = \mathbb{A}, \eta$, then there exists a J such that $J \colon F(\mathsf{cs}(\phi)) \to \mathbb{B}$, and θ agrees with $J \circ \overline{\eta}$ on $\mathsf{fv}(\phi)$.
4. If ϕ is role specific, then $\mathsf{cs}(Tr_F(\phi))$ exists, and $F(\mathsf{cs}(\phi)) = \mathsf{cs}(Tr_F(\phi))$.

Proof. 1. We left-associate conjunctions, so that when ϕ is $\phi_1 \wedge \phi_2$, ϕ_2 is atomic. We also assume that ϕ is written in the order defined before Lemma 4, so every leftmost subformula of ϕ is also role specific. We use structural induction on ϕ.

Base case: If ϕ is the trivially true conjunction with 0 conjuncts, then $Tr_F(\phi)$ is also the null conjunction, which is true in every structure.

Induction step: Let ϕ be $\phi_1 \wedge \phi_2$, where the claim holds for ϕ_1, and ϕ_2 is atomic. When ϕ_2 uses $\mathtt{Prec}, \mathtt{Unq}, \mathtt{UnqAt}, \mathtt{Non}$, or $=$, the claim follows from the definitions.

   If ϕ_2 is a role predicate $\mathtt{RoleName}(s)$, $\eta(s)$ is a strand with at least one node in $\mathbb{A}$, and all of its nodes in $\mathbb{A}$ agree with an initial segment of an instance of the associated role ρ_1. Thus, its F-image in $F(\mathbb{A})$ has at least $g(1)$ nodes in $\mathbb{A}$ and all of its nodes in $\mathbb{A}$ agree with an initial segment of an instance of the corresponding role ρ_2. Hence $F(\mathbb{A}) \models_{\overline{\eta}} Tr_F(\phi_2)$. Position predicates are similar.

   Let ϕ_2 be a parameter predicate $\mathtt{ParamName}(s, t)$. Since ϕ is role specific, there is just one $\mathtt{RoleName}(s)$ with the same s in ϕ_1, and $\mathbb{A} \models_\eta \mathtt{RoleName}(s)$. Thus, $Tr_F(\phi_2)$ is the F-corresponding parameter name predicate, and the F-image of $\eta(s)$ has the same parameter $\eta(t)$. Hence, $F(\mathbb{A}) \models_{\overline{\eta}} Tr_F(\phi_2)$.

   2. $Tr_F(\phi \wedge \psi)$ entails $Tr_F^\phi(\psi)$, and Clause 1 implies $F(\mathbb{A}) \models_{\overline{\eta}} Tr_F(\phi \wedge \psi)$.

   3. By Lemma 4, $\mathsf{cs}(\phi)$ exists. By the properties of cs [16], each strand with nodes in $\mathbb{A}$ is $\eta(s)$ for some distinct s in a role predicate in ϕ. If $\mathbb{A}$ contains i nodes of $\eta(s)$, then there is a node position predicate for i, s, and some n. Moreover, each parameter to the associated role ρ takes an atom or indeterminate as its value in $\eta(s)$, not a concatenation or encryption.

We will construct a $J \colon F(\mathsf{cs}(\phi)) \to \mathbb{B}$. $J = [\phi, \alpha]$ is defined: $\phi(\overline{\eta}(s)) = \theta(s)$. If a is a parameter to $\overline{\eta}(s)$, then $\alpha(a)$ is the corresponding parameter to $\overline{\theta}(s)$. By the universality of $\mathsf{cs}(\phi)$ and of $F(\mathbb{A})$, $J = [\phi, \alpha]$ is a homomorphism.

4. By the syntax, $Tr_F(\phi)$ is role specific, so Lemma 4 implies $\mathsf{cs}(Tr_F(\phi))$ exists. By the previous clause, $J \colon F(\mathsf{cs}(\phi)) \to \mathsf{cs}(Tr_F(\phi))$.

By clause 1, $F(\mathsf{cs}(\phi)) \models_{\overline{\eta}} Tr_F(\phi)$. Thus, Def. 5 entails that $K \colon \mathsf{cs}(Tr_F(\phi)) \to F(\mathsf{cs}(\phi))$. Hence, by the uniqueness in Def. 5, $J \circ K = \mathsf{Id}$. Hence, $F(\mathsf{cs}(\phi))$ and $\mathsf{cs}(Tr_F(\phi))$ are isomorphic. $\qquad\square$

7 Preserving Security Goal Formulas

Π *achieves* a goal formula Γ iff, for all realized Π-skeletons $\mathbb{C}$, $\mathbb{C} \models \Gamma$.

Theorem 2. *Let* $F \colon \Pi_1 \to \Pi_2$, *and let* ϕ *be goal specific with* $\mathbb{A} = \mathsf{cs}(\phi)$.

Suppose Π_1 *achieves the goal* $\Gamma = \forall \overline{x} . (\phi \supset \exists \overline{y} . \psi_1 \vee \ldots \psi_j)$, *and assume there exists a* Δ *and* TLTSs $\leadsto_1$ *and* $\leadsto_2$ *as in Thm. 1, i.e.* $\mathbb{A} \in S(\leadsto_1)$ *and*

1. F, Δ *preserve progress for* $\leadsto_1$ *and* $\leadsto_2$;
2. $\leadsto_1$ *simulates* $\leadsto_2$ *under* F, Δ.

Then Π_2 *achieves* $Tr_F(\Gamma)$.

Proof. $Tr_F(\Gamma)$ is $\forall \overline{x} . (Tr_F(\phi) \supset \exists \overline{y} . Tr_F^\phi(\psi_1) \vee \ldots Tr_F^\phi(\psi_j))$. Suppose that $\mathbb{C}$ is any Π_2-realized skeleton and θ is a variable assignment.

If $\mathbb{C} \not\models_\theta Tr_F(\phi)$, then $\mathbb{C} \models_\theta Tr_F(\phi) \supset Tr_F^\phi(\psi_1) \vee \ldots Tr_F^\phi(\psi_j)$.

So suppose $\mathbb{C} \models_\theta Tr_F(\phi)$. By Lemma 5, Clause 4, $\mathsf{cp}(Tr_F(\phi)) = F(\mathbb{A}), \overline{\eta}$. By Def. 5, there exists $H \colon F(\mathbb{A}) \to \mathbb{C}$, and $\theta \upharpoonright \overline{x} = (H \circ \overline{\eta}) \upharpoonright \overline{x}$.

Case 1. Suppose that H is node-injective. By Thm. 1, there is a Π_1-realized $\mathbb{B}$ such that $\mathbb{A} \leadsto_1 * \mathbb{B}$ and, for some J, K, $F(\mathbb{A}) \xrightarrow{K}_{ni} F(\mathbb{B}) \xrightarrow{J}_{ni} \mathbb{C}$. By Lemma 3, Clause 2, $K = F(L)$ for some $L \colon \mathbb{A} \to \mathbb{B}$. Thus, $\mathbb{B} \models_{L \circ \eta} \phi$.

Since, by assumption, Π_1 achieves Γ, it follows that $\mathbb{B} \models_\zeta \psi_i$, for some ψ_i and some ζ s.t. $\zeta \upharpoonright \overline{x} = (L \circ \eta) \upharpoonright \overline{x}$. By Lemma 5, Clause 2, we can lift this to $F(\mathbb{B})$, so that $F(\mathbb{B}) \models_{\overline{\zeta}} Tr_F^\phi(\psi_i)$. Quantifying existentially, $F(\mathbb{B}) \models_{F(L) \circ \overline{\zeta}} \exists \overline{y} . Tr_F^\phi(\psi_i)$.

Applying J and using $K = F(L)$, we have $\mathbb{C} \models_{J \circ (K \circ \overline{\zeta})} \exists \overline{y} . Tr_F^\phi(\psi_i)$. Since $J \circ K = H$ and $\theta \upharpoonright \overline{x} = (H \circ \overline{\zeta}) \upharpoonright \overline{x}$, we have $\mathbb{C} \models_\theta \exists \overline{y} . Tr_F^\phi(\psi_i)$.

Case 2. H is not node-injective. By [18, Thm. 6.5], there is a $K_0 \colon F(\mathbb{A}) \to \mathbb{D}$ that is universal among homomorphisms equating the nodes that H equates, and for some node-injective H_0, $H = H_0 \circ K_0$. Apply Case 1 to H_0 and $\mathbb{D}$. $\qquad\square$

Related Work. The safe protocol transformation problem is not new. As an idea for protocol design, it goes back at least to Bird et al. [5]. In a key special case, "protocol composition," it dates from the 1990s [21, e.g.]. In the protocol composition case, roles of Π_1 also appear unchanged as roles of Π_2. Since Π_2 may also have additional roles not in the image of Π_2, composition is thus effectively the case in which $\Pi_1 \subseteq \Pi_2$. While there has been an extensive literature devoted to this special case, the more general type of transformation discussed here has seen very little progress. Our view is that the effects of a syntactic change in message structure on protocol behavior are very hard to predict (given an active adversary model). This has made it hard to reason about the full notion of transformation, as opposed to the special case of composition. We have introduced the TLTS as a representation of the protocol analysis problem to tame this complexity.

Focusing then on protocol composition, it has been very successfully treated in a *cryptographic* model. A strong form of composition is reactive simulatability [25,3] or universal composability [7]; weaker forms may still be cryptographically justified [12].

In the *symbolic* model, we previously provided a widely applicable and practically useful criterion [19,14]. Cortier et al.'s criterion is in some ways broader but in other ways narrower than ours [8]; cf. [1]. Our [15] covers the union of [19,8,1]. From one point of view, the contribution of the present paper is to generalize [15] beyond the composition case.

The Protocol Composition Logic PCL considers refinements that preserve security goals [11, Thms. 4.4, 4.8]. A specific proof of a goal formula relies on particular invariants. If a protocol refinement introduces no actions falsifying these invariants, it preserves the security goal. Although PCL was designed to support richer forms of transformation, the existing results are essentially confined to the composition case. [11]'s "parallel" and "sequential" composition amounts to $\Pi_1 \subseteq \Pi_2$. Datta et al.'s "protocol refinement using templates" [10] suggested many of our examples.

By contrast with Distributed Temporal Logic [6], $\mathcal{L}(\Pi)$ is intended to be less expressive about the forms of messages. We wanted to focus only on what is retained under transformation, which concerns the role parameters rather than the forms of the messages. Nevertheless, our logic, unlike DTL, being a quantified logic, satisfaction is undecidable.

Lowe and Auty [23] refine protocols to concrete messages starting from formulas in a Hoare-like logic that represent the effect of messages. Maffei et al. [2] express the effects of messages by abstract tags, and provide constraints on instantiating the tags by concrete messages.

"Protocol compilers" transform their input automatically. Some start with a crypto-free protocol, and transform it into a protocol meeting security goals [9,4]. Others transform a protocol secure in a weak adversary model into protocols satisfying those goals with multi-session, active adversary [20].

Future work. We leave a major gap: What syntactic property of $F\colon \Pi_1 \to \Pi_2$ ensures that F preserves security goals? A clue comes from the "disjoint encryption" property [19,15], cf. [23,8]. Consider a map E from all encrypted units used by Π_1 to a subset of the encrypted units of Π_2. Π_2 should create an encryption $\alpha(E(e))$ on node n only if $n = F(n_0)$ and n_0 creates $\alpha(e)$ in Π_1. Likewise, Π_2 should remove an ingredient from $\alpha(E(e))$ only on a node $n = F(n_0)$ where n_0 removes an ingredient from $\alpha(e)$ in Π_1.

Tool support is also required. CPSA generates some TLTS transition relations. We then construct others, and the simulations, by hand. A variant of CPSA that would explore two protocols in tandem would be of great interest.

Acknowledgments. I am grateful to Dan Dougherty, Dusko Pavlovic, John Ramsdell, Paul Rowe, and Javier Thayer. The simplification of $\mathcal{L}(\Pi)$ vs. [16] arose from a conversation with Ramsdell. Early versions of some of this material were presented at FCS-ARPSA-WITS in 2008 and in Darmstadt in 2010.

Thanks to Siraj Sayani and Soumentra Ghosal, whose hospitality I enjoyed in Coonoor while writing a good part of this paper.

References

1. Andova, S., Cremers, C.J.F., Gjøsteen, K., Mauw, S., Mjølsnes, S.F., Radomirović, S.: Sufficient conditions for composing security protocols. Information and Computation (2007)
2. Backes, M., Cortesi, A., Focardi, R., Maffei, M.: A calculus of challenges and responses. In: FMSE 2007: ACM Workshop on Formal Methods in Security Engineering, pp. 51–60. ACM, New York (2007)
3. Backes, M., Pfitzmann, B., Waidner, M.: A universally composable cryptographic library (2003), http://eprint.iacr.org/2003/015/
4. Bhargavan, K., Corin, R., Deniélou, P.-M., Fournet, C., Leifer, J.J.: Cryptographic protocol synthesis and verification for multiparty sessions. In: IEEE Computer Security Foundations Symposium (2009)
5. Bird, R., Gopal, I., Herzberg, A., Janson, P.A., Kutten, S., Mulva, R., Yung, M.: Systematic design of a family of attack-resistant authentication protocols. IEEE Journal on Selected Areas in Communications 11(5), 679–693 (1993)
6. Caleiro, C., Vigano, L., Basin, D.: Relating strand spaces and distributed temporal logic for security protocol analysis. Logic Journal of IGPL 13(6), 637 (2005)
7. Canetti, R.: Universally composable security: A new paradigm for cryptographic protocols. Report 2000/067, International Association for Cryptographic Research, October 2001. Extended Abstract appeared in Proceedings of the 42nd Symposium on Foundations of Computer Science (FOCS) (2001)
8. Cortier, V., Delaitre, J., Delaune, S.: Safely composing security protocols. In: Arvind, V., Prasad, S. (eds.) FSTTCS 2007. LNCS, vol. 4855, pp. 352–363. Springer, Heidelberg (2007)
9. Cortier, V., Warinschi, B., Zălinescu, E.: Synthesizing secure protocols. In: Biskup, J., López, J. (eds.) ESORICS 2007. LNCS, vol. 4734, pp. 406–421. Springer, Heidelberg (2007)
10. Datta, A., Derek, A., Mitchell, J.C., Pavlovic, D.: Abstraction and refinement in protocol derivation. In: IEEE Computer Security Foundations Workshop. IEEE CS Press, Los Alamitos (2004)
11. Datta, A., Derek, A., Mitchell, J.C., Pavlovic, D.: A derivation system and compositional logic for security protocols. Journal of Computer Security 13(3), 423–482 (2005)
12. Datta, A., Derek, A., Mitchell, J.C., Warinschi, B.: Computationally sound compositional logic for key exchange protocols. In: Computer Security Foundations Workshop, pp. 321–334 (2006)

13. Doghmi, S.F., Guttman, J.D., Javier Thayer, F.: Searching for shapes in cryptographic protocols. In: Grumberg, O., Huth, M. (eds.) TACAS 2007. LNCS, vol. 4424, pp. 523–537. Springer, Heidelberg (2007)
14. Guttman, J.D.: Authentication tests and disjoint encryption: a design method for security protocols. Journal of Computer Security 12(3/4), 409–433 (2004)
15. Guttman, J.D.: Cryptographic protocol composition via the authentication tests. In: de Alfaro, L. (ed.) FOSSACS 2009. LNCS, vol. 5504, pp. 303–317. Springer, Heidelberg (2009)
16. Guttman, J.D.: Security theorems via model theory. EXPRESS: Expressiveness in Concurrency (EPTCS) 8, 51 (2009), doi:10.4204/EPTCS.8.5
17. Guttman, J.D.: Transformations between cryptographic protocols. In: Degano, P., Viganò, L. (eds.) ARSPA-WITS 2009. LNCS, vol. 5511, pp. 107–123. Springer, Heidelberg (2009)
18. Guttman, J.D.: Shapes: Surveying crypto protocol runs. In: Cortier, V., Kremer, S. (eds.) Formal Models and Techniques for Analyzing Security Protocols. Cryptology and Information Security Series. IOS Press, Amsterdam (2011)
19. Guttman, J.D., Javier Thayer, F.: Protocol independence through disjoint encryption. In: Computer Security Foundations Workshop. IEEE CS Press, Los Alamitos (2000)
20. Katz, J., Yung, M.: Scalable protocols for authenticated group key exchange. J. Cryptology 20(1), 85–113 (2007)
21. Kelsey, J., Schneier, B., Wagner, D.: Protocol interactions and the chosen protocol attack. In: Security Protocols Workshop. Springer, Heidelberg (1998)
22. Lamport, L.: Time, clocks and the ordering of events in a distributed system. CACM 21(7), 558–565 (1978)
23. Lowe, G., Auty, M.: A calculus for security protocol development. Technical report, Oxford University Computing Laboratory (March 2007)
24. Needham, R., Schroeder, M.: Using encryption for authentication in large networks of computers. CACM 21(12) (December 1978)
25. Pfitzmann, B., Waidner, M.: Composition and integrity preservation of secure reactive systems. In: Proceedings, Seventh ACM Conference of Communication and Computer Security. ACM Press, New York (November 2000)
26. Ramsdell, J.D., Guttman, J.D.: CPSA: A cryptographic protocol shapes analyzer. In: Hackage. The MITRE Corporation (2009), http://hackage.haskell.org/package/cpsa; see esp. doc subdirectory

Model-Checking Secure Information Flow
for Multi-threaded Programs[*]

Marieke Huisman[1] and Henri-Charles Blondeel[2]

[1] University of Twente, Netherlands
[2] INRIA Grenoble - Rhône-Alpes, France

Abstract. This paper shows how secure information flow properties of multi-threaded programs can be verified by model checking in a precise and efficient way, by using the idea of self-composition.

It discusses two properties that aim to capture secure information flow for multi-threaded programs, and it shows how these properties can be characterised in modal μ-calculus. For this characterisation, a self-composed model of the program is constructed. More precisely, this is a model that contains two copies of the labelled transition system induced by the program, so that the program is executed in parallel with itself. The self-composed model allows to compare two program executions in a single temporal formula that characterises a secure information flow property.

Both the formula and model are translated into the input language for the Concurrency Workbench model checker. We discuss this encoding, and use it for some practical experiments on several simple examples.

1 Introduction

One of the major challenges in the field of application security is multi-threading: the possible interactions between different threads can make the behaviour of an application highly intractable, and therefore multi-threaded applications are notoriously hard to write correctly. Nevertheless, multi-threaded software is omnipresent, and thus the search for formal techniques to establish security properties of multi-threaded software continues. In particular, the following two questions have to be answered: (*i*) what does it mean for a multi-threaded application to respect a security property, and (*ii*) how can we verify this?

This paper concentrates on the latter question: how can we develop a sound and complete technique for the verification of secure information flow (or confidentiality) properties of multi-threaded applications? The most common technique to verify secure information flow properties is to use an information flow type system [18,17,3]; type systems have the advantage that they are efficient, but they are not precise because they use syntactic equalities, and do not consider dependencies between values (see *e.g.*, [1] for more details).

---

[*] This work is partially funded by the EC under the IST-FET-2005-015905 Mobius project, and by NWO under the SlaLoM project. Part of the work done while both authors were at INRIA Sophia Antipolis.

S. Mödersheim and C. Palamidessi (Eds.): TOSCA 2011, LNCS 6993, pp. 148–165, 2012.

Therefore, as an alternative approach, the use of self-composition has been advocated. Self-composition recasts the problem of security verification into a standard program verification problem [1,6]. Originally, this was used for the verification of non-interference [8], a technical property that defines secure information flow of *sequential programs*. Traditionally, non-interference is expressed as a property over two program executions. However, if a program is composed with an independent copy of itself – *i.e.*, where all variables are marked to be different – then non-interference can be stated as a safety property over a single execution of this self-composed program. More precisely, suppose we have a statement S with a single low variable l. Non-interference states that if we have two initial states in which l has the same value, then in the final states, after execution of S, l should still have the same value. More formally: S is non-interfering iff $\forall s, s'.s(l) = s'(l) \land S(s) \leadsto t \land S(s') \leadsto t' \Rightarrow t(l) = t'(l)$. This is a property about two program executions, but self-composition allows to express this as a property over a single program execution. Let S' be a copy of S where all variable names are primed. Thus in particular l in S becomes l' in S'. Then we can say that S is non-interfering iff $\{l = l'\}S; S'\{l = l'\}$, *i.e.*, if we have a pre-state where l and l' are equal and we execute first S and then S', then in the post-state l and l' still have to be equal.

This idea has been exploited further for other definitions of secure information flow. Terauchi and Aiken describe how self-composition of sequential programs can be combined with a type system to characterise non-interference relaxed with information downgrading [21]. Huisman *et al.* [11] describe how secure information flow of multi-threaded applications is characterised by a temporal logic formula. The advantage of the self-composition approach is that since the characterisation is exact, soundness and completeness only depends on soundness and completeness of the verification method for the logic. In particular, if secure information flow is characterised by a temporal logic formula, a model checker can be used to automatically verify secure information flow. In that case, the temporal formula expressing the security property should be defined over a model that is the product of two or more basic models representing a program.

The current paper follows up on the earlier paper by Huisman *et al.* [11]. This earlier paper discusses the definition of observational determinism. Observational determinism was introduced by Zdancewic and Myers as a generalisation of non-interference for multi-threaded programs [23]. Huisman *et al.* show that this definition is not precise, as it accepts programs that leak information, and they propose an improved version. This definition has been further improved by Terauchi [20] — this is the definition we will use in this paper[1]. In addition, Huisman *et al.* also show a CTL* formula that precisely characterises the improved definition of observational determinism. However, there are several shortcomings to the approach: the model over which the property is expressed uses a non-standard composition operator to compose the two independent program copies; and in addition there does not exist a ready-made model checker

---

[1] Terauchi's definition is very restrictive, therefore we have recently proposed an alternative formalisation of observational determinism [10].

for CTL*. To overcome these problems, Huisman *et al.* suggested also characterisations in the modal μ-calculus [12]; however these characterisations turned out not to be correct: they would reject for example a program that looped for ever, while never changing a public variable.

The present paper overcomes these shortcomings as follows:

- It presents a characterisation of observational determinism as proposed by Terauchi [20], in the modal μ-calculus, using a standard composition operator to compose the two program copies;
- It shows that the approach also can be applied to other secure information flow properties, concretely eager trace invariance, as proposed by Roscoe [16];
- The characterisation goes all the way to the model checker: both the program model and the temporal logic formulae are encoded in the input language for the CWB model checker [15];

Several simple example programs are model checked, to show that this approach accepts secure programs that are typically rejected by a type system. From this experience, we draw lessons on what has to be done to make this approach scale to large-scale programs.

Organisation. The remainder of this paper is organised as follows. First, Section 2 introduces the program model. Next, Section 3 presents eager trace invariance and observational determinism. Then, Section 4 discusses their characterisation as temporal logic formulae, and Section 5 discusses how the characterisations are expressed in CWB. Finally, Section 6 concludes, and discusses future work.

Running Example. To illustrate the different definitions and encodings in the paper, throughout we will use the following example programs.

$$h := 0; \text{if } (h = 3) \text{ then } l := h' \text{ else } \epsilon \text{ fi} \parallel l := 3 \qquad (Program\ 1)$$
$$h := 0; \text{if } (h = 3) \text{ then } l := h' \text{ else } \epsilon \text{ fi} \parallel h := 3 \qquad (Program\ 2)$$

We use the convention that variables h and h' contain private data, while the value of l is publicly visible. The first program is secure, but to determine this statically, one has to consider that h is always set to 0, thus the value of h' will never be assigned to l. The second program is not secure: in some interleavings variable h', containing private data, is assigned to the publicly visible variable l.

2   Program Model

This section formally defines syntax and semantics of a simple while language with parallel execution. Individual transitions of the operational semantics are assumed to be atomic. Execution is defined as an infinite sequence of configurations, where configurations contain the (remaining) program to be executed and the global memory. Parallel threads communicate via the global memory. For

$$\frac{\langle S_1, \mu \rangle \to \langle \epsilon, \mu' \rangle}{\langle S_1; S_2, \mu \rangle \to \langle S_2, \mu' \rangle} \qquad \frac{\langle S_1, \mu \rangle \to \langle S_1', \mu' \rangle}{\langle S_1; S_2, \mu \rangle \to \langle S_1'; S_2, \mu' \rangle} \; \text{if } S_1' \neq \epsilon$$

$$\frac{\langle S_1, \mu \rangle \to \langle \epsilon, \mu' \rangle}{\langle S_1 \mid S_2, \mu \rangle \to \langle S_2, \mu' \rangle} \qquad \frac{\langle S_2, \mu \rangle \to \langle \epsilon, \mu' \rangle}{\langle S_1 \mid S_2, \mu \rangle \to \langle S_1, \mu' \rangle}$$

$$\frac{\langle S_1, \mu \rangle \to \langle S_1', \mu' \rangle}{\langle S_1 \mid S_2, \mu \rangle \to \langle S_1' \mid S_2, \mu' \rangle} \; \text{if } S_1' \neq \epsilon \qquad \frac{\langle S_2, \mu \rangle \to \langle S_2', \mu' \rangle}{\langle S_1 \mid S_2, \mu \rangle \to \langle S_1 \mid S_2', \mu' \rangle} \; \text{if } S_2' \neq \epsilon$$

$$\langle \text{if } (b) \text{ then } S_1 \text{ else } S_2 \text{ fi}, \mu \rangle \to \langle S_1, \mu \rangle \quad \text{if } b(\mu)$$

$$\langle \text{if } (b) \text{ then } S_1 \text{ else } S_2 \text{ fi}, \mu \rangle \to \langle S_2, \mu \rangle \text{ if } \neg b(\mu)$$

$$\langle \text{while } (b) \text{ do } S \text{ od}, \mu \rangle \to \langle S; \text{while } (b) \text{ do } S \text{ od}, \mu \rangle \quad \text{if } b(\mu)$$

$$\langle \text{while } (b) \text{ do } S \text{ od}, \mu \rangle \to \langle \epsilon, \mu \rangle \text{ if } \neg b(\mu)$$

$$\langle x := E, \mu \rangle \to \langle \epsilon, \mu[x \mapsto E(\mu)] \rangle \qquad\qquad \langle \epsilon, \mu \rangle \to \langle \epsilon, \mu \rangle$$

Fig. 1. Operational Semantics

simplicity, we do not consider procedure calls, local memory, or synchronisation between threads. Adding these would add more details to the program model, but not essentially change the technical results (but it might of course influence efficiency and performance of the verification). In particular, the characterisation of observational determinism would not change, but only the possible executions that have to be considered for its verification. To characterise eager trace invariance, the operational semantics is extended with extra information, which can straightforwardly be defined for more complex statements.

2.1 Syntax

First we define the syntax of the programming language. Let Var be a set of variables, and $\text{dom}(x)$ the domain of a variable $x \in Var$. Each variable in Var has a security-level *high* or *low* assigned to it[2]. This assignment divides the set Var into two disjoint subsets H and L, containing the variables with high and low security level, respectively.

We do not give any concrete grammar for expressions; we assume that we can write all the usual side-effect-free boolean and integer expressions. Statements ($\in Stmt$) are defined by the following grammar, where $S \in Stmt$, $x \in Var$, e is any expression, b is a boolean expression, and ϵ is the empty statement.

$$S ::= x := e \mid S; S \mid \text{if } (b) \text{ then } S \text{ else } S \text{ fi} \mid \text{while } (b) \text{ do } S \text{ od} \mid S \mid S \mid \epsilon$$

2.2 Semantics

Next we define the semantics of the programming language.

---

[2] As usual, we only consider two security levels, but the approach can easily be generalised to an arbitrary security lattice.

Stores. A store $\in$ *Store* maps *Var* to values, such that each value v belongs to the domain of the corresponding variable x. Formally:

$$Store = \{\mu : Var \rightarrow \bigcup_{x \in Var} \text{dom}(x) \mid x \mapsto v \,,\, v \in \text{dom}(x)\}$$

For $\mu \in Store$, $\mu_{|_L}$ denotes the *restriction* of μ to L, *i.e.,* $\forall x \in L.\mu_{|_L}(x) = \mu(x)$, and $\forall x \in H.\mu_{|_L} x = \perp$. Stores μ and μ' are *L-equivalent*, denoted $\mu \approx_L \mu'$, if $\mu_{|_L} = \mu'_{|_L}$ (*i.e.,* $\forall l \in L.\mu(l) = \mu'(l)$).

Operational semantics. Figure 1 presents the rules of the small step operational semantics of our programming language. Transitions relate program configurations ($\in Conf$), where a configuration $\langle S, \mu \rangle$ consists of a statement S and a store μ. For convenience we use accessor function $\text{store}(\langle S, \mu \rangle) = \mu$. The last (identity) transition rule in Figure 1 applies in case the program has terminated, ensuring that there always is a transition enabled. Thus program behaviour can be considered as a Kripke structure (which makes it suitable for model checking).

Traces. A trace ($\in Trace$) is an infinite sequence of configurations. Given trace $T \in Trace$, T_i denotes the $(i + 1)^{th}$ configuration of $T \in Trace$, that is $T = T_0, T_1, \ldots, T_i, T_{i+1}, \ldots$.

Trace T is a *program trace of S*, starting in the initial store μ, denoted $\langle S, \mu \rangle \Downarrow T$, if (*i*) $T_0 = \langle S, \mu \rangle$, and (*ii*) $\forall i \in \mathbb{N}. T_i \rightarrow T_{i+1}$. Notice that there always is a transition enabled, thus for any initial configuration, an infinite trace exists. Finally, the set of *reachable configurations w.r.t.* a statement S, and a set of stores $\Sigma \subseteq Store$ is formally defined as: $\text{reach}(S, \Sigma) = \{T_i \in Conf \mid \mu \in \Sigma \wedge \langle S, \mu \rangle \Downarrow T \wedge i \in \mathbb{N}\}$.

Example 1. Consider Program 1. Its variables are divided in the sets $H = \{h, h'\}$ and $L = \{l\}$. Suppose we execute this program in initial state $\mu = (h \mapsto 1, h' \mapsto 1, l \mapsto 1)$. A possible execution of this program is (where P_1 denotes the full program):

$$\langle P_1, \mu \rangle \rightarrow \langle \texttt{if} \ldots \parallel l := 3, \mu[h \mapsto 0] \rangle \rightarrow \langle l := 3, \mu[h \mapsto 0] \rangle \rightarrow$$
$$\langle \epsilon, (h \mapsto 0, h' \mapsto 1, l \mapsto 3) \rangle \rightarrow \langle epsilon, (h \mapsto 0, h' \mapsto 1, l \mapsto 3) \rangle \rightarrow \ldots$$

Two other executions are possible, corresponding to the possible interleavings of the two parallel statements. Considering all these executions results in the set:

$$\text{reach}(P_1, \{\mu\}) = \{\langle P_1, \mu \rangle, \langle \texttt{if} \ldots \parallel l := 3, \mu[h \mapsto 0] \rangle, \langle l := 3, \mu[h \mapsto 0] \rangle,$$
$$\langle h := 0; \texttt{if} \ldots, \mu[l \mapsto 3] \rangle, \langle \texttt{if} \ldots, (h \mapsto 0, h' \mapsto 1, l \mapsto 3) \rangle,$$
$$\langle \epsilon, (h \mapsto 0, h' \mapsto 1, l \mapsto 3) \rangle\}$$

3   Secure Information Flow

3.1   Eager Trace Invariance

In 1995, Roscoe observed that one way to guarantee that no private data is leaked, is to require that the public data is deterministic [16]. He defined determinism of public data in two ways: (*i*) *eager trace invariance:* the program's behaviour stripped from all knowledge about private data should be deterministic, or (*ii*) *lazy trace invariance:* the program's behaviour, interleaved with any arbitrary manipulations of private data should be deterministic. In this paper, we further discuss only eager trace invariance[3]. Roscoe's formal definition of eager trace invariance - re-casted for programs - expresses the following: given program P and two sequences of actions (histories) $\mathcal{H}$ and $\mathcal{H}'$ that are equal *w.r.t.* the low actions, *i.e.*, the set of actions associated with low variables, then after P has executed $\mathcal{H}$ or $\mathcal{H}'$, respectively, any possible subsequent sequence of actions should be equal *w.r.t.* the low actions.

To define this formally, we first define the actions of a program. In our program model, parallel threads communicate by reading and writing from the shared store. A sequence of communications describes what a statement "knows" at a particular point, and reading a variable before *or* after a write action on this variable will thus make a difference. Therefore, both read and write actions have to be considered, and we define the following set of *actions* (divided by the security level assignment of variables into Act_L and Act_H):

$$Act = \{\mathsf{write}_{x,v} \mid v \in \mathsf{dom}(x) \wedge x \in Var\} \cup \{\mathsf{read}_{x,v} \mid v \in \mathsf{dom}(x) \wedge x \in Var\}$$

We believe that this choice for the set of actions reflects the definition of eager trace invariance most faithfully in our program model.

Example 2. The different executions of Program 1 from the initial store where all variables are 1 can produce the following actions: $\mathsf{write}_{h,0}, \mathsf{read}_{h,0}, \mathsf{write}_{l,3}$. For Program 2 this would be: $\mathsf{write}_{h,0}, \mathsf{read}_{h,0}, \mathsf{write}_{h,3}, \mathsf{read}_{h,3}, \mathsf{read}_{h',1}, \mathsf{write}_{l,1}$.

To capture the sequence of actions that has been executed, we extend the operational semantics with a history of actions. Single steps can cause multiple actions, or no actions at all to happen, therefore we associate with each step a set of actions. Configurations are extended to the form $\langle S, \mu, \mathcal{H} \rangle$, with accessor function hist, where a history ($\in Hist$) is a sequence of sets of actions. The operational semantics is adjusted to add information to the history; rules that evaluate or write an expression, such as assignment, add new values to the current history.

Example 3. In the extended operational semantics, the first execution of Program 1 becomes (where ϵ is the empty sequence):

$$\langle P_1, \mu, \epsilon \rangle \rightarrow \langle \mathtt{if} \ldots \| \; l := 3, \mu[h \mapsto 0], \{\mathsf{write}_{h,0}\} \rangle \rightarrow$$
$$\langle l := 3, \mu[h \mapsto 0], \{\mathsf{write}_{h,0}\}.\{\mathsf{read}_{h,0}\} \rangle \rightarrow$$
$$\langle \epsilon, (h \mapsto 0, h' \mapsto 1, l \mapsto 3), \{\mathsf{write}_{h,0}\}.\{\mathsf{read}_{h,0}\}.\{\mathsf{write}_{l,3}\} \rangle \rightarrow$$
$$\langle \epsilon, (h \mapsto 0, h' \mapsto 1, l \mapsto 3), \{\mathsf{write}_{h,0}\}.\{\mathsf{read}_{h,0}\}.\{\mathsf{write}_{l,3}\}.\{\} \rangle \rightarrow \ldots$$

Reachability is extended in the obvious way, *i.e.*, reach$(S, \Sigma, \mathcal{H})$ is the set of reachable configurations from S and Σ *whose history equals* $\mathcal{H}$.

---

[3] Lazy trace invariance can also be model checked, but this requires that a special operation is added to the program model that models the arbitrary manipulation of private data.

Example 4. Consider Program 1 and let *Store* be the set of all possible stores. Then for example:

$$\mathsf{reach}(P_1, Store, \{\mathsf{write}_{h,0}\}) = \{\langle \mathtt{if} \ldots \| \, l := 3, \mu[h \mapsto 0], \{\mathsf{write}_{h,0}\}) \mid \mu \in Store \}\rangle$$
$$\mathsf{reach}(P_1, Store, \{\mathsf{write}_{l,3}\}) = \{\langle h := 0; \mathtt{if} \ldots, \mu[l \mapsto 3], \{\mathsf{write}_{l,3}\}) \mid \mu \in Store \})\}\rangle$$
$$\mathsf{reach}(P_1, Store, \{\mathsf{read}_{h,0}\}) = \{\}$$

Two histories $\mathcal{H}_1$ and $\mathcal{H}_2$ are *equivalent w.r.t. a set of actions A*, denoted $\mathcal{H}_1 \equiv_A \mathcal{H}_2$, if they are equivalent up to empty sets, after removing all actions that are not in A. Now we can define eager trace invariance in the context of our program model.

Definition 1 (Eager trace invariance). *Statement S is* eagerly trace invariant *w.r.t. L if*

$$\forall \, \mathcal{H}, \mathcal{H}' \in Hist. \mathcal{H} =_{Act_L} \mathcal{H}'.$$
$$\forall c \in \mathsf{reach}(S, Store, \mathcal{H}).c' \in \mathsf{reach}(S, Store, \mathcal{H}').$$
$$\forall T \in Trace.c \Downarrow T \Rightarrow$$
$$\exists T' \in Trace.c' \Downarrow T' \wedge \forall m \in \mathbb{N}. \, \exists n \in \mathbb{N}. \, \mathsf{hist}(T_m) \equiv_{Act_L} \mathsf{hist}(T'_n)$$

This definition states the following. Suppose we have two histories $\mathcal{H}$ and $\mathcal{H}'$ that correspond to initial executions of S, *i.e.*, there are configurations c and c' reachable by these histories. Then any possible continuation of c can be matched by a continuation of c' - where matching is understood as that the low actions should coincide.

Notice that configurations c and c' are only constrained by histories $\mathcal{H}$ and $\mathcal{H}'$, not by any initial store.

Example 5. Consider again Program 1. The histories that match on the low actions either (*i*) have no low actions at all, or (*ii*) contain the action $\mathsf{write}_{l,3}$. In case (*i*), any possible continuation will contain the low action $\mathsf{write}_{l,3}$; in case (*ii*), any possible continuation will not produce any low action anymore. Thus the program is eagerly trace invariant.

However, if we consider Program 2, the histories $\mathcal{H} = \mathsf{write}_{h,0}.\mathsf{write}_{h,3}$ and $\mathcal{H}' = \mathsf{write}_{h,3}.\mathsf{write}_{h,0}$ are equivalent *w.r.t.* the low actions (as there are none), but their possible continuations are not. For any initial store μ, the first history leads to the configuration $\langle \mathtt{if} \ldots, \mu[h \mapsto 3], \mathcal{H}\rangle$ and this will be continued by the actions $\mathsf{read}_{h,3}.\mathsf{write}_{l,h'}$ (for whatever the value of h' is). However, the history $\mathcal{H}'$ leads to a configuration $\langle \mathtt{if} \ldots, \mu[h \mapsto 0], \mathcal{H}'\rangle$ that will only be continued by the action $\mathsf{read}_{h,0}$. Clearly, these continuations are not equivalent *w.r.t.* the low actions. Thus Program 2 is not eagerly trace invariant.

Notice that if we would change the **then** branch in Program 2 to a statement that would only read the value of l, *e.g.*, $h' := l$, then the program would still not be eagerly trace invariant, because reading of low variables is considered to be a visible action.

3.2   Observational Determinism

Inspired by Roscoe's observation about determinism, Zdancewic and Myers [23] propose that a program has secure information flow if the low traces with public data are independent of the private data, *i.e.*, for any two low-equivalent stores, the traces of low variables are the same, up to stuttering[4]. They call this *observational determinism*.

Several variations of observational determinism have been proposed in the literature. These vary in the definition of low trace equivalence. Zdancewic and Myers define trace equivalence by requiring that the trace for each low variable should be equivalent up to stuttering and prefixing [23]. Later, Huisman *et al.* have shown that this definition is insecure, even for sequential programs [11]. However, Terauchi showed that also Huisman *et al.*'s definition is still insecure: if location traces are considered independently, information can be deduced from the relative order in which two locations are updated. He defines trace equivalence as equality up to stuttering and prefixing of the complete low stores. However, in a forthcoming paper, Huisman and Ngo [10] show that allowing prefixing makes security scheduler-dependent. Therefore, in the definition of observational determinism, we define low trace equivalence, denoted $T \simeq_L T'$ as *equality of the low stores up to stuttering*.

Definition 2. *Statement S is* observationally deterministic *w.r.t. L if*

$$\forall \mu, \mu' \in Store. \, \forall T, T' \in Trace.$$
$$\mu \approx_L \mu' \wedge \langle S, \mu \rangle \Downarrow T \wedge \langle S, \mu' \rangle \Downarrow T' \Rightarrow T \simeq_L T'$$

Example 6. Consider again Program 1. For any two low equivalent stores μ and μ', with initial value l_0 for the variable l, the low store traces are of the following shape: $(l \mapsto l_0) \ldots (l \mapsto 3) \ldots$. Thus clearly, any two traces will be low equivalent, and the program is observationally deterministic.

Consider Program 2. Two low equivalent stores μ and μ' that differ in the value of h' can have traces that are not low equivalent. Suppose that h' is 1 in μ and 2 in μ'. Then a low store trace starting from μ is of the shape $(l \mapsto l_0) \ldots (l \mapsto 1) \ldots$ or $(l \mapsto l_0) \ldots$, while a low store trace starting from μ' is of the shape $(l \mapsto l_0) \ldots (l \mapsto 2) \ldots$ or $(l \mapsto l_0) \ldots$. Thus, clearly not all traces are low store equivalent, and the program is not observationally deterministic.

However, if in Program 2, the **then** branch would be changed to for example $h' := l$ - thus only reading the value of l, then the program would be observationally deterministic. This illustrates the difference with eager trace invariance, where also reading of variables is considered important (*cf.* Example 5).

---

[4] Two traces are said to be equivalent *up to stuttering* if they are the same if all subsequent duplicates are removed (*e.g.*, $xxyyz$ and $xyyyzzz$ are stuttering equivalent, because in both cases removing the subsequent duplicates results in the trace xyz).

$$s \models^T \text{true} \overset{def}{\Leftrightarrow} true \qquad\qquad s \models^T \text{false} \overset{def}{\Leftrightarrow} false$$

$$s \models^T p \overset{def}{\Leftrightarrow} p \in \lambda(s)$$

$$s \models^T \neg\Phi \overset{def}{\Leftrightarrow} \neg(s \models^T \Phi) \qquad s \models^T \Phi \wedge \Psi \overset{def}{\Leftrightarrow} s \models^T \Phi \wedge s \models^T \Psi$$

$$s \models^T \langle\alpha\rangle\Phi \overset{def}{\Leftrightarrow} \exists s' \in S.\, (s \overset{\alpha}{\to} s' \wedge s' \models^T \Phi) \qquad s \models^T [\alpha]\Phi \overset{def}{\Leftrightarrow} \forall s' \in S.\, (s \overset{\alpha}{\to} s' \Rightarrow s' \models^T \Phi)$$

$$s \models^T \mu X.\Phi \overset{def}{\Leftrightarrow} \exists k \in \mathbb{N}.\, s \models^T \mu X^k.\Phi \qquad s \models^T \nu X.\Phi \overset{def}{\Leftrightarrow} \forall k \in \mathbb{N}.\, s \models^T \nu X^k.\Phi$$

$$\mu X^0.\Phi \overset{def}{=} \text{false} \qquad\qquad \mu X^{k+1}.\Phi \overset{def}{=} \Phi[\mu X^k.\Phi/X]$$

$$\nu X^0.\Phi \overset{def}{=} \text{true} \qquad\qquad \nu X^{k+1}.\Phi \overset{def}{=} \Phi[\nu X^k.\Phi/X]$$

Fig. 2. Semantics of modal μ-calculus

4 A Temporal Logic Characterisation of Secure Information Flow

This section first presents the modal μ-calculus [12], the temporal logic used for the characterisation. Then it shows how observational determinism and eager trace invariance are characterised using this logic. The next section shows how the properties and the model are encoded in the input language of the CWB model checker, and uses this to verify secure information flow of some simple examples.

4.1 Modal μ-Calculus

As mentioned above, in earlier work Huisman *et al.* proposed a characterisation of observational determinism, using CTL*. However, no readily available model checker for CTL* exists. Moreover, the characterisation in CTL* used a non-standard composition operator, tailored to the specific property at hand. To make the approach generally applicable, therefore this paper uses the modal μ-calculus [12] instead (whereas the modal μ-calculus characterisation in [11] was not precise enough).

The modal μ-calculus is an extension of Hennessy-Milner logic with fixed-point operators that allow to express recursion. Let $\mathcal{N}$ be a set of variable names, ranged over by X. Let Lab be the set of actions labels, ranged over by α, and let $\mathcal{A}$ be the set of atomic propositions, ranged over by p. Then the syntax of modal μ-calculus formulae is given by the following grammar:

$$\Phi ::= \text{true} \mid \text{false} \mid p \mid X \mid \neg\Phi \mid \Phi \wedge \Phi \mid \Phi \vee \Phi \mid \langle\alpha\rangle\Phi \mid [\alpha]\Phi \mid \mu X.\Phi \mid \nu X.\Phi$$

Figure 2 defines the semantics of modal μ-calculus formulae, *w.r.t.* a labelled transition system $T = (S, Lab, \to, A, \lambda)$, where S is the set of states, Lab the set of transition labels, $\to \subseteq S \times Lab \times S$ the transition relation, A the set of atomic propositions, and $\lambda : S \to 2^A$ the valuation, describing for each state which atomic propositions hold. The symbol s ranges over S. The semantics of fixed-point formulae uses (inductively) defined *fixed-point approximants* [5].

4.2   Observational Determinism in Temporal Logic

To characterise observational determinism in the modal μ-calculus, we first define a set of action labels: $Act = \{c_{x,v} \mid x \in Var \wedge v \in \mathsf{dom}(x)\} \cup \{\tau\}$. Intuitively, a transition is labelled with $c_{x,v}$ if it changes the value of variable x to the value v. Given a set of variables X, we use c_X to abbreviate the set of labels that encode changes to $x \in X$: $c_X = \{c_{x,v} \mid x \in X \wedge v \in \mathsf{dom}(x)\}$.

The operational semantics is updated with these labels: each transition that assigns v to variable x (where v is different from x's former value) is labelled $c_{x,v}$; all other transitions are labelled with the silent transition label τ. Notice that assignment of a non-changed value is not considered as a change – it will be labelled τ. Sequential and parallel composition propagate transition labels.

Example 7. Consider the example execution of Program 1 in example 1. In the updated operational semantics, this execution becomes:

$$\langle P_1, \mu \rangle \xrightarrow{c_{h,0}} \langle \mathtt{if} \dots \mid l := 3, \mu[h \mapsto 0] \rangle \xrightarrow{\tau} \langle l := 3, \mu[h \mapsto 0] \rangle \xrightarrow{c_{l,3}}$$
$$\langle \epsilon, (h \mapsto 0, h' \mapsto 1, l \mapsto 3) \rangle \xrightarrow{\tau} \langle \epsilon, (h \mapsto 0, h' \mapsto 1, l \mapsto 3) \rangle \xrightarrow{\tau} \dots$$

We wish to check whether a program is observationally deterministic. In order to do this, we need to compare two program executions. The trick of self-composition is to compose the program with itself in such a way that the execution of the self-composed program corresponds to the two executions of the individual program copies (originally proposed in [1,6]). In our case, we do this by executing the two program copies in parallel. To be able to extract the two program executions, we clearly separate the program configurations of the two programs in every state.

Thus, the self-composed program model is defined as the labelled transition system $T = (S, Lab, \rightarrow, A, \lambda)$, where we define:

- the set of states $S = Conf \times Conf$, i.e., states contain configurations for both program copies,
- the set of action labels $Lab = \{(a)_j \mid a \in Act \wedge j \in \{1, 2\}\}$, where the index j denotes which program copy performs the action,
- the transition relation $\rightarrow \subseteq S \times Lab \times S$ using the labelled operational semantics described above:

$$\frac{c_1 \xrightarrow{a} c_1'}{(c_1, c_2) \xrightarrow{(a)_1} (c_1', c_2)} \qquad \frac{c_2 \xrightarrow{a} c_2'}{(c_1, c_2) \xrightarrow{(a)_2} (c_1, c_2')}$$

- the set of atomic propositions $A = \{\mathsf{eq}_L\}$, and
- the valuation $\lambda : S \rightarrow P(A)$ such that $\mathsf{eq}_L \in \lambda((c1, c2)) \Leftrightarrow \forall l \in L.\mathsf{store}(c1)(l) = \mathsf{store}(c2)(l)$.

Theorem 1. *A program S is observationally deterministic if and only if, for all stores μ and μ',*

$$(\langle S, \mu \rangle, \langle S, \mu' \rangle) \models^T \Phi_{OD}$$

where: $\Phi_{OD} = \text{eq}_L \Rightarrow \nu X.\text{always}^{(\overline{c_L}_1)} ([(\text{c}_L)_1] \Upsilon)$

$\Upsilon = \text{eventually}^{(-)^L_2} (\text{eq}_L) \wedge \text{always}^{(\overline{c_L})_2} ([(\text{c}_L)_2] (\text{eq}_L \wedge X))$

$(-)^L_i = \{(a)_i \mid \exists l \in L. \, a = \text{c}_l \vee a = \tau\}, i \in \{1, 2\}$

$(\overline{c_L})_i = \{(a)_i \mid a \neq \text{c}_L\}, i \in \{1, 2\}$

$\text{always}^A(\phi) = \nu Y.\phi \wedge (\bigwedge_{a \in A} [a] Y) \qquad \text{eventually}^A(\phi) = \mu Y.\phi \vee (\bigwedge_{a \in A} [a] Y)$

Proof. For space reasons, we refer to Blondeel's Master's thesis [2] for the proof of this theorem[5].

Intuitively, formula Φ_{OD} expresses that if the low stores of the two program copies are the same (eq_L), then the trace corresponding to the transitions of the first part and the trace corresponding to the transitions of the second part are stuttering equivalent. Stuttering equivalence says that whenever the first part changes a variable in L ($[(\text{c}_L)_1] \ldots$), then Υ has to hold, expressing that: (*i*) there is always a point reachable where the second program copy will change a variable in L such that the low stores become equal again ($\text{eventually}^{(-)^L_2} (\text{eq}_L)$), and (*ii*) if the second program copy is the only one to take transitions and those transitions do not change low variables, ($\text{always}^{(\overline{c_L})_2}(\ldots)$), then after the second program copy changes a low variable for the first time ($[(\text{c}_L)_2] \ldots$), the two stores will be equal and the whole formula will hold again ($\text{eq}_L \wedge R$).

4.3   Eager Trace Invariance in Temporal Logic

In a similar spirit, eager trace invariance can be characterised. However, this requires to compose the program with itself *thrice*: a program is eager trace invariant if for every two executions that have the same initial low actions, there exists a third execution that performs *all* initial actions of the second execution and then mimics all future low actions of the first execution. This makes it necessary that the initial store of the third model can remain *undetermined* for a while, therefore we add an uninitialised store $\bot$ to the model, defining $\mathit{Conf}_\bot = \mathit{Stmt} \times (\mathit{Store} \cup \{\bot\})$, together with an explicit initialisation label init.

The temporal logic characterisation of eager trace invariance does not use atomic propositions, so the model is of the form $(S, \mathit{Lab}, \rightarrow)$, where

- states $S = \mathit{Conf}_\bot \times \mathit{Conf}_\bot \times \mathit{Conf}_\bot$,
- labels[6] $\mathit{Lab} = \{\tau\} \cup \{(a)_j \mid a \in \mathit{Act} \cup \{\text{init}\} \wedge j \in \{1, 2, 3\}\}$, and
- transitions $\rightarrow$ are defined as the obvious lifting of the standard operational semantics, extended with explicit initialisation.

The formula abstracts away from the particular kind of high transitions that occur. To model this, we define a so-called high transition relation $\Rightarrow_H$, with corresponding modalities $\langle\langle a \rangle\rangle_H$ and $[a]_H$, respectively, as a variation of standard

---

[5] In fact, this is a proof for the case where the location traces have to be stuttering equivalent, instead of the complete traces - but the main structure of the proof remains unchanged.

[6] Where *Act* is as defined in the definition of eager trace invariance, page 153.

weak transitions and modalities (that abstract over internal transitions). Let a_l be a low action label, and let $\stackrel{(a_h)_j}{\Rightarrow}$ be the standard weak transition relation. Then the high transition relation $\Rightarrow_H$ is defined as follows.

$$s \stackrel{\tau}{\Rightarrow}_H s' \Leftrightarrow s(\Rightarrow_{H'})^* s' \qquad\qquad s \Rightarrow_{H'} s' \Leftrightarrow \exists a_h \in Act_H . \exists j \in \{1,2,3\} . s \stackrel{(a_h)_j}{\Rightarrow} s'$$
$$s \stackrel{a_l}{\Rightarrow}_H s' \Leftrightarrow s \Rightarrow_H \stackrel{a_l}{\Rightarrow} \Rightarrow_H s'$$

Now we can characterise eager trace invariance as well in modal μ-calculus.

Theorem 2. *A program S is eager invariant if and only if*

$$(\bot,\bot,\bot) \models^{T_S} [(init)_1] [(init)_2] \, \Phi_{ETI}$$

where

$$\Phi_{ETI} = [init_1] [init_2] \, (\nu X. \langle init_3 \rangle \, mimic_{3,1} \wedge \bigwedge_{a_h \in Act_H} [(a_h)_1] \, X$$
$$\wedge \bigwedge_{a_h \in Act_H} [(a_h)_2] \, \langle init_3 \rangle \, \langle\!\langle (a_h)_3 \rangle\!\rangle \, \Psi$$
$$\wedge \bigwedge_{a_l \in Act_L} [(a_l)_1] \, [(a_l)_2] \, \langle init_3 \rangle \, \langle\!\langle (a_l)_3 \rangle\!\rangle \, \Psi)$$
$$\Psi = \nu Y. \, mimic_{3,1} \wedge \bigwedge_{a_h \in Act_H} [(a_h)_1] \, Y \wedge \bigwedge_{a_h \in Act_H} [(a_h)_2] \, \langle\!\langle (a_h)_3 \rangle\!\rangle \, Y$$
$$\wedge \bigwedge_{a_l \in Act_L} [(a_l)_1] \, [(a_l)_2] \, \langle\!\langle (a_l)_3 \rangle\!\rangle \, Y$$
$$mimic_{3,1} = \nu Z. \bigwedge_{a_l \in Act_L} [(a_l)_1]_H \, \langle\!\langle (a_l)_3 \rangle\!\rangle_H \, Z$$

Proof. See Blondeel's Master thesis [2] for the proof.

Formula $mimic_{3,1}$ expresses that for all histories generated by model 1, model 3 can generate a history which is low equivalent. Formula Φ_{ETI} and Ψ are identical, except that Ψ assumes that the store of the third model is already initialised. Intuitively, we loop in Φ_{ETI} until $init_3$ has happened, and then we loop in Ψ. Formula Φ_{ETI} and Ψ define all states where $mimic_{3,1}$ should hold. These are all states where (*i*) model 1 and 2 have communicated low equivalent histories, and (*ii*) model 3 has communicated exactly the same history (including high actions) as model 2. In other words, formula Φ_{ETI} and Ψ express that as long as model 1 and model 2 have low equivalent histories (*i.e.*, one of them does a high action, or they do the same low action), model 3 can reproduce the actions that model 2 has done so far (including high actions), and then mimic model 1 in its future low actions.

5   Encoding in the Concurrency WorkBench

As mentioned above, in earlier work, Huisman *et al.* characterised observational determinism using CTL* [11]. However, there is no readily available model checker for CTL*, therefore they experimented with Evaluator in the CADP tool set [7] to model check the property. But since Evaluator only supports alternation-free modal μ-calculus, while observational determinism (as defined by Huisman) only can be expressed as a μ-calculus formula with alternation of greatest and least fixed points, only a stronger property could actually be verified. Thus, it is preferable to use a model checker that supports full modal μ-calculus, such as Concurrency WorkBench (CWB) [15]. This expressiveness is needed, because the properties typically express requirements such as: if one model can do a certain step, the other model (the program copy) has to be able to mimic this step.

We encode our program model and the modal μ-calculus formulations of observational determinism and eager trace invariance in CWB's specification language. The encoding is quite straightforward, to be able to quickly get experimental results.

CWB allows to define agents (or processes) in basic CCS, the Calculus of Communicating Systems [14]. CWB's specification language is quite restrictive, and it does not provide any support for data. Thus there are no parametrised actions, nor conditional statements, and we have to use basic CCS agents to update and lookup variables.

In CCS, when a process performs action a, some parallel process or the environment must simultaneously perform a co-action $'a$ (a corresponds to *receiving* on channel a and $'a$ corresponds to *sending* on channel a). If $'a$ is performed by a parallel process, then a and $'a$ together form a silent action τ. This action corresponds to an *internal choice*, and it is ignored by the weak modalities $\langle\!\langle \alpha \rangle\!\rangle$ and $[\![\alpha]\!]$ of the modal μ-calculus. Internal actions are used to control the behaviour of the agents. All other actions communicate with the environment (*external choices*). For each model, we have exactly one input action: input-mi for model i. After this action, all variables in model i are initialised. The other actions, with "output" in their name, denote a message that is sent to the environment.

Observational determinism and trace invariance assume different actions, therefore we have to give different CCS models. In the sequel, we describe the most important aspects of the modelling of observational determinism. The modelling of eager trace invariance uses a similar approach (and reuses part of the CWB modelling for observational determinism); we refer to Blondeel's Master thesis [2] for details about this.

5.1 CWB Encoding of the Program Model

The first step to encode the program model is to model the store using CCS agents. Each agent is of the form $x-v-$mi, where x is a variable, i a program copy number and v a value in the (finite) domain of x. It is necessary to enumerate all possible values, because CCS can not be parametrised with data. Each agent can output the value, either to the environment, or internally. These actions return the original agent. Further, we model updates, that return a different agent, related with the new value of the variable. Every change is output, both externally and internally. The internal communication ensures that the model of the store is updated. As the updates consist of several actions, we have to ensure that the variable cannot be changed in between. To do this, we introduce 'begin' and 'end' labels for variable updates, that ensure that each complete update is executed atomically. Consequently, the properties that we want to verify have to be adapted for this: instead of checking for a single transition that corresponds to a variable change, they have to match pairs of labels.

Also the individual transitions in the operational semantics (Figure 1) are not atomic in the CCS model. To ensure atomicity of the steps in the operational semantics, a special lock is defined per program model. Each transition in the program model first acquires the lock, then executes the corresponding CCS actions, and then releases the lock. In each model, we have one agent for the assignment of a constant (**AssignValue-mi**) and one agent for the assignment of the value stored in another variable (**AssignVar-mi**), for example:

> agent **AssignValue-mi**(output-begin-change-x-to-v_1-mi, change-x-v_1-mi,
> value-x-v_1-mi, value-x-v_2-mi, Follow-mi) =
> **takeLock-mi**. (value-x-v_2-mi. 'output-begin-change-x-to-v_1-mi.
> 'change-x-v_1-mi. 'output-end-change-mi. +
> value-x-v_1-mi. 'output-nochange-mi).
> **'releaseLock-mi**.Follow-mi;

This agent should be understood as follows: first the lock for model mi is acquired. If the current value of x in the model mi is v_2, then a change to the value v_1 is communicated (both internally and externally), and then the change has finished. If the value of x is already v_1, then no change is communicated. Then the lock is released, and the remainder of the model mi is executed.

All transitions of the operational semantics are modelled, except for those when the program is terminated; this case is handled by the encoding of observational determinism. Each program copy is modelled as the parallel composition of agents modelling the program, the store and the lock mechanism. The complete program is modelled as the parallel composition of two copies of such models.

Example 8. Consider again Program 1. Using our CWB encoding, the first program copy is modelled as the following CCS agent. Notice that instead of using integer values we explicitly encode Boolean values because we do not have any data in CCS, and the modelling is intended as a proof of concept. All text preceded by $*$ are comments:

```
agent Pr1-m1 =
  * h := false
  (AssignValue-m1( c-h-false-out-m1,          * output-begin-change-x-to-v1-m1
                   c-h-false-m1,              * change-x-v1-m1
                   v-h-false-m1, v-h-true-m1, * value-x-v1-m1, value-x-v2-m1
  * if(h = true) then...else ∈ fi
  If-m1( v-h-true-m1, v-h-false-m1, * then-condition, else condition
       * l := h', then branch
       AssignVar-m1( c-l-true-out-m1, c-l-true-m1, c-l-false-out-m1, c-l-false-m1,
                     v-l-true-m1, v-l-false-m1,
                     v-hprime-true-m1, v-hprime-false-m1, 0),
       0))) | * else branch
  * l := true
  (AssignValue-m1( c-l-true-out-m1, c-l-true-m1, v-l-true-m1, v-l-false-m1, 0));
```

This is executed in parallel with the locking mechanism to make the transition steps of the program copy atomic and with the agent modelling the store of the first program copy, after hiding the internal communication actions. Together this results in the agent describing the program model for the first program copy.

> agent **ExPr1-m1** =
>   (**Lock-m1** | **StoreLHHprime-m1** | **Pr1-m1**) \ **InternActions-m1** ;

Program copy 2 is exactly the same, with all **m1** replaced by **m2**. Their parallel composition - the program model of the self-composed program - is then defined as **ExPr1-m1|ExPr1-m2**.

5.2   CWB Encoding of Observational Determinism

To model the observational determinism property in CWB, we first model equality of variables $x \in Var_L$. Because we currently only encode Boolean values, it is sufficient to check whether x in m1 is true if and only if x in m2 is true. This results in the following property definition for **Eq** (where T is CWB notation for *true*, and & is conjunction):

> prop **Eq** =
> $\bigcup_{x \in Var_L}$ (⟨ 'output-value-*x*-*true*-m1⟩T ⇒ ⟨ 'output-value-*x*-*true*-m2 ⟩ T) &
>   (⟨ 'output-value-*x*-*true*-m2⟩T ⇒ ⟨ 'output-value-*x*-*true*-m1 ⟩ T);

To handle termination according to the operational semantics, we express explicitly when a model mi cannot do any action corresponding to the labelled transitions by defining a set **ProgressActions-mi**. We explicitly add a liveness requirement ∼**CanHoldBeforeEnd-mi**, ensuring that there is no path on which Phi always holds until the program terminates (where ∼ is CWB notation for negation, and | for disjunction).

> prop **Finished-mi** = [[**ProgressActions-mi**]]F;
> set **ProgressActions-mi** =
>   { 'output-begin-change-*x*-to-*v*-mi | $x \in Store \wedge v \in \mathsf{dom}(x)$} ∪
>   { 'output-end-change-mi, 'output-nochange-mi};
> prop **CanHoldBeforeEnd-mi**(Phi) =
>   min(X. (Phi & **Finished-mi**) | (Phi & ⟪**ProgressActions-mi**⟫X));

Now we can model observational determinism and its subexpressions.

> prop **ObervationalDeterminism** = [[init-m1]][[init-m2]]**Eq** ⇒ **TraceInd**;
> prop **TraceInd** = max(R. Always-*x*-m1(
>   [[**BeginChangeLowActions-m1**]] [['output-end-change-m1]]
>   **Eventually-m2**(**Eq**) & ∼**CanHoldBeforeEnd-m2**(∼**Eq**) &
>   **Always-*x*-m2**([[**BeginChangeLowActions-m2**]]
>   [['output-end-change-m2]](**Eq** & R))
> set **BeginChangeLowActions-mi** =
>   { 'output-begin-change-*x*-to-*v*-mi | $x \in Store_L \wedge v \in \mathsf{dom}(x)$}

set **Compl-change-x-mi** =
    { 'output-begin-change-y-to-v-mi | $y \in Store - \{x\} \wedge v \in \mathsf{dom}(x)$} $\cup$
    { 'output-end-change-mi, 'output-nochange-mi};
prop **Always-x-mi**(Phi) = max(X. Phi & [[**Compl-change-x-mi**]]X);
prop **Eventually-mi**(Phi) = min(X. Phi | [[**ProgressActions-mi**]]X);

We have verified this property on several simple example programs, including running examples Program 1 and Program 2. Program 1 is observationally deterministic, but typically rejected by a type checker because of the information-leaking then-branch that depends on a private variable - even though the condition will never be true, thus the then branch will never be executed. This is correctly accepted by CWB. Program 2 is not observationally deterministic, and this is indeed rejected by CWB. We have tried the model checker on about 20 small example programs. In all cases, the model checker returns the (correct) answer within milliseconds.

To try the encoding on more realistic examples, the encoding has to be improved, because we would need more than just Boolean values.

6   Conclusions and Future Work

This paper describes a practical exercise in using the self-composition approach to model check secure information flow for multithreaded programs. Concretely, we show how eager trace invariance, proposed by Roscoe [16], and observational determinism, in the version of Terauchi [20], can be characterised as temporal logic formulae and encoded in the Concurrency WorkBench [15]. The encoding can be used to check security of several simple example programs, including examples that would be rejected by a type checker.

As future work, we plan to make the approach scale. For this, we need to improve the modelling of the program model, without an explicit encoding of the data domain. We will study whether parametrised boolean equation systems [4,9] are appropriate for this. If so, we will develop a translation from a program in a general-purpose programming language into such a system.

The properties that we studied in this paper are classical definitions of confidentiality in a multithreaded program. However, they can be overly restrictive, because they require the program behaviour to be completely deterministic. An alternative approach is to define a probabilistic confidentiality property that restricts the likelihood of a certain trace occurring. The literature contains several examples of probabilistic secure information flow properties, *e.g.*, [22,19,17]. We are currently extending our approach to such probabilistic properties, using probabilistic temporal logics and a probabilistic model checker, such as PRISM [13].

Acknowledgements. We thank Ngo Minh Tri and the anonymous reviewers for their useful feedback on earlier versions of this paper.

References

1. Barthe, G., D'Argenio, P., Rezk, T.: Secure information flow by self-composition. In: Computer Security Foundation Workshop (CSFW 2017). IEEE Press, Los Alamitos (2004)
2. Blondeel, H.-C.: Security by logic: characterizing non-interference in temporal logic. Master's thesis, KTH Sweden (2007), ftp://ftp-sop.inria.fr/everest/Marieke.Huisman/blondeel.pdf
3. Boudol, G., Castellani, I.: Noninterference for concurrent programs and thread systems. Theor. Comput. Sci. 281(1-2), 109–130 (2002)
4. Chen, T., Ploeger, S.C.W., van de Pol, J.C., Willemse, T.A.C.: Equivalence checking for infinite systems using parameterized boolean equation systems. In: Caires, L., Vasconcelos, V.T. (eds.) CONCUR 2007. LNCS, vol. 4703, pp. 120–135. Springer, Heidelberg (2007)
5. Dam, M., Gurov, D.: mu-calculus with explicit points and approximations. Journal of Logic and Computation 12, 43–57 (2002)
6. Darvas, Á., Hähnle, R., Sands, D.: A theorem proving approach to analysis of secure information flow. In: Hutter, D., Ullmann, M. (eds.) SPC 2005. LNCS, vol. 3450, pp. 193–209. Springer, Heidelberg (2005)
7. Garavel, H., Lang, F., Mateescu, R., Serwe, W.: CADP 2006: A toolbox for the construction and analysis of distributed processes. In: Damm, W., Hermanns, H. (eds.) CAV 2007. LNCS, vol. 4590, pp. 158–163. Springer, Heidelberg (2007)
8. Goguen, J., Meseguer, J.: Security policies and security models. In: IEEE Symposium on Security and Privacy, pp. 11–20 (1982)
9. Groote, J.F., Orzan, S.: Parameterised anonymity. In: Degano, P., Guttman, J.D., Martinelli, F. (eds.) FAST 2008. LNCS, vol. 5491, pp. 177–191. Springer, Heidelberg (2009)
10. Huisman, M., Ngo, M.T.: A new definition of confidentiality for multi-threaded programs (2010) (manuscript)
11. Huisman, M., Worah, P., Sunesen, K.: A temporal logic characterisation of observational determinism. In: Computer Security Foundations Workshop (2006)
12. Kozen, D.: Results on the propositional μ-calculus. Theoretical Computer Science 27, 333–354 (1983)
13. Kwiatkowska, M., Norman, G., Parker, D.: PRISM: Probabilistic model checking for performance and reliability analysis. ACM SIGMETRICS Performance Evaluation Review 36(4), 40–45 (2009)
14. Milner, R.: A Calculus of Communicating Systems. Springer, Heidelberg (1980)
15. Moller, F., Stevens, P.: Edinburgh Concurrency Workbench user manual (version 7.1), http://homepages.inf.ed.ac.uk/perdita/cwb/
16. Roscoe, A.: CSP and determinism in security modelling. In: Symposium on Security and Privacy, pp. 114–127. IEEE Computer Society Press, Los Alamitos (1995)
17. Sabelfeld, A., Sands, D.: Probabilistic noninterference for multi-threaded programs. In: Computer Security Foundations Workshop, pp. 200–215. IEEE Press, Los Alamitos (2000)
18. Smith, G., Volpano, D.: Secure Information Flow in a Multi-threaded Imperative Language. In: Principles of Programming Languages, pp. 355–364 (1998)
19. Smith, G., Volpano, D.: Confinement properties for multi-threaded programs. Electronic Notes in Theoretical Computer Science 20 (1999)

20. Terauchi, T.: A type system for observational determinism. In: Computer Security Foundation, CSF 2008 (2008)
21. Terauchi, T., Aiken, A.: Secure Information Flow as a Safety Problem. In: Hankin, C., Siveroni, I. (eds.) SAS 2005. LNCS, vol. 3672, pp. 352–367. Springer, Heidelberg (2005)
22. Volpano, D., Smith, G.: Probabilistic noninterference in a concurrent language. Journal of Computer Security 7, 231–253 (1999)
23. Zdancewic, S., Myers, A.C.: Observational determinism for concurrent program security. In: 16th IEEE Computer Security Foundations Workshop (2003)

Multiple Congruence Relations, First-Order Theories on Terms, and the Frames of the Applied Pi-Calculus

Florent Jacquemard[1], Étienne Lozes[1,3,*], Ralf Treinen[2], and Jules Villard[1,4,*]

[1] LSV, ENS Cachan, CNRS UMR 8643 and INRIA, France
[2] PPS, Université Paris Diderot, CNRS UMR 7126, France
[3] MOVES, RWTH Aachen, Germany
[4] Queen Mary University of London, UK

Abstract. We investigate the problem of deciding first-order theories of finite trees with several distinguished congruence relations, each of them given by some equational axioms. We give an automata-based solution for the case where the different equational axiom systems are linear and variable-disjoint (this includes the case where all axioms are ground), and where the logic does not permit to express tree relations $x = f(y, z)$. We show that the problem is undecidable when these restrictions are relaxed. As motivation and application, we show how to translate the model-checking problem of $A\pi\mathcal{L}$, a spatial equational logic for the applied pi-calculus, to the validity of first-order formulas in term algebras with multiple congruence relations.

1 Introduction

Term algebras play a crucial role in the symbolic modeling of cryptographic protocols. In the applied π-calculus [2], a variant of the π-calculus tailored to the study of security protocols, the history of communications at some point of a protocol can be represented by a *frame*, consisting of a set of terms, each representing a message that has been sent, together with a set of *names* that are assumed to be secret at the beginning of the communication. For instance, the encryption of a secret s using someone's public key $pub(k)$ (with the equational axiom $dec(enc(x, pub(k)), k) = x$) can lead to the frame $F_0 := (\{k, s\}, \{u_0 = pub(k), u_1 = enc(s, u_0)\})$ where the first element of the pair is the set of *secret* (or *hidden*) names (here k and s) of the frame. Analyzing frames is crucial to discover potential flaws in security protocols.

Usually, one checks the properties of frames against two particular queries: the deducibility of a term from a given frame, and the static equivalence of two given frames. Assuming passive attackers who can observe messages exchanged on all public channels, deducibility corresponds to what they may infer from these observations, while static equivalence asserts *indistinguishability* between two protocols. These two properties are decidable for a fairly large (at least from a practical perspective) class of underlying equational theories, as shown by Abadi and Cortier [1]. However, many other properties, more tailored to a particular protocol, are imaginable. For instance, in the frame F above, one may ask whether the owner of the private key k will be able to

---

[*] Authors partially supported by the french ANR project PANDA.

S. Mödersheim and C. Palamidessi (Eds.): TOSCA 2011, LNCS 6993, pp. 166–185, 2012.

uncover s. To provide a more general decision procedure that would also apply to these properties, one may wish to use a logic for which the model-checking problem is decidable. Since first-order logics over a term algebra cannot easily express the properties above, other formalisms need be considered.

In this paper, we study the decidability of the model-checking of $A\pi\mathcal{L}$ [20,19], a spatial logic for the applied π-calculus, and more precisely of a fragment $\mathcal{FSL}$ of it we call *frame spatial logic*, that is dedicated to frames. This fragment exposes two of the main ingredients of $A\pi\mathcal{L}$, hidden name revelation and spatial conjunction, which we believe to be generally useful in naturally expressing security properties of frames. For instance, the hidden name revelation can be used to capture the subtler property mentioned above using the formula $Hk. u_0 = pub(k) \wedge (\exists x. Hs. x = s)$, which reads informally as follows: by revealing k, whose public key is published on u_0, one may craft a term x, independent of s but which may depend on k (given the position of the existential quantifier in the formula), such that x is equal to s (here $x = dec(u_2, k)$ would be a valid witness). Spatial conjunction $*$ between two properties expresses the fact that the current frame can be decomposed into two subframes that do not share any hidden name such that each subframe satisfies one of the subformulas. For instance, the formula $1 := \neg\mathbf{0} \wedge \neg(\neg\mathbf{0} * \neg\mathbf{0})$ describes precisely the non-empty frames that may not be decomposed into two non-empty frames. Using this formula, one may express a property Φ about a part of a frame that represents a single session of a protocol (supposing that each session is distinguished from the others by the use of a unique hidden name in each message) with $(1 \wedge \Phi) * true$. Decomposing frames spatially may also help expose which parts of the frame are responsible for the leak of a secret: the formula $(\exists x. Hn. x = n) \wedge \neg(\exists x. Hn. (\Phi_1 * x = n))$ means that a secret name is leaked, but that the messages in the part of the frame described by Φ_1 are necessary to obtain this secret. The frame spatial logic $\mathcal{FSL}$ is also rich enough to express that a given term is deducible from a frame and to characterize a particular frame.

Reducing the model-checking problem of the logic $\mathcal{FSL}$ to a purely equational logic with no spatial connectives gives rise to formulas where *multiple* congruence relations may appear, which come from the various (fragments of) frames $\{u_i = t_i\}_{i \in I}$ under consideration, each introducing additional axioms $u_i = t_i$ to the term algebra. Another, more restricted case of multiple congruence relations can be found in the logic of frames $\mathcal{LF}$ of Hüttel and Pedersen [16], in which one can compare terms either syntactically ($t_1 = t_2$) or according to the underlying equational theory $\mathcal{E}$ ($t_1 =_\mathcal{E} t_2$).

In this paper, we introduce the general framework of first-order constraints systems with *multiple* congruence relations. There exist a number of decidability results for the first-order theory of term algebras, or equivalently finite trees, and more generally for the first-order theory of the quotient of a term algebra by some congruence. Most of these decidability results were obtained by quantifier elimination. One of the key observation for quantifier elimination procedures is that the rule

$$\exists x. (x = t \wedge \phi) \quad \rightsquigarrow \quad \phi[x \leftarrow t] \quad \text{if } x \notin \mathit{Vars}(t)$$

where ϕ is an arbitrary conjunction of literals, and $\phi[x \leftarrow t]$ denotes the formula obtained by replacing every occurrence of the variable x by the term t, requires $=$ to be a congruence relation with respect to all functions and predicates of the structure. However, when faced with several congruence relations, the observation above cannot be naively used as a basis for quantifier elimination. The reason is that, faced with a formula like $\exists x_1, x_2. (x_1 =_1 t_1 \wedge x_2 =_2 t_2 \wedge \phi)$ where $=_1$ and $=_2$ are two different congruence relations of our structure, one cannot simply eliminate x_1 or x_2 as before. Indeed $=_1$ would not necessarily be a congruence with respect to $=_2$, and vice versa, since in general the equational axioms used for defining these equivalence relations would be independent. One might however hope that there is a solution to this problem. If $\{\theta_1, \ldots, \theta_n\}$ is a complete set of unifiers of $x =_1 t_1$, that is for the equational theory $=_1$, then the above formula would be equivalent to $\exists x_2, \bar{y}_1. (x_2 =_2 t_2 \wedge \phi)\theta_1 \vee \ldots \vee \exists x_2, \bar{y}_n. (x_2 =_2 t_2 \wedge \phi)\theta_n$ where $\bar{y}_i$ is the set of extra variables introduced by the unifier θ_i. The question is whether a similar combination result can be achieved for the full first-order theory.

Results. In this paper, we show the decidability of the first-order theory of term algebras with several congruence relations. The predicates of our structure are of the form $x =_i y$, where each $=_i$ is given by a set of linear and variable-disjoint equational axioms. The structure does *not* contain function symbols, and hence does not allow to express relations of the form $x = f(y, z)$. This restriction makes the structure accessible to automata-theoretic techniques, which is a key to our decidability result. We show that decidability no longer holds when we allow term relations like $x = f(y, z)$, or when one generalizes to flat axiom systems. However, our decidability result can be extended to the quotient of the term algebra under a certain class of rewrite systems (which represent underlying equational theories on terms) for which a completion procedure terminates. We show that it is the case for rewrite rules of the form $g \rightarrow x$ where g is a *jack* (see page 174) and all $=_i$ are axiomatized by ground equations. We also show that undecidability is reached as soon as one of the $=_i$ is the tree equality.

From a security point of view, as we will show, this means that deducibility and static equivalence, as well as the model-checking problem of $\mathcal{FSL}$, are all decidable when the underlying equational theory can be expressed as a rewrite system such that the completion procedure mentioned above terminates. This is the case in particular for the theory of pairs and of symmetric and asymmetric encryption with *fixed* keys, but not for the theory of signed messages for instance.

Related work. This paper is the result of two lines of research: decidability results for first-order theories on the one side, and the study of process algebras for security protocols on the other side.

The decidability of the first-order theory of finite trees over a finite signature, with syntactic equality as the only predicate, was first shown by Malc'ev [22], this result was later rediscovered and extended independently by Maher [21] and Comon and Lescanne [10]. Encouraged by this result, several researchers started in the late 80s the program to show decidability of the first-order theory of term algebras with different predicates than just syntactic equality. Research basically went into several directions: one direction was to add relations other than equality to the theory, in particular ordering relations that were useful for ordered rewrite calculi [6,17], or for typing of programming languages [24,18]. Another direction was the addition of predicates that can be recognized by various classes of tree automata [5,8]. A third direction was to replace the syntactic equality relation in the original result by an equality relation modulo a set of equational axioms. The initial optimism was fueled by the fact that for quantifier-free positive constraints, so-called unification systems, the extension of syntactic unification to unification modulo equational theories has led to a rich theory and many useful results (see, for instance, [3] for a survey). The probably strongest result in this direction is the decidability of the theory of term algebras modulo so-called *shallow* equational theories [9]. However, it also turned out that the limits of decidability are met much earlier with first-order theories than with unification problems, and undecidability of the theory of term algebras modulo some important equational theories were shown, among them AC [25,23].

From the perspective of symbolic cryptography, our work can be compared with the one of Abadi and Cortier [1] in which they show that term deduction and static equivalence are decidable for many equational theories. Most of the classes they consider are out of the reach of the techniques presented here; however, our work takes a different approach than theirs: we consider the decision of any property that can be expressed in $\mathcal{FSL}$, for instance the mere existence of a leaked secret name (which amounts to quantifying over the terms that can be deduced from a frame), or more generally of any property expressible in a first-order theory with multiple congruence relations and a background term rewrite system. This makes both results incomparable.

Outline. Section 2 collects the necessary background on term algebras, tree automata, and term rewriting. In Section 3, we establish the decidability of the first-order theory of term algebras with multiple congruence relations, and the undecidability under small relaxations of our hypothesis. In Section 4, we show how to extend the decidability result to a certain class of "background" rewrite systems. Finally, Section 5 introduces the application to the study of the frames of the applied π-calculus.

2   Preliminaries

We assume the usual notions of rewriting. A *signature* Σ is a set of function symbols with arity. The subset of function symbols of Σ of arity n is denoted by Σ_n. A signature Σ is called *monadic* if when it contains only unary and constant function symbols ($\Sigma = \Sigma_0 \cup \Sigma_1$). The set of variables is V; given a signature Σ, we denote by $T(\Sigma, V)$ the set of terms over Σ, and by $T(\Sigma)$ the set of *ground* terms (terms without variables). A term $t \in T(\Sigma, V)$ can be conveniently seen as a function from its set of positions $Pos(t)$ (non-empty set of sequences of positive integers that is closed under prefix and left brother) into $\Sigma \cup V$. Let $Vars(t)$ denote the set of variables of t, $depth(t)$ its depth, $t|_p$ the subterm of t at position p, and $t[s]_p$ the replacement in t of the subterm at position p by s. The term t is called *linear* if every variable of $Vars(t)$ occurs exactly once in t.

Equations are considered non-oriented, that is $\ell = r$ is identified with $r = \ell$. We call an equation $\ell = r$ *ground* when $Vars(\ell) = Vars(r) = \emptyset$, *variable-disjoint* when $Vars(\ell)$ is disjoint with $Vars(r)$, *flat* when $depth(\ell), depth(r) \leq 1$ and *shallow* when every variable of $Vars(\ell) \cap Vars(r)$ occurs at depth at most 1 in ℓ and r. A set of equations is variable-disjoint (resp. ground, flat, shallow) when each of its equations is. Any flat equation is shallow, and any ground equation is both shallow and variable-disjoint, while in general flat or shallow equations are not necessarily variable-disjoint.

Let R be a rewrite system, and E a set of equational axioms. We write $s \xrightarrow{R} t$ when s rewrites to t in one step by R, and $s \xleftrightarrow{E} t$ when s transforms to t in one equational proof step by E. The relations $\xrightarrow{*}{R}$ and $=_E$ are the reflexive and transitive closures of respectively $\xrightarrow{R}$ and $\xleftrightarrow{E}$, that is, in the latter case, $s =_E t$ when s and t are equal modulo the set E of equations. We write $=_{E,R}$ for the reflexive, symmetric and transitive closure of $\xleftrightarrow{E} \cup \xrightarrow{R}$.

Given a finite signature Σ, a (bottom-up) *tree automaton* A is given by (Q, F, Δ) where Q is a finite set of *states*, $F \subseteq Q$ is called the set of *accepting states*, Δ is a set of rewrite rules $f(q_1, \ldots, q_n) \to q$ with $f \in \Sigma_n$, $q_1, \ldots, q_n, q \in Q$. The automaton A *accepts* a tree t iff $t \xrightarrow{*} q \in F$ by the transition rules Δ. The *language* L_A is the set of all trees accepted by A. Tree automata enjoy (almost) all the nice properties of word automata, in particular closure under Boolean operations, decidability of the emptiness problem, determinization, minimization [7].

The *convolution* operation defined below allows to code n-tuples of trees as trees over a signature of n-tuples. Let Σ be a signature with $\square \notin \Sigma$. We define the signature $\Sigma^{[n]}$, for $n \geq 1$, as

$$\Sigma^{[n]} = \{[f_1, \ldots, f_n] \mid f_i \in \Sigma \cup \{\square\}, f_i \neq \square \text{ for at least one } i\}.$$

The arity of $[f_1 \ldots, f_n]$ in $\Sigma^{[n]}$ is the maximum of the arities of those f_i that are in Σ. For $t_1, \ldots, t_n \in T(\Sigma)$, the convolution $t_1 \otimes \ldots \otimes t_n$ is the tree $t \in T(\Sigma^{[n]})$ defined by $Pos(t) = Pos(t_1) \cup \ldots \cup Pos(t_n)$, and for all $\pi \in Pos(t)$, $t(\pi) = [f_1, \ldots, f_n]$ where $f_i = t_i(\pi)$ if $\pi \in Pos(t_i)$, and $f_i = \square$ otherwise. Projection is defined by $\pi_i(t_1 \otimes \ldots \otimes t_n) = t_i$.

For example, let $\Sigma = \{h, f, a\}$, where a is a constant, f unary, and h binary. Then we have that $f(a) \otimes h(a, f(a)) = [f, h]([a, a], [\square, f]([\square, a]))$.

Now, one can define *tree-automatic representations* and *tree-automatic structures* analogously to the definition given in [4] for automata over finite words. This definition applies only to so-called *relational* structures, that is structures that have only predicates in their logical language and no constants or function symbols. This is not a restriction as constants or functions can always be expressed by predicates. Let $\mathfrak{A}$ be a structure over a relational signature with relation symbols $R_1, \ldots, R_n$. A *tree-automatic representation* of $\mathfrak{A}$ is given by

1. a finite signature Σ,
2. a recognizable tree language $L_\delta \subseteq T(\Sigma)$,
3. an onto function $\nu \colon L_\delta \to |\mathfrak{A}|$ ($|\mathfrak{A}|$ denotes the universe of $\mathfrak{A}$),
4. a recognizable tree language $L_R \subseteq T(\Sigma^{[n]})$ for each relation symbol R of the signature of $\mathfrak{A}$, such that for all $t_1, \ldots, t_n \in L_\delta$, $t_1 \otimes \ldots \otimes t_n \in L_R$ if and only if $(\nu(t_1), \ldots, \nu(t_n)) \in R^{\mathfrak{A}}$ –we say that the relation $R^{\mathfrak{A}}$ is *recognizable*.

A structure is *tree-automatic* if it has a tree-automatic representation. The first-order theory of any tree-automatic structure is decidable.

Ground Tree Transducers (GTT) have been introduced in [11]. A GTT is defined by two tree automata A_1 and A_2 over the same signature Σ, and possibly with shared states. The GTT defined by A_1 and A_2 recognizes the pair $(t, t') \in T(\Sigma)^2$ iff there exists a context C, terms $t_i, t'_i \in T(\Sigma)$, and states q_i for $1 \leq i \leq n$, such that $t =$

$C[t_1, \ldots, t_n]$, $t' = C[t'_1, \ldots, t'_n]$, $t_i \xrightarrow{*} q_i$ by A_1 and $t'_i \xrightarrow{*} q_i$ by A_2. Any relation defined by a GTT is recognizable, and the set of GTT-definable relations is closed under iteration (Kleene star) [12].

3   The Case of Several Congruence Relations

Definition 1. *Let Σ be a countable signature with an upper bound on the arities of the function symbols, $(E_i)_{i \in I}$ be a finite family of finite sets of equations over Σ, and $(L_j)_{j \in J}$ a finite family of recognizable tree languages over finite subsets of the signature Σ. The first-order structure $\mathfrak{A}(\Sigma, (E_i)_{i \in I}, (L_j)_{j \in J})$ is defined as follows: the universe is the set of all ground Σ-terms, there are no constant or function symbols, for every $i \in I$ we have a binary relation $=_i$, interpreted as $t_1 =_i t_2$ iff $t_1 =_{E_i} t_2$, for every $j \in J$ we have a unary relation L_j, interpreted as $L_j(t)$ iff $t \in L_j$. The structure $\mathfrak{H}(\Sigma, (E_i)_{i \in I}, (L_j)_{j \in J})$ contains in addition to $\mathfrak{A}(\Sigma, (E_i)_{i \in I}, (L_j)_{j \in J})$ all symbols from Σ as function symbols, interpreted as free constructor symbols.*

Note that first order logic with equality comes as a particular case, when $E_i = \emptyset$ for some i. In this case, we can write $=$ for $=_i$. This definition allows to consider a structure in which every ground term $t \in T(\Sigma)$ exists as a syntactic constant. This would be represented by having in the family of recognizable tree languages, for every $t \in T(\Sigma)$, the language consisting of the single term t only (each such language is of course recognizable). Also, note that the logical language of $\mathfrak{H}(\Sigma, (E_i)_{i \in I}, (L_j)_{j \in J})$ allows to express unification problems like $x = f(y, z)$; however this is not possible in $\mathfrak{A}(\Sigma, (E_i)_{i \in I}, (L_j)_{j \in J})$.

We will show that one can effectively construct, given as input a finite family $(E_i)_{i \in I}$ of linear and variable-disjoint equation systems and a finite family $(L_j)_{j \in J}$ of recognizable tree languages, a tree-automatic representation of $\mathfrak{A}(\Sigma, (E_i)_{i \in I}, (L_j)_{j \in J})$. The first step is to define the encoding of the algebra as trees over a finite signature, the (minor) difficulty here being that the algebra contains trees over a possibly infinite alphabet but with a bounded arity. We elude the details.

The languages L_j, $j \in J$, are recognizable by definition. In order to show that every $=_i$, $i \in I$, is recognizable we construct a Ground Tree Transducer as follows: Given the linear and variable-disjoint equational theory $E = \{s_1 = t_1, \ldots, s_n = t_n\}$, let A_1 be the tree automaton that recognizes the set of instances of s_i in state q_i, for any i, and the set of instances of t_i in state p_i, for any i. Symmetrically, let A_2 be the tree automaton that recognizes the set of instances of s_i in state p_i, for any i, and the set of instances of t_i in state q_i, for any i. These automata can be constructed exactly because each equational axiom is linear. Since the axioms are variable-disjoint, the GTT defined by A_1 and A_2 recognizes a pair of terms (t, t') iff t is obtained from t' by a parallel equational replacement with respect to E. The transitive closure of this relation is exactly the equality relation modulo E, which is again a GTT [12], and hence recognizable. Hence:

Theorem 1. *Let Σ be an arity-bounded countable signature. The following problem is decidable: given a finite family $(E_i)_{i \in I}$ of finite sets of linear variable-disjoint equations over Σ, a finite family $(L_j)_{j \in J}$ of recognizable tree languages over Σ, and a first-order formula ϕ, does $\mathfrak{A}(\Sigma, (E_i)_{i \in I}, (L_j)_{j \in J}) \models \phi$ hold?*

Thm. 1 no longer holds if generalized to the structure $\mathfrak{H}(\Sigma, (E_i)_{i \in I}, (L_j)_{j \in J})$, that is if one also allows relations like $x = f(y, z)$.

Theorem 2. *It is undecidable whether a given existential closed first order formula holds in a given structure* $\mathfrak{H}(\Sigma, (E_i)_{1 \le i \le 3}, (L_j)_{1 \le j \le 3})$ *with* Σ *finite, E_1 and E_2 finite sets of ground equations, and $E_3 = \emptyset$.*

Proof *(sketch).* We encode the problem of acceptance of the empty tape for Turing machines. A configuration of a Turing machine M is represented as a right-comb $c_i = g(c_{i,1}, g(c_{i,2}, \ldots, g(c_{i,k}, \flat) \ldots))$ where g is a binary symbol and the constant symbols $c_{i,j}$ are either letter of the input alphabet of M, or a state of M, used to indicate the position of its head. A computation $c_0, \ldots, c_n$ of M (sequence of successive configurations) is also encoded as a right comb $f(c_0, \ldots, f(c_n, \flat))$. We consider the closed formula ϕ defined as follows:

$$\exists y, y_1, y_2, x.\ L_{sp}(y) \wedge y =_{E_1} y_1 \wedge L_c(y_1) \wedge y =_{E_2} y_2 \wedge L_c(y_2) \wedge L_0(x) \wedge y_1 = f(x, y_2)$$

where L_0 and L_c are the languages of term representations of respectively the initial configurations of M (there are several such representations because we use padding), and sequences of configurations (possibly not successive) of M, ending with a final configuration. The regular language L_{sp} contains roughly the term representation of sequences of convolution products of pairs of successive configurations (roughly, terms of the form $f(c_0 \otimes d_1, \ldots, f(c_{n-1} \otimes d_n, f(c_n \otimes \flat, \flat)))$ where the configuration d_{i+1} is obtained from c_i using a transition of M).

Moreover, E_1 and E_2 define respectively the left and right projections over the signatures of pairs. Hence ϕ holds in $\mathfrak{H}(\Sigma, (E_i)_{i \in 1,2}, (L_{sp}, L_c, L_0))$ iff M admits a successful computation (y_1) starting with an initial configuration.   □

Note that the above problem is decidable for arbitrary first-order formula and structures $\mathfrak{H}(\Sigma, (E_1), \emptyset)$ where E_1 is a shallow equational system [9]. However, Thm. 1 no longer holds when one replaces variable-disjoint equational systems by flat equational systems. The signature considered in the next theorem is monadic, hence the results holds already when considering a domain of words.

Theorem 3. *It is undecidable whether a given existential closed first order formula holds in a given structure* $\mathfrak{A}(\Sigma, (E_i)_{1 \le i \le 3}, (L_j)_{1 \le j \le 2})$ *with* Σ *finite and monadic, E_1 and E_2 finite sets of flat equations, and $E_3 = \emptyset$.*

Proof *(sketch).* We reduce from the Post correspondence problem (PCP). Let $\mathcal{P} = \{(u_i, v_i) \mid u_i, v_i \in \{a, b\}^+, 1 \le i \le N\}$ be an instance of PCP and let $L := \max(|u_i|, |v_i| \mid i \le N)$. We consider a monadic signature containing a constant symbol $\flat$ and unary function symbols a, b and $P_{i,j}$ for all $1 \le i \le N$ and $1 \le j \le L$. The purpose of the symbols $P_{i,j}$ is to represent a "skeleton" of solution of $\mathcal{P}$, *i.e.* a sequence of indexes that will be replaced by letters of the u_i's or v_i's using two sets of flat equations E_1 and E_2. In E_1, we have equations like $P_{i,j}(x) = u_{i,j}(x)$ if $1 \le i \le N$ and $1 \le j \le |u_i|$ ($u_{i,j}$ is the jth letter of u_i) and $P_{i,j}(x) = x$ if $|u_i| < j$, and similarly for v_i in E_2.

Moreover, we have two tree automata: L_α recognizing $\{a, b\}^+\flat$, and L_P recognizing $\{P_{i,1} \cdots P_{i,L} \mid 1 \le i \le N\}^* \flat$. Finally, the closed formula $\phi := \exists x, u, v.\ L_P(x) \wedge$

$x =_{E_1} u \wedge x =_{E_2} v \wedge L_\alpha(u) \wedge L_\alpha(v) \wedge u = v$ holds in $\mathfrak{A}(\Sigma, (E_i)_{1 \leq i \leq 3}, (L_\alpha, L_P))$
iff $\mathcal{P}$ has a solution. $\qquad\qquad\qquad\qquad\qquad\qquad\qquad\qquad\qquad\qquad\qquad\quad$ □

4   Adding a Background Term Rewrite System

In this section we show that Thm. 1 can be extended to the case where all equations are taken modulo an additional term rewrite system with some particular properties. The first property is that the system is *canonical*, that is normalizing and confluent, such that each term has a unique normal form. This allows us to restrict the universe of the logic structure to contain only terms in normal form, and each ground term would be interpreted in that structure as its normal form.

Definition 2. *Let Σ, $(E_i)_{i \in I}$, $(L_j)_{j \in J}$ be as in Def. 1, and R be a canonical, left-linear rewrite system. The first-order structure $\mathfrak{A}(\Sigma, (E_i)_{i \in I}, (L_j)_{j \in J}, R)$ is defined as $\mathfrak{A}(\Sigma, (E_i)_{i \in I}, (L_j)_{j \in J})$ in Def. 1 except that the universe is restricted to R-normal forms and that $t_1 =_i t_2$ is interpreted as $t_1 =_{E_i, R} t_2$.*

Note that the term rewrite system may indeed intervene even when the structure contains only terms in normal form, and when all equational systems are normalized with respect to the rewrite system. Take, for example, a rewrite system R consisting of the rule $left(pair(x, y)) \rightarrow x$ and the equational system $E = \{c = pair(a, b)\}$. The system E is normalized w.r.t. R, and so are the terms a and $left(c)$. However, $left(c) = a$ is a consequence of $E \cup R$ but not of E alone.

We say that there is a *critical pair* (CP) between two rewrite rules $\ell \rightarrow r$ and $g \rightarrow d$ if there exists a substitution σ and a non-variable position p of g such that $g\sigma \mid_p = \ell\sigma$, in that case the critical pair is the equation $g\sigma[r\sigma]_p = d\sigma$.

For the decidability result below we require in addition the rewrite system to be *orthogonal*, that is left-linear and without critical pairs. The set of terms in normal forms is then recognizable as a consequence of left-linearity [7]; absence of critical pairs will be useful in the proof of Thm. 4. Orthogonality implies confluence [15].

The idea is to "complete" any of the given equational systems E_i w.r.t. R, by adding the CP (which are equations) between equations and rules of R. If this process terminates for each of these systems E_i then we can conclude. Given an equation $l = r$ and a rewrite rule $g \rightarrow d$, we consider the following two cases of critical pairs:

cp$_1$) There is a substitution σ and a non-variable position p of g such that $g\sigma \mid_p = l\sigma$, in that case the critical pair is $g\sigma[r\sigma]_p = d\sigma$.
cp$_2$) There is a substitution σ and a non-variable position p of l such that $g\sigma = l\sigma \mid_p$, in that case the critical pair is $r\sigma = l\sigma[d\sigma]_p$.

We say that E' is the *completion* of E by R when E' is the smallest set containing E and that contains all its own critical pairs with R. If this set is finite then it can be calculated from E by successive addition of critical pairs.

Lemma 1. *If R is orthogonal and E' is the completion of E by R then $s =_{E, R} t$ iff $s =_{E'} t$ for all terms s, t in R-normal form.*

Proof. Any E' proof step can be simulated by several E, R proof steps, so the back direction is obvious. For the other direction, first note that when $s =_{E,R} t$ then $s =_{E',R} t$ since $E \subseteq E'$. Any proof of $s =_{E',R} t$ can be transformed into a proof such that any R-rewrite step is either preceded by an R rewrite-step, or by an E-step such that the redex of the rewrite step has a non-trivial overlap with the previous equational step. This is a consequence of the orthogonality of R and the fact that s and t are in R-normal form, since a rewrite step can be commuted with a non-overlapping equational step. If the shortest such proof used an R-step then we could replace the preceding equational step and that rewrite step by one single equational step (their critical pair), which would yield a contradiction. ☐

In order to meet the hypotheses of Thm. 1, we have to assure that the critical pair is again linear and variable-disjoint. Linearity may be violated only by a non-linearity of d (since all other terms are linear), and variable disjointness may be violated in case cp_1 when $g\sigma[\bullet]_p$ is not ground. We obtain together with Lemma 1 and Thm. 1:

Theorem 4. *Let Σ be an arity-bounded countable signature, and R an orthogonal and terminating term rewrite system. There exists a decision procedure for the following problem: given a finite family $(E_i)_{i \in I}$ of finite sets of linear variable-disjoint equations over Σ, such that each E_i has a finite completion by R that is linear and variable-disjoint, given a finite family $(L_j)_{j \in J}$ of recognizable tree languages over Σ, and a first-order formula ϕ, does $\mathfrak{A}(\Sigma, (E_i)_{i \in I}, (L_j)_{j \in J}, R) \models \phi$ hold?*

Example. Let R be the term rewrite system with rules $left(pair(x, y)) \rightarrow x$, $right(pair(x, y)) \rightarrow y$ and let E be the following equational theory: $E = \{pair(a, pair(b, c)) = d\}$. Completion terminates successfully with the following equational system: $E = \{pair(a, pair(b, c)) = d, a = left(d), pair(b, c) = right(d), b = left(right(d)), c = right(right(d))\}$.

We can characterize a simple case in which completion always succeeds: we call a term a *jack* when it is either shallow and linear, or $f(t_1, \ldots, t_i, \ldots, t_n)$ such that some t_i is shallow and linear, and each t_j with $j \neq i$ is a constant.

Lemma 2. *When R is a non-overlapping rewrite system of rules $g \rightarrow x$ where each g is a jack, $x \in Vars(g)$, and E a ground equational system such that no constant occurring on a left-hand side of R is a side of E, then completion of any variable-disjoint and linear equation system is finite.*

Proof. The rewrite system is, as an easy consequence of the hypotheses, terminating and orthogonal. Since any right-hand side is subterm of a left-hand-side, which in turn is linear, all terms involved and hence all CP are linear. If $l = r$ is an equation and $g\sigma_p = l\sigma$ an overlap, then due to the definition of jacks and the third condition in the lemma, $g\sigma[\bullet]_p$ is ground, and hence the CP is variable-disjoint. We elude the termination proof of completion. ☐

Here is an example of a term rewrite system that satisfies the conditions of Lem. 2. This system describes the cryptographic operators of pairing and projection, and asymmetric encryption and decryption for *fixed* keys.

$$left(pair(x, y)) \rightarrow x \quad dec(enc(x, pub(a)), a) \rightarrow x \quad enc(dec(x, pub(a)), a) \rightarrow x$$
$$right(pair(x, y)) \rightarrow y \quad dec(enc(x, b), pub(b)) \rightarrow x \quad enc(dec(x, b), pub(b)) \rightarrow x$$

In this case, equational axioms may not contain a or b (the ground subterms of the left-hand sides of R). The generalization of these axioms to arbitrary keys represented by a variable, *i.e.* $dec(enc(x, pub(y)), y) \to x$ would lead to a left-hand side that is not a jack. Thm. 4 does not hold when the completion is no longer variable-disjoint.

Theorem 5. *It is undecidable whether a given existential closed first order formula holds in a given structure* $\mathfrak{A}(\Sigma, (E_i)_{1 \leq i \leq 3}(L_j)_{1 \leq j \leq 2}, R)$ *with* Σ *finite,* R *containing rules of the form* $f(x, c) \to x$ *for* $f \in \Sigma_2, c \in \Sigma_0$ *and* $x \in V$, E_1, E_2 *finite sets of ground equations over* Σ, $E_3 = \emptyset$.

Proof. Similarly to the proof of Thm. 3, we reduce from PCP. The main difference is that we use binary terms of the form $f(\alpha_1, \ldots f(\alpha_n, b) \ldots)$ instead of unary ones (words). The letters of the PCP alphabet and the auxiliary symbols $P_{i,j}$ are now constant symbols, and the equations of E_1 have the form $P_{i,j} = u_{i,j}$ if $1 \leq j \leq |u_i|$ or $P_{i,j} = \square$ if $|u_i| < j \leq L$ (and similarly for v_i with E_2). The TRS contains only one rule $f(\square, x) \to x$. $\qquad\square$

Note that in the case of the proof of Thm. 5, the completion of an equation $P_{i,j} = \square$ by the rule $f(\square, x) \to x$ yields the non variable-disjoint equation $f(P_{i,j}, x) = x$.

5   Application to the Spatial Logic for Frames

In this section, we recall the definitions of the frames of the applied π-calculus (Aπ for short) and the fragment $\mathcal{FSL}$ of the spatial equational logic $A\pi\mathcal{L}$. We then show how to reduce the model-checking problem of $\mathcal{FSL}$ to the satisfaction of a first-order constraint system with multiple congruence relations and a background equational theory, which allows us to apply the results of the previous section in the context of the study of cryptographic protocols.

5.1   Frames

A *frame* is a record of the current knowledge of the environment in the form of *active substitutions*, each accounting for a message that has been sent over the network. Frames act as snapshots of the history of communications during the reduction of Aπ processes. Their study is useful for the post-mortem analysis of the knowledge leaked by a process as well as for characterizing observationally equivalent processes.

Formally, we suppose given a signature Σ that contains the disjoint and countable sets V^π and N^π representing respectively Aπ variables (not to be confused with *term variables*: from the point of view of the signature, Aπ variables are *constants*) and names. V is the usual set of (first-order) variables, distinct from V^π. A frame is a pair (H, S), where $H \subseteq N^\pi$ is a finite set of hidden names and S is a finite set of ground equations of the form $u = r$, where $u \in V^\pi$ and r is a *ground* term (which can contain aπ variables and names, but no term variables). Following the original definition of the applied π-calculus [2], we only consider frames $F = (H, \{u_1 = r_1, \ldots, u_k = r_k\})$ where the u_i's are pairwise distinct and there is no cycle in the Aπ variables (*i.e.* there is an ordering $(i_1, \ldots, i_k)$ of the indices such that u_{i_j} does not appear in $r_{i_{j'}}$ when $j \leq j'$). The u_i's (resp. r_i) form the *domain* (resp. *codomain*) of F, written $dom(F)$ (resp. $codom(F)$). We suppose fixed an equational theory $\mathcal{E}$, used to model cryptographic primitives (for instance defined as a rewrite system as in the previous section).

Notations. We will use the letters h, n, m, s to refer to elements of $\mathcal{N}^\pi$, u for elements of $\mathcal{V}^\pi$, a for elements of $\mathcal{N}^\pi \cup \mathcal{V}^\pi$ and x, y for elements of V. We write t for arbitrary terms in $T(\Sigma, V)$, and r for ground terms in $T(\Sigma)$. The expressions $fn(t)$ and $fav(t)$ respectively denote the sets of names and $A\pi$ variables of t, defined as usual, and $fnav(t) := fn(t) \cup fav(t)$. These notations are lifted to the sets of free names and $A\pi$ variables of frames and formulas in the standard way, with $fn((H, S)) := fn(S) \setminus H$. The union of *disjoint* sets is denoted by $\uplus$.

Frames are considered up to the following structural congruence relation that accounts for α-equivalence over hidden names, for vacuous hidden names, and for the rewriting of terms using the equational theory:

Definition 3. *Structural congruence* $\equiv$ *is the smallest equivalence relation on frames satisfying the following assertions*[1]:

α-CONV	$(H, S) \equiv (H[n{\leftarrow}n'], S[n{\leftarrow}n'])$	*if* $n \in H$ *and* $n' \notin H \cup fn(S)$
NEW	$(H, S) \equiv (H', S)$	*if* $H \cap fn(S) = H' \cap fn(S)$
REWRITE	$(H, \{u_1 = r_1, \ldots, u_k = r_k\}) \equiv (H, \{u_1 = r'_1, \ldots, u_k = r'_k\})$	
		if $\forall i \in \{1, \ldots, k\}. r_i \xleftrightarrow{*}{\mathcal{E}} r'_i$

Let us now recall the two essential notions of deducibility and static equivalence for frames. Two ground terms r_1 and r_2 are equal in the frame F, written $F \vdash_{\mathcal{E}} r_1 = r_2$ (or $F \vdash r_1 = r_2$ if $\mathcal{E}$ is clear from context) when there exists a frame $(H', S') \equiv F$ such that $fn(r_1, r_2) \cap H' = \emptyset$ and $r_1 \xleftrightarrow{*}{\mathcal{E} \cup S'} r_2$.

Definition 4. *A ground term r is deducible from the frame (H, S) if there exists a term r' such that $fn(r') \cap H = \emptyset$ and $(\emptyset, S) \vdash r = r'$.*

F and F' are statically equivalent, written $F \approx_s F'$, when $dom(F) = dom(F')$ and, for all ground terms r, r', $F \vdash r = r'$ if and only if $F' \vdash r = r'$.

Definition 5. *Two frames $F_1 = (H_1, S_1)$ and $F_2 = (H_2, S_2)$ are orthogonal if $H_1 \cap H_2 = \emptyset$, $dom(F_1) \cap dom(F_2) = \emptyset$, $fn(codom(F_1)) \cap H_2 = fn(codom(F_2)) \cap H_1 = \emptyset$, and $S_1 \uplus S_2$ is acyclic. The composition $F = F_1 * F_2$ of orthogonal frames F_1, F_2 is the frame $(H_1 \uplus H_2, S_1 \uplus S_2)$.*

As usual, we write $F_1 \equiv F_2 * F_3$ if there are F'_1, F'_2, F'_3 such that $F'_1 = F'_2 * F'_3$ and $F_i \equiv F'_i$. For instance, the following equality holds:

$$(\{n\}, \{u_o = pub(n)\}) * (\{n\}, \{u_1 = enc(n, u_0)\})$$
$$\equiv (\{k, s\}, \{u_0 = pub(k), u_1 = enc(s, u_0)\})$$

The composition of two frames requires their rewriting so as to prevent clashes of their respective hidden names, hence $(\{k\}, \{u_o = pub(k)\})$ and $(\{k, s\}, \{u_1 = enc(s, pub(k)\}))$ can be composed into $(\{k, k', s\}, \{u_0 = pub(k), u_1 = enc(s, pub(k'))\})$ but not into $(\{k, s\}, \{u_0 = pub(k), u_1 = enc(s, pub(k))\})$.

---

[1] We slightly deviate from the standard structural congruence defined by Abadi and Fournet [2], as we assume that substitutions of a frame are not taken into account when rewriting the terms of this frame (for instance, in our setting, $(H, \{u_1 = u_2, u_2 = r\}) \not\equiv (H, \{u_1 = r, u_2 = r\})$). This does not change the notions of deducibility and static equivalence.

$$F, v \vDash t_1 = t_2 \quad \Leftrightarrow \quad F \vdash_{\mathcal{E}} t_1 v = t_2 v$$
$$F, v \vDash \mathbf{0} \qquad\quad \Leftrightarrow \quad F \equiv (\emptyset, \emptyset)$$
$$F, v \vDash \textcircled{c}a \qquad \Leftrightarrow \quad \forall F' \equiv F.\, a \in fnav(F')$$
$$F, v \vDash \neg\Phi \qquad\, \Leftrightarrow \quad F, v \nvDash \Phi$$
$$F, v \vDash \Phi_1 \wedge \Phi_2 \quad \Leftrightarrow \quad F, v \vDash \Phi_1 \text{ and } F, v \vDash \Phi_2$$
$$F, v \vDash \Phi_1 * \Phi_2 \quad \Leftrightarrow \quad \exists F_1, F_2.\, F \equiv F_1 * F_2,\, F_1, v \vDash \Phi_1 \text{ and } F_2, v \vDash \Phi_2$$
$$F, v \vDash \exists x.\, \Phi \quad\; \Leftrightarrow \quad \exists r \in T(\Sigma).\, F, (v \cup \{x \rightarrow r\}) \vDash \Phi$$
$$F, v \vDash \textsf{V}a.\, \Phi \quad\; \Leftrightarrow \quad \exists a' \notin fnav(F, v, \Phi).\, F, v \vDash \Phi[a \leftarrow a']$$
$$F, v \vDash \textsf{H}n.\, \Phi \quad\; \Leftrightarrow \quad \exists n' \notin fn(F, v, \Phi).\, \exists (H', S').\, \begin{array}{l} F \equiv (\{n'\} \uplus H', S') \\ \text{and } (H', S'), v \vDash \Phi[n \leftarrow n'] \end{array}$$
$$F, v \vDash \Phi \oslash n \quad\; \Leftrightarrow \quad (\{n\} \cup H, S), v \vDash \Phi$$

Fig. 1. Satisfaction relation of $\mathcal{FSL}$ for a frame $F = (H, S)$

5.2 The Frame Logic $\mathcal{FSL}$

Consider the fragment $\mathcal{FSL}$ of $A\pi\mathcal{L}$ formed by the formulas Φ of the following grammar, where $t_1, t_2 \in T(\Sigma, V)$, $a \in \mathcal{N}^\pi \uplus V^\pi$, $x \in V$, and $n \in \mathcal{N}^\pi$.

$$\Phi ::= t_1 = t_2 \mid \mathbf{0} \mid \textcircled{c}a \mid \neg\Phi \mid \Phi_1 \wedge \Phi_2 \mid \Phi_1 * \Phi_2 \mid \exists x.\, \Phi \mid \textsf{V}a.\, \Phi \mid \textsf{H}n.\, \Phi \mid \Phi \oslash a$$

The semantics of the logic is given by a satisfaction relation between a frame $F = (H, S)$, a valuation v mapping term variables of V to ground terms of $T(\Sigma)$, and a formula Φ. It is shown in Fig. 1, and is devised so as not to distinguish between structurally congruent frames. Intuitively, $t_1 = t_2$ is an equality test under the ambient equational theory $\mathcal{E}$ augmented by the equalities in F, $\mathbf{0}$ describes empty frames, $\textcircled{c}a$ is true whenever the name or $A\pi$ variable a appears free in all the frames structurally congruent to F, $\neg$, $\wedge$ and $\exists$ is the classical first-order fragment, $\textsf{V}a$ is the Gabbay-Pitts quantifier over fresh names or $A\pi$ variables (*i.e.* it quantifies over names–or $A\pi$ variables–that do not appear free in neither the frame nor the remaining formula), $\textsf{H}n$ is a quantifier over hidden names of the frame (intuitively, it reveals a secret name of the frame, which may be vacuous if it does not appear free in the set of equations S of F), $*$ is the spatial conjunction that decomposes F into two orthogonal subframes, and $\Phi \oslash n$ hides the name n in F and proceeds with Φ.

For instance, the deducibility of a secret name (without specifying which one) is expressed by $\exists x.\, \textsf{H}k.\, x = k$: as the term quantification is placed first, the guessed term x cannot mention the revealed name k. The general deducibility problem is also expressible in this fragment, but the formula depends on the frame $F = (\{h_1, \ldots, h_l\}, \{u_1 = t_1, \ldots, u_k = t_k\})$ due to α-conversion issues:

$$\text{deducible}(F, t) := \exists x.\, \textsf{H}h_1, \ldots, h_l.\, (x = t \wedge u_1 = t_1 \wedge \ldots \wedge u_k = t_k)$$

Other security properties are expressible using spatial logics, for instance regarding the quantity of information leaked in a frame: $\exists x.\, \textsf{H}k.\, x = k$ holds if there is at least one secret leaked by the frame, while $\exists x, y.\, \textsf{H}k, k'.\, x = k \wedge y = k'$ asserts that two independent secrets are. The formulas presented in the introduction also fit our fragment.

5.3   From Spatial to Equational

In this section, we reduce the model-checking problem for $\mathcal{FSL}$ to the evaluation of an equational formula over a term algebra. We assume given a signature $\Sigma \supseteq \mathcal{N}^\pi \uplus \mathcal{V}^\pi$ and an equational theory $\mathcal{E}$ defined by an orthogonal, terminating term rewrite system $R_{\mathcal{E}}$. Moreover, we can assume that all the rewrite rules in $R_{\mathcal{E}}$ mention only variables, and no constants, as it is always the case in $A\pi$ equational theories. For every finite set S of ground equations of the form $u = r$, $=_S$ denotes $\xrightarrow{*}_{S \cup \mathcal{E}}$. Consider the first-order logic $\mathcal{L}_{\text{eq}}$ defined by the following grammar (we omit its semantics for brevity):

$$\phi ::= t_1 =_S t_2 \mid n \in fn(t) \mid u \in fav(t) \mid \phi_1 \wedge \phi_2 \mid \neg\phi \mid \exists x.\,\phi \mid \mathsf{V}n.\,\phi$$

Let $\mathfrak{A} := \mathfrak{A}(\Sigma, (=_S)_S, (C_a)_{a\in\mathcal{N}^\pi\uplus\mathcal{V}^\pi}, R_{\mathcal{E}})$ where $C_a := \{t \mid a \in fnav(t)\}$. We give below a translation $H, S, \Phi \mapsto (\!|H, S, \Phi|\!)$ that associates an equational formula in $\mathcal{L}_{\text{eq}}$ to a frame (H, S) and a spatial formula Φ, built by induction on Φ with the following inductive hypothesis:

Lemma 3. *For all v, H, S and Φ, $\mathfrak{A}, v \models (\!|H, S, \Phi|\!)$ if and only if $(H, S), v \models \Phi$.*

Notations. We write $t = t'$ for $\bigwedge_{i=1}^n t_i = t'_i$ (and similarly for sets of terms) and $m \in fn(t)$ for $\bigvee_{i=1}^n m \in fn(t_i)$ (and similarly for $u \in fav(t)$). Arities are implicitly supposed to match: in $\exists t.\,t = codom(S)$, t's size is implicitly chosen to match the size of $codom(S)$. Finally, $\top$ (resp. $\bot$) is a formula that is always true (resp. always false), for instance $n = n$ for some n (resp. $\neg n = n$).

The translation of $\copyright a$ follows its semantics and thus is quite straightforward. It is defined as $\bot$ when $a \in H$, $\top$ when $a \in dom(S)$, and otherwise as

$$(\!|H, S, \copyright a|\!) := \forall \boldsymbol{x}.\,\boldsymbol{x} =_\emptyset codom(S) \Rightarrow a \in fnav(\boldsymbol{x})$$

Hiding a name consists merely of adding h to the set of hidden names, and term quantification is left as-is, since the semantics of $\exists x$ for $\mathcal{FSL}$ and $\mathcal{L}_{\text{eq}}$ are the same. As we know all the hidden names of the frame, we can treat name revelation as a disjunction over those names and a fresh name n', the latter accounting for the fact that one can reveal "fake" hidden names (using NEW):

$$(\!|H, S, \Phi \otimes n|\!) := (\!|H \cup \{n\}, S, \Phi|\!) \qquad\qquad (\!|H, S, \exists x.\,\Phi|\!) := \exists x.\,(\!|H, S, \Phi|\!)$$

$$(\!|H, S, \mathsf{H}n.\,\Phi|\!) := \mathsf{V}n'.\bigvee_{h\in H\uplus\{n'\}} (\!|H \setminus \{h\}, S, \Phi[n\leftarrow h]|\!)$$

To translate an equality $t_1 = t_2$ one has to take care of the hidden names of S, as $\mathcal{L}_{\text{eq}}$ only allows substitutions as parameters of equality tests, and not general frames. To overcome this, we simulate the behavior of hidden names by replacing the names of S that appear in H with fresh names H' such that $H' \cap fn(S, t_1, t_2) = \emptyset$. It is easy to check that these fresh names behave like hidden names for the equality test.

$$(\!|\{h_1, \ldots, h_k\}, S, t_1 = t_2|\!) := \\ \mathsf{V}h'_1, \ldots, h'_k.\,t_1[h_1, \ldots, h_k \leftarrow h'_1, \ldots, h'_k] =_S t_2[h_1, \ldots, h_k \leftarrow h'_1, \ldots, h'_k]$$

To translate $*$, we need to be able to state that the set of hidden names appearing in two subframes are disjoint one from another up to rewriting of terms using the equational theory. This is achieved by the operator $t_1 \perp^H t_2$ below which states that two sets of names t_1 and t_2 may be rewritten so as not to share names in H:

$$t_1 \perp^H t_2 := \exists x_1, x_2. \, x_1 =_\emptyset t_1 \wedge x_2 =_\emptyset t_2 \wedge \bigwedge_{h \in H} (h \in fn(x_1) \Rightarrow h \notin fn(x_2))$$

The translation of frame composition then only needs to quantify over all 2-partitions of the set of active substitutions that yield orthogonal subframes:

$$(\!| H, S, \Phi_1 * \Phi_2 |\!) := \bigvee_{S_1 \uplus S_2 = S} (codom(S_1) \perp^H codom(S_2) \wedge (\!| H, S_1, \Phi_1 |\!) \wedge (\!| H, S_2, \Phi_2 |\!))$$

This particular step of our translation would be unsound if substitutions of the frame could be applied to other substitutions of the frame, like in the original applied π-calculus. Finally, $(\!| H, S, \neg\Phi |\!) := \neg(\!| H, S, \Phi |\!)$, $(\!| H, S, \Phi_1 \wedge \Phi_2 |\!) := (\!| H, S, \Phi_1 |\!) \wedge (\!| H, S, \Phi_2 |\!)$, and $(\!| H, S, \mathbf{0} |\!) := \top$ if $S = \emptyset$ and $\perp$ otherwise. From the inductive hypothesis of Lem. 3 we deduce:

Theorem 6. *For all frame $F = (H, S)$ and formula Φ of $\mathcal{FSL}$ one can effectively compute a formula ϕ of $\mathcal{L}_{eq}$ such that $F \models \Phi$ if and only if $\mathfrak{A} \models \phi$. Moreover, the predicates $=_{S'}$ that appear in ϕ are all such that $S' \subseteq S$.*

5.4 Deciding the Model-Checking of $\mathcal{FSL}$ and Static Equivalence

We now show how to apply Thm. 4 to the decidability of security properties of frames, namely the ones expressible in $\mathcal{FSL}$, as well as static equivalence.

Theorem 7. *Let (H, S) be a frame such that the completion of S under $R_\mathcal{E}$ terminates and is linear and variable disjoint. Then the problem to decide, for a formula $\Phi \in \mathcal{FSL}$, whether (H, S) satisfies Φ is decidable when the comparisons are all of the form $r =_{S'} r'$, $x =_{S'} r$ or $x =_{S'} x'$ where $S' \subseteq S$.*

Proof. Let us write $\mathcal{A}_\phi$ (resp. $\mathcal{S}_\phi$) for the *finite* set of a (resp. S') such that $a \in fn(t)$ or $a \in fav(t)$ (resp. $=_{S'}$) appears in ϕ, and $\mathfrak{A}_\phi$ for $\mathfrak{A}(\Sigma, (=_{S'})_{S' \in \mathcal{S}_\phi}, (C_a)_{a \in \mathcal{A}_\phi}, R_\mathcal{E})$. For ϕ to be a formula over this structure (which does not include function symbols), the comparisons $t_1 =_S t_2$ have to be restricted to those of the forms $r =_S r'$, $x =_S r$ or $x =_S x'$ (where $r, r' \in T(\Sigma)$ denote *ground* terms and $x, x' \in V$ are term variables). This restriction corresponds to the hypothesis of the theorem on Φ, which is satisfied by all the formulas presented in this paper.

Let us observe that one can eliminate Gabbay-Pitts quantifiers in any formula by first rewriting the formula in prenex form (the only non-homomorphic case being $\exists x. \, \mathsf{N}n. \, \phi \Leftrightarrow \mathsf{N}n. \, \exists x. \, (\neg n \in fn(x)) \wedge \phi)$, and then dropping them. Since by hypothesis the completion of S terminates under $R_\mathcal{E}$, the completions of every $S' \subseteq S$ also terminates. Moreover, the equations $=_{S'}$ are over ground terms, hence are trivially linear and variable-disjoint, and the languages C_a are all recognizable. Thus Thm. 4 applies on $\mathfrak{A}_\phi$, which shows that the satisfiability problem $\overset{?}{\models} \phi$ for the logic $\mathcal{L}_{eq}$ is decidable. $\square$

In particular, the model-checking problem of $\mathcal{FSL}$ is decidable whenever the conditions on $R_{\mathcal{E}}$ and S of Lemma 2 are satisfied, hence for the equational theory of pairs or of fixed key symmetric or asymmetric encryption (or any combination thereof), whatever the considered frame S is.

This result also applies with the original definition of structural congruence for frames by Abadi and Fournet [2] (see the footnote page 176). However, our translation of the $*$ logical operator would not produce a finite formula anymore, hence this connector would have to be dropped to retain decidability. One may also easily add the $A\pi$ variable hiding operator of $A\pi\mathcal{L}$ $\Phi \oslash u$, which we omitted to simplify our syntax for frames (in which hidden variables have no meaning), without impairing Thm. 7.

Finally, $\mathcal{L}_{\mathrm{eq}}$ can also express static equivalence between two frames $F = (\{h_i\}_i, S)$ and $F' = (\{h_i'\}_i, S')$ by the following formula, thus providing a decidable way of deciding such a relation when the equational theory obeys the constraints above:

$$F \approx_s F' \text{ iff } \forall x, x'. \bigwedge_{i,i'} \neg h_i h_{i'}' \in \mathit{fn}(x, x') \Rightarrow (x =_S x' \Leftrightarrow x =_{S'} x')$$

6   Conclusion

Classically used decision procedures for first-order theories seem not be applicable when faced with multiple congruence relations defined by independent equational axioms. Automata-based methods, on the other hand, have the advantage that the combination of different predicates, each of them recognizable for the same encoding of the elements of the algebra, comes for free. However, they can handle only restricted classes of equational axioms. Whether it is possible to push the method to, for instance, non left-linear background equational theories like $check(x, pub(k), sign(x, k)) \rightarrow ok$ is up to future work.

As an application, we have obtained a decidability result for the model-checking of a rich fragment of $A\pi\mathcal{L}$ and static equivalence, under a class of realistic equational theories. It is incomparable with previous decidability results obtained for deducibility and static equivalence only [1]. Considering a larger fragment of $A\pi\mathcal{L}$ would be challenging, in particular in the handling of $A\pi$ variable revelation $Hu.\Phi$, which is not supported in our setting as it amounts to quantifying over a new, unknown substitution $u = r$ against which terms can be tested. Such an extension would require not only to consider multiple congruence relations, but also to quantify over them. We conjecture that techniques similar to those exposed in this paper could be applied to the study of the model-checking of the frame logic of Hüttel and Pedersen.

References

1. Abadi, M., Cortier, V.: Deciding Knowledge in Security Protocols under Equational Theories. Theoretical Computer Science 367(1-2), 2–32 (2006)
2. Abadi, M., Fournet, C.: Mobile values, new names, and secure communication. In: POPL 2001 (2001)
3. Baader, F., Snyder, W.: Unification theory. In: Handbook of Automated Reasoning, vol. I, ch. 8, pp. 445–532. Elsevier and MIT Press (2001)

4. Blumensath, A., Grädel, E.: Automatic structures. In: Logic in Computer Science, Santa Barbara, CA, pp. 51–62 (June 2000)
5. Caron, A.-C., Coquide, J.-L., Dauchet, M.: Encompassment properties and automata with constraints. In: Kirchner, C. (ed.) RTA 1993. LNCS, vol. 690, pp. 328–342. Springer, Heidelberg (1993)
6. Comon, H.: Solving symbolic ordering constraints. IJCS 1(4), 387–412 (1990)
7. Comon, H., Dauchet, M., Gilleron, R., Löding, C., Jacquemard, F., Lugiez, D., Tison, S., Tommasi, M.: Tree automata techniques and applications (2007), http://www.grappa.univ-lille3.fr/tata (release October 12, 2007)
8. Comon, H., Delor, C.: Equational formulae with membership constraints. Information and Computation 112(2), 167–216 (1994)
9. Comon, H., Haberstrau, M., Jouannaud, J.-P.: Syntacticness, cycle-syntacticness and shallow theories. Information and Computation 111(1), 154–191 (1994)
10. Comon, H., Lescanne, P.: Equational problems and disunification. Journal of Symbolic Computation 7, 371–425 (1989)
11. Dauchet, M., Tison, S., Heuillard, T., Lescanne, P.: Decidability of the confluence of ground term rewriting systems. In: LICS, pp. 353–359 (1987)
12. Dauchet, M., Tison, S., Heuillard, T., Lescanne, P.: Decidability of the confluence of finite ground term rewrite systems and of other related term rewrite systems. Information and Computation 88(2), 187–201 (1990)
13. Godoy, G., Huntingford, E., Tiwari, A.: Termination of rewriting with right-flat rules. In: Baader, F. (ed.) RTA 2007. LNCS, vol. 4533, pp. 200–213. Springer, Heidelberg (2007)
14. Gurevich, Y., Veanes, M.: Logic with equality: Partisan corroboration and shifted pairing. Information and Computation 152(2), 205–235 (1999)
15. Huet, G.: Confluent reductions: Abstract properties and applications to term rewriting systems. J. ACM 27(4), 797–821 (1980)
16. Hüttel, H., Pedersen, M.D.: A logical characterisation of static equivalence. Electronic Notes in Theoretical Computer Science 173, 139–157 (2007)
17. Jouannaud, J.-P., Okada, M.: Satisfiability of systems of ordinal notation with the subterm property is decidable. In: Leach Albert, J., Monien, B., Rodríguez-Artalejo, M. (eds.) ICALP 1991. LNCS, vol. 510, pp. 455–468. Springer, Heidelberg (1991)
18. Kuncak, V., Rinard, M.C.: Structural subtyping of non-recursive types is decidable. In: Logic in Computer Science, Ottawa, Canada, pp. 96–107 (June 2003)
19. Lozes, É., Villard, J.: A spatial equational logic for the applied π-calculus. In: van Breugel, F., Chechik, M. (eds.) CONCUR 2008. LNCS, vol. 5201, pp. 387–401. Springer, Heidelberg (2008)
20. Lozes, É., Villard, J.: A spatial equational logic for the applied π-calculus. Distributed Computing 23(1), 61–83 (2010)
21. Maher, M.J.: Complete axiomatizations of the algebras of finite, rational and infinite trees. In: LICS, Edinburgh, Scotland, pp. 348–357 (July 1988)
22. Malc'ev, A.I.: Axiomatizable classes of locally free algebras of various type. In: The Metamathematics of Algebraic Systems: Collected Papers 1936–1967, ch. 23 (1971)
23. Marcinkowski, J.: Undecidability of the $\exists^*\forall^*$ part of the theory of ground term algebra modulo an AC symbol. In: Narendran, P., Rusinowitch, M. (eds.) RTA 1999. LNCS, vol. 1631, pp. 92–102. Springer, Heidelberg (1999)
24. Su, Z., Aiken, A., Niehren, J., Priesnitz, T., Treinen, R.: The first-order theory of subtyping constraints. In: POPL, pp. 203–216. ACM, New York (2002)
25. Treinen, R.: A new method for undecidability proofs of first order theories. Journal of Symbolic Computation 14(5), 437–457 (1992)

A   Coping with Countable Signatures

In order to show that $\mathfrak{A}(\Sigma, (E_i)_{i \in I}, (L_j)_{j \in J})$ is an automatic structure we first have to define the encoding of the algebra as trees over a finite signature, the (minor) difficulty here being that the algebra contains trees over a possibly infinite alphabet but with a bounded arity.

If n is the maximal arity of a function symbol in Σ then we can arrange all function symbols of arity n into a (finite or infinite) enumeration. The signature of the automatic representation would consist of a constant 0, a unary function s, and function symbols $f_0, \ldots, f_i$, each f_i being of arity $i + 1$. A function symbol $f(x_1, \ldots, x_n) \in \Sigma$ of arity n, being number i in the enumeration, would be represented for the automatic representation as $f_n(s^i(0), x_1, \ldots, x_n)$. The interpretation function ν is straightforward to define, and the automaton for L_δ would just have to ensure that 0 and s only occur as first argument of the f_i, and that the first argument of any f_i is of the form $s^j(0)$, possibly with a bound on j in case there are only finitely many function symbols of the corresponding arity.

More exactly, let n be the maximal arity occurring in Σ, and let for any $i, 0 \le i \le n$, $m_i \in \mathbf{N} \cup \infty$ be the number of symbols in Σ of arity i. The tree automaton that recognizes all terms that are encoding of a ground Σ-term is $f_i(q_i, q \ldots, q) \to q$ for any i. Here, the state q is the only accepting state that recognizes all encodings of terms. For any i, the state q_i recognizes all encoding of natural numbers that are not larger than m_i: If $m_i = \infty$ then we define $0 \to q_i$ and $s(q_i) \to q_i$, and for $m_i \in \mathbf{N}$ we have that $0 \to p_i^0$, $s(p_i^j) \to p_i^{j+1}$ (when $j < m_i$) and $p_i^{m_i} \to q_i$.

B   Proof of Theorem 2

To prove that the first-order theory of $\mathfrak{H}(\Sigma, (E_i)_{1 \le i \le 3}, (L_j)_{1 \le j \le 3})$ is undecidable for ground equations (Thm. 2), we propose a reduction of the acceptance problem of the empty tape for deterministic Turing machines using a technique of *shifted pairing* [14].

Let M be a deterministic Turing machine computing on a tape bounded on the left and unbounded on the right, with input alphabet $\Gamma \cup \{\flat\}$ ($\flat$ is a special blank symbol), state set S, initial state s_0, final state set S_f, and transition function $\delta : (S \setminus S_f) \times \Gamma \cup \{\flat\} \to S \times \Gamma \cup \{\flat\} \times \{\text{left, right, stay}\}$. Note that it is assumed *wlog* that entering a final state terminates the computation. Moreover, we also assume *wlog* that before entering a final state, M deletes the whole tape (all the symbols of Γ are replaced by $\flat$).

We represent a *configuration* of M as a word c in $\Gamma^* S \Gamma^* \flat^*$, where the unique state symbol $s \in S$ in c indicates the current position of the head of M in the configuration, in the sense that the head of M is on the symbol of $\Gamma \cup \{\flat\}$ immediately following s in c. The length of a word c is denoted $|c|$. The languages of initial and final configurations of M are respectively $C_0 := s_0 \flat^*$ and $C_f := S_f \flat^*$. The transition relation of M, written $\vdash_M$, is the binary relation on configurations such that $c \vdash_M c'$ iff c' is obtained from c according to δ. For instance, if $\delta(s, a) = \langle s', a', \text{left} \rangle$, then $c = \alpha b s a \beta \flat^m$ with $\alpha, \beta \in \Gamma^*$, $b \in \Gamma$ and $c' = \alpha s' b a' \beta \flat^m$, if $\delta(s, a) = \langle s', a', \text{right} \rangle$, then $c = \alpha s a \beta \flat^m$ and $c' = \alpha a' s' \beta \flat^m$, and if $\delta(s, a) = \langle s', a', \text{stay} \rangle$, then $c = \alpha s a \beta \flat^m$ and $c' = \alpha s' a' \beta \flat^m$. A *computation* of M is a finite sequence $c_0, c_1, \ldots, c_n$ of configurations of M such that

$c_0 \in C_0$ and for all $0 \le i < n$, $c_i \vdash_M c_{i+1}$. It is *successful* if the state of c_n is final, *i.e.* $c_n \in S_f\, \flat^*$ by hypothesis.

We shall encode the configurations and computations of M as right-combs built on the signature $\Upsilon := \{f : 2, g : 2, \flat : 0, \# : 0\} \cup \{b : 0 \mid b \in \Gamma \cup S\}$. Let us moreover extend Υ into the signature $\Sigma := \Upsilon \cup \Upsilon_0^{[2]}$ (*i.e.* Σ extends Υ with the set of constant symbols of the form $[a, b]$ with $a, b \in \Sigma_0 \cup \{\Box\}$ such that a or b is not $\Box$).

A computation $c_0, \dots, c_n$ is encoded as a term $f(c_0^t, \dots, f(c_n^t, \flat))$ of $T(\Sigma)$, where for all $0 \le i \le n$, c_i^t is the term encoding of the configuration $c_i = c_{i,1} \dots c_{i,k}$ defined as $c_i^t := g(c_{i,1}, \dots, g(c_{i,k}, \flat))$.

Let $L_0 := \{c_0^t \mid c_0 \in C_0\}$ be the recognizable language of term encodings of initial configurations of M. Let L_c be the recognizable language of terms of the form $f(c_0^t, \dots, f(c_n^t, \flat))$, with $n \ge 0$, such that for all $0 \le i \le n$, c_i is a configuration of M (*i.e.* $c_i \in \Gamma^* S\, \Gamma^* \flat^*$) and c_n is a final configuration of C_f.

For technical convenience, we shall use below a simplified convolution product $\circledast$ defined only on configurations of same length or a configuration and $\flat$:

$$g(a, s) \circledast g(b, t) = g([a, b], s \circledast t) \qquad \flat \circledast \flat = \flat \qquad g(a, s) \circledast \flat = g([a, \Box], s \circledast \flat)$$

It is easy to verify that the set $\{c^t \circledast d^t \mid c \vdash_M d, |c| = |d|\}$ is a recognizable tree language of $T(\Sigma)$. Hence, the following set is also a recognizable tree language (called shifted pairing language):

$$L_{sp} := \Big\{ f(c_0^t \circledast d_1^t, \dots, f(c_{n-1}^t \circledast d_n^t, f(c_n^t \circledast \flat, \flat))) \mid \forall 0 \le i < n. \; \left\{ \begin{array}{l} |c_i| = |d_{i+1}| \\ \& \;\; c_i \vdash_M d_{i+1} \end{array} \right\} .$$

Note that in the definitions of L_{sp} and L_c, the configurations $c_0, \dots, c_n$ and $d_1, \dots, d_n$ are arbitrary. In particular it is not required that the sequence $c_1, \dots, c_n$ is a computation of M (otherwise the languages would not be recognizable!).

We define two ground equational theories describing roughly the left and right projections on terms of L_{sp}. More precisely, these theories E_1 and E_2 are defined by

$$
\begin{aligned}
E_1 &:= \{[a_1, a_2] = a_1 \mid [a_1, a_2] \in \Upsilon_0^{[2]}\} \qquad\qquad E_3 := \emptyset \\
E_2 &:= \{[a_1, a_2] = a_2 \mid a_1, a_2 \in \Sigma_0\} \\
&\quad \cup \; \{g([\flat, \Box], \flat) = \#, \quad g([\flat, \Box], \#) = \#\} \\
&\quad \cup \; \{f(g([s^f, \Box], \#), \flat) = \flat\} \quad (s^f \in S_f)
\end{aligned}
$$

Let us now consider the following closed first-order formula ϕ over $\mathfrak{H}(\Sigma, (E_i)_{1 \le i \le 3}, (L_\otimes, L_c))$, and establish now the correctness of the reduction.

$$\exists y, y_1, y_2, x. \; L_{sp}(y) \wedge y =_{E_1} y_1 \wedge L_c(y_1) \wedge y =_{E_2} y_2 \wedge L_c(y_2) \wedge L_0(x) \wedge y_1 = f(x, y_2)$$

Lemma 4. ϕ *is satisfiable in* $\mathfrak{H}(\Sigma, (E_i)_{i \in 1,2}, (L_{sp}, L_c, L_0))$ *iff* M *admits a successful computation starting with a blank tape.*

Proof. For the *if* direction, assume that there exists a finite computation $c_0, \dots, c_n$ of M with $c_0 \in C_0 = s_0 \flat^*$ and $c_n \in S_f\, \flat^*$. We can assume moreover that the configurations $c_0, \dots, c_n$ have all the same length, using if necessary some padding with $\flat$'s at the right.

Let $y = f(c_0^t \circledast c_1^t, \ldots, f(c_{n-1}^t \circledast c_n^t, f(c_n^t \circledast \flat, \flat)))$. By definition, $y \in L_{sp}$.

Let $y_1 = f(c_0^t, \ldots, f(c_n^t, \flat))$ and $y_2 = f(c_1^t, \ldots, f(c_n^t, \flat))$. We can observe easily that $y_1 \in L_c$, $y =_{E_1} y_1$ and $y =_{E_2} y_2$. Moreover, with $x_0 = c_0^t$, we have $x_0 \in L_0$ and $y_1 = f(x_0, y_2)$. Hence ϕ is satisfiable in $\mathfrak{H}(\Sigma, (E_i)_{i \in 1,2}, (L_{sp}, L_c, L_0))$.

For the *only if* direction, assume that ϕ is satisfiable, and let y, y_1, y_2, x_0 be terms such that $y \in L_{sp}$, $y =_{E_1} y_1$, $y =_{E_2} y_2$. $y_1 \in L_c$, $y_2 \in L_c$, $x_0 \in L_0$ and $y_1 = f(x_0, y_2)$.

Let $y = f(c_0^t \circledast d_1^t, \ldots, f(c_{n-1}^t \circledast d_n^t, f(c_n^t \circledast \flat, \flat)))$ with $n \geq 0$, and for all $0 \leq i < n$, $|c_i| = |d_{i+1}|$ and $c_i \vdash_M d_{i+1}$ (*). Since $y =_{E_1} y_1$ and $y_1 \in L_c$, it holds that $y_1 = f(c_0^t, \ldots, f(c_n^t, \flat))$. Moreover $c_n \in C_f$ (set of final configurations) by definition of L_c. Since $y =_{E_2} y_2$ and $y_2 \in L_c$, we have necessarily $y_2 = f(d_1^t, \ldots, f(d_n^t, \flat))$ (the terms of L_c do not contain the symbols $\square$ or $\#$).

Finally, $y_1 = f(x_0, y_2)$ implies that $x_0 = c_0^t$ and $d_i^t = c_i^t$ for all $1 \leq i \leq n$. From (*), it follows that $c_i \vdash_M c_{i+1}$ for all $0 \leq i < n$. Hence $c_0, \ldots, c_n$ is a successful computation of M starting with a blank tape since $x_0 \in L_0$.   □

C   Proof of Theorem 3

The proof is by reduction of the Post correspondence problem (PCP). The principle of the reduction presented here follows an idea used in [13] for showing undecidability of another problem (termination of shallow term rewriting systems).

Let us consider the following instance of PCP without empty words given by a finite set of pairs of words: $\mathcal{P} := \{(u_i, v_i) \mid u_i, v_i \in \{a, b\}^+, 1 \leq i \leq N\}$. A solution of $\mathcal{P}$ is a finite sequence $(i_j)_{0 \leq j \leq k}$ with $1 \leq i_0, \ldots, i_k \leq N$, such that $u_{i_0} u_{i_1} \ldots u_{i_k} = v_{i_0} v_{i_1} \ldots v_{i_k}$. The problem of the existence of a solution is undecidable. For all $1 \leq i \leq N$, let $u_i = u_{i,1} \ldots u_{i,|u_i|}$ and $v_i = v_{i,1} \ldots v_{i,|v_i|}$. Let $L := \max(|u_i|, |v_i| \mid i \leq N)$, and let us define the signature $\Sigma := \{a : 1, b : 1, \flat : 0\} \cup \{P_{i,j} : 1 \mid 1 \leq i \leq N, 1 \leq j \leq L\}$. For the sake of readability, we shall write the terms of $T(\Sigma)$ as words of $\Sigma_1^* \Sigma_0$. The purpose of the symbols $P_{i,j}$ in the words P_i is to represent a "skeleton" of solution of $\mathcal{P}$, *i.e.* a sequence of indexes that will be replaced by letters of the u_i's or v_i's by the following two sets of flat equations

$$
\begin{aligned}
E_1 = &\{ P_{i,j}(x) = u_{i,j}(x) \mid 1 \leq i \leq N, 1 \leq j \leq |u_i| \} \\
&\cup \{ P_{i,j}(x) = x \mid 1 \leq i \leq N, |u_i| < j \leq L \} \\
E_2 = &\{ P_{i,j}(x) = v_{i,j}(x) \mid 1 \leq i \leq N, 1 \leq j \leq |v_i| \} \\
&\cup \{ P_{i,j}(x) = x \mid 1 \leq i \leq N, |v_i| < j \leq L \}
\end{aligned}
$$

Let $E_3 = \emptyset$. For all $1 \leq i \leq N$, let P_i be the word $P_{i,1} \cdots P_{i,L}$. Let us consider two tree automata: L_α recognizing $\{a, b\}^+ \flat$, L_P recognizing $\{P_i \mid 1 \leq i \leq N\}^* \flat$. Finally, let us show that the reduction is correct, where ϕ is the following closed formula:

$$\phi := \exists x, u, v. \ L_P(x) \wedge x =_{E_1} u \wedge x =_{E_2} v \wedge L_\alpha(u) \wedge L_\alpha(v) \wedge u = v.$$

Lemma 5. *ϕ is satisfiable in $\mathfrak{A}(\Sigma, (E_i)_{1 \leq i \leq 3}, (L_\alpha, L_P))$ iff $\mathcal{P}$ has a solution.*

Proof. For the *if* direction, assume that $\mathcal{P}$ admits a solution $(i_j)_{0 \leq j \leq k}$ with $1 \leq i_0, \ldots, i_k \leq N$, and $u_{i_0} u_{i_1} \ldots u_{i_k} = v_{i_0} v_{i_1} \ldots v_{i_k}$. Let $x = P_{i_0} \cdots P_{i_k} \flat$ and let $u = u_{i_0} u_{i_1} \ldots u_{i_k} \flat$ and $v = v_{i_0} v_{i_1} \ldots v_{i_k} \flat$. Hence $u = v$. Moreover, $x \in L_P$, $u, v \in L_\alpha$, and $x =_{E_1} u$, $x =_{E_2} v$. Therefore ϕ is satisfiable.

For the *only if* direction, assume that ϕ is satisfiable, and let x, u, v be terms such that $x \in L_P$, $x =_{E_1} u$, $x =_{E_2} v$, $u \in L_\alpha$, $v \in L_\alpha$, and $u = v$. Let $x = P_{i_0} \cdots P_{i_k} \flat$ for some $1 \leq i_0, \ldots, i_k \leq N$. From $x =_{E_1} u$ and $u \in L_\alpha$, it follows that necessarily $u = u_{i_0} u_{i_1} \ldots u_{i_k} \flat$. Note that the equations of E_1 can be applied in both direction, i.e. $P_{i,j}$ can be replaced by $u_{i,j}$ (or deleted) but also $u_{i,j}$ can be replaced by another $P_{i',j'}$ when $u_{i,j} = u_{i',j'}$. But this $P_{i',j'}$ will eventually be placed by $u_{i,j}$ in order to get $u \in L_\alpha$ (there are no other replacement possible). Similarly, $v = v_{i_0} v_{i_1} \ldots v_{i_k} \flat$. From $u = v$, it follows that $(i_j)_{0 \leq j \leq k}$ is a solution of $\mathcal{P}$.   □

D   Termination of Completion

Lemma 6. *Let R be a non-overlapping rewrite system of rules $g \to x$ where each g is a jack, $x \in Vars(g)$, and E a ground equational system such that no constant occurring on a left-hand side of R is a side of E, then completion of any variable-disjoint and linear equation system terminates.*

Proof. In the special situation of this lemma, critical pairs are formed as follows:

1. there is a substitution σ and a non-variable position p of g such that $g\sigma \mid_p = l$, in that case the critical pair is $g[r]_p = d\sigma$.
2. there is a substitution σ and a position p of l such that $g\sigma = l \mid_p$, in that case the critical pair is $r = l[d\sigma]_p$.

First note that addition of critical pairs maintains the invariant that no constant occurring on a left-hand side of R is a side of E. This is due to the fact that, in the first case, g cannot be a constant.

Let G denote the set of ground subterms of the left-hand sides of R. We define, for any term t, $\phi(t)$ as the size of t, where all terms in G are understood to have size 0. More precisely,

$$\phi(t) = \begin{cases} 0 & \text{if } t \in G \\ 1 + \Sigma_{i=1}^{i=n} \phi(t_i) & \text{if } t = f(t_1, \ldots, t_n) \notin G \end{cases}$$

For any n there exist only finitely many terms t with $\phi(t) \leq n$ since G is finite. We will show that when superposition of $l = r$ with the rewrite rule $g \to d$ leads to addition of the critical pair $l' = r'$ then $\phi(l') + \phi(r') \leq \phi(l) + \phi(r)$. As a consequence, only finitely many critical pairs can be added. We consider the two cases above:

1. In that case we have, by the form of the rewrite system, that p is of length at most 1. Hence, $g[\bullet]_p$ is of the form $f(t_1, \ldots, t_{i-1}, \bullet, t_{i+1}, \ldots, t_n)$ where $t_i \in G$. As a consequence, $\phi(r') = \phi(g[r]_p) \leq \phi(r) + 1$.
   On the other hand, l cannot be an element of G since no side of the equational system is a ground subterm of a left-hand side of R, and hence $\phi(l) > 0$. We have that $l' = d\sigma$ is a proper subterm of l, and hence that $\phi(l') < \phi(l)$.
2. First note that $g\sigma$ cannot be an element of G since the rewrite system is orthogonal. Hence, $\phi(l') < \phi(l)$, and we conclude in this case since $r = r'$.   □

Automated Code Injection Prevention for Web Applications

Zhengqin Luo, Tamara Rezk, and Manuel Serrano

INRIA Sophia Antipolis, France
{zluo,trezk,mserrano}@inria.fr

Abstract. We propose a new technique based on multitier compilation for preventing code injection in web applications. It consists in adding an extra stage to the client code generator which compares the dynamically generated code with the specification obtained from the syntax of the source program. No intervention from the programmer is needed. No plugin or modification of the web browser is required. The soundness and validity of the approach are proved formally by showing that the client compiler can be fully abstract. The practical interest of the approach is proved by showing the actual implementation in the HOP environment.

1   Introduction

The impact of the Web 2.0 on sensitive aspects of daily life (home banking, e-commerce, social websites such as Facebook or Twitter, e-voting, etc.) has triggered an unprecedented demand of means for writing highly secured web applications. Unfortunately, their multitier architecture makes the security difficult to enforce. Usually web applications are written in a main language (*e.g.,* PHP, JSP) that executes in the main-tier and dynamically generates programs in a target language (*e.g.,* SQL, HTML, JavaScript) that executes in the target-tier. Furthermore, to enhance the interaction experience between users and web applications, main-tier programs may accept (untrusted) user input. The input may be stored in a database or a persistent variable, and later on be used to generate other target-tier programs. This *dynamic* generation of target-tier programs using untrusted inputs may represent a serious application vulnerability when input is "confused" with the original code of the application to be executed. This kind of attack is known as code injection and more generally, it can be seen as an integrity violation [20]. In spite of several efforts from the security community to avoid code injection attacks, recent statistics [6,31] show that these kind of attacks (*e.g.,* cross-site scripting, SQL injection) are still the most common security vulnerabilities for web applications.

Multitier languages [29,8,10,7] have recently emerged as a response to the need of simplifying the development of web applications. A multitier language provides a unified syntax for server code and client code. Its runtime environment compiles the source into the various formats supported by the tiers. For instance, the runtime system of the HOP programming language contains three

S. Mödersheim and C. Palamidessi (Eds.): TOSCA 2011, LNCS 6993, pp. 186–204, 2012.

dynamic compilers. The first generates server-side byte code. The second generates JavaScript code. The third generates HTML. Multitier languages provide natural tools to solve code injection problems, as they allow global reasoning to be applied to the web applications.

We propose a methodology for preventing code injection in multitier languages which consists in modifying the client code compilers at the point of dynamic generation for comparing the generated code with the specification extracted from the syntax of the the source program. The methodology follows the technique for SQL injection by Su and Wasserman [30], and it also applies to other target-tier languages such as XQuery or LDAP. The methodology complements that of [30] by the following added value:

- The programmer is freed from making any intervention in order to achieve security guarantees. Indeed the expected syntax structure is not provided by the programmer, since it is already given by the syntax of the multitier program.
- Proofs are given by means of standard language-based techniques and programming language semantics. We use the multitier programming language formal semantics in order to prove that the HOP compiler is certified regarding code injection prevention. We formally prove the validity of our approach by showing that the client compiler is fully abstract.

Related Work. The WebSSARI [13], and Pixy [15,16] tools propose tainted-flow static analysis for PHP to identify where untrusted input should be validated. Xie and Aiken [34] develop a finer approximation of tainted flow at the intra-block, intra-procedural, and inter-procedural level. However, tainted flow does not guarantee proper validation of untrusted data, since any pre-defined validation procedure or user-defined filter will be considered as correct. Based on tainted flow analysis, other works propose sophisticated string analysis for assessing the correctness of the validation procedure [23,3,33,32] for SQL or web applications. Those analysis are over-approximations of the possible set of output strings that may be injection attacks. Those approaches above, whether sound or not, require explicit intervention of programmers to deal with untrusted inputs by proper validation. Our approach, on the other hand, does not require any intervention of programmer to be sound with respect to injection attacks.

Other approaches dynamically detect and prevent injection attacks. Perl's *tainted mode* [25] is one of the earliest dynamic mechanisms for disallowing untrusted input to be used in a security-sensitive context. Xu and his colleagues [35] present a policy-based solution for dynamic detection of insecure tainted information flow, where a source-to-source translation instruments programs to track tainted data. Nguyen-Tuong and his colleagues propose similar dynamic flow monitoring with a modified PHP interpreter. Run-time instruction-set randomization [17] prevents SQL injection by randomly masking SQL query keywords, making it difficult to change the intended syntax structure of query by untrusted input. Most of the solutions to prevent code injection (*e.g.*, tainted flow analysis, static string analysis, syntax embedding, etc) either do not free the programmer from doing sanitization by themselves or require browser modifications. The work by Su and Wassermann [30] is the closest one to ours. They prevent SQL injection by comparing constructed SQL queries with given policies at run-time when the query is submitted to a database back-end. Besides the fact that the syntactic structure of SQL code does not change dynamically as is the case of generated JavaScript programs, the difference with respect to our work is that they require a separate grammar specification, whereas our approach takes source semantics directly as specification for programs to be executed in the target-tier. The work by Robertson and Vigna [27] propose a framework that uses typing to identify where untrusted inputs are used in an output HTML page, therefore to use a sanitization function to prevent the structure of the output page from being modified. However the sanitization function in their proposal is not proved to be sound. There are other alternatives to tackle the code injection problem from the client side [14,21,36,26,19]. Swift [9] and SELinks [11] use information flow security analysis to detect code injection attacks, among other techniques such as partitioning of code (in the case of Swift) and typing or filtering (in the case of SELinks). Our technique is significantly different from theirs since it does not require any integration of program static analysis. Moreover, its implementation in multitier compilers is simple and no effort is required to adapt to any target-tier language (it is not dependent of or limited to HTML+JavaScript) provided that the multitier language includes appropriate target-tier language constructors at the source level and that a parser for the target-tier language is available at compilation time.

Blueprint [22] and xJS [2] are two tools that focus on keeping the intended syntax structure of server generated document when untrusted inputs are present. In both systems, untrusted content is parsed at the server-side (eliminating dynamic content), and then encoded as a model in a safe alphabet which does not trigger script evaluation. On the client-side, a safe library function is invoked to recover the untrusted content. As a result, no script evaluation will be triggered by untrusted content. In contrast to our approach, their approach works for existing developing framework of web applications, but requires the programmer to identify untrusted inputs and the context where untrusted input is output. Furthermore, there are performance penalties both on the server-side and client-side. Our solution does not require any programmer's intervention for identifying untrusted sources or context and it has no performance penalty on the client-side.

Contents. In Section 2 we give an overview of the proposed compilation technique. In Section 3 we present the HOP language and its semantics for globally describing web applications. This semantics can be thought as a high-level description of the server and (specially) the client code. In Section 4 we define a compiler from HOP programs to client code (HTML+JavaScript). In Section 4.2 we introduce the compilation extension that allows us to prove the result. We discuss the HOP implementation and some practical JavaScript issues in Section 5. We conclude in Section 6.

2 Overview

In this section we give an overview of multitier web programs and informally present our approach to prevent code injection by compilation.

Web 2.0 applications are commonly composed of three tiers: the server tier or web server contains and executes server code, the client tier or browser executes client code, and the database tier contains a database and a database management system (DBMS) to execute queries.

One of the characteristics of modern web applications is the dynamic generation of code. The web server may generate a particular HTML page based on input from the client for example. Typically, without using a multitier language, dynamic generation of client code is obtained by manipulating strings. Generally the server represents HTML as a text template with holes that are to be filled with dynamic content, as shown in the following example of server code written in Java:

```
1 public class Greeting extends HttpServlet {
2   public void doGet(HttpServletRequest req,
3                     HttpServletResponse res){
4     res.setContentType("text/html");
5     PrintWriter out = res.getWriter();
6     String name = req.getParameter("name");
7     out.println("<HTML>\n<BODY>\n");
8     out.println("Greeting from " + name + "\n");
9     out.println("</BODY>\n</HTML>\n");}}
```

The web service corresponding to the code above, after receiving a request from a client with a parameter "name", will respond with a HTML page to be displayed in the browser, containing a greeting. Multitier programming languages, such as HOP, follow a different path mainly to harmonize the programming of the client and the server. They support a coherent unique syntax and semantics for both ends of the applications. This in general, involves supporting a Document Object Model (henceforth *DOM*) for HTML on the client as well as on the server as shown in Figure 1. This approach has proved to have some advantages over HTML textual representations. It eases the creation and manipulation of HTML documents that are represented as a regular data structures of the language. It also allows to separate the creation of a document from its actual external representation which can vary from one client to another. For instance, a HTML5 capable client might receive a document expressed in that particular HTML version while another one, less skilled, might receive it in XHTML.

In a multitier language, a semantically equivalent program, can be written using constructs from the language, as shown in the following HOP example:

```
1 (define-service (greeting name)
2   (<HTML>
3     (<BODY>
4       "Greeting from" name)))
```

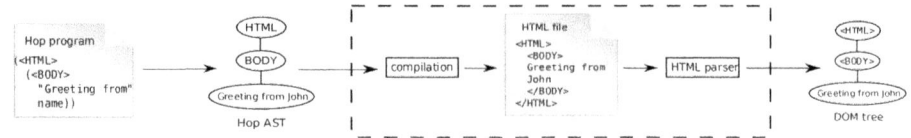

Fig. 1. AST and DOM generated trees after client request

As before, the code above will respond to a client request by a HTML page containing a greeting, but the difference is that <HTML> and <BODY> are regular library functions of the language.

In response to a client request, a HOP program generates a response which can either be *static*, for example a simple static file or string, or *dynamic*. In that case the server executes user code to dynamically generate the response content as in the example above. Only this kind of response is liable to code injection which occurs when the input of the server side computation is inserted in the generated response as a client-side executable code. A typical attack consists in stealing the client's cookies and redirecting then to an adversary's website (see for instance Figure 2). In this example, the input name binds to a malicious string "<script>win...</script>". Therefore the HOP AST (Abstract Syntax Tree) obtained from server-side run-time environment is different from the DOM tree obtained by parsing the generated HTML document in the client's browser. Prevention of code injection only requires to add additional treatment to dynamic responses, no special treatment being required for other responses.

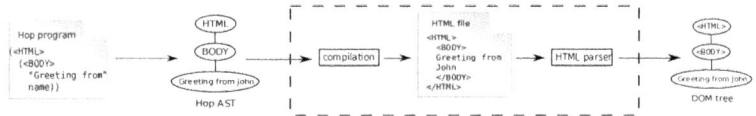

Fig. 2. Mismatch between AST tree and DOM tree

Splitting apart dynamic HTTP requests and being provided with a server-side HOP AST makes code injection detection easier: it is only needed to reproduce the DOM tree that is generated on the client-side and compare it with the HOP AST. This tree can be easily obtained by parsing the HTML document generated from the HOP AST *on the server-side* using a standard HTML parser. Then it is sufficient to compare the two trees to detect code injection attacks. If the two trees have the same shape, the program is safe and the response is sent to the client. If the two trees differ, code has been injected and an exception is raised.

In terms of compiler re-writing, code injection detection only requires to extend the code of the compiler that is in charge of delivering dynamic content.

In order to prove that this eliminates unexpected behaviors from the dynamically generated pages, we use the HOP program semantics, that abstracts away from compilation processes, as the specification of what expected behavior is.

$$str \in String$$

$$p, q, r \ldots \in Pointer$$

$$s ::= x \mid w \mid (s_0\, s_1) \mid {\sim}t \mid (\langle tag \rangle) \mid (\text{dom-appchild!}\, s_0\, s_1)$$

$$t ::= x \mid (\text{lambda}\,(x)\,t) \mid () \mid str \mid p \mid (t_0\, t_1) \mid \$x$$

$$w ::= (\text{lambda}\,(x)\,s) \mid {\sim}c \mid () \mid str \mid p$$

$$c ::= x \mid v \mid (c_0\, c_1)$$

$$v ::= (\text{lambda}\,(x)\,c) \mid () \mid str$$

$$tag ::= \text{HTML} \mid \text{DIV} \mid \cdots$$

Fig. 3. Simplified HOP Syntax

In the rest of the paper, we describe the formalization and code injection soundness proofs (correspondence of the behavior of generated client code with respect to the client HOP semantics) for a subset of the HOP language. However, the implementation of the technique, that is made publicly available from the HOP web page[1], is applied to the full-fledged language, including a non-trivial set of HTML attributes and constructs, as well as CSS files and JavaScript functions.

3 A Multitier Language

We present a core of the HOP language limited to a minimal set of web programming abstractions that are enough to present our compilation technique and develop its formal correctness (a larger formal description of the language that includes constructors for defining services on the server-side, calling services from the client, events handler such as "onclick" in web pages, and event loops as a form of cooperative multithreading [1], can be found in [5]).

3.1 Syntax

The syntax is given in Figure 3, where x denotes any variable. We assume given a set *String* of strings; a set *Pointer* of pointers. Those sets are mutually disjoint, and are also disjoint from the set of variables. Pointers are run-time values for denoting HTML tree nodes. The simplified HOP syntax is stratified into *server code* s and *tilde code* t. The former is basically Scheme [18] code enriched with a construct ${\sim}t$ to ship (tilde) code t to the client, and constructs to dynamically build HTML trees. The latter may include references $\$x$ to server values, and will be translated into *client code* c, before being shipped to the client.

A server expression usually contains sub-expressions of the form ${\sim}t$. As we said, t represents code that will be executed on the clients. This code may use values provided by the server, by means of sub-expressions $\$x$. When the latter are absent (that is, when they have been replaced by a value bound to x), a t

---

[1] http://hop.inria.fr

expression reduces to a client expression c. Notice that for the server an expression $\sim c$ is a value, meaning that the evaluation of code c is delayed until installed on a client site. Server code syntax is enriched with some basic HTML constructs, written in Scheme style, and operations supported by the DOM. Here we confine ourselves to consider the HTML and DIV tags, and the (dom-appchild! s_0 s_1) construct – the other ones are similar (see [12]). The general form of HTML constructors in HOP is $(\langle tag \rangle\ [:attr])$ where $attr$ is an optional list of attributes. For simplicity, we only consider here the cases $(\langle tag \rangle)$ where there is no attribute. A more general form of creating a node with an arbitrary number of children can be defined as syntactic sugar. For example, creating a node with one child can be defined as follows:

$$(\langle tag \rangle\ s) ::= ((\text{lambda}\ (x)\ (\text{dom-appchild!}\ (\langle tag \rangle\ )\ x))\ s)$$

Values also include strings and (), which is a shorthand for the *unspecified* Scheme run-time value. As usual (lambda $(x)\ s$) binds x in the expression s.

A HOP *program* is a *closed* expression s, meaning that it does not contain any free variable. We shall consider expressions up to α-conversion, that is up to the renaming of bound variables, and we denote by $s\{y/x\}$ the expression resulting from substituting the variable y for x in s, possibly renaming y in sub-expressions where this variable is bound, to avoid captures. The operational semantics of the language will be described as a transition system, where at each step a (possibly distributed) *redex* is reduced. As usual, this occurs in specific positions in the code, that are described by means of *evaluation contexts*. The syntax of evaluation contexts is as follows:

$$\mathbf{S} ::= [] \mid (\mathbf{S}\ s) \mid (w\ \mathbf{S}) \mid (\text{dom-appchild!}\ \mathbf{S}\ s) \mid (\text{dom-appchild!}\ w\ \mathbf{S})$$
$$\mathbf{C} ::= [] \mid (\mathbf{C}\ c) \mid (v\ \mathbf{C})$$

As usual, we denote by $\mathbf{S}[s]$ (resp. $\mathbf{C}[c]$) the result of filling the hole [] in context $\mathbf{S}$ (resp. $\mathbf{C}$) with expression s (resp. c).

3.2   Hop Web Application Semantics

The semantics of a HOP web application is represented as a sequence of transitions between configurations. Specific features that are modeled in the semantics in order to capture the behaviour of web applications include: dynamic client code generation and delivery, script nodes execution from a DOM tree, dynamic DOM tree modification. A configuration consists in

- a server configuration S, together with an environment μ providing the values for the variables occurring in the server configuration. For simplicity, we consider that the server configuration consists in a single thread at the time executing server's code to answer client's requests to services.
- a client configuration C, which consists in one running client (extension to multiple clients is straightforward [5] but we prefer to simplify notation here). A client is a tuple $\langle c, \mu, r \rangle$ where c is the client code and μ is the local

environment for the client distinct from the one of the server (the client and the server do not share any state). The pointer r is the *root* of the HTML page that is displayed at the client site by the browser.

- a HOP environment ρ, which binds URLs to services s (we assume given a set Url of names denoting URLs);

Then a configuration Γ has the form $((S, \mu), C, \rho)$. However, to simplify the semantic rules, and to represent the concurrent execution of the various components, we shall use the following syntax for configurations:

$$\Gamma ::= \mu \mid \rho \mid s \mid \langle c, \mu, r \rangle \mid (\Gamma \parallel \Gamma)$$

We assume that parallel composition $\parallel$ is commutative and associative, so that the rules can be expressed following the "chemical style" of [4]:

$$\frac{\Gamma \rightarrow \Gamma'}{(\Gamma \parallel \Gamma'') \rightarrow (\Gamma' \parallel \Gamma'')}$$

meaning that if the components of Γ are present in the configuration, which can therefore be written $(\Gamma \parallel \Gamma'')$, and if these components interact to produce Γ', then we can replace the components of Γ with those of Γ'.

Before introducing and commenting the reaction rules, we define an auxiliary function transforming tilde code into client code. As we said a sub-expression $\sim t$ in server code is *not* evaluated at server side, but will be shipped to the client, usually as the answer to a service request. Since the expression t may contain references $\$x$ to server values, to define the semantics we introduce an auxiliary function Ξ that takes as arguments an environment μ and an expression t, and transforms it into a client expression c. The Ξ transformation consists in replacing $\$x$ by the value bound to x in μ. For example, if $\mu = \{x \mapsto$ "text"$\}$, then we have

$$\Xi(\mu, \sim((\text{lambda}\,(y)\,y)\,\$x)) = \sim((\text{lambda}\,(y)\,y)\,\text{"text"})$$

(The interested reader can check for a formal definition in a previous paper [5]). One should notice that a function, that is a (lambda $(x)\,s$), or client code c cannot be sent to the client this way, because this would in general result in breaking the bindings of free variables that may occur in such an expression. Then this has to be considered as an error. The semantics of the $(\langle tag \rangle)$ construct is that it builds a node of a tree in a *forest*. In order to define this, we assume given a specific null pointer, denoted α, which is not in $Pointer$. We use π to range over $Pointer \cup \{\alpha\}$. Then a forest maps (non null) pointers to pairs made of a (possibly null) pointer and an expression of the form $(\langle tag \rangle\,c_1 + \cdots + c_n)$. The pointer $q \in Pointer$ assigned to p is the *ancestor* of the node, if it exists. If it does not, this pointer is α. Such a node is labeled *tag* and has n children, which are either leaves (labeled with some client code or value) or pointers to other nodes in the tree. For simplicity we consider here the forest as joined to the environment providing values for variables. That is, we now consider that μ is a mapping from a set $\mathsf{dom}(\mu)$ of variables and (non null) pointers, that maps variables to values, and pointers to pairs made of a (possibly null) pointer and a *node* expression. The syntax for node expressions a is as follows:

$$a ::= (\langle tag \rangle \, \ell)$$
$$\ell ::= \varepsilon \mid c \mid (\ell_0 + \ell_1)$$

where ε is the empty list. In what follows we assume that $+$ is associative, and that $\varepsilon + \ell = \ell = \ell + \varepsilon$. We shall also use the following notations in defining the semantics, assuming that the pointers occurring in the list ℓ are distinct:

$$(\langle tag \rangle \, \ell) + p = (\langle tag \rangle \, \ell + p)$$
$$(\langle tag \rangle \, \ell_0 + p + \ell_1) - p = (\langle tag \rangle \, \ell_0 + \ell_1)$$

Given a forest μ, and $p \in \mathsf{dom}(\mu)$, we denote by $\mu[p \mapsto (\pi, a)]$ the forest obtained by updating the value associated with p in μ. For $r \in \textit{Pointer}$, we also define $\mu \lceil r$ to be the part of the forest that is reachable from r (a formal definition can be found in [5]). For example:

$$\mu = \begin{bmatrix} r \mapsto (\alpha, \langle \mathsf{HTML} \rangle \, \text{"text"} + p), \\ p \mapsto (r, \langle \mathsf{DIV} \rangle \, \text{"text"}), \\ q \mapsto (\alpha, \langle \mathsf{DIV} \rangle \, \text{"text"}) \end{bmatrix}, \mu \lceil r = \begin{bmatrix} r \mapsto (\alpha, \langle \mathsf{HTML} \rangle \, \text{"text"} + p), \\ p \mapsto (r, \langle \mathsf{DIV} \rangle \, \text{"text"}) \end{bmatrix}$$

An excerpt of the semantics rules is given in Figure 4. Rules for variable look-up and function application are standard and left out (a complete set of rules can be found in [5]) . The TILDE rule transforms tilde code containing $\$x$

$$\frac{\Xi(\mu, t) = c}{\mathbf{S}[\sim t] \parallel \mu \rightarrow \mathbf{S}[\sim c] \parallel \mu} \text{ (TILDE)} \qquad \frac{\mu(r) = (\alpha, (\langle \mathsf{HTML} \rangle \, \ell))}{r \parallel \mu \parallel \langle \emptyset, \emptyset, \alpha \rangle \rightarrow \mu \parallel \langle \emptyset, \mu \lceil r, r \rangle} \text{ (SERVRET)}$$

$$\frac{\rho(u) = w \quad v \neq (\mathsf{lambda} \, (x) \, c)}{\rho \rightarrow (w \, v) \parallel \langle \emptyset, \emptyset, \alpha \rangle \parallel \rho} \text{ (INIT)}$$

$$\frac{R(r, p, \mu) \quad \mu(p) = (q, (\langle tag \rangle \, \ell_0 + c + \ell_1))}{\langle v, \mu, W, r \rangle \rightarrow \langle c, \mu[p \mapsto (q, (\langle tag \rangle \, \ell_0 + \ell_1))], W, r \rangle} \text{ (SCRIPT)}$$

$$\frac{p \notin \mathsf{dom}(\mu)}{\mathbf{S}[(\langle tag \rangle)] \parallel \mu \rightarrow \mathbf{S}[p] \parallel \mu \cup \{p \mapsto (\alpha, (\langle tag \rangle \, \varepsilon))\}} \text{ (TAGS)}$$

$$\frac{\mu(p) = (\pi, a_0) \quad \mu(q) = (q', a_1) \quad \mu(q') = (\pi', a_2) \quad p \neq q' \quad \neg R(q, p, \mu)}{\mathbf{S}[(\mathsf{dom\text{-}appchild!} \, p \, q)] \parallel \mu \rightarrow \mathbf{S}[()] \parallel \mu \begin{bmatrix} p \mapsto (\pi, a_0 + q), \\ q \mapsto (p, a_1), \\ q' \mapsto (\pi', a_2 - q) \end{bmatrix}} \text{ (APPENDS1)}$$

Fig. 4. Excerpt of HOP Semantics

expressions into a server value. The SERVRET rule is the key rule in the semantics that, in the case of the high-level semantics, allows us to specify which code is executed on the client site. The SERVRET rule can be used once a service in the server has finished its evaluation, and its result is shipped to the client. The kind of service results we are interested in are pointers representing a HTML fragment or document, possibly containing one or more script nodes to execute. In the high-level semantics, the HTML document with script nodes is constructed by HOP HTML constructors. Tilde codes are dynamically evaluated by possibly embedding values obtained with $x expressions. The SERVRET rule sets the root of the client document to be the result value pointer r and the client environment to $\mu \lceil r$ that represents exactly the HTML tree that hangs from pointer r in the server store.

The INIT rule creates a new instance of a service and initializes its execution with any argument v. This rule is intentionally made non-deterministic to model that the client can provide any input to the service. This argument is (untrusted) input provided by the client. On the client site, there is the SCRIPT rule that models execution of script node contained in the client HTML document. We use the predicate $R(r, p, \mu)$ to state that pointer p is a descendant of r in μ, and that the code that we find at node p, and which is to be triggered, is the leftmost one in the tree $\mu \lceil r$ determined by r. (We should also check that this tree is still a valid HTML document. We do not formally define this predicate here – this is straightforward.) An example illustrates the predicate R in Figure 5. Finally the APPENDS1rule modifies the DOM by appending a child to an existing node in the store. Notice that the rule preserves the uniqueness of pointers in list presentation.

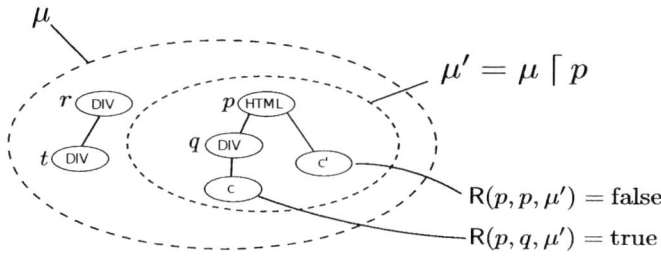

Fig. 5. Example: The predicate R

3.3 A More Fine-Grained Semantics

The high-level SERVRET rule abstractly defines HOP client code and its intended behavior, that is, the HTML tree should be delivered intact to the client. We present a more detailed semantics that consists in a dynamic compilation phase compiling a HOP AST tree to HTML + JavaScript code to transfer the document constructed in the server's store to a client thread. This appears in a new version of the rule SERVRET. At the client-side, the HTML parser (in the browser) interprets this HTML document, possibly invoking the JavaScript engine to execute script nodes.

$$str \ \in \ String \qquad\qquad\qquad string$$

$$c_{js} ::= x \ | \ v_{js} \ | \ c_{js}(c'_{js}) \qquad\qquad code$$

$$v_{js} ::= \mathsf{function}(x)\{\mathsf{return} \ c_{js}\} \ | \ () \ | \ str \quad values$$

Fig. 6. JavaScript (abstract) Syntax

Client-side JavaScript Syntax and Semantics. We give a formal treatment to the syntax and semantics of JavaScript in order to prove correctness in following sections. The abstract syntax of a small core of JavaScript is shown in Figure 6. Its syntax is self-explanatory. We omit usual definitions such as variable substitution. The evaluation context is defined as follows:

$$\mathbf{J} ::= [] \ | \ \mathbf{J}(c_{js}) \ | \ v_{js}(\mathbf{J})$$

We overload notation $C = \langle c_{js}, \mu, r \rangle$ for client configuration in the low-level semantics, where c_{js} and μ are JavaScript code and store, respectively. The definition of list ℓ for node representation is also updated, since in the low-level semantics script nodes are now JavaScript expressions. The shape of a server configuration and global configuration are left unchanged. As shown in Figure 7, rule VARJS and APPJS are unsurprising, which evaluate redex for client-side JavaScript code.

Client Dynamic Compilation. The dynamic compilation is parametrized with a HOP client compiler C and a HTML parser P. The HOP client compiler C transforms a server HOP store and a pointer that represents an abstract HOP tree with HOP client code ($\mu \lceil r$) into an actual HTML document that contains JavaScript code. The HTML parser P (which includes a JavaScript parser), on the client-side, will parse any HTML document and produce a pair of store and root pointer (μ_c, p) as the DOM tree to be rendered (see Figure 1). As shown in Figure 7, instead of abstractly transferring part of the server's store $\mu \lceil r$, the new SERVRETLOW rule first use HOP client compiler to compile the abstract tree into a HTML document *doc*. Then it uses the HTML parser P to parse *doc*, in order to produce a DOM tree for the client. The network transmission of

$$\frac{\mu(x) = v_{js}}{\langle \mathbf{J}[x], \mu, p \rangle \rightarrow \langle \mathbf{J}[v_{js}], \mu, p \rangle} \ (\text{VARJS})$$

$$\frac{y \notin \mathsf{dom}(\mu)}{\langle \mathbf{J}[\mathsf{function}(x)\{\mathsf{return} \ c_{js}\}(v_{js})], \mu, p \rangle \rightarrow \langle \mathbf{J}[c_{js}\{y/x\}], \mu \cup \{y \mapsto v_{js}\}, p \rangle} \ (\text{APPJS})$$

$$\frac{doc = \mathsf{C}(\mu, r) \quad \mathsf{P}(doc) = (\mu_c, p) \quad \mu_c(p) = (\alpha, (\langle \mathsf{HTML} \rangle \ \ell))}{\mu \ \| \ \langle (), \emptyset, \alpha \rangle \rightarrow \mu \ \| \ \langle p, \mu_c, p \rangle} \ (\text{SERVRETLOW})$$

Fig. 7. Low-level semantics

the HTML document is made implicit in the rule. The rest of the rules are left unchanged from the high-level semantics.

4   Client-Code Compilation

In this section we first show that a naive compiler may cause the fine-grained semantics to have more undesired behaviors than the high-level semantics, which are code injection attacks. Then we show how to modify the naive compiler by using the *tree-comparison technique* to obtain a secured HOP client compiler that prevents code injection attacks. We give formal proof that the secured compiler is code-injection free, that is, it has no more behavior than the high-level semantics.

4.1   A Naive Client Compiler

The compiler C_a translates a server's store and a pointer to a HTML document *doc* by simply concatenating HTML tags and content. It also uses a JavaScript compiler C_j that compiles HOP client code into JavaScript. This naive compiler is defined in Figure 8(c), in which letters in typewriter font represent string characters and "." represent string concatenation (omitted when unambiguous)[2].

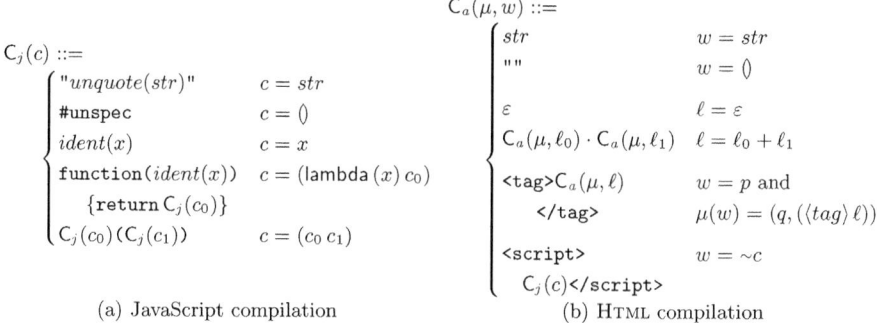

(a) JavaScript compilation   (b) HTML compilation

Fig. 8. HOP dynamic compilation

Example. Let us illustrate how the fine-grained semantics has more behaviors than the high-level one. Figure 9(a) shows a HOP program constructing a simple HTML document depending on input **name**. The compilation using C_a is shown in Figure 9(b), if the input provided is the string **Alice**. Furthermore, the initial client configuration obtained by SERVRETLOW rule is $\langle \mu_c, \emptyset, p \rangle$, where $str =$ **Alice**, and

$$\mu_c = \{p \mapsto (\alpha, (\langle \mathsf{HTML} \rangle\, q)), q \mapsto (p, (\langle \mathsf{DIV} \rangle\, str))\}$$

---

[2] In JavaScript compiler C_j, we assume that the *unquote* function escapes a string to its string literal representation (*e.g.,* "a"b" is escaped to "a\"b"), and *ident* is a bijection that maps each variable name to a unique string (*e.g.,* variable name x is mapped to x).

```
1 (lambda (name)          1 <HTML>
2     (<HTML>             2   <DIV>
3         (<DIV>          3     Alice
4             name)))     4   </DIV>
                          5 </HTML>
```

(a) Hop program (b) Compilation results

Fig. 9. Example: Fine-grained Semantics

We can observe that the store obtained by SERVRETLOW rule and SERVRET are equivalent up to pointer renaming.

However, the fine-grained semantics is not simulated by the high-level semantics presented in the previous section, since more behaviors may appear on the client side by means of a code injection attack [3]. If input name is

<script>function(x){return x;}("str")</script>

we would obtain a HTML page by compilation as follows:

```
1 <HTML><DIV><SCRIPT>
2 function(x){return x;}("str")
3 </SCRIPT></DIV></HTML>
```

Observe that the corresponding store μ_c obtained by SERVRETLOW rule and the parser P is :

$$\mu_c = \{p \mapsto (\alpha, (\langle \mathsf{HTML} \rangle\, q))\}$$
$$\cup\{q \mapsto (p, (\langle \mathsf{DIV} \rangle\, str + \mathsf{function}(x)\{\mathsf{return}\ x\}(str)))\}$$

The same configuration cannot be obtained by the SERVRET rule in the high-level semantics.

4.2   A Secure Client Compiler

In order to define a secure HOP client compiler, we need to introduce a relation $\approx$ between a high-level client store μ and a low-level client store μ'. Informally, two stores are in the relation if their tree structures are the same. Definition of $\approx$ is given in Figure 10. For simplicity, we assume in the definition that two pointers are indistinguishable if they are equal (however, this assumption could be easily relaxed by standard indistinguishability definitions up to a bijection on pointer names). Note that pointers are used here just to describe tree representations in the semantics. In the actual implementation, the parser does not return a store but rather a DOM tree. The translation $\mathcal{C}_{js}$ from HOP client code to JavaScript is as follows:

$$\frac{}{\mathcal{C}_{js}(\emptyset) = \emptyset} \quad \frac{}{\mathcal{C}_{js}(str) = str} \quad \frac{\mathcal{C}_{js}(c) = c_{js} \quad \mathcal{C}_{js}(c') = c'_{js}}{\mathcal{C}_{js}((c\,c')) = c_{js}(c'_{js})}$$

---

[3] This attack is not particular harmful. This is just for demonstrating that the adversary has the ability to inject code.

$$\frac{}{\varepsilon \approx \varepsilon} \qquad \frac{\mathcal{C}_{js}(c) = c_{js}}{c \approx c_{js}}$$

$$\frac{\ell_0 \approx \ell_0' \quad \ell_1 \approx \ell_1'}{\ell_0 + \ell_1 \approx \ell_0' + \ell_1'} \qquad \frac{\ell \approx \ell'}{(p, (\langle tag \rangle \ell)) \approx (p, (\langle tag \rangle \ell'))}$$

$$\frac{\mathrm{dom}(\mu) = \mathrm{dom}(\mu') \qquad \forall p \in \mathrm{dom}(\mu).\mu(p) \approx \mu'(p)}{\mu \approx \mu'}$$

Fig. 10. Tree indistinguishability

$$\frac{\mathcal{C}_{js}(c) = c_{js}}{\mathcal{C}_{js}((\mathsf{lambda}\,(x)\,c)) = \mathsf{function}(x)\{\mathsf{return}\ c_{js}\}}$$

The secure HOP client compiler is then defined as follows:

$$\mathsf{C}_s(\mu, r) = \begin{cases} \mathsf{C}_a(\mu, r) & \text{if } \mathsf{P}(\mathsf{C}_a(\mu, r)) = (\mu_c, p) \text{ and } \mu \lceil r \approx \mu_c \\ & \text{and } p = r \\ \bot & \text{otherwise} \end{cases}$$

It is built on top of the naive compiler C_a. The secure version of the compiler returns the result generated by C_a, only if the source tree $(\mu \lceil r, r)$ is indistinguishable from the tree (μ_c, p) obtained by parsing (on the server-side) the generated document. Otherwise, it returns $\bot$, which raises an exception on the server-side.

Assumption on the HTML *parser.* Our technique requires just a standard HTML parser on the server-side. The implication is that only *valid* HTML page is delivered. Therefore injection attacks caused by ill-formed HTML and browser parsing quirks are not possible in our approach, since ill-formed HTML is never output to the client.

Formal correctness. We use $\to_h$ to denote high-level semantics transitions, and $\to_l$ to denote low-level semantics transitions in order to distinguish them in the following definition. We define the simulation $\Gamma \succ \Gamma'$, where Γ is a high-level configuration and Γ' is low-level configuration.

Definition 1. *Let* $\Gamma_0 = ((S_0, \mu_0), C_0, \rho_0)$ *and* $\Gamma_1 = ((S_1, \mu_1), C_1, \rho_1))$. *The simulation* $\succ$ *is the largest relation* $\mathcal{S}$ *on configurations such that* $\Gamma_0 \, \mathcal{S} \, \Gamma_1$ *implies:*

1. $\mu_0 = \mu_1$
2. $C_0 = \langle c, \mu, r \rangle$, $C_1 = \langle c_{js}, \mu_{js}, r \rangle$ *such that* $\mu \approx \mu_{js}$

and if $\Gamma_1 \to_l \Gamma_1'$, *then there exists* Γ_0' *such that* $\Gamma_0 \to_h \Gamma_0'$ *and* $\Gamma_0' \, \mathcal{S} \, \Gamma_1'$.

Finally, we state a theorem that implies that the client secure compiler is fully abstract, given the correctness of the HOP to JavaScript compiler.

Theorem 1. *Let* $\Gamma = \Gamma' = ((\epsilon, \epsilon), \epsilon, \rho)$, *where* Γ *is a high-level configuration and* Γ' *is a low-level configuration, and* ρ *is a* HOP *services environment. If the fine-grained semantics use the secured client compiler* C_s, *we have* $\Gamma \succ \Gamma'$.

The theorem claims the soundness of our approach to eliminate code injection attacks. The proof is a standard simulation proof: we show that the semantics of delivered client code (standard HTML+JavaScript) simulates the high-level semantics of client HOP code. The proof can be found in an accompanying technical report[4].

5   Practical Discussion

In this section we report about an experiment that evaluates the penalty imposed by the integrity enforcement, and we discuss how the tree comparison technique can be applied to traditional programming languages for Web applications. In Appendix A we discuss some practical issues of the implementation.

Performance. We have compared the execution times of several Hop programs with security enforcement enabled and disabled (Figure 11). We have measured the time needed by the server to deliver dynamic contents. Using the `httperf` tools [24], we have exercised the server with a repeated request up to an execution time (`usr + sys`) of about 10 seconds for the unchecked version. All requests are sent in the same HTTP connection using HTTP keep-alive annotations. The server is executed on an Intel Xeon W3570 running at 3.2GHz with 6GB of memory. For each execution, we report on the execution time expressed in seconds. Here is a short description of each tested program. `Hoppanel` (700 loc) generates a web page presenting all the installed HOP programs on a host. `Hopclock` (1100 loc), is a web wall clock. `Hoppmt` (160 loc) is a web loan calculator. `Hoptris` (740 loc) is Tetris on a web browser. `Hopstick` (800 loc) provides stickers on a web browser. `Hopphoto` (2130 loc) is a web photo browser. `Hopfile` (550 loc) is a web server-side file browser.

The impact on the performance of security enforcement depends on the nature of the executed programs, and can be noted only on the server side. Once the code is installed on the browser, there is no performance cost with respect to unsecure programs. The slowdown ratio in the server ranges from 1.38 to 4.23. We believe, however, these are not significant performance penalty for several following reasons.

1. It must be noted that at this early stage of the implementation no optimization is applied to the tree comparison. The security manager writes and parses the entire HTML documents. This is expensive when the documents are large. Minimizing this cost will be subject of future work and may include sound sanitization techniques for untrusted inputs.

---

[4] http://www-sop.inria.fr/members/Zhengqin.Luo/papers/acipwa-long.pdf

benchmark	secure	unsecure	δ
hoppanel	43.56s	10.29s	4.23
hopclock	31.77s	10.50s	3.02
hoppmt	34.68s	12.59s	2.75
hoptris	33.57	12.56s	2.67
hopsticker	14.43	9.98s	1.45
hopphoto	16.36	11.87s	1.38
hopfile	23.97s	10.44s	2.30

Fig. 11. This performance evaluation measures the impact of security enforcement in Hop. The *secure* column reports on the execution times with security enforcement. The *unsecure* column reports on the execution times in seconds without security enforcement. The column δ shows the slowdown ratio.

2. It must be observed that these measures represent worst cases because for this experiment only the times to get the dynamic parts of the applications have been measured. For displaying this page in the browser, there are several other static content to be load, such as Hop run-time library and images. Since those content are not dynamically generated, there is no run-time penalty for these content. By counting the time that the server need to deliver them, we can bring down the overall run-time penalty.

3. As already demonstrated in a previous experiment [28], HOP can be more than one order of magnitude faster than common web platforms based on Apache or Tomcat for delivering dynamic documents. Hence, even with security enforcement enabled, HOP still is one of the fastest runtime environments for delivering Web 2.0 content.

Remarks on Other Programming Languages. The tree comparison technique presented in Section 4 can also be applied to other traditional programming languages for Web applications, with additional efforts. For example, to apply this technique on a Web server that supports PHP requires to modify the Web server in a non-trivial way:

1. For each PHP program that generates a HTML page, associate it with a separate function that computes an AST as specification depending on given inputs.

2. Upon receiving a HTTP request from a client of a PHP program, the Web server invokes the corresponding specification function on received input, obtaining an AST. It then executes the PHP program with a PHP interpreter, and parses the output of the program with a HTML parser, obtaining another HTML tree. The server delivers the HTML output only if the trees are of the same shape.

Comparing to the multitier programming languages approach, applying tree comparison technique on traditional programming languages for the Web requires further modification on Web servers and programmers' intervention to write specification function.

6   Conclusion

We have shown that multitier languages provide appropriate tools to eliminate code injection. In particular these kind of languages provide an essential ingredient to detect code injection: the intended semantics of the web application. We propose a compilation technique and prove its correctness in the HOP language. The technique does not require any kind of browser modification nor any annotation from the programmer. We believe that its simplicity makes it suitable for any kind of multitier compiler.

References

1. Abadi, M., Plotkin, G.D.: A model of cooperative threads. In: Shao, Z., Pierce, B.C. (eds.) POPL, pp. 29–40. ACM, New York (2009)
2. Athanasopoulos, E., et al.: xJS: Practical XSS Prevention for Web Application Development. In: Proceedings USENIX Conference on Web Application Development (WebApps 2010), Boston, USA (June 2010)
3. Balzarotti, D., Cova, M., Felmetsger, V., Jovanovic, N., Kirda, E., Kruegel, C., Vigna, G.: Saner: Composing static and dynamic analysis to validate sanitization in web applications. In: IEEE Symposium on Security and Privacy, pp. 387–401 (2008)
4. Berry, G., Boudol, G.: The chemical abstract machine. In: Proceedings of the ACM International Conference on Principle of Programming Languages (POPL), pp. 81–94. ACM Press, New York (1990)
5. Boudol, G., Luo, Z., Rezk, T., Serrano, M.: Towards reasoning for web applications: an operational semantics for hop. In: APLWACA 2010, pp. 3–14 (2010)
6. Cenzic Inc. Web application security trends report Q1-Q2, 2009 (2010), http://www.cenzic.com/
7. Chlipala, A.: Ur: Statically-Typed Metaprogramming with Type-Level Record Computation. In: PLDI (2010)
8. Chong, S., Liu, J., Myers, A., Qi, X., Vikram, K., Zheng, L., Zheng, X.: Building secure web applications with automatic partitioning. Communications of the ACM 52(2), 79–87 (2009)
9. Chong, S., Liu, J., Myers, A.C., Qi, X., Vikram, K., Zheng, L., Zheng, X.: Secure web application via automatic partitioning. In: SOSP, pp. 31–44 (2007)
10. Cooper, E., Lindley, S., Wadler, P., Yallop, J.: Links: Web programming without tiers. In: de Boer, F.S., Bonsangue, M.M., Graf, S., de Roever, W.-P. (eds.) FMCO 2006. LNCS, vol. 4709, pp. 266–296. Springer, Heidelberg (2007)
11. Corcoran, B.J., Swamy, N., Hicks, M.W.: Cross-tier, label-based security enforcement for web applications. In: SIGMOD Conference, pp. 269–282 (2009)
12. Gardner, P., Smith, G., Wheelhouse, M., Zarfaty, U.: DOM: Towards a formal specification. In: Proceedings of the ACM SGIPLAN workshop on Programming Language Technologies for XML (PLAN-X), California, USA. ACM Press, New York (January 2008)
13. Huang, Y.-W., Yu, F., Hang, C., Tsai, C.-H., Lee, D.-T., Kuo, S.-Y.: Securing web application code by static analysis and runtime protection. In: WWW, pp. 40–52 (2004)
14. Jim, T., Swamy, N., Hicks, M.: Defeating script injection attacks with browser-enforced embedded policies. In: WWW, pp. 601–610 (2007)

15. Jovanovic, N., Kruegel, C., Kirda, E.: Precise alias analysis for static detection of web application vulnerabilities. In: PLAS 2006: Proceedings of the 2006 Workshop on Programming Languages and Analysis for Security, pp. 27–36. ACM, New York (2006)
16. Jovanovic, N., Krügel, C., Kirda, E.: Pixy: A static analysis tool for detecting web application vulnerabilities (short paper). In: IEEE Symposium on Security and Privacy, pp. 258–263 (2006)
17. Kc, G.S., Keromytis, A.D., Prevelakis, V.: Countering code-injection attacks with instruction-set randomization. In: ACM Conference on Computer and Communications Security, pp. 272–280 (2003)
18. Kelsey, R., Clinger, W.D., Rees, J.: Revised[5] report on the algorithmic language scheme. SIGPLAN Notices 33(9), 26–76 (1998)
19. Kirda, E., Kruegel, C., Vigna, G., Jovanovic, N.: Noxes: a client-side solution for mitigating cross-site scripting attacks. In: SAC 2006: Proceedings of the 2006 ACM Symposium on Applied Computing, pp. 330–337. ACM, New York (2006)
20. Li, P., Mao, Y., Zdancewic, S.: Information integrity policies. In: Proceedings of the Workshop on Formal Aspects in Security & Trust (FAST) (September 2003)
21. Livshits, V.B., Erlingsson, Ú.: Using web application construction frameworks to protect against code injection attacks. In: PLAS, pp. 95–104 (2007)
22. Louw, M.T., Venkatakrishnan, V.N.: Blueprint: Robust prevention of cross-site scripting attacks for existing browsers. In: IEEE Symposium on Security and Privacy, pp. 331–346 (2009)
23. Minamide, Y.: Static approximation of dynamically generated web pages. In: WWW, pp. 432–441 (2005)
24. Mosberger, D., Jin, T.: httperf: A tool for Measuring Web Server Performance. In: First Workshop on Internet Server Performance, pp. 59–67. Association for Computing Machinery (ACM), New York (1998)
25. The Perl Programming Language, http://www.perl.org
26. Reis, C., Dunagan, J., Wang, H.J., Dubrovsky, O., Esmeir, S.: Browsershield: Vulnerability-driven filtering of dynamic html. ACM Trans. Web 1(3), 11 (2007)
27. Robertson, W.K., Vigna, G.: Static enforcement of web application integrity through strong typing. In: USENIX Security Symposium, pp. 283–298 (2009)
28. Serrano, M.: HOP, a fast server for the diffuse web. In: Field, J., Vasconcelos, V.T. (eds.) COORDINATION 2009. LNCS, vol. 5521, pp. 1–26. Springer, Heidelberg (2009)
29. Serrano, M., Gallesio, E., Loitsch, F.: HOP, a language for programming the web 2.0. In: Proceedings of the First Dynamic Languages Symposium, DLS, Portland, Oregon, USA (October 2006)
30. Su, Z., Wassermann, G.: The essence of command injection attacks in web applications. In: POPL, pp. 372–382 (2006)
31. The MITRE Corporation. 2010 CWE/SANS top 25 most dangerous programming errors
32. Wassermann, G., Su, Z.: Sound and precise analysis of web applications for injection vulnerabilities. In: PLDI, pp. 32–41 (2007)
33. Wassermann, G., Su, Z.: Static detection of cross-site scripting vulnerabilities. In: ICSE, pp. 171–180 (2008)
34. Xie, Y., Aiken, A.: Static detection of security vulnerabilities in scripting languages. In: USENIX Security Symposium, pp. 179–192 (2006)
35. Xu, W., Bhatkar, E., Sekar, R.: Taint-enhanced policy enforcement: A practical approach to defeat a wide range of attacks. In: In 15th USENIX Security Symposium, pp. 121–136 (2006)
36. Yu, D., Chander, A., Islam, N., Serikov, I.: Javascript instrumentation for browser security. In: POPL, pp. 237–249 (2007)

A   Practical Code Injection Prevention in Hop

A code is considered to be injected when a user input string ends up being interpreted by the browsers as a client-side expression. To prevent this HOP imposes that all client-side codes should be generated by the HOP client-side compiler.

In HTML there are two ways to specify client-side expressions: *i)* by using SCRIPT nodes in the HTML tree, and *ii)* by including JavaScript expressions in the HTML nodes attributes. HOP handles these two situations differently.

First, the tree comparison presented in this paper ensures that no SCRIPT node is maliciously generated by the untrusted input in the server. The security enforcement takes place during the compilation of the AST into HTML. Prior to generating the actual text of a HTML response, a pre-processor first writes that response into a temporary file, parses it back, and compares the spine of the two trees. The response tree is immune to code injection if and only if the spines of the two trees are equivalent.

Second, a simple filtering rejects all attributes of nodes. In the HTML specification, those attribute strings as event handler will be interpreted as script expressions. HOP imposes that these attributes are bound to HOP client-side expressions, not to strings. For instance, it rejects

(<DIV> :onclick "alert(msg)" ...)

but it accepts

(<DIV> :onclick ~(alert msg) ...)

Since HOP offers no means for transforming a string of characters into a *tilde code* expression, this simple filtering technique ensures that attributes as event handlers cannot be used to inject arbitrary expressions.

Beyond the HTML specification, most browsers interpret attributes values prefixed with the string `javascript:` as listener attributes. For instance, the following HTML link, when clicked, evaluates the `alert` function call.

<A href="javascript:alert('foo')">click me</a>

Obviously this extension could also lead to code injection. To solve that problem we have adopted a conservative solution that disables this extension by forbidding the `javascript:` prefix for all attributes. This is enforced by HOP for HTML trees as well as for CSS declarations.

Finally, HOP also ensures that pure client-side manipulation cannot yield to executing new codes. For that, the client-side runtime library only binds JavaScript functions that are safe. For instance, if functions such as `eval` or `document.write` were accessible in HOP they could be used to evaluate arbitrary user forged code. The dangerous functions are either not included or slightly modified. For instance facilities such as `innerHTML` that parses an inserted string to a HTML tree is kept, but its argument must be a HTML node instead of a string.

Soundness of Removing Cancellation Identities in Protocol Analysis under Exclusive-OR

Sreekanth Malladi

Dakota State University
Madison, SD 57042, USA
Sreekanth.Malladi@dsu.edu

Abstract. In [Mil03, LM05], Millen-Lynch-Meadows proved that, under some restrictions on messages, including identities for canceling an encryption and a decryption within the same term during analysis will be redundant. i.e., they will not lead to any new attacks that were not found without them. In this paper, we prove that slightly modified restrictions are sufficient to safely remove those identities, even when protocols contain operators such as the notorious Exclusive-OR operator that break the free algebra assumption with their own identities, in addition to the identities considered by Millen-Lynch-Meadows.

Keywords: Cryptographic protocol analysis, Free algebras, Equational theories, Constraint solving, Exclusive-OR.

1 Introduction

1.1 Background

Consider the following protocol:

$$\begin{aligned}
\text{Message 1.} \quad & A \to B \; : \; [K_{AB}]_{sh(A,B)} \\
\text{Message 2.} \quad & C \to A \; : \; [N]_{sh(B,C)} \\
\text{Message 3.} \quad & A \to B \; : \; [[N]_{sh(B,C)}]_{sh(A,B)} \\
\text{Message 4.} \quad & B \to C \; : \; N.
\end{aligned}$$

(*Notation*: A, B, C are agent variables; K_{AB} is a session-key variable; N is a nonce variable; $sh(X, Y)$ represents the long-term shared-key of agents X and Y; $[t]_k$ represents t encrypted with k using a symmetric cipher).

Suppose A and B are played by two honest agents a and b, while C is played by a dishonest agent c. Then the following attack is possible:

$$\begin{aligned}
\text{Message 1.} \quad & a \to b \; : \; [k_{ab}]_{sh(a,b)} \\
\text{Message 2.} \quad & c \to a \; : \; [n]_{sh(b,c)} \\
\text{Message 3.} \quad & c(a) \to b \; : \; [k_{ab}]_{sh(a,b)} \quad \text{(replaying Message 1)} \\
\text{Message 4.} \quad & b \to c \; : \; [k_{ab}]_{sh(b,c)}^{-1}.
\end{aligned}$$

(*Note*: We use all lower-case symbols now since this is a protocol execution. $c(a)$ denotes c spoofing as a).

S. Mödersheim and C. Palamidessi (Eds.): TOSCA 2011, LNCS 6993, pp. 205–224, 2012.

The protocol and the attack were inspired from the example in [Mil03]. Basically, in the attack, c replays the first message to b as the third message. Since b does not know that the plain-text of the encryption is a session-key k_{ab}, not the encryption that it was expecting, it would innocently decrypt it using $sh(a, b)$, then with $sh(b, c)$, and send $[k_{ab}]_{sh(b,c)}^{-1}$ to[1] c, thinking it sent n. Agent c can happily encrypt it with $sh(b, c)$ that it shares with b, to learn k_{ab}.

This vulnerability could be found when $[K_{AB}]_{sh(A,B)}$ and $[[N]_{sh(B,C)}]_{sh(A,B)}$ are unified, whence it would be apparent that N should be substituted with $[K_{AB}]_{sh(B,C)}^{-1}$. However, we would not discover it, if the unification algorithm did not include the identity $[[p]_r^{-1}]_r = p$. i.e., an Explicit Decryption Operator (EDO) identity.

Protocol analysis techniques that adopt an identity-free (or free algebra) model such as [THG98, MS01, HS02] miss attacks that exploit identities. Others like the NRL analyzer [Mea92, Mea96] that do include such identities would discover them.

Millen considers this issue in [Mil03] and notes that, if protocols are designed without terms like $[\_]_\_^{-1}$ (called *pure* protocols) and[2] do not contain terms of the form $[X]_\_$ at all where X is a variable (called *EV-Free* protocols), then we would never have terms of the form $[[\_]_\_^{-1}]_\_$ during analysis, in which case, the EDO identity is never used. For instance, in the above protocol, if message 3 is changed to $[[N, B]_{sh(B,C)}]_{sh(A,B)}$, agent B would expect to see a pair after decrypting with $sh(A, B)$ and $sh(B, C)$. If not, it would reject the message. Hence, the attack exploiting the EDO identity would not exist.

Similarly, Lynch & Meadows extended Millen's result to the asymmetric encryption case [LM05]. They showed that if protocols do not use private encryption keys or public signature keys explicitly in messages and do not contain terms of the form[3] $[X]_\_^{\rightarrow}$, then cancellations in asymmetric encryptions will not be possible and the corresponding identities, e.g. $[[t]_{pv(a)}^{\rightarrow}]_{pk(a)}^{\rightarrow} = t$ will be redundant during analysis. They call such protocols, *pk-pure*, and *PEV-free*.

The point here is not that the example attack above is a realistic scenario, but the conditions in which an identity-free analysis is sound. Indeed, it is well-known that encryptions should have some redundancy to ensure correct decryption and to use some random number in the plain-text as well, since deterministic encryption is insecure. Millen-Lynch-Meadows show that the same principles are sufficient for identity-free analysis, and hence their restrictions are not additional — they are a must anyway for secure protocols. But the lesser

---

[1] $[t]_k^{-1}$ denotes t decrypted with k using a symmetric cipher; the notation might seem strange, but it is motivated by the fact that decryption in symmetric ciphers uses the same key as encryption, but the process is inverted (or reversed).

[2] Following Lowe [Low99], we use underscore (_) when the value in that place is irrelevant in a formula; this helps the reader to focus on the important values.

[3] We use a superscript $\rightarrow$ to indicate the use of an asymmetric cipher, because the key inverse is used for encryption/decryption, but the process is the same as encryption (there is not a reverse process for decryption).

the identities used in protocol analysis, the easier and faster analysis becomes, so Millen-Lynch-Meadows results are quite useful for protocol analysis.

1.2   The Problems and Our Contributions

We wanted to find out whether Millen-Lynch-Meadows results hold when more operators are used in protocols that have their own identities, in addition to those considered by Millen-Meadows-Lynch. For instance, the Exclusive-OR (XOR) operator is one such operator that possesses ACUN (Associativity, Commutativity, existence of Unity and Nilpotence) identities. To be precise, the main questions we were concerned about were:

1. *Can we still conduct protocol analysis without the identities considered by Millen-Meadows-Lynch when protocols use operators such as XOR that have their own identities?*
2. *Are the restrictions given by Millen-Meadows-Lynch sufficient in such protocols or do we need more restrictions?*

It is very important to find these out since many protocols used in real-life such as SSH and SSL use the XOR operator. This operator is also notorious since its ACUN identities were used to reveal surprising attacks that were not discovered without them [RS98]. Further, contemporary research efforts are focusing on these kind of problems. For instance, in a very recent work [SEMM10], the theory of ACUN with public-key/private-key cancellation was used to show new attacks. [SEMM10] also emphasized the importance of studying combinations of theories, quite strongly.

We found that EV-freedom doesn't necessarily help under XOR. For instance, if the third message in our example protocol was $[[N \oplus B]_{sh(B,C)}]_{sh(A,B)}$, it is EV-Free. But the attack is still possible, by replaying message 1 into message 3, since b cannot check the format of the XOR term inside. In fact, b would decrypt the replayed message with $sh(a, b)$, then with $sh(b, c)$, and send $[k_{ab}]_{sh(b,c)}^{-1} \oplus b$ as the fourth message (thinking it sent just n). Agent c can obtain k_{ab} by xoring it with b, followed by encrypting with $sh(b, c)$.

But if the third message in the protocol is changed to some $[[1, N \oplus B]_{sh(B,C)}]_{sh(A,B)}$, the attack is thwarted, since B would look for a pair after decrypting with $sh(A, B)$ and $sh(B, C)$. Using this concept, we make the following contributions:

1. A combination and unification of the results in [Mil03] and [LM05] who dealt with symmetric and asymmetric encryption respectively, but not both;
2. We show that when protocols adopt a new, slightly modified version of EV-Freedom, called **EVX-Freedom**, and the other restriction of Millen-Lynch-Meadows called *purity*, using identities to cancel encryptions do not reveal any new attacks under XOR (Section 3);
3. We also show that if protocols obey another scheme that is a slight modification of a scheme in [LM05] called **Structure** (independent of purity and EVX-Freedom), cancellation identities again do not reveal any new attacks;
4. We fix a few minor errors in [Mil03] and [LM05].

2   Protocol Model

In this section, we will define the term algebra in Section 2.1, attacker deductions in Section 2.2, and constraint solving for protocol analysis in Section 2.3.

2.1   Term Algebra

We assume the existence of a set of variables denoted *Vars*. The signature Σ contains the set of nullary functions symbols denoted *Constants* and another set of symbols to construct more terms: $\{tuple, senc, sdec, penc, sign, xor\}$.

senc and *sdec* represent symmetric encryption and decryption operators respectively. *penc* represents asymmetric key encryption. There is no *pdec*, since as we noted before, in most asymmetric ciphers, the process of decryption is the same as encryption but using the inverse key. *sign* represents the signature of a term such that $sign(t, k)$ is a signature of t that is to be verified using the inverse of k.

We will call the terms created with operators *senc*, *sdec*, *penc* and *sign* as "encrypted terms". We will also use a predicate encrypted() that returns true only if the argument supplied to it is an encrypted term.

Cumulatively, we define the infinite set *Terms* as,

$$Terms = Vars \cup Constants \cup \{f(t_1, \ldots, t_n) \mid f \in \Sigma \wedge t_1, \ldots, t_n \in Terms\}.$$

Syntactically, $tuple(t_1, \ldots, t_n) = [t_1, \ldots, t_n]$, $senc(t, k) = [t]_k$, $sdec(t, k) = [t]_k^{-1}$, $penc(t, k) = [t]_k^{\rightarrow}$, $sign(t, k) = [t]_k^{\leftrightarrow}$, $xor(t_1, t_2) = t_1 \oplus t_2$.

We use a superscript $\mapsto$ for signatures, since although they use asymmetric ciphers, they are different from asymmetric encryptions, since they encrypt a hash of the text, not the text itself.

In contrast to [Mil03, LM05] who used a functional notation throughout, we use the above syntactic sugar to denote terms, which we believe helps in following the proofs. For instance, [LM05] denotes the asymmetric encryption of X with a private-key K_1 and public-key K_2 as $pe(pk(K_2, pub, enc), pe(pk(K_1, priv, enc), X))$, which might be easier to follow if denoted as $[[X]_{pv(K_1)}^{\rightarrow}]_{pk(K_2)}^{\rightarrow}$.

We will call t in $[t]_k$ or $[t]_k^{\rightarrow}$ or $[t]_k^{\leftrightarrow}$ as the "plain-text" of those terms and k as their "key". We use functions $plaintext()$ and $key()$ to refer to the plain-text and key of encrypted terms.

Using AC properties of *xor*, we write $xor(t_1, xor(t_2, t_3))$ simply as $t_1 \oplus t_2 \oplus t_3$.

The *subterm* relation $\sqsubseteq$ is defined as,

$$(t' \sqsubseteq t) \text{ iff } (t' = t) \vee (\exists f \in \Sigma; t_1, \ldots, t_n; t'') \left(\begin{array}{c} (t = f(t_1, \ldots, t_n)) \wedge \\ (t'' \in \{t_1, \ldots, t_n\}) \wedge (t' \sqsubseteq t'') \end{array} \right).$$

We will denote the subterms of a term t as $SubTerms(t)$. We will denote the subterms of t that are encrypted as $EncSubTerms(t)$. A *ground term* is a term with no variables as subterms.

By $pk(k)$ and $spk(k')$ we denote the keys k and k' being used as public-keys for asymmetric encryption. Similarly, $pv(k)$ and $spv(k')$ as private keys. The use of functions pk, pv, spk, spv helps in distinguishing the purpose of the keys and define the identities and deductions accordingly. For instance, our identities and deductions will not allow $[t]^{\rightarrow}_{pk(k)}$ to be decrypted with $spv(k)$.

Note also that $pk(k)$ (and similarly $pv(k)$, $spk(k)$, $spv(k)$) does not mean that k is necessarily an agent identity; it can be any term. i.e., $pk(k)$ is not necessarily an atomic key where $pk()$ is a look-up function on agents' public-keys. It only denotes k being used is a key for asymmetric encryption that is known to everyone and that it possesses an inverse denoted $pv(k)$ that is known to some or only one agent.

We define the following set of identities that reflect cancellation of asymmetric/symmetric encryption/decryption rounds, denoted $E_1=\{E_{S1}, E_{S2}, E_{P1}, E_{P2}, E_{P3}, E_{P4}\}$ where,

$$E_{S1} : [[t]^{-1}_k]_k = t, \; E_{P1} : [[t]^{\rightarrow}_{pk(k)}]^{\rightarrow}_{pv(k)} = t, \; E_{P3} : [[t]^{\rightarrow}_{spv(k)}]^{\rightarrow}_{spk(k)} = t$$
$$E_{S2} : [[t]_k]^{-1}_k = t, \; E_{P2} : [[t]^{\rightarrow}_{pv(k)}]^{\rightarrow}_{pk(k)} = t, \; E_{P4} : [[t]^{\rightarrow}_{spk(k)}]^{\rightarrow}_{spv(k)} = t$$

We also give the ACUN identities, denoted $E_2 = \{E_A, E_C, E_U, E_N\}$ where,

$$E_A : t_1 \oplus (t_2 \oplus t_3) = (t_1 \oplus t_2) \oplus t_3, \; E_U : t \oplus 0 = t,$$
$$E_C : t_1 \oplus t_2 = t_2 \oplus t_1, \qquad\qquad E_N : t \oplus t = 0.$$

We denote $E = E_1 \cup E_2$. We will denote by $R/R_1/R_2$ the rewriting rules to be applied on a term to reduce it using the identities $E/E_1/E_2$ respectively. R can be shown to be confluent. R_1 can be shown to be convergent using techniques described in [Mea92]. R_2 will not be convergent because of E_C. Hence, when we refer to irreducibility under E_2, we mean the irreducibility under E_2 modulo E_A, E_C. We will denote the normal form of a term t (or set of terms) modulo a set of rewriting rules R as $t \downarrow_R$.

The main results in this paper show that R_1 are inapplicable on terms under some syntactic restrictions. This would mean that when R are applied on terms, effectively only R_2 are applied.

We will use a predicate $\texttt{irred}(,)$ taking parameters a term/set of terms/substitution and a set of identities/rewrite rules that returns $\texttt{true}$ if the former is irreducible modulo the latter. E.g. If t is a term, $\texttt{irred}(t, R_1)$ is true if t is irreducible modulo R_1.

2.2 Attacker Deductions

Our attacker deduction model is based on Lowe's model in [Low04]. We model single step attacker deduction rules through the relation $\vdash$, defined as:

$$\vdash \;::\; \mathcal{P}(\textit{Terms}) \times \textit{Labels} \times \textit{Terms}$$

such that, $S \vdash_l s$ represents that the attacker can deduce s from S using the action label l belonging to the set $\textit{Labels}$.

We use two different sets of deduction rules to achieve two different results in Sections 3 and 4. We define them separately in those sections.

We define the *derivation* of a term s from a set of terms S using deduction rules L, identities E that are represented by rewrite rules R, using the relation $\models$: Let S be irreducible by R. Then,

$$
\begin{aligned}
& S \models_{E,L} s \Leftrightarrow \\
& (\exists \langle S_1 \vdash s_1, \ldots, S_n \vdash s_n \rangle) \\
& \left((\forall i \in \{1, \ldots, n\}) \begin{pmatrix} (S_1 = S) \wedge (s_n = s) \wedge \\ (S_{i+1} \subseteq S_i \cup \{s_i \downarrow_R\}) \wedge \\ (\exists l \in L; \sigma; T \vdash_l t)((T\sigma =_E S_i \sigma \wedge t\sigma =_E s_i \sigma)). \end{pmatrix} \right).
\end{aligned} \tag{1}
$$

Read $S \models_{E,L} s$ as s is *derivable* from S using the deduction rules L and identities E.

2.3 Protocol Analysis Using Constraint Solving

We now define strands to model protocols and constraint solving for protocol analysis.

Definition 1 (Node, Strand, Protocol, Semi-bundle)
A node *is a tuple* $\langle \pm, t \rangle$, *where* $+$ *and* $-$ *denote "sending" and "receiving" a term* t *respectively. A* strand *is a sequence of nodes. A* protocol *is a set of strands. A* semi-bundle *is a collection of strands from a protocol, after applying some substitutions to some of the variables in the strands.*

We will overload the function $SubTerms()$ to return all the subterms in a set of strands.

A constraint is denoted $m : T$ where m is a term and T is a set of terms. Protocol analysis on semi-bundles using constraint solving can reveal vulnerabilities on protocols.

Definition 2 (Constraints, Satisfiability)
A constraint $m : T$ *is* satisfiable *using a substitution* σ, *identities* E *and deduction rules* $\mathcal{D}$ *if* $T\sigma$, $m\sigma$ *are ground terms, and* $T\sigma \models_{E,\mathcal{D}} m\sigma$:

$$\text{satisfiable}(\sigma, E, \mathcal{D}, m : T) \Leftrightarrow T\sigma \models_{E,\mathcal{D}} m\sigma.$$

A constraint sequence $C = \langle m_1 : T_1, \ldots, m_n : T_n \rangle$ *is from a semi-bundle* S *if*

- *every* $m : T \in C$ *is such that*
  - m *is a term on a receiving node in* S;
  - *every* $t \in T$ *is a term on a sending node in* S;
  - *if* m *and* t *are on the same strand, then* t *precedes*[4] m;
- *for all* m_i, m_j *where* $i, j \in \{1, \ldots, n\}$, m_i *precedes* m_j *if they are both on the same strand;*
- $(\forall i \in \{1, \ldots, n-1\})(T_i \subseteq T_{i+1})$.

---

[4] t_i *precedes* t_j *if* $\langle t_1, \ldots, t_n \rangle$ *is a strand and* $t_i, t_j \in \{t_1, \ldots, t_n\}$ *s.t.* $i < j$.

C is satisfiable *with σ under (E, D), iff every constraint in C is satisfiable with the same substitution:*

$$\text{satisfiable}(\sigma, E, D, C) \Leftrightarrow (\forall c \in C)(\text{satisfiable}(\sigma, E, \mathcal{D}, c)).$$

We denote all possible constraint sequences from a semi-bundle S as $ConSeq(S)$.

We assume that every protocol has a set of variables that are intended to be kept secret in each execution of the protocol. We denote them $SecVars(Pr)$. We also denote the constants substituted to those variables as $secrets(S)$ if S is a semi-bundle of Pr such that $S = Pr\sigma_S$ for some substitution σ_S.

A protocol has an attack on secrecy if a constraint sequence from a semi-bundle of a protocol after an artificial constraint with a secret as the target term to the end of the constraint sequence is satisfiable:

Definition 3 (Insecurity for secrecy)
A protocol Pr is insecure for secrecy under identities E and deduction rules $\mathcal{D}$ if

- $C = \langle \_ : \_, \ldots, \_ : T \rangle \in ConSeq(S)$ *such that S is a semi-bundle of Pr and*
- $C^\frown \langle m : T \rangle$ *is[5] satisfiable where $m \in secrets(S)$.*

i.e.,

$$\text{insecureForSecrecy}(Pr, E, \mathcal{D}) \Rightarrow \left(\begin{array}{c} (\exists \sigma; \sigma_S; C; S) \\ (S = Pr\sigma_S) \wedge (m \in secrets(S)) \wedge \\ (C = \langle \_ : \_, \ldots, \_ : T \rangle \in ConSeq(S)) \wedge \\ \text{satisfiable}(\sigma, E, \mathcal{D}, C^\frown \langle m : T \rangle) \end{array} \right).$$

3 Purity and EVX-Freedom Imply Soundness

In this section, we will prove that syntactic restrictions called purity and EVX-Freedom on terms are sufficient to ensure that no new attacks can be found by exploiting identities E_1 given in Section 2.1.

3.1 Attacker Deduction Rules, $\mathcal{D}$ and $\mathcal{DE}$

We first give rules $\mathcal{D}$ and $\mathcal{DE}$ that we will consider, starting with $\mathcal{D}$:

$$[t_1, \ldots, t_n] \vdash_{ex_i} t_i \qquad \{t, k\} \vdash_{senc} [t]_k \qquad \{t, pk(k)\} \vdash_{pkenc} [t]^{\rightarrow}_{pk(k)}$$
$$\{t_1, \ldots, t_n\} \vdash_{comb} [t_1, \ldots, t_n] \quad \{[t]_k, k\} \vdash_{sdec} t \qquad \{[t]^{\rightarrow}_{pk(k)}, pv(k)\} \vdash_{pkdec} t$$
$$\{t_1, t_2\} \vdash_{xor} t_1 \oplus t_2 \qquad \{t, spv(k)\} \vdash_{pvsigenc} [t]^{\leftrightarrow}_{spv(k)} \quad \{[t]^{\leftrightarrow}_{spv(k)}, spk(k)\} \vdash_{pvsigdec} t$$

Rules in $\mathcal{DE}$ include all the ones in $\mathcal{D}$ and some additional ones below:

$$\{t, k\} \vdash_{sdenc} [t]^{-1}_k \quad \{t, pv(k)\} \vdash_{pvenc} [t]^{\rightarrow}_{pv(k)} \quad \{t, spk(k)\} \vdash_{pksigenc} [t]^{\leftrightarrow}_{spk(k)}$$

---

[5] $\frown$ is the sequence concatenation operator.

Notice that we don't have the following deductions:

- $\{[t]_k^{-1}, k\} \vdash_{sddec} t$, since it can be simulated with *senc* and the identity $E_{S1} : [[t]_k^{-1}]_k = t$.
- $\{[t]_{pv(k)}^{\rightarrow}, pk(k)\} \vdash_{pvdec} t$ since it can be simulated with *penc*, and E_{P2}; similarly, *pksigdec*, which can be simulated with *pvsigenc* and E_{P4} respectively;
- $\{t_1 \oplus t_2, t_1\} \vdash t_1$ and others involving $\oplus$, that can be simulated with *xor* and E_2.

3.2   Purity and EVX-Freedom Requirements

We now define the syntactic requirements of purity and EVX-Freedom on protocols that we claim void the deductions $\mathcal{DE} \setminus \mathcal{D}$ and identities E_1 during protocol analysis.

Definition 4 (Purity and EVX-Freedom).
A term t is pure *if it does not have subterms of the form* $[\_]^{-1}$, $pv(\_)$ *or* $spk(\_)$:

$$\texttt{pure}(t) \Leftrightarrow (\not\exists [\_]^{-1}_\_, pv(\_), spk(\_) \sqsubseteq t).$$

A term t is EVX-Free *if the plain-texts of all its encrypted subterms are not variables or* XOR *terms:*

$$\texttt{EVXF}(t) \Leftrightarrow (\forall t' \sqsubseteq t)(plaintext(t') \notin Vars \wedge plaintext(t') \neq \_ \oplus \ldots \oplus \_).$$

The definition of purity might seem "non-uniform": since it prohibits private encryption keys $pv(\_)$, it might seem natural to prohibit private signature keys $spv(\_)$ as well. But we need to permit either $spv(\_)$ or $spk(\_)$, not both, in order to prevent the use of identities E_{P3} and E_{P4}. We choose to keep $spv(\_)$, since one uses $spk(k)$ to verify $[\_]_{spv(\_)}^{\mapsto}$, not vice-versa. If we prohibit $spv(\_)$, we would have to expect people to possess other's private signature keys!

Another alternative is to simply allow only terms of the form $[t]_{spk(k)}^{\mapsto}$ in the term algebra, with the intention that it represents that the signature of t is verified with $spk(k)$. But in that case, we would have to remove any deductions in $\mathcal{D}$ and $\mathcal{DE}$ that use $spv(\_)$, which is not unreasonable since signatures are only verified — decrypting them will not serve any purpose since people encrypt the hash of messages when signing, not the message itself.

We will call a protocol Pr as pure or EVX-Free if $SubTerms(Pr)$ are pure or EVX-Free respectively. We will assume that if a protocol is pure or EVX-Free, then every semi-bundle from it is also pure and EVX-Free.

3.3   Soundness Proofs

In this section we will prove our main claim. We will start with a few lemmas that assist us in the proof of the main theorem at the end.

The first lemma is the most crucial, lynchpin lemma.

Lemma 1 (Purity and EVX-Freedom ensure irreducibility under R_1)
Let t be a term and σ a substitution. Then,

$$\mathtt{pure}(t) \wedge \mathtt{EVXF}(t) \wedge \mathtt{irred}(\sigma, R) \Rightarrow (t\sigma) \downarrow_R = (t\sigma) \downarrow_{R_2} .$$

Proof. A term is reducible under R_1 if it has a subterm that resembles:

- $[[\_]\_^{-1}]\_, [[\_]^{\to}_{pv(\_)}]^{\to}_{pk(\_)}, [[\_]^{\to}_{pk(\_)}]^{\to}_{pv(\_)}, [[\_]^{\mapsto}_{spv(\_)}]^{\mapsto}_{spk(\_)}, [[\_]^{\mapsto}_{spk(\_)}]^{\mapsto}_{spv(\_)};$ or
- $[t]\_, [t]^{\to}_{pk(\_)}, [t]^{\mapsto}_{spv(\_)},$ such that a substitution to the term t can result in the term matching a term in the first case, after rules in R_2 are applied.

But both these cases are not possible when a term is pure and EVX-Free by definition.

Note that purity and EVX-Freedom do not prevent reducibility under R_2, but only R_1. For instance, as in the example given in the Introduction, $[1, X \oplus A \oplus b]_k$ is pure and EVX-Free, but it is reducible under R_2 with a substitution $\sigma = \{b/A\}$. But this is not of concern to us, since we are not trying to prove that our syntactic restrictions prevent attacks that exploit ACUN identities, but only the ones that exploit cancellation of symmetric/asymmetric encryption/decryption operations (R_1).

Next, we define a new rewrite system P that "purifies" a term by replacing all subterms of the form $[X]_Y^{-1}$ to $[X]_Y$. It also replaces those of the form $[X]^{\to}_{pv(Y)}$, $[X]^{\mapsto}_{spk(Y)}$ with X, since the decryption keys for those terms are publically available anyway.

$$
\begin{aligned}
&\textbf{(a)} \quad [t]_k^{-1} \to [t]_k \\
&\textbf{(b)} \quad [t]^{\to}_{pv(k)} \to t \\
&\textbf{(c)} \quad [t]^{\mapsto}_{spk(k)} \to t
\end{aligned}
$$

P can be applied on any impure term to convert it into a pure term. Obviously, every pure term t is irreducible modulo P. i.e., if t is pure, then $t \downarrow_P = t$. Also, every pure term is irreducible with R_1.

The idea behind defining purification is to subsequently use it to show that any breach of security in an "impure" analysis (using $\mathcal{DE}, E$) can also be simulated in a "pure" analysis (using $\mathcal{D}, E_2$) after purifying the terms.

The next lemma is similar to Lemma 1 except that only purity of a term is assumed, not EVX-Freedom.

Lemma 2 (Irreducibility preserved under purification)
Let t be a term and σ be a substitution. Then,

$$\mathtt{pure}(t) \wedge \mathtt{irred}(\sigma, P) \Rightarrow \mathtt{irred}(t\sigma, P).$$

Proof. Under the symmetric case, since t is pure, it does not have a subterm t' such that t' resembles $[\_]\_^{-1}$. Since σ is irreducible, it does not have such a term either. Hence, $t\sigma$ will not have such terms and hence is irreducible under P.

Similarly, for the asymmetric case, being pure, t does not have any private keys or public signature keys as subterms. Since σ doesn't have such terms either (being irreducible under P), we have that $t\sigma$ is irreducible under P.

Corollary 1. *We can infer from the lemma that if t and σ are irreducible under P, it does not matter whether we purify $t\sigma$ with P or first purify σ with P and then apply it to t. i.e., $(t\sigma) \downarrow_P = t(\sigma \downarrow_P)$.*

The next step is to show that every single deduction in $\mathcal{DE}$ on a set of terms S that are irreducible under R_1 is also possible in $\mathcal{D}$ when necessary (i.e., if the deduced term is not already in S), if S has been purified using P.

Theorem 1 (Deductions preserved under purification)
Let S be a set of terms. Then,

$$\begin{pmatrix} (S \vdash_l s) \wedge (l \in \mathcal{DE}) \wedge \\ \mathtt{irred}(S, R_1) \end{pmatrix} \Rightarrow \begin{pmatrix} (\exists l' \in \mathcal{D})(S \downarrow_P \vdash_{l'} s \downarrow_P) \vee \\ (s \downarrow_P \in S \downarrow_P). \end{pmatrix}$$

Proof (Sketch)
The detailed proof can be found in Appendix A, Theorem 4.

We show that for each deduction in $\mathcal{DE}$, there is an equivalent deduction in $\mathcal{D}$.

Deductions that deduce terms irreducible under R_1 are trivial. Some of these are, ex_i, $comb$, xor, and $pkdec$.

For the other deductions, there are two possibilities: either the deduced term is irreducible under R_1 or reducible:

- If it is irreducible, we have a corresponding deduction in $\mathcal{D}$ when S and s are purified. For instance, consider the following deduction using the rule $sdenc$ in $\mathcal{DE}$: $\{t, k\} \vdash_{sdenc} [t]_k^{-1}$.
  If $\mathtt{irred}([t]_k^{-1}, R_1)$, then we can have a deduction using rule $senc$ in $\mathcal{D}$:

$$\{t \downarrow_P, k \downarrow_P\} \vdash_{senc} [t \downarrow_P]_{k \downarrow_P}.$$

- If it is reducible, then we have another deduction in $\mathcal{D}$ which simulates the combination of the equation that it is reducible with, and the deduction in $\mathcal{DE}$. For instance, in the same example as the first case, suppose $t = [t']_k$ (here t' must be irreducible under R_1, since t is). Then, $[[t']_k]_k^{-1} =_{E_1} t'$. Hence, for the deduction below:

$$\{[t']_k, k\} \vdash_{sdenc} [[t']_k]_k^{-1}$$

we have the following deduction using rule $sdec$ in $\mathcal{D}$:

$$\{[t']_{k \downarrow_P}, k \downarrow_P\} \vdash_{sdec} t'.$$

We are now ready to achieve the main result for this section.

Theorem 2 (Main Result 1)
If a protocol Pr is pure and EVX-Free and if Pr is insecure for secrecy under $(E, \mathcal{DE})$, it is also insecure for secrecy under $(E_2, \mathcal{D})$.

Proof (Sketch)

The detailed proof is in Appendix A. Briefly, since Pr is insecure for secrecy, from Def. 3, we have that a constraint sequence C of a semi-bundle from Pr is satisfiable after an artificial constraint with its target as a secret term is added to C.

From Theorem 1, we have that if a constraint in C is satisfied using $\models_{E,\mathcal{DE}}$, it can also be satisfied using $\models_{E_2,\mathcal{D}}$, if all the terms in C are purified using the purifying rewrite system P.

Hence, we have that Pr is also insecure for secrecy under $(E_2, \mathcal{D})$.

4   Structured Protocols

We now define the other requirement on protocols, namely "structured terms":

Definition 5. *A term is* structured *iff the plaintext of each of its encrypted subterms is not a variable, an* XOR *term or an encrypted term;*

$$\mathsf{structured}(t) \Leftrightarrow (\forall t' \sqsubseteq EncSubTerms(t)) \begin{pmatrix} (plaintext(t') \notin Vars) \wedge \\ (plaintext(t') \neq \_ \oplus \ldots \oplus \_) \wedge \\ \neg \mathsf{encrypted}(plaintext(t')) \end{pmatrix}.$$

A protocol Pr is structured *or* structured(Pr) *iff every term in $SubTerms(t)$ is structured.*

A simple way to ensure that terms are structured is by adding constants as tags to plain-texts of all encryptions that are not tuples, along the lines of [HLS03, RS05, ML09].

Structured protocols need not be pure and they are EVX-Free by definition. Structure achieves the effects of both purity and EVX-Freedom in preventing cancellations.

Lack of purity allows cancellation after substitution. For instance, $[[t]_{X\oplus b}^{-1}]_k$ which will not occur in pure protocols is reducible when $X = k \oplus b$. Similarly, for asymmetric encryptions, for pure protocols, $[[\_]_{pv(\_)}^{\rightarrow}]_{pk(\_)}^{\rightarrow}$ do not occur, and $[[\_]_{spv(\_)}^{\rightarrow}]_{pk(\_)}^{\rightarrow}$ that could occur do not cancel because we assume $spv(k) \neq pv(k)$, for all k and $spk(k) \neq pk(k)$ as well. In this section, structure inhibits such cancellations even in impure terms. We show that attacks found on structured protocols using R can also be found using R_2 alone, with additional deductions to make up for R_1.

4.1   Attacker Deductions

Like in Section 3, we first define the attacker deduction rules that we will consider. The first set of rules is $\mathcal{DS}$, which are used only with E_2. These include those in $\mathcal{D}$ and some additional ones below:

$$\{t, k\} \vdash_{sdenc} [t]_k^{-1} \quad \{t, pv(k)\} \vdash_{pvenc} [t]_{pv(k)}^{\rightarrow} \quad \{t, spk(k) \vdash_{pksigenc} [t]_{spk(k)}^{\rightarrow}$$

These were not part of $\mathcal{D}$ because of purity, but they were a part of $\mathcal{DE}$, because they were needed to be used in conjunction with R_1.

$\mathcal{DS}$ also includes two more rules below:

$$\{[t]^{\rightarrow}_{pv(k)}, pk(k)\} \vdash_{pvdec} t \quad \{[t]^{\leftrightarrow}_{spk(k)}, spv(k)\} \vdash_{pksigdec} t$$

These were not in $\mathcal{D}$ because such terms do not appear in pure terms. But now we do not assume purity. They were also not included in $\mathcal{DE}$ because they can be simulated by combining a deduction rule and a reduction rule in R_1.

We define $\mathcal{DSE}$ to include those in $\mathcal{DS}$ but excluding $pkdec$, $pvsigdec$, $pvdec$, and $pksigdec$. $\mathcal{DSE}$ are used along with the identities E for deducing terms. The excluded rules can be simulated with other rules and E. For instance, $pkdec$ - $\{[t]^{\rightarrow}_{pk(k)}, pv(k)\} \vdash_{pkdec} t$ can be simulated with $pvenc$ - $\{t, pv(k)\} \vdash_{pvenc} [t]^{\rightarrow}_{pv(k)}$ by using $[t]^{\rightarrow}_{pk(k)}$ in place of t, whence, $[t]^{\rightarrow}_{pv(k)}$ becomes $[[t]^{\rightarrow}_{pk(k)}]^{\rightarrow}_{pv(k)} = t$ by virtue of E_{P1}.

4.2 Proofs

We first prove a lemma that is analogous to Lemma 1.

Lemma 3 (Irreducibility by R_1 preserved for structured protocols)
Let t be a term and σ a substitution. Then,

$$\mathtt{structured}(t) \wedge \mathtt{irred}(\sigma, R) \Rightarrow (t\sigma) \downarrow_R = (t\sigma) \downarrow_{R_2} .$$

Proof. The only way $t\sigma$ can be reducible under R_1 is if it was of the form $[[\_]^{-1}_\_]_\_$, $[[\_]^{\rightarrow}_{pv(\_)}]^{\rightarrow}_{pk(\_)}$, $[[\_]^{\rightarrow}_{pk(\_)}]^{\rightarrow}_{pv(\_)}$, $[[\_]^{\leftrightarrow}_{spv(\_)}]^{\leftrightarrow}_{spk(\_)}$, $[[\_]^{\leftrightarrow}_{spk(\_)}]^{\leftrightarrow}_{spv(\_)}$.

But these forms are possible only if t had an encrypted subterm of these forms or an encrypted subterm with its plaintext a variable, XOR term or an encrypted term so that $t\sigma$ will resemble those forms. None of these are possible when t is a structured term.

Hence, we have, $(t\sigma) \downarrow_R = (t\sigma) \downarrow_{R_2}$.

We are now ready to prove the main theorem on structured protocols. We do not need to use any purification of terms using P now, since the theorem applies for pure and impure protocols alike.

There was an error in the proof of a similar theorem in [LM05, Theorem 3]. They claim they consider the deduction $pkenc$, but they actually consider $pvenc$ (most likely inadvertently). We fix it here.

Theorem 3 (Main Result 2)
If a structured protocol Pr is insecure for secrecy under $(E, \mathcal{DSE})$, it is insecure for secrecy under $(E_2, \mathcal{DS})$.

Proof. We first prove that if S is a set of terms irreducible under R_1, then if a term s can be deduced from S using rules in $\mathcal{DSE}$, it can also be deduced using rules in $\mathcal{DS}$:

$$(\forall l \in \mathcal{DSE}) \big(\mathtt{irred}(S, R_1) \wedge (S \vdash_l s \downarrow_{R_1}) \Rightarrow (\exists l' \in \mathcal{DS})(S \vdash_{l'} s) \big). \quad (2)$$

This is straightforward for deductions like ex_i, $comb$, and xor, which deduce terms that are irreducible under R_1. For instance, consider $comb$, which is possible in $\mathcal{DSE}$ and $\mathcal{DS}$ alike, since

$$\{s_1 \downarrow_{R_1}, s_2 \downarrow_{R_1}\} \vdash_{comb} (s_1 \downarrow_{R_1}, s_2 \downarrow_{R_1})$$

is the same as $\{s_1, s_2\} \vdash_{comb} (s_1, s_2)$, given that $\mathrm{irred}(S, R_1)$ from hypothesis.

For the other deductions, we have to show that any result of a deduction in $\mathcal{DSE}$ that is reducible under R_1 can be deduced using a deduction rule in $\mathcal{DS}$ that was removed in $\mathcal{DSE}$.

For instance, consider $senc$:

$$\{t \downarrow_{R_1}, k \downarrow_{R_1}\} \vdash_{senc} [t]_k \downarrow_{R_1},$$

where $[t]_k$ is reducible by R_1. Then, t must be some $[t']_k^{-1}$ where t' and k are irreducible. So the deduction is now: $\{[t']_k^{-1} \downarrow_{R_1}, k \downarrow_{R_1}\} \vdash_{senc} [[t']_k^{-1}]_k \downarrow_{R_1} = t'$.

But this is the same as: $\{[t']_k^{-1}, k\} \vdash_{sddec} t'$.

(recall that $sddec$ belongs to $\mathcal{DS}$, but not $\mathcal{DSE}$).

Similarly, consider $penc$: If $[t]_{pk(k)}^{\rightarrow}$ is reducible to t' such that $t = [t']_{pv(k)}^{\rightarrow}$, then

$$\{t \downarrow_{R_1}, pk(k \downarrow_{R_1})\} \vdash_{penc} [t]_{pk(k)}^{\rightarrow} \downarrow_{R_1}$$

is the same as $\{[t']_{pv(k)}^{\rightarrow}, pk(k)\} \vdash_{pvdec} t'$.

Similar reasoning applies for $pvsigenc$ which can be simulated by $pksigdec$ if the result $[t]_{spv(k)}^{\rightarrow}$ were to be reducible.

We have included a formal version of the rest of the proof in Appendix A, since it is similar to Theorem 2.

Informally, since Pr is insecure for secrecy, from Def. 3, we have that a constraint sequence C of a semi-bundle from Pr is satisfiable after an artificial constraint with its target as a secret term is added to C.

From above, we have that if a constraint in C is satisfied using $\models_{E,\mathcal{DSE}}$, it can also be satisfied using $\models_{E_2,\mathcal{DS}}$, if all the terms in C are purified using the purifying rewrite system P.

Hence, we have that Pr is also insecure for secrecy under $(E_2, \mathcal{DS})$.

5   Related Work

There has been a great amount of interesting research published in the last decade combining algebraic properties with intruder deductions. For instance, Basin et al. present a uniform and modular approach to handling algebraic properties in protocol analysis [BMV05]. A good coverage of such results is given in the survey by Cortier et al. [CDL06].

It seems that research in protocol analysis under algebraic properties at this point is split largely into two directions:

- Results showing how the properties can be included while developing analysis or verification tools. Extensions to the constraint solver, Maude-NPA, ProVerif and other tools are being undertaken world-wide in this direction;
- Parallel results showing how to safely remove some identities, aiding in the development and effective use of tools.

Our contributions in this paper clearly fall in the second category. While it is not possible to cover all the related articles here, below are some results in the same spirit:

- In a very significant result, Comon and Delaune describe how the presence of the "finite variant property" which holds for theories such as Abelian groups ensures that some algebraic properties can be safely removed [CD05];
- In [KT08], Kuesters-Truderung demonstrate the $\oplus$-linearity property for protocols to reduce the protocol verification problem to free algebra verification, when verifying using ProVerif;
- In [ML09, Mal10] we have shown that under the restriction of tagging messages (similar to the tagging in this paper), the role of ACUN identities during unification is restricted so that unifiers result only from syntactic unification. The net effect being that removing type-flaw and multi-protocol attacks from consideration during analysis is sound.

6   Conclusion

In this paper, we proved that every attack found by including cancellation identities for symmetric and asymmetric encryption/decryption can also be found without them, under some reasonable syntactic restrictions on protocols, even when they use operators like Exclusive-OR that possess their own identities.

The basic concept behind EV-Freedom [Mil03], PEV-Freedom [LM05], EVX-Freedom, and Structure is the same: Protocols should be designed so that agents will be able to verify some property of messages after decryption, such as their number in the protocol, operators used to create them etc. This is a prudent engineering practice [AN94], has been used to guarantee protocol security against important forms of attacks [HLS03, GT00, ML09, Mal10] and ensure decidability [Low99, RS05].

Exclusive-OR is just one of many similar operators and theories that we can extend the results under. Especially, theories that are disjoint with the standard algebra[6] like monoidal theories can be similarly considered and the main results can be easily achieved. Only Lemmas 1 and 3 would have to be changed for other theories.

Identities such as $[a, b] = a$, $[a, b] = a \oplus b$ etc. cannot be similarly considered, since the lynchpin Lemmas 1 and 3 cannot be extended when E_2 contains those equations. But such identities are usually quite unrealistic and impractical, so

---

[6] i.e., those that do not use free operators like tuples in their identities.

it is probably not worth the trouble to invent restrictions that would preserve soundness of analysis under them anyway.

As pointed out in [LM05], our results on purity and EVX-Freedom cannot be extended directly to other trace properties, in particular, authentication. This is because, they involve purification that alters the protocol specification. For instance, authentication of an agent that she is indeed Alice might depend on determining if the agent possesses $[secret]^{\rightarrow}_{pv(\text{Alice})}$ according to the protocol. But our main theorem 1 in Section 3 purifies the term into $secret$, removing the encryption layer. Therefore, its derivation in a purified protocol doesn't imply that authentication is violated under $(E_2, \mathcal{D})$ in the original protocol as well, since it is sent in plain anyway. This is not a problem for the main theorem 2 on structured protocols though, since there is no purification or alteration of protocol there. That result can be extended to authentication by a suitable definition for that property, analogous to Def. 3 for secrecy.

The results in this paper are part of an ongoing effort to scale the security analysis of protocols hierarchically following [Mea03], starting with the most basic model. Extensions of results would require extending proofs in the base model appropriately with additional operators, theories and attacker capabilities. While Millen's result [Mil03] was the initial base for this result, Lynch-Meadows was the next step in the hierarchy. Our contribution is about extending both [Mil03] and [LM05] appropriately with an additional equational theory, and extending their proofs accordingly by strategically introducing the theory at crucial points.

We believe that future research in protocols will have to be similarly conducted, building on the work in the base model, extending it to the desired level in the hierarchy.

Acknowledgments. I am greatly indebted to Chris Lynch (Clarkson University) for helpful comments on the paper, and many clarifications on [LM05]. Thanks also to the anonymous reviewers whose comments helped in improving the presentation.

This work was conducted as a result of funding from the International Institute of Information Technology (IIIT) during summer of 2010. I am grateful to Kishore Kothapalli, Bezawada Bruhadeshwar (faculty, CSTAR, IIIT) and Prof. Rajeev Sangal (Director, IIIT) for their support.

References

[AN94]   Abadi, M., Needham, R.: Prudent Engineering Practice for Cryptographic Protocols. In: Proc. IEEE Symposium on Research in Security and Privacy, pp. 122–136. IEEE Computer Society Press, Los Alamitos (1994)

[BMV05]   Basin, D., Mödersheim, S., Viganò, L.: Algebraic intruder deductions. In: Sutcliffe, G., Voronkov, A. (eds.) LPAR 2005. LNCS (LNAI), vol. 3835, pp. 549–564. Springer, Heidelberg (2005)

[CD05]   Comon-Lundh, H., Delaune, S.: The finite variant property: How to get rid of some algebraic properties. In: Giesl, J. (ed.) RTA 2005. LNCS, vol. 3467, pp. 294–307. Springer, Heidelberg (2005)

[CDL06]   Cortier, V., Delaune, S., Lafourcade, P.: A of algebraic properties used in cryptographic protocols. Journal of Computer Security 14(1), 1–43 (2006)

[GT00]   Guttman, J.D., Thayer, F.J.: Protocol Independence through Disjoint Encryption. In: 13th IEEE Computer Security Foundations Workshop, pp. 24–34 (July 2000)

[HLS03]   Heather, J., Lowe, G., Schneider, S.: How to prevent type flaw attacks on security protocols. Journal of Computer Security 11(2), 217–244 (2003)

[HS02]   Heather, J., Schneider, S.: Equal to the task? In: Gollmann, D., Karjoth, G., Waidner, M. (eds.) ESORICS 2002. LNCS, vol. 2502, pp. 162–177. Springer, Heidelberg (2002)

[KT08]   Küsters, R., Truderung, T.: Reducing protocol analysis with xor to the xor-free case in the horn theory based approach. In: ACM Conference on Computer and Communications Security, pp. 129–138 (2008)

[LM05]   Lynch, C., Meadows, C.: On the relative soundness of the free algebra model for public key encryption. Electr. Notes Theor. Comput. Sci. 125(1), 43–54 (2005)

[Low99]   Lowe, G.: Towards a completeness result for model checking of security protocols. Journal of Computer Security 7(2-3), 89–146 (1999)

[Low04]   Lowe, G.: Analysing protocols subject to guessing attacks. Journal of Computer Security 12, 83–98 (2004)

[Mal10]   Malladi, S.: Protocol independence through disjoint encryption under exclusive-or. In: Workshop on Foundations of Computer Security and Privacy, FCSPrivMod (2010)

[Mea92]   Meadows, C.: Applying formal methods to the analysis of a key management protocol. Journal of Computer Security 1(1), 5–36 (1992)

[Mea96]   Meadows, C.: Analyzing the Needham-Schroeder public-key protocol: A comparison of two approaches. In: Bertino, E., Kurth, H., Martella, G., Montolivo, E. (eds.) ESORICS 1996. LNCS, vol. 1146, pp. 351–364. Springer, Heidelberg (1996)

[Mea03]   Meadows, C.: Towards a hierarchy of cryptographic protocol specifications. In: FMSE 2003: Formal Methods in Security Engineering. ACM Press, New York (2003)

[Mil03]   Millen, J.: On the Freedom of Decryption. Information Processing Letters 86(6), 329–333 (2003)

[ML09]   Malladi, S., Lafourcade, P.: How to prevent type-flaw attacks under algebraic properties. In: Workshop on Security and Rewriting Techniques, Affiliated to CSF 2009 (July 2009)

[MS01]   Millen, J., Shmatikov, V.: Constraint solving for bounded-process cryptographic protocol analysis. In: Proc. ACM Conference on Computer and Communication Security, pp. 166–175. ACM Press, New York (2001)

[RS98]   Ryan, P.Y.A., Schneider, S.A.: An attack on a recursive authentication protocol. a cautionary tale. Inf. Process. Lett. 65(1), 7–10 (1998)

[RS05]   Ramanujam, R., Suresh, S.P.: Decidability of context-explicit security protocols. Journal of Computer Security 13, 135–165 (2005)

[SEMM10]   Sasse, R., Escobar, S., Meadows, C., Meseguer, J.: Protocol analysis modulo combination of theories: A case study in maude-npa. To Appear, Sixth International Workshop on Security and Trust Management (STM). ERCIM (European Research Consortium in Informatics and Mathematics) (2010)

[THG98]   Thayer, F.J., Herzog, J.C., Guttman, J.D.: Strand spaces: Why is a security protocol correct? In: Proc. IEEE Symposium on Research in Security and Privacy, pp. 160–171. IEEE Computer Society Press, Los Alamitos (1998)

A   Detailed Proofs

Theorem 4 (Deductions preserved under purification)
Let S be a set of terms. Then,

$$\left(\begin{array}{c} (S \vdash_l s) \wedge (l \in \mathcal{DE}) \wedge \\ \mathtt{irred}(S, R_1) \end{array} \right) \Rightarrow \left(\begin{array}{c} (\exists l' \in \mathcal{D})(S \downarrow_P \vdash_{l'} s \downarrow_P) \vee \\ (s \downarrow_P \in S \downarrow_P). \end{array} \right).$$

Proof. We will prove the theorem for each deduction in $\mathcal{DE}$.

ex_i, $comb$: For deductions ex_i and $comb$, that every deduction in $\mathcal{DE}$ has a corresponding deduction in $\mathcal{D}$ is obvious. For instance, if $\{s_1, s_2\} \vdash_{comb} [s_1, s_2]$, then there can be a corresponding deduction in $\mathcal{D}$ such that $\{s_1 \downarrow_P, s_2 \downarrow_P\} \vdash_{comb} [s_1 \downarrow_P, s_2 \downarrow_P]$.

$senc$: Suppose $\{t, k\} \vdash_{senc} [t]_k$. Then, we have two cases:

$\mathtt{irred}([t]_k, R_1)$: In this case, we can have a deduction
$\{t \downarrow_P, k \downarrow_P\} \vdash_{senc} [t \downarrow_P]_{k \downarrow_P}$.

$\neg\mathtt{irred}([t]_k, R_1)$: In this case, since $\mathtt{irred}(t, R_1)$, suppose $t = [t']_k^{-1}$, where $\mathtt{irred}(t', R_1)$. Then, $[t]_k =_{E_1} [[t']_k^{-1}]_k = t'$. We will then use $sdec$ on $t \downarrow_P, k \downarrow_P$ such that $\{t \downarrow_P, k \downarrow_P\} = \{[t']_k^{-1} \downarrow_P, k \downarrow_P\} = \{[t' \downarrow_P]_{k \downarrow_P}, k \downarrow_P\} \vdash_{sdec} t'$.

$sdec$: If $\{[t]_k, k\} \vdash_{sdec} t$, then $\mathtt{irred}(t, R_1)$ since $\mathtt{irred}([t]_k, R_1)$. Therefore, we can have a deduction $\{[t \downarrow_P]_{k \downarrow_P}\} \vdash_{sdec} t \downarrow_P$.

$sdenc$: If $\{t, k\} \vdash_{sdenc} [t]_k^{-1}$, we have two cases:

$\mathtt{irred}([t]_k^{-1}, R_1)$: Then, we can have a deduction
$\{t \downarrow_P, k \downarrow_P\} \vdash_{senc} [t \downarrow_P]_{k \downarrow_P}$.

$\neg\mathtt{irred}([t]_k^{-1}, R_1)$: Then, suppose $t = [t']_k$, where $\mathtt{irred}(t', R_1)$, since $\mathtt{irred}(t, R_1)$. Then, $[[t']_k]_k^{-1} =_{E_1} t'$. Hence, for $\{[t']_k, k\} \vdash_{sdenc} [[t']_k]_k^{-1}$, we have $\{[t']_{k \downarrow_P}, k \downarrow_P\} \vdash_{sdec} t'$.

xor: If $\{t_1, t_2\} \vdash_{xor} t_1 \oplus t_2$, then we can have: $\{t_1 \downarrow_P, t_2 \downarrow_P\} \vdash_{xor} t_1 \downarrow_P \oplus t_2 \downarrow_P$.

$pkenc$: $\{t, pk(k)\} \vdash_{pkenc} [t]_{pk(k)}^{\rightarrow}$. We have two cases:

$\mathtt{irred}([t]_{pk(k)}^{\rightarrow}, R_1)$: Then, we have $\{t \downarrow_P, pk(k \downarrow_P)\} \vdash_{pkenc} [t \downarrow_P]_{pk(k \downarrow_P)}^{\rightarrow}$.

$\neg\mathtt{irred}([t]_{pk(k)}^{\rightarrow}, R_1)$: Let $t = [t']_{pv(k)}^{\rightarrow}$. Then, $\{[t']_{pv(k)}^{\rightarrow} \downarrow_P, pk(k \downarrow_P)\} = \{t \downarrow_P, pk(k \downarrow_P)\}$ which implies $t' \downarrow_P \in S \downarrow_P$. Similar reasoning applies for $pvsigenc$.

$pkdec$: Suppose, $\{[t]_{pk(k)}^{\rightarrow}, pv(k)\} \vdash_{pkdec} t$. Then, we have, $\{[t \downarrow_P]_{pk(k \downarrow_P)}^{\rightarrow}, pv(k \downarrow_P)\} \vdash_{pkdec} t \downarrow_P$. Similar reasoning applies for $pvsigdec$.

$pvenc$: Suppose, $\{t, pv(k)\} \vdash_{pvenc} [t]_{pv(k)}^{\rightarrow}$. We have two cases:

$\mathtt{irred}([t]^{\rightarrow}_{pv(k)}, R_1)$: Then, $[t]^{\rightarrow}_{pv(k)} \downarrow_P = t \downarrow_P$, which belongs to $\{t \downarrow_P, pv(k \downarrow_P)\}$.

$\neg\mathtt{irred}([t]^{\rightarrow}_{pv(k)}, R_1)$: Then, let $t = [t']^{\rightarrow}_{pk(k)}$. So we can have, $\{[t' \downarrow_P]^{\rightarrow}_{pk(k\downarrow_P)}, pv(k \downarrow_P)\} \vdash_{pkdec} t' \downarrow_P$. Similar reasoning applies for $pksigenc$.

Theorem 5 (Main Result 1)

If a protocol Pr is pure and EVX-Free and if Pr is insecure for secrecy under $(E, \mathcal{DE})$, it is also insecure for secrecy under $(E_2, \mathcal{D})$.

Proof. Since Pr is insecure for secrecy under $(E, \mathcal{DE})$, from Def. 2, suppose $C = C'^{\frown}\langle m : T_n \rangle$, where $m \in secrets(S)$, $S = Pro_S$, $C' = \langle m_1 : T_1, \dots, m_n : T_n \rangle \in ConSeq(S)$ where:

$$(\exists \sigma)\left((\forall m : T \in C)(T\sigma \models_{E,\mathcal{DE}} m\sigma)\right). \tag{3}$$

Consider a constraint $m : T \in C$. Let $T\sigma = X$, and $m\sigma = x$. If $T\sigma \models_{E,\mathcal{DE}} x$, then by the definition of $\models$ (Eq. 1) we have:

$$\left((\forall i \in \{1,\dots,n\})\begin{pmatrix}(\exists\langle S_1 \vdash s_1, \dots, S_n \vdash s_n\rangle) \\ (S_1 = X) \wedge (s_n = x)\wedge \\ (S_{i+1} \subseteq S_i \cup \{s_i \downarrow_R\})\wedge \\ (\exists l \in \mathcal{DE}; \sigma; T \vdash_l t)(T\sigma =_E S_i\sigma \wedge t\sigma =_E s_i\sigma).\end{pmatrix}\right). \tag{4}$$

Since m and T are pure, EVX-Free, if σ is irreducible modulo R, from Lemma 1 we have:

$$(\forall t \in T\sigma \cup \{m\sigma\})(t \downarrow_R = t \downarrow_{R_2}). \tag{5}$$

which implies $\mathtt{irred}(T\sigma \cup \{m\sigma\}, R_1)$ and also that

$$(\forall t \in T\sigma \cup \{m\sigma\})((t =_E t') \Rightarrow (t =_{E_2} t')). \tag{6}$$

Combining (4) with (5), (6) and Theorem 1 we have:

$$\left((\forall i \in \{1,\dots,p\})\begin{pmatrix}(\exists\langle S_1' \vdash s_1', \dots, S_p' \vdash s_p'\rangle) \\ (p \leq n)\wedge \\ (S_1' = X \downarrow_P) \wedge (s_p' = x \downarrow_P)\wedge \\ (S_{i+1}' \subseteq S_i' \cup \{s_i \downarrow_{R_2}\})\wedge \\ (\exists l' \in \mathcal{D}; \sigma; T \vdash_{l'} t)(T\sigma =_{E_2} S_i'\sigma \wedge t\sigma =_{E_2} s_i'\sigma).\end{pmatrix}\right). \tag{7}$$

which implies $X \downarrow_P \models_{E_2,D} x \downarrow_P$. i.e., $(T\sigma) \downarrow_P \models_{E_2,D} (m\sigma) \downarrow_P$.
Using this in Corollary 1 we have, $T\sigma \downarrow_P \models_{E_2,D} m\sigma \downarrow_P$.
Applying this in (3) above, we have:

$$(\exists \sigma)\left((\forall m : T \in C)(T\sigma \downarrow_P \models_{E_2,\mathcal{D}} m\sigma \downarrow_P)\right). \tag{8}$$

From Def. 3, this implies that Pr is insecure for secrecy under $(E_2, \mathcal{D})$. Hence, the result.

Theorem 6 (Main Result 2)
If a structured protocol Pr is insecure for secrecy under $(E, \mathcal{DSE})$, it is insecure for secrecy under $(E_2, \mathcal{DS})$.

Proof. We first prove that if S is a set of terms irreducible under R_1, then if a term s can be deduced from S using rules in $\mathcal{DSE}$, it can also be deduced using rules in $\mathcal{DS}$:

$$(\forall l \in \mathcal{DSE})\left(\texttt{irred}(S, R_1) \wedge (S \vdash_l s \downarrow_{R_1}) \Rightarrow (\exists l' \in \mathcal{DS})(S \vdash_{l'} s)\right). \qquad (9)$$

This is straightforward for deductions like ex_i, $comb$, and xor, which deduce terms that are irreducible under R_1. For instance, consider $comb$, which is possible in $\mathcal{DSE}$ and $\mathcal{DS}$ alike, since

$$\{s_1 \downarrow_{R_1}, s_2 \downarrow_{R_1}\} \vdash_{comb} (s_1 \downarrow_{R_1}, s_2 \downarrow_{R_1})$$

is the same as $\{s_1, s_2\} \vdash_{comb} (s_1, s_2)$, given that $\texttt{irred}(S, R_1)$ from hypothesis.

For the other deductions, we have to show that any result of a deduction in $\mathcal{DSE}$ that is reducible under R_1 can be deduced using a deduction rule in $\mathcal{DS}$ that was removed in $\mathcal{DSE}$.

For instance, consider $senc$:

$$\{t \downarrow_{R_1}, k \downarrow_{R_1}\} \vdash_{senc} [t]_k \downarrow_{R_1},$$

where $[t]_k$ is reducible by R_1. Then, t must be some $[t']_k^{-1}$ where t' and k are irreducible. So the deduction is now:

$$\{[t']_k^{-1} \downarrow_{R_1}, k \downarrow_{R_1}\} \vdash_{senc} [[t']_k^{-1}]_k \downarrow_{R_1} = t'.$$

But this is the same as: $[t']_k^{-1}, k\} \vdash_{sddec} t'$ (recall that $sddec$ belongs to $\mathcal{DS}$, but not $\mathcal{DSE}$).

Similarly, consider $penc$: If $[t]_{pk(k)}^{\rightarrow}$ is reducible to t' such that $t = [t']_{pv(k)}^{\rightarrow}$, then $\{t \downarrow_{R_1}, pk(k \downarrow_{R_1})\} \vdash_{penc} [t]_{pk(k)}^{\rightarrow} \downarrow_{R_1}$ is the same as $\{[t']_{pv(k)}^{\rightarrow}, pk(k)\} \vdash_{pvdec} t'$.

Similar reasoning applies for $pvsigenc$ which can be simulated by $pksigdec$ if the result $[t]_{spv(k)}^{\rightarrow}$ were to be reducible.

Since Pr is insecure for secrecy under $(E, \mathcal{DSE})$, from Def. 2, suppose $C = C'^\frown \langle m : T_n \rangle$, where $m \in secrets(S)$, $S = Pr_{\sigma_S}$, $C' = \langle m_1 : T_1, \ldots, m_n : T_n \rangle \in ConSeq(S)$ such that:

$$(\exists \sigma)\left((\forall m : T \in C)(T\sigma \models_{E, \mathcal{DSE}} m\sigma)\right). \qquad (10)$$

Consider a constraint $m : T \in C$. Let $T\sigma = X$, and $m\sigma = x$. If $T\sigma \models_{E, \mathcal{DSE}} x$, then by the definition of $\models$ (Eq. 1) we have:

$$\left(\begin{array}{l} (\exists \langle S_1 \vdash s_1, \ldots, S_n \vdash s_n \rangle) \\ (\forall i \in \{1, \ldots, n\}) \left(\begin{array}{l} (S_1 = X) \wedge (s_n = x) \wedge \\ (S_{i+1} \subseteq S_i \cup \{s_i \downarrow_R\}) \wedge \\ (\exists l \in \mathcal{DSE}; \sigma)((T \vdash_l t \wedge \\ (T \cup \{t\})\sigma =_E (S_i \cup \{s_i\})\sigma)). \end{array}\right) \end{array}\right). \qquad (11)$$

Since m and T are structured, if σ is irreducible modulo R, from Lemma 3 we have:

$$(\forall t \in T\sigma \cup \{m\sigma\})(t \downarrow_R = t \downarrow_{R_2}). \tag{12}$$

which implies $\mathtt{irred}(T\sigma \cup \{m\sigma\}, R_1)$ and also that

$$(\forall t \in T\sigma \cup \{m\sigma\})((t =_E t') \Rightarrow (t =_{E_2} t')). \tag{13}$$

Combining (11) with (12), (13) and (9) we have:

$$\left((\forall i \in \{1,\ldots,n\}) \begin{pmatrix} (\exists \langle S_1' \vdash s_1', \ldots, S_n' \vdash s_n' \rangle) \\ (S_1' = X) \wedge (s_n' = x) \wedge \\ (S_{i+1}' \subseteq S_i' \cup \{s_i \downarrow_{R_2}\}) \wedge \\ (\exists l' \in \mathcal{DS}; \sigma)((T \vdash_{l'} t \wedge \\ (T \cup \{t\})\sigma =_{E_2} (S_i' \cup \{s_i'\})\sigma)). \end{pmatrix} \right). \tag{14}$$

which implies $X \models_{E_2, DS} x$. i.e., $T\sigma \models_{E_2, DS} m\sigma$.
Applying this in (10) above, we have:

$$(\exists \sigma)\left((\forall m \; : \; T \in C)(T\sigma \models_{E_2, \mathcal{DS}} m\sigma) \right). \tag{15}$$

From Def. 3, this implies that Pr is insecure for secrecy under $(E_2, \mathcal{DS})$. Hence, the result.

Author Index